Library of
Davidson College

THE COMPLETE WORKS
OF
WALTER SAVAGE LANDOR

VOLUME V

Dying speech of an philosopher.

I think is none for more my wants gift.
Nature I loved and, next to Nature, Art;
I warm'd both hands before the fire of Life;
It sinks; and I am ready to depart.

Walter Savage Landor

THE
COMPLETE WORKS
OF
WALTER SAVAGE LANDOR

EDITED BY

T. EARLE WELBY

VOLUME V

BARNES & NOBLE, Inc.
New York
METHUEN & CO. Ltd
London

This edition, published in 1969

by Barnes & Noble, Inc., New York
and Methuen & Co., Ltd. London

is reproduced from the edition
published by Chapman & Hall, Ltd.
between 1927 and 1936

828
W261c
v.5

Manufactured in the United States of America

76-9945

CONTENTS

IMAGINARY CONVERSATIONS

ENGLISH (continued)

		PAGE
XXV.	SAMUEL JOHNSON AND JOHN HORNE (TOOKE)	1
XXVI.	WINDHAM AND SHERIDAN	102
XXVII.	MR. PITT AND MR. CANNING	110
XXVIII.	ROMILLY AND WILBERFORCE	126
XXIX.	SOUTHEY AND PORSON	139
XXX.	ROMILLY AND PERCEVAL	214
XXXI.	ELDON AND ENCOMBE	221
XXXII.	SOUTHEY AND LANDOR	230

IMAGINARY CONVERSATIONS

ENGLISH—(*continued*)

XXV. SAMUEL JOHNSON AND JOHN * HORNE (TOOKE)

(*Imag. Convers.*, ii., 1824; ii., 1826; *Wks.*, i., 1846; *Wks.*, iv., 1876.)

TOOKE.[1] Doctor Johnson, I rejoice in the opportunity, late as it presents itself, of congratulating you on the completion of your great undertaking: my bookseller sent me your *Dictionary* the day it came [2] from the press, and it has exercised ever since [3] a good part of my time and attention.

JOHNSON. Who are you, sir?

TOOKE. My name is Horne.

JOHNSON. What is my *Dictionary*, sir, to you? [4]

TOOKE. A treasure.[5]

JOHNSON. Keep it then at home and to yourself, sir, as you would any other treasure, and talk no more about it than you would about that. You [6] have picked up some knowledge, sir; but out of dirty places. What man in his senses would fix his study on the hustings? When a gentleman takes it into his head to conciliate the rabble, I deny his discretion and I doubt his honesty. Sir, what can you have to say to me?

* J. Horne assumed the name of Tooke after the supposed date of this Conversation.—W. S. L.

[1] 1st ed. reads: "TOOKE. Permitt me to congratulate you, Dr. Johnson, on the completion," etc.

[2] 1st and 2nd eds. read: "issued."

[3] 1st ed. reads: "since a considerable." 2nd ed. reads: "since, (and some years have now elapsed) a considerable."

[4] For Horne Tooke's opinion of the Dictionary see his *Diversions of Purley*: "his Dictionary is the most imperfect and faulty . . . of his productions." Boswell records Johnson's admission that he would have liked to adopt some of Horne's etymologies.

[5] 1st and 2nd eds. read: "A treasure, I doubt not."

[6] From "You" to "me" added in 3rd ed.

IMAGINARY CONVERSATIONS: ENGLISH

TOOKE. Doctor, my studies have led me some little way into etymology, and I am interested in whatever contributes to the right knowledge of our language.

JOHNSON. Sir, have you read [1] our old authors?

TOOKE. Almost [2] all of them that are printed and extant.

JOHNSON. Prodigious! do you speak truth?

TOOKE. To the best of my belief.

JOHNSON. Sir, how could you, a firebrand [3] tossed about by the populace, find leisure for so much reading?

TOOKE. The number of English books printed before the accession of James the First, is smaller than you appear to imagine; and the manuscripts, I believe, are not numerous; certainly in the libraries of our Universities they are [4] scanty. I wish you had traced in your preface all the changes made in the orthography [5] these last three centuries, for which about five additional pages would have been sufficient. The [6] first attempt to purify and reform the tongue was made by John Lyly, in a book entitled *Euphues and his England*,* and a most fantastical piece of fustian it is. This Author has often been confounded with William Lily, a better grammarian, and better known. Benjamin Jonson did somewhat, and could have done more. Although our governors have taken no pains either to improve our language or to extend it, none in Europe is spoken habitually by so many. The French boast the universality of theirs: yet the Germans, the Spaniards, and the Italians may contend with them on this ground: for as the Dutch is a dialect of the German, so is the Portuguese of the Spanish, and not varying in more original words

---

[1] 1st ed. reads: "redd." In this Conversation, for an obvious reason, the spelling of the 1st ed. is noted marginally.

[2] "Almost" not in 1st or 2nd ed.

[3] 1st and 2nd eds. read: "firebrand tossed about by the rabble, a restless spirit, a demogorgon, find," etc.

[4] 1st and 2nd eds. insert: "rather."

[5] 1st and 2nd eds. read: "language."

[6] From "The" to "known" added in 2nd ed. From "Benjamin" to "more" added in 3rd ed. From "Although" to "Tuscan" added in 2nd ed. From "The *lingua*" to "Italian" added in 3rd ed. From "The languages" to "English" added in 2nd ed. From "and" to "people" added in 3rd ed. From "We" to "seam" added in 2nd ed. From "and" to "soreness" added in 3rd ed. From "JOHNSON" to "particulars" added in 2nd ed.

* Among the works of Charles de St. Pierre is *Projet pour réformer l'Orthographie des Langues de l'Europe:* he must not be confounded with Barnardin de St. Pierre, fanciful as is the treatise.—W. S. L.

JOHNSON AND HORNE (TOOKE)

than the Milanese and Neapolitan from the Tuscan. The *lingua franca*, which pervades the coasts of the Mediterranean, the Ionian, and the Ægean seas, is essentially Italian. The languages of the two most extensive empires in Europe are confined to the fewest people. There are not thirteen millions who speak Turkish, nor fifteen who speak Russian, though branches of the Sclavonic are scattered far. If any respect had been had to the literary glory of our country, whereon much of its political is and ever will be dependent, many millions more would at this time be speaking in English; and the Irish, the Welsh, and the Canadians, like the Danes and Saxons, would have forgotten they were a conquered peole.

We should be anxious both to improve our language and to extend it. England ought to have no colony in which it will not be soon the only one spoken. Nations may be united by identity of speech more easily than by identity of laws : for identity of laws only shows the conquered that they are bound *to* another people, while identity of speech shows them that they are bound *with* it. There is no firm conjunction but this ; none that does not retain on it the scar and seam, and often with much soreness.

JOHNSON. So far, I believe, I may agree with you, and remain a good subject.

TOOKE. Let us now descend from generalities to particulars. Our spelling hath undergone as many changes as the French, and worse.

JOHNSON. And [1] because it hath undergone many, you would make it undergo more ! There is a fastidiousness in the use of language that indicates an atrophy of mind. We must take words as the world presents them to us, without looking at the root. If we grubbed under this and laid it bare, we should leave no room for our thoughts to lie evenly, and every expression would be constrained and crampt. We should scarcely find a metaphor in the purest author that is not false or imperfect, nor could we imagine one ourselves that would not be stiff and frigid. Take now for instance a phrase in common use. *You are rather late.* Can anything seem plainer ? Yet *rather*, as you know, meant originally *earlier*, being the comparative of *rathe ;* the " rathe primrose " of the poet recalls it. We can not say, *You are sooner late :* but who is so troublesome and silly as to question the propriety of saying, *You are rather late ?* We

---

[1] From " And " to " more " added in 2nd ed. From " There " to " What ! " (in Johnson's speech beginning, " And are you, sir, more acute ") added in 3rd ed.

IMAGINARY CONVERSATIONS: ENGLISH

likewise say, *bad orthography* and *false orthography* : how can there be false or bad *right-spelling ?*

TOOKE. I suspect there are more of these inadvertencies in our language than in any other.

JOHNSON. Sir, our language is a very good language.

TOOKE. Were it not, I should be less solicitous to make it better.

JOHNSON. *You* make it better, sir !

TOOKE. By reverencing the authority of the learned, by exposing the corruptions of the ignorant, and by reclaiming what never ought to have been obsolete.

JOHNSON. Sir, the task is hopeless : little can be done now.

TOOKE. And because little can be done, must we do nothing ? Because with all our efforts we are imperfect, may not we try to be virtuous ? Many of the anomalies in our language can be avoided or corrected : if many shall yet remain, something at least will have been done for elegance and uniformity.

JOHNSON. I hate your innovations.

TOOKE. I not only hate them, but would resist and reject them, if I could. It is only such writers as you that can influence the public by your authority and example.

JOHNSON. Sir, if the best writer in England dared to spell three words differently from his contemporaries, and as Milton spelt them, he would look about in vain for a publisher.

TOOKE. Yet Milton is most careful and exact in his spelling, and his ear is as correct as his learning. His language would continue to be the language of his country, had it not been for the Restoration.

JOHNSON. I have patience, sir ! I have patience, sir ! Pray go on.

TOOKE. I will take advantage of so much affability ; and I hope that patience, like other virtues, may improve by exercise.

On the return of Charles from the Continent, some of his followers may really have lost their native idiom, or at least may have forgotten the graver and solider parts of it ; for many were taken over in their childhood. On their return to England, nothing gave such an air of fashion as imperfection in English : it proved high breeding, it displayed the court and loyalty. Home-bred English ladies soon acquired it from their noble and brave gallants ; and it became the language of the Parliament, of the Church, and of the Stage. Between the last two places was pretty equally distributed all the facetiousness left among us.

JOHNSON AND HORNE (TOOKE)

Johnson. Keep clear of the Church, sir, and stick to language.

Tooke. Punctually will I obey each of your commands.

Johnson. Did South and Cowley and Waller fall into this slough?

Tooke. They could not keep others from it. I peruse their works with pleasure: but South, the greatest of them, is negligent and courtly in his spelling, and sometimes, although not often, more gravely incorrect.

Johnson. And pray now what language do you like?

Tooke. The best in all countries is that which is spoken by intelligent women, of too high rank for petty affectation, and of too much request in society for deep study. Cicero praises more than one such among the Romans; the number was greater among the Greeks. We have no writer in our language so pure as Madame de Sévigné. Indeed we must acknowledge that the French far excell us in purity of style. When have we seen, or when can we expect, such a writer as Le Sage? In our days there is scarcely an instance of a learned or unlearned man who has written gracefully, excepting your friend Goldsmith and (if your modesty will admit my approaches) yourself. In your *Lives of the Poets*, you have laid aside the sceptre of Jupiter for the wand of Mercury, and have really called up with it some miserable ghosts from the dead.

Johnson. Sir, I desire no compliments.

Tooke. Before, I offered not my compliment but my tribute; I dreaded a repulse; but I little expected to see, as I do, the finger of Aurora on your face.

Johnson. If the warmth of the room is enough to kindle your poetry, well may it possess a slight influence on my cheek. The learned men, I presume, are superseded by your public orators.

Tooke. Our parliamentary speakers of most eminence are superficial in scholarship, as we understand the word, and by no means dangerously laden with any species of knowledge. Burke is the most eloquent and philosophical of them; Fox the readiest at reply, the stoutest debater, the acutest disputant.

Johnson. Rebels! but what you say of their knowledge is the truth. I have said it of one party, and I know it of the other, else I would trounce you for your asseveration.

Tooke. You yourself induced me to make the greater part of my remarks; more important, as being on things more important, than transitory men; such is language.

IMAGINARY CONVERSATIONS: ENGLISH

JOHNSON. How, sir, did I?

TOOKE. By having recommended in some few instances a correcter mode of spelling. Bentley and Hall and Dryden, though sound writers, are deficient in authority with me; when, for example, they write *incompatible* for *incompetible*: we want both words, but we must be careful not to confound and misapply them. Dryden and Roscommon formed a design of purifying and fixing the language: neither of them knew its origin or principles, or was intimately or indeed moderately versed in our earlier authors, of whom Chaucer was probably the only one they had perused. It is pretended that they abandoned the design from the unquietness of the times: as if the times disturbed them in their studies, leaving them peace enough for poetry, but not enough for philology.

JOHNSON. And are you, sir, more acute, more learned, or more profound? What![1] because at one time our English books were scanty, you would oppose the scanty to the many, with all the rashness and inconsistency of a republican.

TOOKE.[2] Bearing all your reproofs and reproaches with equanimity and submission, I converse with you on this subject because you have given up much time to it: with another I should decline the discussion. I am hopeful of gaining some information and of suggesting some subject for inquiry. Illiterate, inconsiderate, irreverent, and overweening men will be always disregarded by me. Like children and clowns, if they see a throne or a judgment-seat, they must forsooth sit down in it. Such people set themselves above me, and enjoy the same feelings as those in the one-shilling gallery who look down on Garrick. He is only on the stage, no higher than the footlights, and plays only for others; whereas they have placed themselves at the summit, and applaud and condemn to please their fancies. It is equitable that coarse impudence should be met with calm contempt, and that Wisdom should sit down and lower her eyes, when Impudence trips over the way to discountenance her, or Ignorance starts up to teach her.

JOHNSON. Coxcombs and blockheads always have been, and always will be, innovators; some in dress, some in polity, some in language.

TOOKE. I wonder whether they invented the choice appellations you have just repeated.

---

[1] End of passage added in 3rd ed.
[2] From "TOOKE" to "your own principles," p. 7, last line, added in 3rd ed.

JOHNSON AND HORNE (TOOKE)

JOHNSON. No, sir! Indignant wise men invented them.

TOOKE. Long ago then. Indignant wise men lived in the time of the Centaurs: such combinations have never existed since. Your remark however on the introducers of new words into our language, is, I apprehend, well-founded: but you spoke generally and absolutely, and in this (I think) incorrectly. Julius Cæsar, whom you ought to love and reverence for giving the last blow to a republic, was likewise an innovator in spelling; so was Virgil; and to such a degree, that, Aulus Gellius tells us, he spelled the same word differently in different places, to gratify his ear. Milton has done the same.

JOHNSON. And sometimes injudiciously: for instance, in writing *Hee* emphatically; *He* less so. He also writes *subtile*, as a scholar should do; and *suttle*, as the word is pronounced by the most vulgar.

TOOKE. Cicero, not contented with new spellings, created new words. Now the three Romans have immemorially been considered the most elegant and careful writers in their language: and we confer on our countryman but a small portion of the praises due to him, in asserting that both in poetry and prose his mastery is above them all. Milton is no factitious or accrete man; no pleader, no rhetorician. Truth in him is the parent of Energy, and Energy the supporter of Truth. If we rise to the Greek language, the most eloquent man on record, Pericles, introduced the double *t* instead of the double *s*: and it was enamelled on that golden language to adorn the eloquence of Aspasia, and to shine among the graces of Alcibiades. Socrates bent his thoughtful head over it, and it was observed in the majestic march of Plato. At the same time Thucydides and the tragedians, together with Aristophanes, contributed to form, or united to countenance, the *Middle Attic*. One would expect that Elegance and Atticism herself might have rested and been contented. No: Xenophon, Plato, Æschines, Demosthenes, were promoters of the *New Attic*, altering and softening many words in the spelling. With such men before me, I think it to be deeply regretted that coxcombs and blockheads should be our only teachers, where we have much to learn, much to obliterate, and much to mend.

JOHNSON. Follow your betters, sir!

TOOKE. Such is my intention: and it is also my intention that others shall follow theirs.

JOHNSON. Obey the majority, according to your own principles.

IMAGINARY CONVERSATIONS: ENGLISH

You reformers will let nothing be great, nothing be stabile. The [1] orators you mention were deluders of the populace.

TOOKE. And so were the poets, no doubt: but let us hope that the philosophers and moralists were not, nor indeed the writers of comedy. Menander was among the reformers: so was Plautus at Rome: the most highly estimated for his rich Latinity by Cicero and all the learned. Our own language had, under the translators of the Bible and of the Liturgy, reached the same pitch as the Latin had in the time of Plautus; and the sanctitude of Milton's genius gave it support, until the worst of French invasions overthrew it. Cowley, Sprat, Dryden, imported a trimmer and succincter dress, stripping the ampler of its pearls and bullion. Arbuthnot and Steele and Swift and Addison added no weight or precision to the language, nor were they choice in the application of words. None of them came up to their French contemporaries in purity and correctness; and their successors, who are more grammatical, are weak competitors with the rival nation for those compact and beautiful possessions. De Foe has a greater variety of powers than they, and he far outstrips in vigor and vivacity all the other pedestrians who started with him. He spells some words commendably, others not.[2] Of the former are *onely, admitt, referr, supplie, relie, searcht, wisht;* of the latter *perticulars, perusall, speciall, vallues.* Hurd, very minute and fastidious, in like manner writes often reprehensibly, though oftener well. Do you tolerate his "*catched*"?

JOHNSON. Sir, I was *teached* better.

TOOKE. He also writes "under these circumstances."

JOHNSON. Circumstances are things *round about;* we are *in* them, not *under* them.

TOOKE. We find "those who *had* rather *trust* to the equity" for "*would* rather." I believe he is the last writer who uses the word *wit* for *understanding*, although we continue to say "he is out of his *wits*." He very properly says *encomiums*, to avoid a Grecism. We never say "rhododendra," but "rhododendro*ns*." In our honest old English, all's well that ends well: and *encomiums, phenomenons,*

---

[1] From "The" to "yesterday" (in Tooke's speech beginning, "We must lead happy lives") added in 3rd ed.

[2] I am indebted to Mr. Stephen Wheeler for the information that, with two exceptions, all the words noted by Landor are in Defoe's letter to Harley, given in William Hazlitt's edition of 1841, Landor's own copy of which is in the possession of his descendants.

JOHNSON AND HORNE (TOOKE)

memorandums, sound thoroughly and fully English. Hurd is less so in his use of the word *counterfeit*, which we are accustomed to take in an unfavorable sense. " Alexander suffered none but an Apelles and a Lysippus to *counterfeit* the form and features of his person." The sentence is moreover lax. I am glad, however, to find that he writes *subtile* instead of *subtle*. He has the merit too of using *hath* instead of *has*, in many places, but is so negligent as to omit it sometimes before a word beginning with *s*, or *ce* and *ci*, and *ex*. This is less bad than before *th*. Like Middleton, he writes *chast*.

JOHNSON. Improperly. Nobody writes *wast* for *waste*. In all such words the vowel is pronounced long, which his spelling would contract. Dr. Hurd writes plainly, and yet not ignobly. His criticisms are always sensible, never acute; his language clear, but never harmonious.

TOOKE. We cease to look for Eloquence; she vanished at the grave of Milton.

JOHNSON. Enough of Milton. Praise the French, sir! A republican is never so much at his ease as among slaves.

TOOKE. We must lead happy lives then. But you were pleased to designate us as enemies to greatness and stability. What is it I admire in Milton but the greatness of his soul and the stability of his glory? Transitory is everything else on earth. The minutest of worms corrodes the throne; a slimier consumes what sat upon it yesterday. I know not the intentions and designs of others: I know not whether I myself am so virtuous that I should be called a republican, or so intelligent that I should be called a reformer. In regard to stability, I do however think I could demonstrate to you, that what has a broad basis is more stabile than what has a narrow one, and that nothing is gained to solidity by top-heaviness. In regard to greatness, I doubt my ability to convince you. Much in this is comparative. Compared with the plain, the mountains are indeed high: compared with what is above them in the universe of space, they are atoms and invisibilities. Such too are mortals. I do not say the creatures of the cannon-foundry and the cutlery; I do not say those of the jeweller and toyman, from whom we exclude light as from infants in a fever, and to whom we speak as to drunken men to make them quiet; but the most intellectual we ever have conversed with. What are they in comparison with a Shakespeare or a Bacon

IMAGINARY CONVERSATIONS: ENGLISH

or a Newton? You however seemed to refer [1] to power only. I have not meditated on this subject so much as you have, and my impression from it is weaker: nevertheless I do presume to be as hearty and as firm a supporter of it, removing (as I would do) the incumbrances from about it, and giving it ventilation.

JOHNSON. Ventilation! yes, forsooth! from the bellows of Brontes and Steropes and Pyracmon.

TOOKE. Come, Doctor, let us throw a little more dust on our furnace, which blazes fiercelier than our work requires. The word *firy* comes appositely: why do we write it *fiery*, when *wire* gives *wiry?* The [2] word rushes into my mind out of Shakespeare,

> And the *delighted* spirit
> To bathe in *fiery* floods.

Truly this would be a very odd species of delight. But Shakespeare never wrote such nonsense: he wrote *belighted* (whence our *blighted*), struck by *lightning:* a fit preparation for such bathing. Why do we write *lieutenant*, when we write, "I would as *lief*"? Would [3] there be any impropriety or inconvenience in writing end*e*vor and *demeanor* as we write *tenor*, omitting the *u?*

JOHNSON. Then you would imitate cards of invitation, where we find *favor* and *honor*.

TOOKE. We find *ancestor* and *author* and *editor* and *inventor* in the works of Doctor Jonson,[4] who certainly bears no resemblance to a card of invitation. Why can not we place all these words on the same bench? Most people will give us credit for knowing that they are derived from the Latin; but the wisest will think us fools for ending them like *hour*, *sour*, and *flour*, pronounced so differently. I look upon it as a piece of impudence to think we can correct the orthography of such writers as Selden and Milton. They wrote not only *honor*, *favor*, *labor*, but likewise *brest*, *lookt*, and *unlookt-for*, *kinde*, *minde*. To spell these differently is a gross absurdity.

JOHNSON. By removing a single letter from the holy word *Saviour*, you would shock the piety of millions.

TOOKE. In that word there is an analogy with others, although the class is small: *paviour* and *behaviour*, for instance.

[1] 2nd ed. reads: "referr."   [2] From "The" to "bathing" added in 3rd ed.
[3] From "Would" to "rust" (in Tooke's speech beginning, "We never censure") added in 3rd ed.
[4] *Wks.*, 1846, reads: "Johnson."

JOHNSON AND HORNE (TOOKE)

JOHNSON. It now occurs to me that *honor* was spelt without the *u* in the reign of Charles I., with it under his successor. Perhaps *armour* should be *armure*, from the low Latin *armatura*.

TOOKE. If we must use such words as *reverie*, why not oblige them to conform with their predecessors, *travesty* and *gaiety*, which should have the *y* instead of the *i*. When we, following Cowley, write *pindarique*, we are laughed at; but nobody laughs at *picturesque* and *antique*, which are equally reducible to order.

JOHNSON. It is an awful thing to offend the Genius of our language. We can not spell our words as the French spell theirs. No other people in the world could reduce to nothing so stiff and stubborn a letter as *x*, which they do in *eaux*.

TOOKE. We never censure them for writing *carême*, which they formerly wrote *caresme*, more anciently *quaresme*, and other words similarly: yet they have one language for writing, another for speaking, and affect a semblance of grammatical construction by a heap of intractable letters. While three suffice with us (*a, m, a*), they use eight (*aimaient*), of which the greater part not only are unprofitable, but would, in any language on earth, express a sound, or sounds, totally different from what they stand for: *r, s, t,* end words whose final sound is our *a*. We never censure the Italians for writing *ricetto*, as they pronounce it, without a *p*, and *benedetto* without a *c*: we never shudder at the danger they incur of losing the traces of derivation. The most beautiful and easy of languages assumes no appearance of strength by the display of harshness, nor would owe its preservation to rust. Let us always be analogical when we can be so without offence to pronunciation. There are some few words in which we are retentive of the Norman laws. We write *island* with an *s*, as if we feared to be thought ignorant of its derivation. If we must be reverential to custom, let it rather be in the presence of the *puisne* judge. There are only the words *puisne, isle, island, demesne, viscount*, and the family name *Grosvenor*, in which an *s* is unsounded. I would omit [1] it in these.[2] The French

---

[1] 2nd ed. reads: "omitt."
[2] 2nd ed. has a footnote as follows:—" I rejoice in this opportunity of paying my respects to Mr. Mitford, living or dead. The only judicious thing I find in his history is the spelling of *iland*. His ignorance and falsehood are beyond all match and measure: several instances of each are to be found within a few pages, in his invective against Demosthenes. If he be living, I entreat our ministers to grant a pension, or to devise an appointment,

have set us an example here, rejecting the useless letter. They also write *dette*, which we write " debt." I know not why we should often use the letter *b* where we do. We have no need of it in *crumb* and *coomb* : the original words being without it.

JOHNSON. King Charles I. writes *dout*. In the same sentence he writes *wherefor*.* But to such authority such men as you refuse allegiance even in language. Your *coomb* is sterile, and your *crumb* is dry ; as such minutenesses must always be.

TOOKE. So are nuts ; but we crack and eat them. They are good for the full, and for those only.

JOHNSON. The old writers had strange and arbitrary ways of spelling, which makes them appear more barbarous than they really are. There [1] are learned men who would be grieved to see removed from words the traces of their origin .

TOOKE. There are learned men who are triflers and inconsiderate. Learning, by its own force alone, will never remove a prejudice or establish a truth. Of what importance is it to us that we have derived these words from the Latin through the French ? We do not preserve the termination of either. Formerly if many unnecessary letters were employed, some were omitted. *Ea* and *oa* were unusual. In various instances the spelling of Chaucer is more easy and graceful and elegant than the modern. He avoids the diphthong in *coat, green, keen, sheaf, goat;* writing *cote, grene, kene, shefe, gote.* Sackville, remarkable for diligence and daintiness of composition, spells " delights " *delites*, and " shriek " *shreek*. He also writes *bemone, brest, yeeld*. What we foolishly write *work* was formerly spelt *werke*, as we continue to pronounce it. Formerly there was such a

---

in recompense of his hatred against the ancient liberties of his country : and if this should be inconvenient, to recommend him to the Pacha of Egypt as the most proper officer to remove from their native soil the wives, daughters, and infant-sons, of the Greeks ; praying that he may be confirmed in his situation, until a sufficient number of Nubians and Arabs be put into quiet and legitimate possession of the Peloponnesus, and until envoys have arrived from the Christian kings and princes to reside near such regular government, as the wisdom of their brother and cousin shall have established under God, for the happiness of his people."

* Letter to P. Rupert. See Forster's Life of Cromwell, in his *Statesmen of the Commonwealth.*—W. S. L.

[1] From " There " to " innovation " (in Tooke's speech beginning, " I know little about poetry ") added in 3rd ed. 1st and 2nd eds. read : " are. TOOKE. You have now brought me to a question, which if you will favour me, we will discuss. I perceive," etc.

word as *shew*: we still write it, but we pronounce it *show*, and we should never spell it otherwise. There is another of daily occurrence which we spell amiss, although we pronounce it rightly. *Coxcomb* in reality is *cockscomb*, and Ben Jonson writes it so, adding an *e*. He who first wrote it with an *x* certainly did not know how to spell his own name. In a somewhat like manner we have changed our *pennies* into *pence*, and our *acquaintants* into *acquaintance*. Now what have these gained by such exchange? Latterly we have run into more unaccountable follies; such as *compel* for *compell*, and I have seen *inter* for *interr*. Nobody ever pronounces the last syllables of these words short, as the spelling would indicate. You would be induced to believe such writers are ignorant that their *inter* and our *enter* are of a different stock. In the reign of Charles I. *parliament* was usually, though not universally, spelt *parlement*: how much more properly! What we write *door* and *floor* the learned and judicious Jonson wrote *dore* and *flore*. I find in his writings *cotes, profest, spred, partrich, grone, herth, theater, fórraine, diamant, phesants, mushromes, banisht, rapt, rackt, addrest, ake, spred, stomack, plee, strein* (song), *windore, fild* (filled), *moniment, beleeve, yeeld, scepter, sute* (from sue), *mist* (missed), *grone, crackt, throte, yong, harbor, harth, oke, cruze, crost, markt, minde* (which it is just as absurd to write *mind*, as it would be to write *time tim*), *taught, banisht, cherisht, heapt, thankt*. It is wonderful that so learned a man should be ignorant that *spitals* are hospitals. He writes: "Spittles, post-houses, hospitals." Had he spelt the first properly, as he has done all the other words, he could not have made this mistake. Fairfax writes *vew, bow* (bough), *milde, winde, oke, spred, talkt, embrast*. Fleming, in his translation of the Georgics, *ile, oke, anent;* (which latter word, now a Scotticism, is used by Philemon Holland); *gote, feeld, yeeld, spindel*. Drayton, and most of our earlier writers, instead of *thigh*, write *thie*. Milton in the Allegro,[1]

Where the bee with honied *thie*.

I perceive that you yourself, in your letter to Lord Chesterfield, have several times written the word *til;* and I am astonished that the propriety of it is not generally acknowledged after so weighty an authority. *Sent*, for *scent*, is to be found in old writers, following the derivation. There are several words now obsolete which are more

[1] *Sic*. Read: "Penseroso."

elegant and harmonious than those retained instead. *Gentleness* and *idleness* are hardly so beautiful as Chaucer's *gentilesse* and *idlesse*. We retain the word *lessen*, but we have dropped *greaten*. Formerly good authors knew its value.

I wish I were as sure that

>Multa renascentur quæ jam cecidere,

as I am that,

>>cadentque
>Quæ nunc sunt in honore vocabula.[1]

I am unacquainted with any language in which, during the prosperity of a people, the changes have run so seldom into improvement, so perpetually into impropriety. Within another generation, ours must have become so corrupt, that writers, if they hope for life, will find it necessary to mount up nearer to its sources.

JOHNSON. And what will they do when they get there? The leather from the stiff old jerkin will look queerly in its patches on the frayed satin.

TOOKE. Good writers will suppress the violence of contrast. They will rather lay aside what by its impurity never had much weight, than what has lost it by the attrition of time; and they will be sparing of such expressions as are better for curiosities than for utensils. You and I would never say " by *that* means " instead of *these;* nor " *an* alms "; yet Addison does. He also says a " *dish* of coffee," yet coffee never was offered in a dish, unless it was done by the fox to the crane after the dinner he gave her. We hear of our *lyrical* poetry, of our *senate*, of our *manes*, of our *ashes*, of our *bards*, of our British *Muse*. Luckily the ancients could never run into these fooleries; but their judgment was rendered by discipline too exact for the admission of them. Only one valuable word has been received into our language since my birth, or perhaps since yours. I have lately heard *appreciate* for *estimate*.

JOHNSON. I am an antigallican in speech as in sentiments. What we have fairly won from the French let us keep, and avoid their new words like their new fashions. Words taken from them should be amenable, in their spelling, to English laws and regulations. *Appreciate* is a good and useful one; it signifies more than *estimate* or *value;* it implies to " value *justly*." All words are good which come

[1] Hor., *Ars Poet.*, 70.

JOHNSON AND HORNE (TOOKE)

when they are wanted ; all which come when they are not wanted, should be dismissed.

TOOKE. Let us return from new words to the old spellings of Benjamin Jonson, which other learned men followed : *deprest, speke, grete, fede, reson, reper, sheves, relefe, leve, grene, wether, erthe, breth, seke, seson, sege, meke, stepe, rome, appere, dere, throte, tothe, betwene, swete, deth, hele, chere, nere, frende, tretise, teche, conceve, tonge, bere, speche, stere.* Altogether there are about forty words, out of which the unnecessary diphthong is ejected. He always omits the *s* in *island* and *isle;* he writes *sovrane, subtil, childe,* and *werke.* He would no more have written *sceptre* than *quivre.*

JOHNSON. Milton too avoided the diphthong ; he wrote *drede* and *redy.* Mandevile wrote *dede,* and *grane* of incense.

TOOKE. You tell us that the letter *c* never ends a word according to English orthography ; yet it did formerly both in words of Saxon origin and British, as *Eric, Rod-eric, Caradoc, Madoc. Wenlock,* the name of a town in Shropshire, formerly ended in *c,* and Hume always writes *Warwic.*

JOHNSON. Sir, do not quote infidels to me. Would you write *sic* and *quic ?*

TOOKE. I would, if we derived them from the Greek or Latin.

JOHNSON. Without the authority of Ben Jonson, on whom you so relie ?

TOOKE. There is in Jonson strong sense, and wit too strong ; it wants airiness, ease, and volatility. I do not admire his cast-iron ornaments, retaining but little (and that rugged and coarse-grained) of the ancient models, and nothing of the workmanship. But I admire his judgment in the spelling of many words, and I wish we could return to it. In others we are afraid of being as English as we might be and as we ought to be. Some appear to have been vulgarisms which are no longer such. By vulgarism I mean what is unfounded on ratiocination or necessity : for instance *underneath.*

JOHNSON. Our best writers have used it.

TOOKE. They have ; and wisely ; for it has risen up before them in sacred places, and it brings with it serious recollections. It was inscribed on the peasant's grave-stone, long before it shone amid heraldic emblems in the golden lines of Jonson, ushering in

Pembroke's sister, Sydney's mother.[1]

---
[1] *Sic.* Another misquotation of Ben Jonson is on page 16.

IMAGINARY CONVERSATIONS: ENGLISH

Beside, it is significant and euphonious. Either half conveys the full meaning of the whole. But it is silly to argue that we gain ground by shortening on all occasions the syllables of a sentence. Half a minute, if indeed so much is requisite, is well spent in clearness, in fulness, and pleasureableness of expression, and in engaging the ear to carry a message to the understanding. *Whilst* is another vulgarism which authors have adopted, the last letter being added improperly. *While* is " the *time* when "; *whiles* " the time*s* when."

JOHNSON. I am inclined to pay little attention to such fastidiousness, nor does it matter a straw whether we use the double *e*, instead of *ete*, in *sweet*, and the other words you recited from good authors. But I now am reminded that *near* is *nigher*, by Sir Thomas More writing " *never* the *nere*." However, you are not to suppose that I undervalue the authority of Benjamin Jonson. I find sometimes his poetry unsatisfactory and troublesome; but his prose is much better, and now and then almost harmonious; which his verses never are for half a dozen lines together.

TOOKE. I know little about poetry; but it appears to me that in his, where he has not the ague he has the cramp. Nearly all his thoughts are stolen. The prettiest of his poems,

Drink to me only with thy eyes,

is paraphrased from Scaliger's version of Aristænetus. He collected much spoil from his campaign in the Low Countries of Literature. However, his English for the most part is admirable, and was justly looked up to until Milton rose, overshadowing all England, all Italy, and all Greece. Since that great man's departure we have had nothing (in style I mean) at all remarkable. Locke and Defoe were the most purely English: and you yourself, who perhaps may not admire their simplicity, must absolve them from the charge of innovation. I perceive that you prefer [1] the spelling of our gentlemen and ladies now flourishing, to that [2] not only of Middleton but of Milton.

JOHNSON. Before [3] I say a word about either, I shall take the liberty, sir, to reprehend your unreasonable admiration of such

---

[1] 1st and 2nd eds. read: " preferr."
[2] 1st and 2nd eds. read: " that of Middleton and Milton."
[3] From " Before " to " let him alone " added in 3rd ed.

JOHNSON AND HORNE (TOOKE)

writers as Defoe and Locke. What, pray, have they added to the dignity or the affluence of our language?

TOOKE. I would gladly see our language enriched as far as it can be without depraving it. At present we recur to the Latin and reject the Saxon. This is strengthening our language just as our empire is strengthened, by severing from it the most flourishing of its provinces. In another age we may cut down the branches of the Latin to admit the Saxon to shoot up again : for opposites come perpetually round. But it would be folly to throw away a current and commodious piece of money because of the stamp upon it, or to refuse an accession to an estate because our grandfather could do without it. A book composed of merely Saxon words (if indeed such a thing could be) would only prove the perverseness of the author. It would be inelegant, inharmonious, and deficient in the power of conveying thoughts and images, of which indeed such a writer could have but extremely few at starting. Let the Saxon however be always the groundwork.

JOHNSON. Is Goldsmith plain and simple enough for you?

TOOKE. I prefer him to all our writers now living ; but he has faults such as we do not find in less men, Louth for instance, and Hurd. In his *Essay on the Present State of Polite Literature*, he thus terminates a sentence : " Without a friend to drop a tear on their *unattended obsequies*." Now what are *obsequies* but funeral attendance? And surely he is a bad philosopher and a worse historian who says,

> A time there was, ere England's griefs began,
> When every rood of ground maintain'd its man.[1]

There never was any such time ; and if ever there should be, we who believe that " England's griefs " have more than begun already, are fortunate in being born at the present day.

JOHNSON. He writes more correctly than Middleton ; so let him alone. Middleton is not so correct a writer as you fancy. He was an infidel, sir, and, what is worse, a scoffer. He [2] wants the sweetness of Pope and Addison, the raciness of Dryden and Cowley, the compression of Swift and Hobbes, the propriety and justness and elevation of Barrow, the winning warmth and affectionate soul of

---

[1] *The Deserted Village.*
[2] From " He " to " overtops it " added in 2nd ed.

IMAGINARY CONVERSATIONS: ENGLISH

Jeremy Taylor, the terseness of Junius, the vivacity of Burke, clinging to a new idea like a woodbine to a young tree, till he embraces every part of it and overtops it.

TOOKE.[1] I was apprehensive of your insisting that we have nothing so classical in our language as the *Life of Cicero:* for such, I understand, is the opinion of our scholars at the Universities. I have detected many inaccuracies in Middleton; not in his reasonings and conclusions, for in these he is clear and strong, but in expression.[2] He says in his *Letter from Rome,* " The temple of some heathen deity *or* that of the Paphian Venus," [3] as if the Paphian Venus was not a heathen deity. " Popery, *which* abounds with instances of the grossest forgeries both of saints and reliques, *which* have been *imposed for genuine,* &c." [4] To have been *forgeries,* they must have been *imposed for genuine :* here is also a confusion in the repetition of *which,* relating to two subjects; as again, " The prejudices *which* the authority of so celebrated a writer may probably *inject* to the disadvantage of my argument, *which,* &c." [5]

JOHNSON. If Warburton had been as discerning [6] in language as he was acute in argument, he would have exposed to ridicule the [7] expression, " *inject a prejudice.*"

TOOKE. His acuteness seems usually to have forsaken him the

---

[1] 1st ed. reads: " TOOKE. You will acknowledge that we have nothing . . . *Life of Cicero,* nothing at once so harmonious and so unaffected. JOHNSON. Do you assert that Izaac Walton, who also wrote biography, is not equally unaffected ? TOOKE. Unaffected he is, and equally so, but surely less harmonious. Allow me to join with you in admiration of this most natural writer and most virtuous man, whose volumes I read with greater pleasure than any excepting Shakespear's. There is indeed, as you appear to indicate, no similitude between them; no more, I confess it, than there is between a cowslip and the sun that shines upon it; but there is a perpetually pleasant light, if I may use the expression, reflected from every thought and sentence, and no man ever redd him without being for a time both happier and better. I, like yourself, have detected a few inaccuracies," etc. 2nd ed. reads identically from " You " to " Shakespear's," and then : " JOHNSON. This would appear an absurdity, to those who are ignorant that the wisest books do not always please most the wisest men ; and that, if there are some which we want in our strength, there are others which we want in our infirmities. Fortunate is he who, in no hour of relaxation or of idleness, takes up, to amuse or pamper it, a worse book than Walton. TOOKE. There is, indeed . . . between Walton and Shakespear; no more . . . inaccuracies," etc.

[2] 1st ed. reads : " expressions of small importance."
[3] 1st ed. here inserts : " p. 134." [4] 1st ed. here inserts : " p. 171."
[5] 1st ed. here inserts : " p. 224."
[6] 1st ed. reads : " elegant." [7] 1st ed. reads : " such an."

JOHNSON AND HORNE (TOOKE)

moment he lost his malignity. As [1] some beasts muddy the water by tramping it before they drink, so nothing is palatable to Warburton but what he has made turbid. Nothing is weaker than his argument on this question, nothing more inelegant than his phraseology.[2] In another place he writes " *d*enounced " for " *a*nnounced." Our pugnacious bishop, although he defended the divine legation of Moses, would have driven the chariot of Pharaoh against him into the Red Sea. He says, in reference to Middleton, " How many able writers have employed *their* time and learning to prove Christian Rome to have borrowed *their* superstitions from the pagan city ? " He means *her* superstitions, and not the superstitions of the *able writers*, which the words, as they stand, designate. He surely could not dissent from Middleton, with whom nearly all the papists agree, drawing however far different inferences.

JOHNSON. On this ground I go with Middleton : he states a historical fact : he states a thing visible : but while he pretends to approach Religion for the sake of looking at her dress, he stabs her. Come, sir ! come, sir ! philology rather than this !

TOOKE. A little more then of philology : but first, let me suggest to you that no stab, my good Doctor, can inflict a dangerous wound on Truth. Homer had probably the design of impressing some such sentiment, when he said that gashes in celestial bodies soon unite again. If you have ever had the curiosity to attend a course of lectures on chemistry, or have resided in the house of any friend who cultivates it, you may perhaps have observed how a single drop of colourless liquid, poured on another equally colourless, raises a sudden cloud and precipitates it to the bottom : so, unsuspected falsehood, taken up as pure and limpid, is thrown into a turbid state by a drop ; and it does not follow that the drop must be of poison.

I [3] wish it were possible on all occasions to render the services we

[1] From "As" to "turbid" added in 3rd ed.
[2] 1st ed. reads : " phraseology . . . Sea. You remember the verses, I know not by whom.

>If Warburton by chance should meet
>The twelve apostles in the street,
>He'd pick a quarrel with 'em all,
>And shove his Saviour from the wall.

He says," etc. The verses, which are incorrectly given by Crump, were retained in 2nd ed., but deleted in *Wks.*, 1846.

[3] From " I " to " disapprove of the rest " added in 2nd ed. 1st ed. continues : " Middleton is once or twice vulgar : he writes '*for good and all,*' p. 286. This is," etc.

IMAGINARY CONVERSATIONS: ENGLISH

owe to criticism, without the appearance of detracting from established or from rising reputations. Since however the judicious critic will animadvert on none whose glory can be materially injured by his strictures, on none whose excellence is not so great and so well-founded that his faults in the comparison are light and few, the labour is to be endured with patience. For it is only by this process that we can go on from what is good to what is perfect. I am in the habit of noting down the peculiarities of every book I read; and, knowing that I was to meet you here, I have placed in the fold of my sleeve [1] such as I once collected out of Middleton.

JOHNSON. I shall be gratified, sir, by hearing them; and much more [2] than by dissertations, however rich and luminous, on his character and genius, which prove nothing else to me than the abilities of the dissertator.[3]

TOOKE. I will begin them with his orthography. He writes constantly *intire, onely, florish, embassador, inquire, genuin, tribun, troublesom, chast, hast* for *haste, wast* for *waste*.

JOHNSON. Pronouncing the three last as the common people do universally, and as others beside the common people do in his native county, Yorkshire. I approve of [4] the five first; I disapprove of the rest.

TOOKE. We [5] who condemn the elision of the final *e* in these words, in which the pronunciation requires it, elide it where it must likewise be pronounced. Our better authors in a wiser age never wrote *find, mind, kind, blind*, without the final vowel.

JOHNSON. It is wonderful we ever should have consented to part with it, having once had it, and knowing its use.

TOOKE. To return to Middleton. He writes *battel, sepulcher, luster, theater*.

JOHNSON. I do not blame him. Milton,[6] and most of our best

---

[1] 2nd ed. reads: " glove."
[2] 2nd ed. reads: " more so, let me assure you, than," etc.
[3] 2nd ed. reads: " declamer."
[4] 2nd ed. reads: " of the rest; I disapprove of these."
[5] From " We " to " To return to Middleton " added in 3rd ed. From " He " to " theater " added in 2nd ed.
[6] From " Milton " to " famous *theater* " added in 2nd ed. From " TOOKE " to " writer " added in 2nd ed. From " or " to " scholar " added in 3rd ed. From " TOOKE. He " to " *grandeur* " added in 2nd ed. From " the only " to " with Middleton " added in 3rd ed.

JOHNSON AND HORNE (TOOKE)

scholars, have done the same. Addison saw at Verona the famous *theater*.

TOOKE. He writes the verb *rebell* with a single *l*.

JOHNSON. The fault must surely be the printer's; and yet several final consonants have lately been omitted in our verbs, either by the ignorance and indifference of the writer, or by the unrebuked self-sufficiency of the compositor. I was unaware that the corruption began so early, and with a scholar.

TOOKE. He writes *grandor* in preference to *grandeur;* the only word of the kind which we persist in writing as the French do. Their *honneur* and *faveur* are domesticated with us and invested with our livery, while the starveling *grandeur* is left alone like a swallow on the house-top, when all the others have flown away. *Grandor* sounds more largely and fully than that puny offspring of the projected jaw. The authority of Milton, were there no other and better, ought to eliminate so ungainly an anomaly: for *liqueur* is not yet Englished.

JOHNSON. No, sir! we have *dram*. But whatever we would be ashamed of expressing in English, we call in French.

TOOKE. Of the three words *soup, group, troop,* borrowed from the French, there is only one which we have fairly naturalised. If *troop* is written with a double *o*, instead of *ou*, why should not the others?

JOHNSON. Why, indeed?

TOOKE. *Creature* has only two syllables, *creator* three. Why not write *creture*, as we pronounce it? correcting an anomaly so easily.

Now to go on again with Middleton. He[1] confuses *born* and *borne*, which indeed are of the same origin, but differently spelt in their different significations. As these two participles are the same, so are the two substantives *flower* and *flour;* which we may see the more plainly by removing them a little out of our own language, and placing them at the side of a cognate word in another. An academy of Tuscany, still in existence I think, entitled *Della Crusca*, chose for its emblem a sieve, and for its motto, *Il più bel fior ne coglie*.

JOHNSON. True enough: and now indeed I perceive the reason, indifferently versed as I am in the Italian language, why the members of that academy have been universally called, of late years, *coglioni*.

TOOKE. Whenever I hear a gentleman addressed by that title, I

[1] From "He" to "No, truly" added in 2nd ed.

shall bow to him as to a personage of high distinction, if I should travel at any time so far as Florence.

JOHNSON. Rightly judged, sir! A *coglione* in all countries is treated (I doubt not) with deference and respect.

TOOKE. Middleton writes *clame, proclame, exclame;* I think properly; as *pretense* and *defense.* He never uses the word *boast,* but *brag* instead of it; and the word *ugly,* in itself not elegant, most inelegantly. " There are many ugly reports about him," " which Cicero calls an ugly blow," " an ugly precedent," " an ugly disturbance broke out." He uses *proper* too as only the vulgar do. " Cicero never speaks of him with respect, nor of his government but as of a *proper* tyranny." " *A proper apotheosis.*"

JOHNSON. I did not imagine him to be so little choice in his expressions; you have collected a number that quite astonishes me.

TOOKE. May I read on?

JOHNSON. Are there more still upon that small piece of paper? Pray satisfy my curiosity.

TOOKE. Will you admit [1] a *southsayer?*

JOHNSON. No, truly; although [2] in the days of Elizabeth many wrote it so.

TOOKE. And many wrote them more idiomatically and more analogically than at present. What we write *monarch* and *tetrarch,* they wrote *monark* and *tetrark,* as we find in Aylmer and all the learned. Why should they be spelt like *arch* and *march* and *starch?*

JOHNSON. I agree with you: we did spell several words better in the reigns of Elizabeth and James than we do now. The learned were recognised then, and inferiors submitted to legitimate authority.

TOOKE. Yet, Doctor, you inform us in your preface that if the authors who write *honor, labor, explane, declame,* &c., have done no good, they have done little harm, because few have followed them, and because they innovated little. In fact, the writers to whom you refer have not innovated at all, but have followed the best authorities: and attempted to do good by substituting the better for the worse. A man or a writer is not the less good because he is not followed. There was a time, we read, when all went wrong, excepting one family. Every one of the words you have cited was written by learned, harmonious, and (I will add) considerate and elegant writers,

---

[1] 2nd ed. reads: " admitt."
[2] From " although " to " taught to *write* " added in 3rd ed.

JOHNSON AND HORNE (TOOKE)

excepting *red*, to which two unnecessary letters were added; of these the last has been rejected by universal consent. The double *d* was retained to distinguish the preterite of the verb from the adjective *red*; but the sense alone would always do that. Some other words are without the same advantage. We frequently find the adverb *still*, where it is doubtful whether it is an adverb or an adjective: for which reason, as well as for analogy, I would write *stil*. We write *until*, and should, as you have done, write *til*. In the same preface you inform us that " our language has been exposed to the corruptions of ignorance and the caprices of innovation." This is true, and to an extent which few men have the organs to see clearly. You commend the spelling of *highth* by Milton; and at the same time you are reluctant to correct our worst anomalies, declaring your unwillingness to " disturb upon narrow views, or for minute propriety, the orthography of our fathers." But if our fathers were licentious, and encroached on the patrimony of our grandfathers, what is to be done? Would it not be well to recover, by any obvious and honest means, as much as may be? If my father was a hairdresser, and chatted agreeably but wrote vilely, would it not be better to imitate my grandfather, who was a curate, and who spoke with seriousness and wrote with precision?

JOHNSON. Perhaps you are right. I have had my fling at Middleton; now take yours again.

TOOKE. Do you prefer a Gallicism or a Latinism? However, you shall have both. " Not *obnoxious* to Clodius's law," for not *amenable, liable*, or *subject*. Then " he dresses up in a clear and agreeable style ": then he goes on to " depreciate a *name*, so highly revered for its patriotism, and *whose* writings, &c." Now in what school-room was a *name* ever taught to *write*. " The [1] senate had no stomach to meddle with an affair so delicate."

JOHNSON. The delicacy of a thing in general is no reason why the stomach is disinclined to meddle with it.

TOOKE. " An oath which Cato himself, though he had publicly declared that he would never do it, was forced at last to swallow. He had digested many things against his will."

JOHNSON. He [2] might have swallowed them against his will, but surely he must have been the more glad at having digested them in

[1] From " The " to " will " added in 2nd ed.
[2] From " He " to " hardness " added in 3rd ed.

IMAGINARY CONVERSATIONS: ENGLISH

proportion to their hardness. If [1] he digested them against his will, the digestion could not have been forced nor difficult. The evil is, when we have the will and can not do it! But I hope we may now leave the dining-room.

TOOKE. In [2] Middleton's time it was usual to call Cicero by the familiar name of *Tully*, and we continue to say *Tully's Offices*. A mere Englishman, and only to such should we think we are speaking when we speak in English, would never comprehend the meaning of the title.

JOHNSON. Why not call the book *Cicero on Moral Obligations*, or, in one word, on *Duties?*

TOOKE. It might deceive some purchasers, on seeing only the title-page. *Duties*, in our days, signify *taxes*. Whenever we talk of the duties simply and solely, the taxes are understood: these being the only duties which statesmen inculcate on the people. The Roman names have fared among us worse than the Greek. Several retain their full proportions. Mark Antony has no Roman feature: such a name is more applicable to an English coal-heaver or mackerel-crier than to the great orator or the celebrated triumvir.

JOHNSON. In a translation from the Latin, wherever the Romans are introduced as speakers, I should think it more dignified to pronounce the names at full. I would not offer my money in a clipped and sweated state.

TOOKE. We retain the folly of turning the Greeks into Romans, and ending in *us* what ought to end in *os;* as Anyt*us* and Melit*us*. This is absurder than naturalising them at once. Are you inclined to look again at the coarseness and clumsiness of Middleton?

JOHNSON. Drag him out, by all means.

TOOKE.[3] "I did not take him to be a rascal." "Such clauses were only bugbears." "The occasion was so pat." "Shall I do it, *says I*, in my own way?" and two lines lower, "I will move the senate then, *says I*"; and three after, "So I thought, *says I*." Cicero is the speaker! "Cross the Tyber," for *across*. "I *had* rather *have* him the comrade of Romulus than of the Goddess Safety." "To try what fortunes he could *carve* for himself." "He seems to

---

[1] 2nd ed. reads: "Then they could not have been hard of digestion. The evil is . . . dining-room."

[2] From " In " to " by all means " added in 3rd ed.

[3] From " TOOKE " to " inert " added in 2nd ed.

JOHNSON AND HORNE (TOOKE)

be hard *put to it,* for a pretext." "Part *with without* regret." "*Dressing up* an impeachment." " If any other fate *expect me.*" " They would submit their conduct to the judgment of Cato, and deposit four thousand pounds *apiece* in his hands."

JOHNSON. *Apiece,* although Hooker has once applied the expression to men, ought never in such cases to be used instead of *each.* Its proper sense is of things saleable, inert or alive, but rather of the inert.

TOOKE. In [1] that case it might do very well for his senate or ours. I [2] find in most writers the word *each* used indiscriminately for *every :* this is wrong in prose : *each* ought never to be employed but in reference to persons or things mentioned before.

JOHNSON. I never heard that.

TOOKE. It may be wrong ; consider it. Middleton translates the word *innocens,* which, when spoken of military men, signifies their forbearance and moderation, into *innocent,* a term quite ridiculous when thus applied in English. In Cato's letter to Cicero, about his intended triumph, we find it thrice. " Young *Cæsar flowed* from the source of my counsels." " What *flows* from the result."

JOHNSON. False metaphor !

TOOKE. " If ever they *got the better.*" " To *give* the *exclusion.*" " Coming *forward towards.*"

JOHNSON. Redundant and very inelegant !

TOOKE. He always writes *oft* instead of *often.*

JOHNSON. Poetry alone has this privilege.

TOOKE. " The high office *which* you fill, and the eminent distinction *that* you bear."

JOHNSON. Much better without both *which* and *that.*

TOOKE. He uses the superlative *freest.*

JOHNSON. Properly the word *free* has no comparative nor superlative : for all monosyllables are made dissyllables by them, which could not be in *freer* and *freest.* I [3] do not willingly write *re-establish* or *re-edify.* The better word for the one would be *restablish*, if *restore* and *refix* are inadequate, and for the other *reconstruct.* It is bad enough to be affected, but it is intolerable to be at once affected

---

[1] From " In " to " ours " added in 3rd ed.
[2] From " I " to " *freer* and *freest* " added in 2nd ed.
[3] From " I " to " rightly " (and the footnote) added in 3rd ed. The peccant line of Byron is also cited in the second Conversation of Southey and Porson.

IMAGINARY CONVERSATIONS: ENGLISH

and uncouth. Justly may he be laughed at who falls into that slough which with a troublesome mincing gait he would avoid. They who might be shocked at *reappear* as a dissyllable, tolerate *ideal* as one, and *real* as a monosyllable.* Yet they would pronounce *reality* and *ideality* rightly. Many [1] of Middleton's political and religious, and some of his moral and historical reflections, do not please me.

TOOKE. A [2] scholar, as he was, should never have countenanced the sentence of Valerius Maximus on Marius. " Arpinum," he says, " had the singular felicity to produce the most *glorious contemner*, as well as the most illustrious improver, of the arts and eloquence." A singular kind of felicity indeed! If this glory had had its followers, the greater part of the world would at this time have been a forest. He places strange and discordant ideas in close apposition. Speaking of Sylla, he says, " He employed himself particularly in *reforming the disorders* of the state, by putting his new *laws* in execution, and in *distributing the confiscated lands of the adverse party* among his legions: so that the republic seemed to be once more seated on a *legal basis*, and the laws and judicial proceedings began to flourish in the forum." Confiscation [3] is a pretty legal basis, no doubt. Here he brings me to the Rostra. *Rostra* must be plural: I wonder he wrote " *that* rostra." There is an idle and silly thought in the Preface. Romulus, he tells you, seems to have *borrowed* the plan of his new state from the old government of Athens, as it was instituted by Theseus. What could Romulus know of Theseus or of Athens? The people were in the same state of civilisation, had the same wants, and satisfied them alike. Romulus borrowed the houses, harvests, and wives, of those near him: he borrowed no more from Athens than from 'Change-Alley. The laws of Solon were known to Numa first among the Romans, if [4] indeed Numa

---

* We find in Byron " *real* " a monosyllable. Neither he nor anyone else ever made " *reality* " a trisyllable. He caught it from a Scotch mother, quite uneducated. His grammar is very incorrect: for instance,

" Let *he* who made thee answer that." *Cain*.—W. S. L.

[1] From " Many " to " please me " added in 2nd ed.
[2] From " A " to " forum " added in 2nd ed.; " TOOKE " inserted in 3rd ed.
[3] From " Confiscation " to " rostra " added in 3rd ed. 2nd ed. reads: " forum ' (v. i. p. 35). TOOKE. There is an idle," etc., from " There is " to " Romans " having been added in that ed.
[4] From " if " to " fictitious " added in 3rd ed. From " JOHNSON. Leave politics " to " adapted " added in 2nd ed.

JOHNSON AND HORNE (TOOKE)

was a Roman, and not rather a Corinthian. The name seems fictitious.

JOHNSON. Leave politics alone: let history lie quiet. What I remarked, some time since, on comparatives and superlatives, makes me desirous that we had a collection of Latin and English comparatives, the former terminating in the masculine and feminine by *ior,* the latter in *er.* It would show us at a glance to what words the Roman writers, and our own, thought it better to prefix *magis* and *more,* instead of the comparative by the termination; and we should see, what never occurred to me until now, that the ancient and elegant chose the simpler mode preferably. Middleton, whom you have been quoting and examining so attentively, writes, *honester, modester:* Milton, *virtuousest.*

TOOKE. With all my veneration for this extraordinary and exemplary man, I would never use the word; and with all the preference I give, whenever it can be given, to the comparative formed by the final syllable, I never would admit it, nor the superlative, in words ending with *ous:* such as *virtuous, pious, religious.*

JOHNSON. Nor I truly: but perhaps our contemporaries are somewhat too abstemious in words to which it might be more gracefully adapted.

TOOKE. Middleton [1] writes " for good and all." This is somewhat in the manner of your friend Edmund Burke, who uses the word *anotherguess;* in which expression are both vulgarity and ignorance: the real term is *another-guise:* there is nothing of *guessing.* Beside [2] *another-guise* we have *another-gates.*

> When Hudibras about to enter
> Upon *anothergates* adventure, &c.

JOHNSON. Edmund Burke, sir, is so violent a reformer that I am confident he will die a Tory. I am surprised that anything he does or says should encounter your disapprobation. He, sir, and Junius should have been your favourites, if indeed they are not one and the same: for Edmund writes better when he writes for another, and any character suits him rather than his own. Shenstone, when he forgot his Strephons and Corydons and followed Spenser, became

---

[1] 1st ed. reads: " Middleton is once or twice vulgar: he writes '*for good and all,*' p. 286. This," etc.
[2] From " Beside " to " adventure " added in 3rd ed.

IMAGINARY CONVERSATIONS: ENGLISH

a poet. Your old antagonist Junius [1] wears an elegant sword-knot, and swaggers bravely. What think you?

TOOKE.[2] His words are always elegant, his sentences always sonorous, his attacks always vigorous, and rarely (although I may be a sufferer by admitting it) misplaced.[3] However, those only can be called great writers, who bring to bear on their subject more than a few high faculties of the mind. I require in him whom I am to acknowledge [4] for such, accuracy of perception, variety of mood, of manner, and of cadence; imagination, reflection, force, sweetness, copiousness, depth, perspicuity. I require in him a princely negligence of little things, and a proof that although he seizes much, he leaves much (alike within his reach) unappropriated [5] and untouched. Let me see nothing too trim, nothing quite incondite. Equal solicitude is not to be exerted upon all ideas [6]; some are brought into the fulness of light, some are adumbrated: so on the beautiful plant of our conservatories, a part is in fruit, a part in blossom; not a branch is leafless, not a spray is naked. Then come those graces and allurements, for which we have few and homely names, but which among the ancients had many, and expressive of delight and of divinity, *lepores, illecebræ, veneres*, &c.: these, like the figures that hold the lamps on staircases, both invite us and show us the way up: for, write as wisely as we may, we cannot fix the minds of men upon our writings unless we take them gently by the ear.

JOHNSON. On [7] this we meet and agree; but you exact too much. You include too many great properties within your stipulations.

TOOKE. Several of these in Junius were uncalled for; some that would have been welcome were away; and he is hardly a great writer in whom anything that is great is wanting.

JOHNSON. Sometimes even Cicero himself is defective both in ratiocination and in euphony.

---

[1] 1st ed. reads: " Junius (what makes you smile, sir?) wears."
[2] 1st ed. reads: " TOOKE. Of Junius I would say little, for more reasons than one. His," etc.
[3] 1st ed. reads: " misplaced. Still however those."
[4] 1st ed. reads: " acknowledge so, accuracy."
[5] 1st and 2nd eds. read: " unappropriated. Let me."
[6] 1st ed. reads: " ideas alike; some."
[7] 1st ed. reads: " Here we."

JOHNSON AND HORNE (TOOKE)

Tooke. It [1] can not be controverted that, even in this most eloquent author, there are sentences which might be better.

Johnson. For instance, in the monkish canticle,

> Bellum autem ita *suscipiatur*
> Ut nihil aliud nisi pax quæsita *videatur*.

Tooke. By writing *susceptum sit*, he would have avoided the censure he has here incurred too justly. Toward the end of his dialogue *De Claris Oratoribus*, he runs into the tautology, " *Hic me dolor tangit ; hæc me cura solicitat.*" Can anything be more self-evident, and therefore more unnecessary to state and insist on, than *that those are worthy of friendship in whom there is a reason why they should be our friends !*

> Digni autem sunt amicitiâ, quibus in ipsis inest causa cur diligantur :

or indeed much more so, than *that old age comes on by degrees ;* which he expresses in words redundant with the letter *s*.

> Sensim sine sensu ætas senescit.

And I wish I could think it were free from the ambition of an antithesis, in the *sensim sine sensu*.

Johnson. He is the only Latin prose writer in whom you will find a pentameter.

> Quid dominus navîs ? eripietne suum ?

And I doubt whether in any other the tenses of *possum* are repeated seven times in about fourteen lines,* as they are here, with several of the same both before and after.

Tooke. This [2] pentameter is not his only one.

Johnson. Stop there. We write pentameter with the *e* before the *r*, and *metre* inversely. I throw out this fresh bone to you in my largess.

Tooke. In the third book *De Oratore*, where he reproves the fault,

---

[1] From " It " to " justly "added in 2nd ed. From " Toward " to " *solicitat* " added in 3rd ed. From " Can " to " after " added in 2nd ed. In 2nd ed. this passage is given wholly to Johnson.

* *De Officiis*, l. ii, beginning at the close of the paragraph, " Adde ductus aquarum, etc."—W. S. L.

[2] From " This " to " deserved " added in 3rd ed. In 2nd ed. Tooke continues : " Doctor, let us try to think as rightly as Cicero, and to express our thoughts," etc.

IMAGINARY CONVERSATIONS: ENGLISH

he commits it. If you never have remarked the passage, you will wonder at finding both a hexameter and pentameter, and in sequence.

> Complexi plus multo etiam vidisse videntur
> Quam quantum nostrorum ingeniorum acies, &c.

Milton puts several verses together in his prose. At the conclusion of the second book of his *Treatise against Prelaty*, are nearly four of the most powerful and harmonious he ever wrote.

> When God commands to take the trumpet, &c.[1]

In another place he likewise writes as prose,

> The blessed meekness of his lowly roof,
> Those ever open and inviting doors, &c.

But these last, although good, fair verses, are only to the pitch of *Paradise Regained*.

JOHNSON. The dog barked at bishops; and Cicero praised those who slew his benefactor.

TOOKE. We have nothing to do at present with the politics of either, although we have raised into a blaze the tenets of the one, and have slain more friends than the other ever conciliated or deserved. Let us try to express our thoughts as clearly; we may then as easily pardon those who discover a few slight faults in our writings, as he would pardon us, were he living, for pointing them out in his. The two most perfect writers (I speak of style) are Demosthenes and Pascal; but all their writings put together are not worth a third of what remains to us of Cicero; nor can it be expected that the world will produce another (for the causes of true eloquence are extinct) who shall write at the same time so correctly,[2] so delightfully, and so wisely.

JOHNSON. Let him give way, sir, let him give way, for your rump-parliament and regicide. The causes of true eloquence are extinct! I understand you, sir: rump and regicide for ever!

TOOKE. Doctor, I am not one of those who would agitate so idle a question, as, whether it is the part of a contemptible man, much less whether it is that of a criminal one, to scoff at superstitions forbidden by the religion of our country, or to punish with death and ignominy,

---

[1] Used by Landor on the title-page of *The Italics*, 1848.
[2] 1st ed. reads: " correctly, so clearly, so," etc.

JOHNSON AND HORNE (TOOKE)

a torturer, a murderer, a tyrant, a violator of all his oaths and a subverter of all his laws!

JOHNSON. That sentence, sir, is too graceful for mouths like yours. *Burn, sink, and destroy*, are words of better report from the hustings.

TOOKE. I presume you mean, Doctor, when they are directed by pious men against men of the same language and lineage: for words, like ciphers and persons, have their value from their place. I am sorry you seem offended.

JOHNSON. It is the nature of the impudent never to be angry.

TOOKE. Impudence, I find, is now for the first time installed among the christian virtues.

JOHNSON. No, sir: impudence is to virtue what cynicism is to stoicism. Nothing is harder or crueler; nothing seems less so.

TOOKE. Doctor, let me present to you this cup of tea.

JOHNSON. Why! the man wears upon his mind an odd party-coloured jacket; half-courtier, half-rebel. I do not think I have flattered him very much; yet he bowed as if he was suing me to dance with him.

I[1] can listen, sir, while you talk rationally: but I am angry that a gentleman of your abilities should be so inordinately fond of change. Do you think anything correct in any author whatsoever?

TOOKE. Once[2] I was of opinion that nothing in Pascal could be corrected or improved: this opinion I have seen reason to change, still considering him more exact and elaborate than the best English writers. In the second sentence of his *Provincial Letters*, he says, "Tant d'assemblées d'une compagnie aussi célèbre qu'est la Faculté de Théologie à Paris, et où il s'est passé tant de choses *si extraordinaires* et *si* hors d'exemple, en font concevoir une *si* haute idée qu'on ne peut croire qu'il n'y en ait un sujet bien *extraordinaire*. Cependant vous serez bien surpris, quand vous apprendrez par ce récit à quoi se termine un *si* grand éclat."

JOHNSON. These repetitions indeed appear inelegant.

TOOKE. In the first sentence, a few lines above, he used *bien abusé*, and afterward *bien important*. I shall make no observation on the disagreeable recurrence of sound in *surpris* and *récit*. Similar sounds have sometimes a good effect; but it must be an exquisite ear that

---

[1] From "I" to "whatsoever" added in 3rd ed.
[2] From "Once" to end of Conversation not in 1st ed.

distinguishes the proper time. Permit me to continue the period. " Et c'est ce que je vous dirai en peu de mots, après m'en être parfaitement instruit."

JOHNSON. Here I can detect no fault.

TOOKE. It lies in the reasoning: Pascal says plainly, " You will be much surprised, when you learn by my recital how such a bustle terminates; and I will tell you it in few words, when I am perfectly informed of it."

JOHNSON. I have not yet seen the error.

TOOKE. How can Pascal say positively that his correspondent will be *much surprised*, at the result of a thing which he is about to relate, when he himself does not well know what that result will be? That he does not, is evident; because he says he will tell him *after* he has discovered the matter of fact. He makes another promise too, rather hazardous: he promises that he will tell it in few words. Now, not seeing the extent of the information he may receive on it, few words perhaps might not suffice.

JOHNSON. I doubt whether the last objection be not hyper-criticism.

TOOKE. Better that than *hypocriticism;* the vague and undisciplined progeny of our Mercuries, which run furiously from the porter-pot to the tea-pot, and then breathe their last. There can be no hypercriticism upon such excellent writers as Pascal. Few suspect any fault in him; hardly one critic in a century can find any. Impudence may perch and crow upon high places, and may scratch up and scatter its loose and vague opinions: this suits idlers: but *we* neither talk to the populace nor stand in the sun pointing out what they heed not, and what they could never perceive.

Another [1] fault of his comes into my recollection, and could never come more opportunely than after my expression of esteem for him. " C'est le motif de tous les hommes, jusqu'à ceux qui se tuent *et qui se pendent*." As if he who hangs himself is different from him who kills himself, and has another motive. Were the volumes of Pascal before me, I might lay my finger on other small defects, some in expression, some in reasoning: and I should do it: for you would not suffer him to fall thereby in your esteem, nor even to mingle in the crowd of high literary names. He stands with few; and few will ever join him.

[1] From " Another " to " motive " added in 3rd ed.

JOHNSON AND HORNE (TOOKE)

JOHNSON. Good scholars and elegant writers may sometimes lapse. Gray is both : yet he says,

> Their name, their years, spelt by the unlettered Muse, &c.

There were nine, mythologists tell us ; but they have forgotten to inform us which was the unlettered one. We might as well talk of the powerless Jupiter, the lame Mercury, and the squinting Venus. In another poem, *the court was sat* is not English ; nor is the note, in the *Ode to Music*, on Mary de Valence, " of whom tradition says that her husband " : tradition does not speak here of *her*, but of the husband. I[1] have attempted to demonstrate some improprieties of expression in other places.

TOOKE. You are supposed by many inconsiderate readers to have been too severe on him.

JOHNSON. A critic is never too severe when he only detects the faults of an author. But he is worse than too severe when, in consequence of this detection, he presumes to place himself on a level with genius. A rat or a serpent can find a hole in the strongest castle : but they could about as much construct it as he could construct the harmonious period or " the lofty rhyme." Severity lies in rash exaggeration and impudent exposure. Such as fall into it cut their own fingers, and tie them up so clumsily as to make them useless. He who exults over light faults betrays a more notable want of judgment than he censures. Sir, have I been too minute in my examination of Gray ?

TOOKE. I think you have not ; but I doubt whether you have assigned to him that place among the poets (I dare hardly say the men of genius) to which he is entitled. Expunge from his *Elegy* the second and third stanza, together with all those which follow the words

> Even in our ashes live their wonted fires,

and you will leave a poem with scarcely a blemish : a poem which will always have more readers than any other in any language. Every church-yard contains a monument of Gray inscribed with everlasting characters.

---

[1] From " I " to " Wimbledon common " added in 3rd ed. In 2nd ed., after " husband," TOOKE proceeds : " Gray was a very learned man, and no mean poet. I wish he had not written
> Ah happy hills ! ah pleasing shades," etc.

IMAGINARY CONVERSATIONS: ENGLISH

Johnson. You are enthusiastic for once.

Tooke. No poetry can make me that: and I am quite as sensible of Gray's imperfections as you are. He is often very harsh, and, what is wonderful in so laborious a composer, incorrect.

Johnson. Come hither, young lady! Have you Gray's poems? Go fetch them. Now give them this gentleman. Sir! you need not kiss her hand: she is not the queen.

Tooke. That graceful curtsey might have well deceived me.

Johnson. Sir! you make the girl blush.

Tooke. If so, I implore you not to look so stedfastly at her, pointing me out for so great a criminal.

Johnson. Whisper less loudly. She caught every syllable, and walked away smiling. And now she is standing before the fire, to lay all her blushes upon that.

Tooke. Doctor, you are surely the nicest of observers. Turn, if you please: here are the words we want:

> Fair Venus' train.

Johnson. Ay, indeed, that is harsh enough.

Tooke.
> Yet hark how through the peopled air
> The busy murmur glows.

Johnson. He might as well have said, *Hark!* what fantastic green palings and dingy window-shutters!

Tooke. "The azure flowers that blow," are precisely the azure flowers that never did blow.

> Hard unkindness' altered eye

is harsh, ungrammatical, unpoetical, and worse than nonsense. If her eye were altered, it must be altered for the better.

> Gay Hope is theirs, by Fancy fed,
> Less pleasing when possest.

Unless they possessed it, how is it theirs? He means the *object* of Hope, not Hope.

> Nor second he that *rode sublime*
> Upon the seraph wings of ecstacy
> *The secrets of the abyss to spy.*

This is just as if I should ride to Highgate or Harrow for the purpose of looking into the hold of a lighter on the Thames. Who would ride

JOHNSON AND HORNE (TOOKE)

sublime to spy what lies low, even in an abyss? particularly to spy its secrets? Speaking of Dryden he mentions his "*bright-eyed fancy.*" Vigorous sense and happy expression are the characteristics of Dryden, certainly not fancy.

> Thoughts that *breathe*.

It is no great matter to say that of them.

> Loose his beard.

Beards were never tied up like the tails of coach-horses.

> Hark! how each giant oak and desart cave
> Sighs to the torrent's awful voice beneath;
> O'er thee, O king, their hundred arms they wave.

Who wave their hundred arms? Why, the giant oaks, to be sure. True enough; but not the desert caves, nor the torrent's awful voice; and never was sighing more in vain than theirs.

> The thread is *spun*.

The thread must have been spun before they began *weaving*.

> And gorgeous dames and statesmen old
> In bearded majesty appear.

What! the gorgeous dames too? Where were their scissors?

> Nor envy base, nor creeping gain,
> Dare the muse's walk to *stain*.

One would think he had before his eyes the geese on Wimbledon common. And [1] I wish he had not written

> Ah happy hills! ah pleasing shades!
> Ah fields beloved in vain!

JOHNSON. Why so? the verses are tender.

TOOKE. In the next breath he tells us plainly that they were *not* beloved in vain; quite the contrary; that they soothed his weary soul and breathed a second spring. What [2] could he have more from them?

JOHNSON. Rent, sir, rent. I have graver things to adduce against him. He has dared to talk about the *star of Brunswick*.

---

[1] From "And" to "hammer" added in 2nd ed.
[2] Crump reads: "When."

IMAGINARY CONVERSATIONS: ENGLISH

Tooke. Doctor, I entreat you, as a lover of loyalty, to let every man be loyal in his own way. Obedience to the existing laws is a virtue: respect and reverence of misfortune is another. Only cast out from the pale of loyalty those who espouse the interests of a part rather than of the whole. Whenever I see a person whose connections are plebeian, strive and strain for aristocracy, I know what the fellow would have: he would sacrifice the interests of his friends and class for his own profit. Generosity may induce the high-born man to drop behind his family, and to concern himself in bettering [1] the condition of those below him. Officiousness and baseness are the grounds on which the plebeian moves, who wrangles and fights for [2] certain men more powerful than enough without him. This is the counterfeit loyalty on which I would gladly see descend your reprobating stamp and hammer. The [3] star of Brunswick is no more censurable than the star of Brentford, and very like it both in brilliancy and magnitude.

Johnson. Return to philology: even Cicero himself, as we have seen, speaks incorrectly.

Tooke. Sometimes. Yet my estimation of his good sense and eloquence is undiminished by his inattention and negligence, which rarely occur, and on unimportant matters. The [4] English use *infinity* for *innumerability*, which word he uses: and it is curious, as being the only word in the whole compass of latinity which (with its enclitic) contains nine syllables. "Infinitatem locorum *innumerabilitatemque* mundorum." I never can think that the word *infinitior* is founded on reason. What is infinite cannot be *more* infinite. I do not object so strongly to *perfectissimus*: this is only a mode of *praising* what is perfect, which, like infinity, cannot be extended or increased. There are words, however, which neither in their sense nor their formation seem capable of a comparative or superlative. There [5] are properly no such words as *resistless, relentless, exhaustless*, which we often find not only in poetry but in prose: for all adjectives ending in *less*, of which the first to strike us authors is *moneyless*, are formed from substantives. Yet we can not say *more* or *most* peer*less*; *more* or *most* penni*less*. We often find indeed a *most* care*less* servant,

---

[1] 2nd ed. reads: "meliorating."
[2] 2nd ed. reads: "for those who are."
[3] From "The" to "magnitude" added in 3rd ed.
[4] From "The" to "mundorum" added in 3rd ed.
[5] From "There" to "Yet" added in 3rd ed.

JOHNSON AND HORNE (TOOKE)

a *most* thought*less* boy : but the expression is at least inelegant and unhappy : I should even say vicious, if celebrated writers did not check and control [1] me by their authority.

JOHNSON. Sir, this is quibbling.

TOOKE. If correctness be the best part of eloquence, and as ninety-nine to a hundred in it, which I think it is, then this is no quibble. When our servants or tradesmen speak to us, it is quite enough that we understand them; but in a great writer we require exactness and propriety. Unless we have them from him, we are dissatisfied, in the same manner as if the man who refuses to pay us a debt should offer us a present. I am ready for eloquence when I find correctness. You complain, and [2] justly, of that affected and pedantic expression of Milton, where he says that Adam was the most comely of men ever born since, and Eve the fairest of her daughters.

JOHNSON. Ay, certainly.

TOOKE. Yet you understand what he means. We [3] employ in our daily speech an expression equally faulty. We say, " You of all *others* ought not, &c." Now surely *you* are not one of *others*. Correctly spoken, the phrase would be, " You of all men." On reading Milton's verses the other day, I recollected a parallel passage in Tacitus on Vespasian : " Solus omnium *ante se* principum in melius mutatus " : and fancying that I had seen it quoted by La Rochefoucauld, I had the curiosity to inquire in what manner he translated it : for he leaves none without a French version. His words are, " Il fut le seul des empereurs, *ses prédécesseurs*, qui changea en mieux." Here we see how two acute men [4] pass over, without observing it, a preposterous perversion of language and plain sense.

JOHNSON. There are faults committed by pedants for the mere purpose of defending them.

TOOKE. Writers [5] far removed from pedantry use expressions which, if we reflect on them, excite our wonder.[6]

JOHNSON. Better [7] those than vulgarisms.

[1] 2nd ed. reads : " controll."
[2] 2nd ed. reads : " and very justly."
[3] From " We " to " men " added in 3rd ed.
[4] 2nd ed. reads : " men that ever existed (for such they certainly were in the anatomy of the human heart) pass over," etc.
[5] 2nd ed. reads : " People."
[6] 2nd ed. reads : " wonder more strongly still."
[7] 2nd ed. reads : " Psha ! vulgarisms ! vulgarisms ! TOOKE. A proof of their extensive use. No expression," etc.

IMAGINARY CONVERSATIONS: ENGLISH

TOOKE. There we disagree. No expression can become a vulgarism which has not a broad foundation. The language of the vulgar hath its source in physics: in known, comprehended, and operative things: the language of those who are just above the vulgar is less pure, as flowing from what they do not in general comprehend. Hence the profusion of broken and ill-assorted metaphors, which we find in the conversation of almost all who stand in the intermediate space between the lettered and the lowest. I will go further, and venture to assert that you will find most of the expressions in daily use among ourselves to be ambiguous and vague. Your servant would say, *a man told me so :* the most learned and elegant of your acquaintance would probably say, on the same occasion, *a certain person informed me.* Here the person is not *a certain* but an *uncertain* one, and the thing told may have nothing in it of *information*. A farmer would say, *a deal of money for a galloway :* a minister of state, *a considerable sum*, speaking of the same. Reflection demonstrates clearly that, although the sum may have been the double of the value, it could not be an object of *consideration*, which word, however abused, is equivalent to *contemplation ;* another [1] word strangely degraded and misapplied. *Certain* then is *uncertain*, and *considerable* is *inconsiderable*. These words, you cannot fail to have observed, are the signs and figures whereby we denote the very two things which, in one form or other, are the most operative on the human mind ; magnitude and truth. As [2] *considerable* is *inconsiderable*, and *certain* is *uncertain*, so *doubt* is used for *believe*. " I *doubt* you are wrong," is said for " I *believe* you are wrong." This is elliptical. " I come to the conclusion, or the suspicion, by doubting on points about it, that you are wrong."

JOHNSON. We will return, at some future time, to the metaphysical of language. The [3] new and strange word an *individual* seems rather to signify a *dividual* or *par*ticular. Pray tell me now, since you have always a word in defence of the vulgar, what the fools can mean by a *dead heat*, when racers reach the goal together, and a *dead hand*, speaking [4] of a man apparently the most alive and active : as a *dead hand* at quoits or tennis ?

---

[1] From " another " to " misapplied " added in 3rd ed.
[2] From " As " to " wrong " added in 3rd ed.
[3] From " The " to " particular " added in 3rd ed.
[4] From " speaking " to " tennis " added in 3rd ed.

JOHNSON AND HORNE (TOOKE)

TOOKE. Add also *dead level*. *Dead* is *finished, accomplished;* in that sense the same as *deed; deed* is *fact,* and *fact* implies *certainty.* A *dead level* is an exact one.

JOHNSON. *Deed* however is no adjective.

TOOKE. Nor is *net*, nor is *life :* yet we say a *net*-income and a *life*-interest. I have sometimes thought that *net* might be *neat.*[1] I am however more inclined to believe that it means *purse* in this instance, a thing of the same texture ; and my reason is, that we say ordinarily, " he *netted* so much." Since [2] you have admitted me into court as advocate for the vulgar, let me remark that we laugh at those who pronounce an aspirate where there should be none : but are not we ourselves more ridiculous, who deliberately write it before words in which it never is pronounced ? If we are to pronounce it, why put *an* to it ? as *an* honest, *an* honourable, *an* hour. The simple *a* denotes that it is wanted ; as in *a* harp, *a* heart, *a* house, *a* home, *a* harness. Unprofitably do we employ *an* before words beginning with the aspirate ; and much is it to be regretted that we see broken up and dissevered this household of familiar words. All that are aspirated should have *a* rather than *an* prefixed. There are other things also we often see in print, but never say : for instance, *an unicorn, an university, an use, an ewe, an yew-tree.* We properly say *an only son*, improperly *such an one ;* because in *only* the *o* has simply its own sound, in *one* it sounds as if *w* were before it. Exactly half our vowels are occasionally consonants. Who would venture to say *an* year ago, or *an* youth, or *an yelping* cur, or *an yesterday's* newspaper ?

JOHNSON. Proceed, sir, proceed : but I do not expect much regularity in your proceedings.

TOOKE. Look on me as on a fox-hunter in the field. I cannot go straightforward continually. At one time there is a quickset hedge before me ; at another there are rotten stakes ; here a deep ditch, there a quagmire, and farther onward a wide morass. I will mention words for your consideration as they arise before me, and not in such order as a grammar would require. We are walking in a forest, where the climate is genial, where the soil is rich, and where the fruits are growing wild : we will not at present take the trouble to assort

---

[1] 2nd ed. reads : " *neat ;* we know the two words are the same as adjectives. I," etc.

[2] From " Since " to " *fac-totum* " added in 3rd ed.

IMAGINARY CONVERSATIONS: ENGLISH

them. As here you find a quince next to a cedar, and there peach-blossoms dropping on a yew, so here we may catch a substantive and an adverb close together, both ready for correction.

JOHNSON. Have it so, and go on.

TOOKE. If we write *entrance*, why not *uttrance?* than which nothing can be expressed harsher. We should always write " enter-ance," were it only to make a distinction between this substantive and the verb *entrance*. Shakespeare has done it in *Macbeth:*

> The raven himself is hoarser [1]
> That croaks the fatal enterance of Duncan
> Under my battlements:

and many other words on the same principle: for example, the verse in *All 's Well that Ends Well:* [2]

> And lasting in her sad rememberance.

JOHNSON. Shakespeare has indeed thus written; but what man dares always to be right?

TOOKE. *Simile* is not an English word, nor a Latin one, as a substantive. *Simily* should replace it. But of all the inelegances in pages professedly English, *fac-simile* is the vilest; worse in its conformation than its twin-brother *fac-totum*. In our language there are other parts of speech used somewhat promiscuously. Some verbs with us are French nouns and particles united. What think you of *engross? en gros*. It means in one sense, as probably you have remarked in your *Dictionary*, what is written in *thick* characters by lawyers; in another, that appropriation to themselves of what is not theirs by right; attributing to the means (the engrossing, or writing in *thick* letters) what is done by the employer of those means, the lawyer. Colloquially, and sometimes in graver business, we say *on all sides*.

JOHNSON. Why not?

TOOKE. How many sides have we? I should have believed that we had two only, if a certain compound did not twitch me by the skirt and lay claim to a third.

JOHNSON. Sir, a man has but two sides from which that expression

---

[1] The same emendation is made in the second Conversation of Southey and Porson.

[2] *Sic.* See *Twelfth Night*, I. i. 31.

could have been deduced; for *outside* and *inside* have nothing to do with it. They however show us that *side* in their case signifies *part*; and it has this signification when we say *on all sides*. *Side*, in this sense, is the same as the Latin *situs*, the Italian *sito*. *Usum loquendi populo concessi.*

TOOKE. *Scientiam mihi reservavi.* We have only two *halves*; yet we say on my *behalf*, on your *behalf*, and on his *behalf*, when the same matter is in litigation among three persons. Chaucer says, *on this halfe God;* on this side of God; and *four halves*, four *sides*, as his interpreter expresses it.

JOHNSON.[1] Would you, who are a stickler for propriety, use such an expression as *somehow or other*, which we hear spoken and find written continually?

TOOKE. I would not; because *somehow* expresses the whole meaning, and other *how* is not English. We, who are not vulgar, say *brother-in-law*, *son-in-law*, &c. wherein we appear to vie in folly with the French and Italians, and even to exceed them. An Italian calls *cognato* what we call *brother-in-law*, neither of which is true. He is not cognate to us, nor is he a brother by the laws. The *beaufrère* of the Frenchman is ludicrous; so is the *parent;* but not so much as our *grandson*, one day old. A Frenchman must speak more ridiculously still if he would speak of a horse-shoe made of anything but iron: as Voltaire in *Zadig:* " Des fers *d'argent* à onze deniers de fin." From the same poverty and perversion of language, he attributes *sense* to dust or clouds: " Nuages agités en *sens* contraires," meaning *direction.* There [2] is also an odd expression for " I have it in my power," *Je suis à même:* oddness, but not corruption, as in many of ours. We say *coadjutor* where there is only one helper. And [3] there are expressions which in themselves are very incorrect, yet give an idea not to be mistaken: such for instance is, *Round your fireside.* You can not be round a side.

JOHNSON. " Round the fire " would be better.

TOOKE. Not at all. We can not be round it in our houses, unless some of us are behind the chimney. We say, *Light the fire.* Nothing has less need of lighting. The Italians say, *Light the chimney.* Now for an impropriety or two in verbs. *Originate*, a deponent,

---

[1] From " JOHNSON " to " English " added in 3rd ed.
[2] From " There " to " ours " added in 3rd ed.
[3] From " And " to " verbs " added in 3rd ed.

IMAGINARY CONVERSATIONS: ENGLISH

is become active. People of fashion say *He originated the measure*.

JOHNSON.[1] Scholars will always say *The measure originated from him*.

TOOKE. There is another word which we use improperly. We say, " Such a person was *executed* for robbery ": now the *person* is *prosecuted*, the *sentence executed*. One would imagine that *executioner* should designate the *judge*, him who executes the laws; not him who executes only one decision of them; but in our jurisprudence we have the hangman so perpetually before us that the expression is accountable and reasonable. *Execution* then stands with us for *juridical death*, and not for the completion of any other sentence. We employ it again on the seizure of goods under a warrant.

JOHNSON. Within the last year or two, I have heard the expression " a man of *talent*," instead of " a man of *talents* ": and I am informed by my friend, Sir Joshua Reynolds, who quickly discerns an inelegance and strongly disapproves an innovation, that an *artist* now signifies a *painter*, and *art painting*, exclusively.*

TOOKE. Ignorant people, I myself have remarked, are beginning to speak so: the fashion cannot continue. We might as well call a Doctor of Physic a doctor of rhubarb, and a Doctor of Laws a doctor of subpœnas. And yet we smile at the expressions of the vulgar. You would think me vulgar, if I called a man a *desperate* fool, or a house a *desperate* big house.

---

[1] 2nd ed. reads : " measure : scholars," etc., and " There is," etc., the speech being given to TOOKE.

* Since the time of Johnson, the establishment of an academy for painting in England has much infected our language. If we find five metaphors in a chapter, four of them are upon trust from the oil-and-colour man.—W. S. L.

[In 2nd ed. this footnote continues : " When people attend to the meaning of a sentence as much as to the sound of it, what absurdity must they discover in the following !

'The sun shone in full splendour, and, while it softened the rugged aspect of the surrounding mountains, threw a glow of transparency over the majestic ruins.'—Coxe's *Monmouthshire*.

The slang of the painter comes crudely from the mouth of the tourist. How ridiculous is the application here ! *Glow* and *transparency* are pretty words; but a glow of transparency ! what is that ? or how is it to be thrown *over* majestic ruins. Are the majestic ruins made transparent ? And yet this is the writer who is to discriminate the scenery of one country from the scenery of another ; whose precision of language is to instruct us on the state of manners, of learning, of civilization, and of policy."]

JOHNSON AND HORNE (TOOKE)

JOHNSON. Ay, indeed I should.

TOOKE. Come [1] along, my learned and affable preceptor. Be it as pleasant for you to be released from the columns of a dictionary as for me to escape from the chapters of a grammar. We will expatiate freely over the wide and varied field before us, here trampling down a troublesome thistle, and there raising up again a neglected flower. We will make hay while the sun shines; and I perceive already that the clouds are rolling off. We will toss it about, lightly and easily; which is the true meaning of the word *discuss*; we will let in plentifully light and air, and inhale a fresh fragrance at every heaving of the rake. Others may cart it, lay it on the stack, press it, trim it, truss it, and carry it to market. Even if I should assist you but little, think it somewhat to have drawn around you so many stedfast and inquiring eyes, so many fair heads, each radiant with its circle of glory, like angels about some beatified saint.

JOHNSON. Don't play the fool.

TOOKE. Alas! it is the only game I have ever learnt to play: but I dislike to play it single-handed. Come along, Doctor! We have many words implying intensity, now gone or going out of use among the middling classes, and lapsed entirely from the highest. Such as *mighty* (for *very*) which exactly corresponds with the Latin *valde;* and *desperate*, in the same sense, for which they had a relative in *insanus*, used by Cicero before the senate in designating the terraces of Clodius, which he calls " *insanas* substructiones." The vulgar now use *mortally* as Cicero uses *immortally*, an expression of intensity and vehemence. " Te a Cæsare quotidie plus diligi *immortaliter* gaudio."

JOHNSON. There is hardly any writer who does not sacrifice elegance to force, when he has occasion. Addison says that Virgil " *strained hard* to outdo Lucretius in the description of the plague."

TOOKE. Addison, in the same sentence, which I remember for its singular weakness, says also that " if the reader would see with what success, he may find it at large in Scaliger."

JOHNSON. He might.

TOOKE. Could he not find it equally at large in Lucretius and Virgil; or is Scaliger nearer at hand, presenting a more authentic document than the original? Addison is not only an inconsiderate and superficial critic, but is often vulgar and mean: he is sometimes

---

[1] From " Come " to " single-handed " added in 3rd ed.

ungrammatical. He is both in that verse by which he has expressed how much more useful the senate was in Thessaly than at Rome.

JOHNSON. I remember none such.

TOOKE.
>The *corps* of half her senate
>*Manure* the fields of Thessaly.

The grammatical fault would not have been committed, if the word *corps* had been written, as it should be, with a final *e*. In his *Poem to the King* he hath several times used the word *corps* in the plural. On the contrary he has added *s* to the word *seraphim*. The bathos was never so well illustrated by Swift, as it might have been if he had taken his examples of it from Addison alone. What think you of this?

>Thus Ætna, when in fierce eruption *broke*,
>Fills heaven with ashes—and the earth with smoke.

Look now at his *Saint Cecilia*. The imbecility of the first line we will pass over: in the second, where is the difference between the voice and the accents?

>Cecilia's name does all our numbers grace,
>From every voice the tuneful accents fly.

What does the word *it* relate to, in the next? certainly not to *the accents*, probably not to *voice*, for the *every* stands in the way.

>In soaring trebles now *it* rises high,
>And now it sinks and dwells upon the base.

Doctor, I am a dealer in words, a *word-fancier*; excuse me then if I premise to you, in the spirit of trades and callings, the importance I attach to mine.

JOHNSON. Let us hear what you have to say. Wisdom is founded on words; on the right application of them.

TOOKE. We have two which we use indifferently; *on* and *upon*. It appears to me that those who study elegance, by which I always mean precision and correctness, may give a specimen here. I would say *upon a tower*: on the same principle I would say *on a marsh*. There would indeed be no harm in saying *on a tower*; but there would be an impropriety in saying *upon a marsh*; for *up*, whether we are attentive or inattentive, whether we have been a thousand times wrong or never, means *somewhat high*, somewhat to which we ascend.

JOHNSON AND HORNE (TOOKE)

I should speak correctly if I said, " Doctor Johnson *flew on* me," incorrectly, if I said " he *fell upon* me." Custom is a rule for everything but contradiction. We have hardly three writers of authority.

JOHNSON. How ! sir ! hardly three ! People of your cast in politics are fond of vilifying our country. Is this your whigship ?

TOOKE. Whigship it is indeed : but not mine. Consider me as holding out a cake of meal and honey to appease you, when I bring to your recollection that the Romans have but one. For however great is the genius of Sallustius and Livius and Tacitus, faults have been detected in their style by those who could judge better of it than we can. Almost every elegant verse, almost every harmonious sentence in poetry and prose among the Romans, was written within half a century. The comic authors were imitators of the Greeks : nothing national is to be found in Plautus himself, in whose pieces every sentence bears the impression of its Attic mint. The great work of Lucretius and the greater of Ovid were the first and last deserving the name of poems, great [1] as was the vigour and high the spirit of Ennius. Judging by the language, one would imagine that several centuries had intervened between them ; yet the same reader might have been living the day when each was edited. The most beautiful flowers grow in clusters. Lucretius, Catullus, and Calvus, the loss of whose works is the greatest that latinity has sustained : then Virgil, Ovid, Horace, and Cassius of Parma, the next great loss : for desirous as every man must be to recover the rest of Cicero and Livius, yet he perceives that there is enough of them before him to judge of their genius quite correctly : the remainder would afford him only the same pleasure as what he enjoys. In the lost poets the sources of it are cut off altogether: they can afford us no delight, and we can render them no justice.

JOHNSON. Addison has exhausted your stock.

TOOKE. I had forgotten him again. Since however you bring him back to me, I will endeavour to prove that he has exhausted neither my justice nor my patience. His spelling is villanous : *coffy-house*, *bin* (for been), *evry*, *instanc'd*, *inclin'd*. He is fond of the word *hint*, which, as a substantive, no poet has used, or ever will use.

> Music can noble hints impart.

---

[1] From " great " to " Ennius " added in 3rd ed.

IMAGINARY CONVERSATIONS: ENGLISH

What is merely a hint, can hardly be noble.

> The Almighty listens to a tuneful tongue,
> And seems well pleased and courted with a song.

If these lines had been translated from Voltaire, you would have cried out against his impiety. I know not your opinion of Chaucer.

JOHNSON. I do not read what I should read with difficulty.

TOOKE. Addison says of him,

> In vain he jests in his unpolished strain,
> And tries to make his readers laugh in vain.

The verses are a tautology, and the remark an untruth. In his observations on Cowley there is a bold conceit, which I think must have been supplied by a better poet.

> He more had pleased us had he pleased us less.

This, if it is nonsense, is more like the nonsense of Dryden than of Addison, and is such as conveys an idea. Here comes *hint* again.

> What muse *but* thine can equal *hints* inspire.

To make it English, we must read some other word than *but*.

> And plays in *more unbounded* verse, &c.

Unbounded has in itself the force of a superlative, and cannot admit the comparative *more*. On Milton he expresses your sentiments, but not as you would have expressed them.

> O had the poet ne'er profaned his pen
> To varnish o'er the guilt of faithless men,
> His other works *might* have deserved applause,
> But now the language can't support the cause.

JOHNSON. I confess that here he has reversed the matter, and that his own cause can not support his language.

TOOKE. What has *the cause* to do with the *other* works?[1] He might forsooth have succeeded in scenes of grandeur, if he *never* had written in defence of the commonwealth. It is indeed time that Addison should "*bridle in his struggling muse*."

---

[1] 2nd ed. reads: "works? If Milton was a republican, is that a reason why, while his bad angels are in hell, his good ones should be in purgatory? He might," etc.

JOHNSON AND HORNE (TOOKE)

JOHNSON. Sir, let us call the ostler and put her into the stable for the night. She has a good many blemishes, and winces more than one would have suspected from her sleek and fleshy appearance.

TOOKE. She gives some indication too of having been among the vetches.

JOHNSON. To be grave on it, metaphor is inapplicable to personification.

TOOKE. Hurd [1] is among the most conceited writers of the present day. He has imitated in prose the metaphor so justly ridiculed in these verses of Addison. In his *Dialogue on Sincerity*, he represents Waller saying, " After a few wanton circles, as it were to *breathe* and exercise my *muse*, *I drew her in* from these amusements to a stricter *manage*."

JOHNSON. His criticisms on others are usually sound and sensible. In his manners he is courtly; but in his language he mistakes vulgarity for ease, and inaccuracy for freedom. I remember an instance of his employing that word *manage* ambiguously. Instead of leaving it French he must give it an English spelling. With an English spelling it ought to have an English meaning, which it has not, but quite the contrary. His words are, " To the Hollanders indeed she could *talk big ;* and it was not her humour to *manage* those over whom she had gained an ascendant." Now surely this expresses the very reverse of what the learned prelate wished to say. " *Look big* " recurs just below : and soon after " much *indevoted* to the court," and " misconceived *of*," and " a *great means* of the hierarchical *greatness*." *Means* is plural. " To both your *satisfactions* " : for " to the satisfaction of you both." Since you have mentioned Dryden, let me remark to you that his spelling is negligent. He writes *look'd, traduc'd, describ'd, supply'd, assur'd, polish'd, civiliz'd*. In his preface to the translation of the *Pastorals*, we find " Is there anything more *sparkish* and better humour'd than Venus *her* addressing her son, &c." And he spells *icicles* " ycicles."

Are these the limbs for *y*cicles to tear.

TOOKE. He is rather to be followed in his *cou'd* and *wou'd* and *shou'd ;* because so it is, and so it was then, pronounced. Addison too has written the same words in the same manner. I wish he had

[1] From " TOOKE " to " defiance " (in Johnson's speech beginning " Very true ") added in 3rd ed.

sanctioned by his authority more of our usages, and older and better. But our vicious spelling, and everything else that is vicious in language, is likely to deepen; for every fresh shoal of novelists raises up some muddiness and wriggles against some weed. Of all the absurdities that ever were compressed into one word, surely the greatest is in the word *chiselled* when applied to features. If they who employ it mean to signify a fineness and delicacy, let them be taught that the chisel does only the rougher work, and that the polish is given by attrition. There is no such a thing in existence as a man or a woman; they are turned into *persons* and *individuals*. Nothing is given or granted; everything is *accorded*. Weapons are out of use: but a pistol or a sword is become an *arm*.

JOHNSON Very true. And soldiers are not encamped; they are *biv—biv*. Do pronounce the word; you have flexible organs, and can pronounce the hardest in *Gulliver's Travels*. As for spelling it, I set the two Universities at defiance.

TOOKE. I hear, Doctor, what anyone may easily suppose, that your acquaintance is greatly sought among the ladies. Now, for their benefit, and for the gentlemen too who write novels and romances, I would request you to exert your authority in repressing the term *our hero*. These worthy people seem utterly unaware that the expression turns their narrative into ridicule. Even on light and ludicrous subjects it destroys that illusion which the mind creates to itself in fiction; and I have often wished it away when I have found it in Fielding's *Tom Jones*, although used jocularly. While we are interested in a story we wish to see nothing of the author or of ourselves.

JOHNSON. I detest, let me tell you, your difficulties and exceptions, your frivolity and fastidiousness; I[1] have employed the word myself. You admit one great writer in one language! three or four in another! pray how many do you allow to Greece?

TOOKE. I would not interrupt you, Doctor; thinking it of all things the most indecorous. England has many great writers, Rome has many: but languages do not retain their purity in the hands even of these. Whenever I think of Greece, I think with astonishment and awe; for the language and the nation seem indestructible. Long before Homer, and from Homer to Epictetus, there must have been an uninterrupted series of admirable authors, although we have lost

[1] From " I " to " myself " added in 3rd ed.

JOHNSON AND HORNE (TOOKE)

the earliest of them, both before the poet and after. For no language can hold its breath one whole century: it becomes, if not extinct, very defective and corrupted, if no great writer fosters it and gives it exercise in that period. What a variety of beauty, what a prodigality and exuberance of it in the Greek! Even in its last age it exists in all its freshness. The letter which the mother of Saint Chrysostom addressed to that enthusiast in his youth, is far more eloquent, far more powerful in thought and sentiment, than anything in Xenophon or Plato. That it is genuine cannot be doubted; for it abounds in tenderness, which saints never do, and is concise, which Chrysostom is not.

JOHNSON. Greece ought to be preserved and guarded by the rulers of the world, as a cabinet of gems, open and belonging to them all. Whatever is the fate of other countries, whatever changes may be introduced, whatever laws imposed, whatever tributes exacted, she should preserve her lineaments uneffaced. Her ancient institutions and magistracies should be sanctioned to her, in gratitude for the inestimable blessings she has conferred on us. There is no more danger that republicanism would be contagious from it, than from a medal of Cimon or Epaminondas. To Greece is owing the conversation we hold together; to Greece is owing the very city in which we hold it; its wealth, its power, its equity; its liberality. These are among her earlier benefits: her later are not less. We owe to her the better part of that liturgy by which the divine wrath (let us hope) may be averted from the offences of our prosperity.

TOOKE. I would rather see this regeneration, than Viscount Corinth or Marquis Lacedæmon; than conduct to her carriage the Duchess Œnoanda, or even than dance with Lady Ogygia or Lady Peribœa. We may expect the worthy baronet, Sir Acamas Erechthyoniades, High Sheriff of Mycenæ, if more fashionable systems should prevail, to be created Lord Lieutenant and Custos Rotulorum of that county.

JOHNSON. How much better and how much easier is it, to remove the dirt and rubbish from around this noble statue, and to fix on it again the arm that is broken off and lies under it, than to carve it anew into some Gothic form, and to set it up in the weedy garden of an ignorant and drunken neighbour.

TOOKE. The liberation of Greece is the heirloom of our dreams, and comes not under the cognisance even of imagination when awake. To suppose that she could resist the power of Turkey one year, would be to suppose her more valiant and heroic than she ever was. If this were possible, the most despotic governments, the most friendly to her enslaver, the most indifferent to glory, the most deaf to honour, the very dead to Christianity, would lend an arm to support and save her. Nothing could be more politic, for England in particular, than to make her what Rhodes was formerly, what Malta should now be, equipped if not for the faith, equipped and always under sail against piracy; and religion would not induce her, as it would the knights of those islands, to favour the Catholics in case of war.

JOHNSON. Here our political views converge. Publish your thoughts; proclaim them openly; such as these you may.

TOOKE. It would cost me three thousand pounds to give them the requisite weight; and I believe there are some other impediments to my entrance into the House of Commons. Nothing is fitted to the hands of a king's minister but what is placed in them by a member of that honourable house. They take my money, which serves them little, while my advice, which might do some good, they would reject disdainfully. As where there is omniscience there is omnipotence, so wisdom (we seem to think) is always in proportion to power. A great man feels no want of it; and faulty arguments are only to be discovered through a hole in the dress.

JOHNSON. If[1] your observations were always as just and your arguments as innocent, I never should decline your conversation; but, on the contrary, I should solicit from you a catalogue of such peculiarities and defects, as a profound insight into our language, and a steady investigation of its irregularities and intricacies, have enabled you to remark.

TOOKE. And now, Doctor Johnson, you are at last in good-humour,[2] I hope to requite your condescension by an observation more useful than any I have yet submitted to you. Annibal Caracci,

---

[1] From "If" to "remark" is the concluding speech in 1st ed. In 2nd ed. the speech of TOOKE continues: "a hole in the coat or breeches. We are two somnambulists who have awakened each other by meeting. We will return to our old quarters and pick up words again now our eyes are open.

> ... 'I would not hear a word,
> Should lessen thee in my esteem,'"

etc., as in what in 1846 became the second Conversation.

[2] 2nd ed. reads: "humour with me. I hope," etc.

JOHNSON AND HORNE (TOOKE)

I know not whether in advice or in reproof, said to a scholar, *What you do not understand you must darken*. Are not we also of the Bologna school, my dear Doctor ? Do not we treat men and things in general as Caracci would have the canvas treated ? What we cannot so well manage or comprehend, we throw into a corner or into outer darkness. I do not hate, believe me, nor dislike you for your politics : whatever else they prove, they prove your constancy and disinterestedness. Nor do I supplicate you for a single one more of those kind glances which you just now vouchsafed me. The fixedness of your countenance, frowning as it is, shows at least that you attend to me, which, from a man of your estimation in the world, is no slight favour. Contented as I ought to be with it, I would yet entreat for others in the same condition, that you may be pleased to consider those writers whose sentiments are unpopular, as men walking away spontaneously from the inviting paths of Fortune, and casting up the sum of an account which [1] is never to be paid or presented.

JOHNSON. I did not think there was so much wisdom in you.

TOOKE. Nor was there until this conversation and this strong hand created it.

JOHNSON. How ! have I then shaken hands with him ? and so heartily ?

SECOND CONVERSATION [2]

TOOKE. I am lying in my form, a poor timid hare, and turning my eyes back on the field I have gone through : has not Doctor Johnson a long lash to start me with ?

JOHNSON. Take your own course.

TOOKE. Expect then a circuitous and dodging one. Our hospitable friend, by inviting me so soon again to meet you, proves to me his high opinion of your toleration and endurance.

JOHNSON. Sir, we can endure those who bring us information and are unwilling to obtrude it.

[1] 2nd ed. reads : " which (we know) is," etc.
[2] The single Conversation of 1824, expanded in 1826, was divided into two in *Wks.*, 1846, the continuation containing but little of the matter of 1824. The opening is subsequent to 1826 ; the 1826 text becomes the basis from the quotation ending, " Should lessen me in your esteem."

IMAGINARY CONVERSATIONS : ENGLISH

TOOKE. I can promise the latter only. We are two somnambulists who have awakened each other by meeting. Let us return to our old quarters, and pick up words, as before, now our eyes are open.

JOHNSON. Is your coat-sleeve well furnished with little slips and scraps, as it was when we met last?

TOOKE. I am much afraid, that I may have forgotten what I then brought forward ; and if by chance I should occasionally make the same remark over again on the same word, I must bespeak your indulgence and pardon.

JOHNSON. I wish, sir, you had not bowed to me in that manner when you spoke your last words : such an act of courtesy brings all the young ladies about us. They can not be much interested by our conversation.

TOOKE. That must entirely depend on you. But as our language, like the Greek, the Latin, and the French, may be purified and perfected by the ladies, I hope you will interest them in the discussion, to which this evening I bring only slight materials.

You frown on them, Doctor! but you would not drive them away; and they know it. They fear your frown no more than the sparrows and linnets, in old times, feared the scythe and other implements of the garden god.

" Hanged, drawn, and quartered." Such is the sequence of words employed in the sentence on traitors.

JOHNSON. And, sir, are you here to remark it?

TOOKE. It seems so ; and not without the need.

JOHNSON. Traitors must first have been *drawn* to the place of punishment.

TOOKE. True ; and hence a vulgar error in the learned. A sportsman will tell you that a hare is *drawn* when its entrails are taken out. The traitor was *drawn*, surely enough, to the block or gallows ; but the law always states its sentences clearly, although its provisions and enactments not so. The things to be suffered come in due order. Here the criminal is first hanged, then *drawn*, then his body is cut into quarters.

JOHNSON. I believe you may be right. You have not answered me whether you come supplied with your instruments of torture, your grammatical questions.

TOOKE. I have many of these in my memory, and some on the back of a letter. Permit me first to ask whether we can say, *I had hear?*

JOHNSON AND HORNE (TOOKE)

JOHNSON. You mean to say *heard*.

TOOKE. No; I mean the words *I had hear*.

JOHNSON. Why ask me so idle a question?

TOOKE. Because I find in the eighth chapter of *Rasselas*, " I *had* rather *hear* thee dispute." The intervention of *rather* can not make it more or less proper.

JOHNSON. Sir, you are right. I hope you do not very often find such inaccuracies in my writings. Can you point out another?

TOOKE. I should do it with less pleasure than ease; and I doubt whether there is one in fifty pages; which is indeed no moderate concession, no ordinary praise: for we English are less attentive to correctness and purity of style than any other nation, ancient or modern, that ever pretended to elegance or erudition.

JOHNSON. Sir, you have reason on your side.

TOOKE. In having Doctor Johnson with me.

JOHNSON. I have observed the truth of what you say, and I wonder I never have published my remark.

TOOKE. Permit me, my dear sir, to partake of your wonder on this subject; you have excited mine on so many. But since you authorise me to adduce an instance of your incorrectness, for which I ought to be celebrated among the great discoverers——

JOHNSON. No flattery, sir! no distortion of body! stand upright and speak out.

TOOKE. The second paragraph in *Rasselas* is this: " Rasselas was the fourth son of the mighty Emperor in whose dominions the father of waters begins his course; whose bounty, &c." Now *whose* must grammatically appertain to " the mighty Emperor." But we soon discover by the context that it belongs to " the father of waters."

JOHNSON. I am afraid you are correct.

TOOKE. My dear sir! let us never be afraid of any man's possessing this advantage, but always of his having fraud and falsehood. Reason will come over to our side if we pay her due respect when we find her on the side of an adversary. But I am not yours: let her sit between us, and let us enjoy her smiles and court her approbation.

JOHNSON (*aside*). Strange man! it is difficult to think him half so wicked as he is. But I am inclined to believe that we may be marvellously infatuated by a mountebank's civility.

TOOKE. Doctor, if your soliloquy is terminated, as your turning

IMAGINARY CONVERSATIONS: ENGLISH

round to me again seems to indicate, may I ask whether the Nile is legitimately the father of waters? The Ocean seems to possess a prior right: and the Eridanus has enjoyed the prescriptive title, *King of Rivers*, from collecting a greater number of streams than any known among the ancients. But the Nile, as far as the ancients knew, collected none.

JOHNSON. Insufferably captious!

TOOKE. The captious are never insufferable where nothing is to be caught. Let us set others right as often as we can, without hurting them or ourselves. If this is to be done in either, the setting right is an expensive process.

JOHNSON. Begin, sir.

TOOKE. We will begin our amicable engagement in the same manner as hostilities in the field are usually begun. A few straggling troops fire away first, from hedges and bushes. As far indeed as I am concerned, there will be no order throughout the whole, from first to last. Whatever the part of speech may be, it pretends to the advantages of no lineal descent, and claims no right of appointing a successor. As we appeal to the Roman laws in grammar rather than to the custom of the land: pray why are not "resist*a*nce," and "attend*a*nce," spelt with *e*, like "resid*e*nce" and "perman*e*nce," all proceeding from participles of the same form, "resist*e*ns," "attend*e*ns," "resid*e*ns," "perman*e*ns"? We write "correspond*e*nt." "stud*e*nt," "penit*e*nt," "resid*e*nt," yet we always find "assist*a*nt."

JOHNSON. This, like most irregularities, arises from inattention and slovenliness, not from ignorance or perverseness. Is it not also strange that *won* should be the preterite of win? when "beg*u*n" is the preterite of "begin."

TOOKE. Strange indeed. Ben Jonson uses *wun* in his comedy of *Every Man in his Humour*. So if we write *said* and *paid*, why not *staid* and *praid*? If we write *laid* why not *allaid* and *delaid*? Now, for a substantive or two. South properly writes "beg*g*er." Waller, in the same age, "veget*a*ls," which I think is preferable to "vegetables." There is a reason why the word "eatables" is better spelt as at present. We want "contra*dictive*" for the person, as well as "contra*dicting*" for the thing. We had it and have lost it, while we see other old words brought into use again very indiscreetly. Among the rest the word *wend*. There is no need of it, unless in poetry. In certain new books we find *wended*. There is properly no such word:

JOHNSON AND HORNE (TOOKE)

Spenser has coined it unlawfully. *Went* is the preterite of *wend*, as *lent* of *lend*, *spent* of *spend*, *bent* of *bend*. These are among the few verbs which do not possess two forms of the preterite; the one ending in *ed*, the other in *t*: as *pass, passed, past; ceases, ceased, ceast*. There can be no such word as " pass'd," " ceas'd," though we find them printed. We write, " I talk*ed*, I walk*ed*, I march*ed*," but such words never existed, for these words never were pronounced, and the others never could be. Writing is but the sign of speech; and *such* writing is a false signal. No word ought to be so written that it can not be pronounced; but when we have the same word before us written plainly, it is a strange perversion to reject the commodious spelling. It is as improper to write *alledge* or *abridge* (abrege) as *colledge* or *knowledge*. *Kerchief* also is wrongly spelt; it has nothing to do with " chief." Milton writes in the *Penseroso*

Kercheft in a comely cloud.

We, in imitation of the French, say, " ten *times* as *high* "; the Italians " ten *turns* " (dieci *volte*); the Romans and Greeks expressed it by the simple adverb. *Highth* has nothing to do with time: here is an ellipsis, " ten times *told*." I now proceed to a favourite word of yours, which is wrongly spelt: *allegiance*. In its present form it appears to come from *allege*, or (as we write it) *alledge*; whereas it comes from *liege*, and should be spelt " alli*e*geance."

JOHNSON. You have asked me many questions; let me ask you one. What think you of calling a female writer an *author*, in which the terminating syllable expresses the noun masculine?

TOOKE. Since we in English have no nouns masculine by declension, I see no reason why we should not extend the privileges of those we adopt: a queen may be called a governor, and a god-mother a sponsor: I wish we had authority for terminating the words in *ess* as we have for writing others which usually end in *or*. As our English terminations in few words designate the genders, I should not hesitate.

JOHNSON. Do you hesitate at anything?

TOOKE. At differing in opinion from a superior.

JOHNSON. Superior! do you admit superiors?

TOOKE. I do not admit that a ducal coronet may constitute one, nor that men can make great him whom God has made little: the attempt is foolish and impious. But whoever has improved by

IMAGINARY CONVERSATIONS: ENGLISH

industry the talents his Maker has bestowed on him, to a greater amount than I have done, is my superior. If brighter wit, if acuter judgment, if more creative genius, are allotted him, I reverence in his person a greater than I am, and believe that Almighty God has granted me the sight of him and conversation with him, that I may feel at once my own wants and my own powers : that I may be at once humble and grateful.

JOHNSON. You ? you ?

TOOKE (*bows*). Accept the sign of both, however inadequate the expression.

JOHNSON. This is really stooping to conquer. I was wrong and rude. I will not offend so again.

TOOKE. I am encouraged to pursue my inquiries. What do you think of *horse-godmother* and *horse-laugh* ?

JOHNSON. Expressions of coarseness. The Greeks, instead of *horse*, employed *ox*. *Boumastos*, the *bumastus* of Virgil's *Georgics*, is a large species of grape : *boupais* is our *booby*.

TOOKE. Very true, Doctor ! but may I whisper in your ear my suspicion that the *horse* has nothing to do with the *godmother* or the *laugh*. Indeed I believe no animal has less the appearance of laughter, or is less liable to those outward and visible signs of sickness which sometimes are attributed to him in the comparison, " Sick as a horse." The *godmother* of the personage I whispered to you may readily be imagined a very coarse and indelicate one ; her *laughter* suitable to her character; and her *house* by no means salubrious : and *horse* is designated by the possessive *s*, as in Saint Clement'*s*, Saint Paul'*s*.

JOHNSON. I have been looking into a few old authors for their modes of spelling ; and remembering the better one of writing *stil*, and the many instances where, by being spelt with a double *l*, it might easily be mistaken for the adjective, I took the trouble to write them down. There was indeed an age in our literature when such confusion was thought a beauty. Sir Philip Sidney, in the best of his poems, says

> Now be *still* ; yet *still* believe me, &c.

In another poem of a later author I find

> Lie *still*, sweet maid, and wait the Almighty will ;
> Then rise unchanged and be an angel *still*.

JOHNSON AND HORNE (TOOKE)

How much better would these verses be if the first words were

Rest here, sweet maid.

TOOKE. Unquestionably. But perhaps the learned author had Sir P. Sidney in his eye, and was not undelighted with the pleasurable vices of poetry in such company.

JOHNSON. We need not poke into holes nor pry into corners for old expressions or old modes of spelling. They lie open, on a wide field, in full sunshine. Cowley always writes the preterites and participles *extinguisht, possest, disperst, refresht, nourisht, stopt, knockt, dreamt, burnt, usurpt, reacht.* Daniel and Drayton, among the poets; Waller, Cleaveland, and Cowley, in prose; are the first who wrote as easily as we write at present. The only poetry I can bring to memory which is perfectly such in regard to language as might be written at the present day, is Daniel's

> I must not grieve my love, whose eyes should read,
> Lines of delight, &c.

TOOKE. Permit me to return with you to the verbs. To *lead* is *led* in the preterite, so should *read* be *red*. We have wisely curtailed the final *e*, and may just as wisely curtail the unnecessary reduplication of *d:* for nobody can mistake in any sentence the verb for the adjective. In such words as *amerced, coerced,* &c., the abbreviators of the last and present age usually omit the *e;* but the earlier wrote *amerst, coerst,* to designate that one syllable was added unnecessarily. I have seen letters from the historian Hume, in which he constantly writes *talkt, remarkt, lavisht, askt.* In his printed works the compositor and publisher would never permit it.

JOHNSON. What improvement, in style or anything else, can be expected from a free-thinker?

TOOKE. Among a thousand deteriorations I remember but one improvement in writing since my childhood.

JOHNSON. What is that?

TOOKE. Of late I have remarked that the generality of authors no longer write every substantive with a capital letter.

JOHNSON. It makes an unseemly appearance in the type.

TOOKE. The unseemliness is not equal to the absurdity; nor does it matter whether this letter or that letter be pretty in its form, or

IMAGINARY CONVERSATIONS: ENGLISH

whether it vault with its head above the surface, or dive with its feet under.

JOHNSON. I see indeed no reason why we should employ the capital letter in the middle of the sentence, unless in proper names, in the names of people and countries, in the months, the days, and in the appellations and attributes of the Deity.

TOOKE. The French, if I may venture an opinion, are more elegant than we are in their usage, when they curtail the number of capitals.

JOHNSON. The wretches do not write even *Dieu* with one!

TOOKE. No doubt they are very wretched in this oversight: but perhaps they believe that God is hardly to be made greater by a great letter.

JOHNSON. This is scoffing: I scorn to answer it. And pray, sir, in your reviling, what would you do with *Angels* and *Sirens?*

TOOKE. As they happen to be present, pray ask of themselves what I should do with them, and assure them I am all compliance.

LADY (*to another*). The impudent creature! Did you ever hear the like?

LADY (*in answer*). How should I? I am married.

JOHNSON. If you terminate your preterites and participles in *est* instead of *essed*, which you may do, as there is no innovation in it, you must, to be consistent, spell several of those ending in *ed* without the *e*, as *improv'd*.

TOOKE. Certainly some others; not those; for the vowel gives here the grave sound which the syllable requires. Negligent and thoughtless writers have done it; so they have even in *amerced, coerced*. But if they take away a letter where it is wanted, they put one where it is not; and we continue in this extravagance when we write " worshi*pp*ers " and " counse*ll*ors," for which we have less plea than our predecessors, who wrote " worshi*ppe* " and " counse*ll*."

JOHNSON. Although I agree with you on many points, after reflecting upon the matter, I cannot give my assent to the Anglicising of Greek plurals, such as *phenomena, scholia, encomia*. How would you manage some Latin one? such for instance as *genii*.

TOOKE. We retain the plural *genii* when we refer to the imaginary beings of Oriental fable; that there may be a distinction between these and such real and solid ones as Doctor Johnson, which, according to our idiom and custom, we call *geniuses*. If you insist on retaining the terminations of Greek nouns, then, Doctor, the pleasing

JOHNSON AND HORNE (TOOKE)

task must devolve on you of teaching ladies the Greek grammar. But if they do not accept the plurals of other languages, why should they of this? They say *signors*, and not *signori*.

Now we find ourselves dropt suddenly on designations in society, is it not wonderful that we should apply to the clergy two names so extremely different in their import as the *divine* and the *cloth*. Among the well-dresst gentlemen we may have happened to meet in society, I doubt whether a single one would be contented to be called a piece of haberdashery : and as for a *divine*, the young lady yonder, I mean the tall and slender one, with soft, dark, pensive eyes, and eye-brows not too arched nor too definite, is incomparably more one to my fancy than his Grace the Archbishop of Canterbury.

JOHNSON. I do not see nor heed the girl.

TOOKE. If you could do the one without the other, you would have more philosophy than our discourse requires.

JOHNSON. My worthy sir ! I do request you will be somewhat more circumspect in your observations.

TOOKE. Many thanks, Doctor ! some of them for the advice, and others for two suggestions. *Worth* and *worthy* are subjected to the same construction. I would say, for distinction-sake, " *worth* any price," and " worthy of my esteem." The *of*, which is now omitted after *worthy*, would be only as wrongly added after *worth*. The other day I received a letter from a person who really can read and write rather better than you would suppose, and I found in it mar*quess* instead of *marquis*.

JOHNSON. Sir, the word *marquess* will be a very proper term for *marquis* whenever, by some miraculous power, he becomes his own wife. I wonder that no writer of common sense has remarked that mar*quess* for the lady is better than march*ioness*. My reason is plain enough : it is more proper to assimilate it to its native French than to barbarous Latin : neither the French nor the Italian authorise the form of *marchioness*.

TOOKE. Would not *circumspective* be a better form than *circumspect*? as corresponding with *prospective* and *retrospective*?

JOHNSON. It would. I can not but think that so irregular a locution was at first occasioned by abbreviation in manuscripts : *circumspect* would otherwise be a substantive, like *prospect* and *retrospect*. Now why do you not draw up into a regular and orderly composition these remarks?

IMAGINARY CONVERSATIONS: ENGLISH

Tooke. Even if the thing were worth it, I would never take the trouble, well knowing how impatient an English public is of any changes for the better. And yet by some unaccountable chance, we have latterly made one improvement in our language, among infinite deteriorations.

Johnson. What is it?

Tooke. The restoration of *that* or *which*, in cases of need. The omission is peculiarly observable among the dramatists; the later follow the older, and limp awkwardly in the rear. Addison and Rowe for instance,

> I would not hear a word
> Should lessen thee in my esteem.

And,

> Curse on the innovating hand attempts it.[1]

Custom[2] can never make English of this, because it never can make sense of it. In fact, the relative should only be omitted where a pronoun is concerned. On the other hand, the insertion of it, where it can be well avoided, is among the principal blemishes of ordinary writers. In[3] most places I would eradicate this stiff, hard, thriftless plantain which overruns our literature.

Johnson. At some time, I doubt not, these observations will be carefully collected and duly estimated.

Tooke. The Sibylline leaves, which contain the changes of an empire, as these do of a language, were disconnected and loose. The great difference is that, although mine may be refused at their value, a light breath will not scatter and confuse them, blow it whence it may.

Johnson. Your former conversation has made me think repeatedly what a number of beautiful words there are of which we never think of estimating the value, as there are of blessings. How carelessly, for example, do we (not we, but people) say, " I am delighted to *hear from you*." No other language has this beautiful expression, which, like some of the most lovely flowers, loses its charms for want of close

---

[1] Rowe, *Jane Shore*, iii., i. 197. Quoted also in *High and Low Life in Italy*.

[2] 2nd ed. reads: " This fault of omitting the relative *that* or *which* is not unusual with dramatic writers; in the more ancient it is common: but we find it even in the elegant Rowe. ' Curse on,' " etc.

[3] From " In " to " frequenter " (in Tooke's speech beginning, " Ne'er in this ") added in 3rd ed.

JOHNSON AND HORNE (TOOKE)

inspection. When I consider the deep sense of these very simple and very common words, I seem to hear a voice coming from afar through the air, breathed forth, and entrusted to the care of the elements, for the nurture of my sympathy.

TOOKE. Since we are become a learned nation, not only the words we have cast aside, but also those we have substituted in the place of them, are mostly injudicious ; and such others as we have taken the trouble to construct are unskilful botches. What think you of the word *scientific?* which doubtless some *scientific* man brought into the world ?

JOHNSON. What should I think about it ?

TOOKE. That it is *unscientific.* Now *fic* comes from *fingere* and means *making.* *Prolific* is *making* a progeny : *scientific* is not *making* a science, but adding to the improvement or advancement of one already made.

There are other forms so long and so well established in the mind, that we would hardly alter them if we could. For instance, *eve* and *evening* are the same : so are *morn* and *morning.* Christmas eve is the *evening* or (largely used) the *day* before Christmas. Yet we should be stared at if we said *Monday evening* or *eve*, meaning Tuesday. Nevertheless, if we were always bound by strict analogy, we should speak so. I would be guided by analogy no farther than where I am in danger of being led into ambiguities by neglecting it. A man would be stared at who should call *this morning, to-morrow.*

Among the phrases lately brought back again into use, is the very idle and inefficient *ever and anon.* An apparition at once so grave and so shadowy makes an unseemly figure in the frippery and tinsel of a circulating library.

JOHNSON. I wonder that the expression was *ever* formed ; and that having been formed, it was not *anon* exposed and left to perish.

TOOKE. But the oddest expression in our language is *many a one.* The Italians have *tutti e tre :* for *all three*, " all *and* three," *tutti e quattro*, &c.

JOHNSON. We have also a strange expression in *never* for *no ;* thus, " *ne'er a one of them.*"

TOOKE. *Ne'er* in this instance has no reference to time, but properly to person : *ne'er* here is an awkward contraction of *nowhere.* This is intelligible to all, however few at first sight may be able to account for it. Ambiguity is worse than stiffness : but stiffness is bad enough, and much more common. Nothing [1] of this kind in our authors is frequenter than the subjunctive : " if it *be*, unless it *be* " : which ought never to be used where the doubt is not very strong : for it should be a very strong doubt to supplant idiom. Our best writers use *who* and *whom*, only in speaking of intellectual beings. We [2] do not properly say *the tree who, the horse who ;* in fable however it would be right ; for there they reason and speak.

JOHNSON. The French and other moderns, I believe, never omit those words of theirs whereby they express the relative *which* or *that*.

TOOKE. So we are taught, and in regard to the French, truly. But in the best of the Italian writers *che* is omitted. Machiavelli, whom you will allow me to quote where politics sit idle, has omitted it twice in one sentence. " Monstrale l'amore le porti, dicale il bene le vuoi." *Mandrag.* 4. " I am happy to find from the letter you wrote me, that you enjoy good health." Here *that* is omitted rightly after letter, which it could not well be between the words *me* and *you*. The rejection of it in the proper place is a cause of peculiar elegance ; for it bears heavily on our language. The Romans were fortunate to avoid it by means of the *infinitive* of their verbs ; and perhaps more fortunate still in having so many words to express *but*, another sad stumbling-block to us. Our language is much deformed by the necessity of its recurrence ; and I know not any author who has taken great pains to avoid it where he could.

JOHNSON. Nothing is right with you : in language as in government we yield to Greeks and Romans. One would imagine that Addison, a Whig, might please you.

TOOKE. Doctor, I never ask or consider or care of what party is a good man or a good writer. I have always been an admirer of Addison, and the oftener I read him, I mean his prose, the more he pleases me. Perhaps it is not so much his style, which however is easy and graceful and harmonious, as the sweet temperature of thought in which we always find him, and the attractive countenance, if you will allow me the expression, with which he meets me upon every occasion. It is very remarkable, and therefore I stopped to notice it, that not only what little strength he had, but all his grace

---

[1] 2nd ed. reads, continuing Tooke's remarks on omission of the relative : " blemishes of ordinary writers ; another is the too frequent subjunctive," etc.

[2] 2nd ed. has a footnote : " Fashionable writers discard such rigorous authorities. ' At a spot marked with the feet of horses *who* were conducted to it. . . .' *Old Mortality*."

JOHNSON AND HORNE (TOOKE)

and ease, forsake him when he ventures into poetry: he is even coarse and abject, and copies the grammatical faults of his predecessors, without copying anything else of their manner, good or bad. Were I inclined to retaliate on you, I might come against you in the rear of others, and throw my stone at you on the side of Gray; and [1] where you would least expect it for indulgence. Prejudiced or unprejudiced against him, I wonder you did not catch at the beard of his bard streaming *like a meteor*. He did not take the idea from the *Moses* of Michel-Angelo, nor from the *Padre Eterno* of Raffael in his Vision of Ezekiel, but from the *Hudibras* of Butler.

> This *hairy meteor* did denounce
> The fall of sceptres and of crowns.

Here we have the very words.

Until you pointed out to me my partiality for the Greeks and Romans, I never had suspected it, having always thought ten pages in Barrow worth all their philosophy put together, and finding more wisdom and thought in him, distinct from theology, than [2] in any of them, excepting Aristoteles. If his eloquence is somewhat less pure than that of Demosthenes and Thucydides, who have reached perfection, his mind is as much more capacious and elevated as the Sun is than the Moon and Mercury.

JOHNSON. It is better and pleasanter to talk generally on great and high subjects than minutely. Who would examine that could expatiate?

TOOKE. None can expatiate safely who do not previously examine; and we are not always to consider in our disquisition what is pleasantest, but sometimes what is usefullest. I wonder, in matters of reason, how anything little or great can excite ill humour: for, as many steps as they lead us toward reason, just so many, one would think, they should lead us away from passion. Why should these dry things have discomposed you? If I ride a broomstick, must I, like a witch, raise a storm? In reality a great deal of philosophy, a great deal not only of logic but of abstruse and recondite metaphysics will be found in etymology; the part least pleasing to you in our conversation. I do not wonder that such men as Varro and Cæsar studied it and wrote upon it; but I doubt whether the one or the

---

[1] From "and" to "indulgence" added in 3rd ed.
[2] 2nd ed. reads: "than in any other man. If," etc.

IMAGINARY CONVERSATIONS : ENGLISH

other went very deeply into the business. It is astonishing that the more learned among the Greeks knew absolutely nothing of it. Admirably as they used the most beautiful of languages, they cared no more about its etymologies than a statuary cares about the chemical properties of his marble.

Doctor,[1] in your travels, did you ever happen to see gossamer?

JOHNSON. In my English travels, I saw it formerly in Needwood Forest, five miles from Lichfield: latterly my travels were in Scotland, where there was no plant to support it.

TOOKE. I am unwilling to take so great a freedom as to contest a derivation with you personally, but permit me to suggest the possibility, that many words in what is called low Latin which resemble our English words, are not their parents. Certainly there is a certain resemblance of *gossipium* and *gossimer*. But *gorse*, which in many parts of the country is also called *furze* or *whin*, appears to me to be its root. Chaucer and Shakespeare spell it *gossamour*; Drayton of the same county and age, *gossamere*. Now, if we consider that the common people universally, and the greater part of others, treat the letter *r* very gently, and that you never heard a farmer call *gorse* otherwise than *goss*; if you then consider how large a number of our plants take their names from sentiments, perhaps you may incline to think it possible that *gossamour* is *gorse's-love, gors-amour*. For love seems to be nowhere more faithful than between the plant and its daily visitant in spring, summer, and autumn : on no other do you see it so frequently. The name was given in the first incubation of the French upon the Saxon.

JOHNSON. Sir, this is fanciful.

TOOKE. I am invested with a new quality by the partiality of Doctor Johnson. You mention in your *Dictionary* the word *gossipium* as of low Latinity. I find it nowhere but in Pliny; and he was certainly a man of the highest rank and best education. He mentions it as bearing cotton, which is very different from the *gorse*. There are a few words (but *gossipium* is not one of them) which we believe to be of the latest Latinity, and which in reality are of the earliest. The readers of Apuleius are taught that several of his words are provincial, and of very base and very recent coinage; whereas they were carried into Africa with the first Roman settlers,

---

[1] From " Doctor " to " film " (in Johnson's speech beginning, " I should like to know whether ") added in 3rd ed.

JOHNSON AND HORNE (TOOKE)

and retained their vitality in that country when they had lost it at Rome; just as several of our noblest families are extinct in England, but branch off vigorously in Ireland. The Romans called a goose a gander; they forgot the female name: the Italians in country places never lost it; and to this day *auca* is called *occa*.

JOHNSON. I should like to know whether the man is in earnest; but that I never shall.

In return for this illusory and unsubstantial film, I will present to you a curiosity in the Latin: for surely it is curious that the Romans should have used two words of origin quite contrary for the same thing. To *promise*, was not only *promittere*, but *recipere;* the authority is Cicero.

TOOKE. The reason is plain.

JOHNSON. As you are fond of reasons and innovations, I would consign to you willingly two or three words on which to exercise your ingenuity. I would allow you to write *monsterous* and *wonderous* with an *e*, on the same principle as we write *treacherous* and *ponderous*.

TOOKE. Liberally offered and gratefully accepted. Incroachment may sometimes be the follower of kindness: am I going too far, in asking that *rough, tough, sough, enough,* may be guided by *bluff, rebuff, cuff?* Why should not *cough* be spelt *coff?* why not *dough* and *although, dow* and *altho;* for the benefit of strangers and learners, to say nothing of economy in letters; the only kind of economy on which we reformers can ever hope to be heard? As there is also a cry against the letter *s*, I would remove it from *onwards, towards, forwards, backwards, afterwards,* where it is improper, however sanctioned by the custom of good authors, and I would use it only where the following word begins with *d* or *t*, for the sake of euphony. On the same principle I approve of *saith*, &c. instead of *says*, &c. where the next word begins with *s*, or *z*, or *ce* and *ci*. Hobbes [1] is the last who writes with this termination, and neither he nor his predecessors abstained from it before another *th*. Persons [2] very unlearned, such as Swift and others, have from their natural acuteness perceived the utility of *fixing*, as they call it, our language.

JOHNSON. Sir, I have been patient: I have heard you call Swift a very unlearned man. Malignity of whiggism! I give him up to you, however: he was not very learned. But you ought to have spared

[1] From "Hobbes" to "*th*" added in 3rd ed.
[2] From "Persons" to "language" preserved from 1st ed.

IMAGINARY CONVERSATIONS: ENGLISH

and favoured him; for he was irreverential to the great, and to his God.

TOOKE. An [1] ill-tempered, sour, supercilious man may nevertheless be a sycophant; and he was one. He flattered some of the worst men that ever existed, and maligned some of the best. Of all inhumanities and cruelties, his toward two women who reposed their affections on so undeserving an object, was in its nature the worst and the most unprovoked. But, Doctor, I am inclined to believe that God is as fond of his lively children as of his dull ones; and would as willingly see them give their pocket-money to the indigent and afflicted, as offer their supplications or even their thanks to him. I may be mistaken: so many wiser men have been, that in all these matters I deliver my opinion, but do not inculcate nor insist upon it. When I spoke of Swift and others as very unlearned, I meant in the etymologies and diversities of our language. Swift wrote admirably.

JOHNSON. Yes, sir, and was more original than you and all your tribe.

TOOKE. I am willing that a tory should for ever be an original, and be incapable of having a copyist. But, when I was younger, I read Swift as often as perhaps any other may have done; not for the sake of his thoughts and opinions, but of his style, which I would carry with me and employ.

JOHNSON. Addison's is better.

TOOKE. What I admire in Addison I cannot so easily make use of. If you or I attempted to imitate the mien and features of a Cupid or a Zephyr, I doubt whether we should quite succeed. Perhaps [2] when we meet again, if that pleasure is reserved for me, I may carry in the spacious sleeves of this coat seventy or eighty expressions culled from Addison, at which you will shake your head. At present let me treat you with one sentence, the only one of them I can perfectly recollect. "When we had done eating *ourselves*, the knight called a waiter to him, and *bid* him carry the remainder to the waterman, &c." Now, when they had done *eating themselves*, the waterman would hardly thank them for the remainder, and probably their voices would be but little intelligible to the

---

[1] From "An" to "But" added in 3rd ed. 2nd ed. reads: "God. TOOKE. Doctor, I am inclined," etc.

[2] From "Perhaps" to "to the waiter" added in 3rd ed.

JOHNSON AND HORNE (TOOKE)

waiter. Swift is not so original as you think him. He was a peruser of rare books; for, zealous as he appears in favour of the classics, he liked nothing that was not strange. In one of his searches probably after such reading, he tells us he first met Harley. I do not mention Cyrano de Bergerac, and some others who have given him ideas on the ground-plan of his works; but I mean to bring you where you may find the thoughts. The most beautiful of them is owing to Plutarch. That simile [1] of the geographers and sands of Africa is taken from the first sentence in the *Life of Theseus*: I have traced a great number of his other fancies and reflections, in writers less known and less esteemed.

JOHNSON. Plutarch has many good ones.

TOOKE. Yes, Doctor; and although his style is not valued by the critics, I could inform them that there are in Plutarch many passages of exquisite beauty in regard to style, derived perhaps from authors more ancient.

JOHNSON. Inform them of nothing, sir, if you wish to live peaceably. Let them take from you, but do not offer it. They will pass over your freshest thoughts as if they had been long and intimately known to them, and display your abstruser (to them incomprehensible) as the only ones worthy of remark.

TOOKE. Among these hogs of Westphaly there is not one with a snout that can penetrate into my inclosure, prompt as they are to batten on it and bespatter it, and to trample it down as they grunt and trot along. Doctor, you have been keeping admirable time to my words with your head and body.

JOHNSON. Is that sentence yours? I like the period.

TOOKE. Let anyone claim it whom it suits as well: I grant and resign it freely. Periods I willingly throw away; but not upon things like these. A [2] wise man is shown clearly, distinctly, and advantageously, when he is seen walking patiently by the side of an unwise one; but only on some occasions and to some extent. To quarrel on the road, to twitch him by the coat at every slip he makes, and to grow irritated in irritating him, proves to the unwise man that there is one in the world unwiser than he.

JOHNSON. And now, sir, what plan have you for fixing our language?

---

[1] 2nd ed. reads: "simily."
[2] From " A " to " than he " added in 3rd ed.

IMAGINARY CONVERSATIONS: ENGLISH

Tooke. This [1] is impossible in any; but it is possible to do much, and an authority like yours would have effected it by perpetuating the orthography. On the contrary, I observe in your *Dictionary* some quotations in which the words are spelt differently from what I find them in the original; nor have you admitted all those in Littleton, who compiled his *Latin Dictionary* at a recent period.

Johnson. First, I wrote the words as people now receive them; then, as to Littleton, many of his are vulgar.

Tooke. The more English for that. No expression, be it only free from indecency, is so vulgar that a man of learning and genius may not formerly have used it: but there are many so frivolous and fantastical that they cannot, to the full extent of the word, ever become vulgar. There are but four [2] places where such bad language is tolerated and acknowledged; the cock-pit, the boxing-ring, the race-course, and the House of Commons.

Johnson. I could wish our Senate to have deserved as well of ours as the Roman did of theirs. Illiterate men, and several such are among the correspondents of Cicero, write with as much urbanity and purity as himself; and it is remarkable that the only one of them defective in these qualities is Marcus Antonius the triumvir. But pray give me some more instances in which the spelling should be improved.

Tooke. Many must escape me, and others are but analogical: I will then bring forward only those which occur principally. The word which has just escaped my lips, *occur*,[3] is written improperly with a single *r*.[4] The same may be remarked on the finals of *rebel, compel*, &c.

Johnson. Why should the compound have this potency? It would be more reasonable (however little so) to write *sel* and *fil*, as B. Jonson and many others did; because there could be no ambiguity in the pronunciation.

Tooke. On the same system, if system it can be called, we write

---

[1] From "This" to "instances in which the spelling" preserved from 1st ed.
[2] 1st ed. reads: "three," and excludes "the cock-pit."
[3] 2nd ed. reads: "*occurr.*"
[4] 1st and 2nd eds. read: "single *r*. This impropriety is demonstrated by its preterite, which would be *occured*; for the sign of the preterite is *ed*, in similar verbs, not *red*. The same may be remarked on the verbs *rebel, compel*, etc., *aver, demur, acquit* ... syllable. We ourselves ... rudeness," the speech from "Many" to "rudeness" being given to Tooke.

JOHNSON AND HORNE (TOOKE)

aver, demur, appal, acquit, permit, refit, confer, &c. If these were printed as they ought to be, strangers would more easily know that the accent is on the final syllable. I wish we wrote *drole* instead of *droll*, *drolery* instead of *drollery*, which are discountenanced by the French, and unsupported by our pronunciation. In like manner, why not *controle?* In the time of Elizabeth good authors wrote *vittals*: and long afterward *applie, allie, relie*, which we should do if we wrote *lie*. *Haughty* and *naughty* may drop some useless letters, and appear characteristically *hauty* and *nauty: heinous* is *hainous* by descent.

We ourselves in some instances have lost the right accent of words. In my youth he would have been ridiculed who placed it upon the first syllable of *confiscated, contemplative, conventicle*,* at which the ear revolts: in many other compounds we thrust it thus back with equal precipitancy and rudeness.[1] We have sinned and are sinning most grievously against our fathers and mothers. We shall "rèpent," and " rèform," and " rèmonstrate," and be " rèjected " at last.

JOHNSON.[2] Certainly it does appear strange that the man who habitually says " dèmonstrate " should never say " rèmonstrate."

TOOKE. Sackville, a great authority, writes

> Tossed and tòrmented with tedious thought.

Milton's exquisite ear saved him in general from harshness. He writes " Travèrsing the colure." How much better is aggràndise than àggrandise ! Dryden, in the *Annus Mirabilis*, writes

> Instructed ships shall sail to quick commèrce.

We have suffered to drop away from us the beautiful and commodious word bequeathed to our language by this author, the word

---

* A clever poet of our day writes,
  " Of the plebeian àspirant,"
and
  " We dèsignate the practical."—W. S. L.

[1] 2nd ed. has a footnote :—
" We have arrived at such barbarism, that it was necessary for Wordsworth to place an accent on the second syllable of *indùrated. Memorials of a Tour on the Continent*, p. 43. Such consequence having been given to *cons* and *ins*, we cannot with justice refuse it to *ens* and *disses*. We shall be *en*nobled and others be *dis*pleased. I have been out of England ten years, but I think I can recollect a *convènticle* being called a *cònventicle*."

[2] From " JOHNSON " to " antiquity " added in 3rd ed.

IMAGINARY CONVERSATIONS: ENGLISH

painture. Surely it corresponds more closely with *sculpture* and *architecture* than the participle we convert into a substantive to replace it. On the same principle why not *dancery* for *dancing*, as we find it in Chapman? How refreshing, how delicious, is a draught of pure home-drawn English, from a spring a little sheltered and shaded, but not entangled in the path to it, by antiquity!

Among the words of which the accent has been transposed to their disadvantage, are *confessor* and *convex*, from the second to the first. *Sojourn* is by no means inharmonious if you place the accent where it ought to be, as in *adjourn*; but you render it one of the harshest in our language by your violation of *analogy* in perverting it. *Adverse*[1] is accented on the first syllable, *reverse* and *perverse* on the second: pray, why? Milton writes

> That heard th' *Advèrsary*, who roving stil, &c.

Shakespeare writes *aspèct, uprìght, upròar.** The magnificent word *upròar* is used by Milton: how different from the *ùproar* of the streets! He uses *aspèct* as Shakespeare did, and *uprìght*. He also has the fine adjective *deform*. Who does not see that *uprìght* is better than *ùpright?* Then let him read the noble lines of Milton upon Man.

> Who, indued
> With sanctity of reason, might erect
> His stature, and uprìght with front serene
> Govern the rest, self-knowing, and from thence
> Magnanimous to correspond with Heaven.

JOHNSON. I agree with you, sir. *Arístocrat, concordance, contrary, industry, inímical, contémplate, cónculcate, détail, Alexander, sónorous, súblunary* (what becomes of Milton's " *interlunar* cave "?) *désultory, péremptory*, and many more, are now pronounced by the generality (who always adopt some signal folly), differently from the custom of our fathers, and accentuated on the first syllable.

TOOKE. But even the Greeks, at a time when eloquence was highly flourishing, threw back the accent. In the words ὁμοιος and τροπαιον it rested on the second syllable with Æschylus and Thucydides; on

---

[1] From "*Adverse*" to " mother " added in 3rd ed.

* Our living poets have contributed much to throw back the accent: Wordsworth in particular. Even Southey, solid and many-sided as a basaltic column, lends his support here. He writes *èxploits* three several times, and *pròmulgate* and *còntemplate*.—W. S. L.

the first with Plato and Aristoteles. The very same word was differently accentuated in its different senses: for instance, μητρόκτονος, slain *by* a mother: μητροκτόνος, the slayer of a mother. The common people still pronounce *contrary* with the accent where it should be. We throw it back on the first in *acceptable*, and not in *accessible*; yet it is on the second in *accept*, and on the first in *access*. We [1] continue to say *recèss*, but we begin to say *àccess*: the first innovation was in *process*. Dryden writes

> Swift of despatch and easy of access.

Shakespeare very properly lays the accent on the second syllable of *importune*.

> Have you impòrtuned him?

In conversation we often, indeed mostly, use *'em* for *them*: why not in writing? I would always do it after *th*; as *with 'em*. In the Scotch dialect *wi'* for *with* has peculiar grace.*

Nothing is absurder than that, writing the aspirate, we should use it in some words, omit it in others. In polished society I have remarked none aspirated very distinctly, excepting *happy* and *hard*, with the substantives, though *a* precedes many, not *an*. Is it that we sigh (for to aspirate is nothing else in the mode of utterance) as much at what we wish in the former as at what we feel in the latter?

JOHNSON. I do not know: if your observation is just, it must be so: though the remark seems out of your line and beyond your feeling. The [2] common people are fond of aspirates, and only omit them when they ought not.

TOOKE. It is curious that *fortune* and *happiness* are in no language allied, nearly or remotely, to virtue or merit. In ours they are both of them named from chance.

> What if within the moon's fair shining sphere,
> What if in every other star unseen,
> Of other worlds he *happily* should hear

for *haply*.

[1] From "We" to "impòrtuned him?" added in 3rd ed.
* In the [1] ode of Burns, how incomparably better are the words *Scots wha hae wi'* than *who have with*! —W. S. L.
[2] From "The" to "ought not" added in 3rd ed.

---

[1] In 2nd ed. footnote reads: "In that animated ode of Burns, the most animated that ever issued from the lips of man," etc.

IMAGINARY CONVERSATIONS: ENGLISH

The Greeks were more pious, one would imagine, than our ancestors. They entertained the same opinion about fortune, but believed that happiness was the gift of good genii, or Gods, *eudaimonia*.

JOHNSON. Pray tell me now, sir, what we should do? Will you put me upon your knee and teach me? Should we pronounce all our aspirated syllables as such, or none?

TOOKE. Certainly we should no more add a mark of aspiration to a word wherein it is not used, than a mark of interrogation.

JOHNSON. You are a strange man, sir; why, this is true too! Can you be still a whig?

TOOKE. No, Doctor, nor ever was. I wore one livery, and threw it off as an incumbrance; I will not wear another which is both an incumbrance and a disgrace. I have never been even a swindler; now I must not only be a swindler, but a gambler too,[1] if I sit down among the knaves who have so cheated us.

JOHNSON. Swindler, as we understand it, is the worse character of the two.

TOOKE. By no means so in fact. Any gambler may gamble every day and night in the seven, and most of them do, while few swindlers can swindle above the half. And their stakes are lighter, and such as can affect only their personalities: an hour's attendance on the public when they have nothing else to do, and from a station no less secure than commanding, and then immediately a quiet and long recess from the management of affairs. Gambling [2] is the origin of more extensive misery than all other crimes put together: and the mischief falls principally on the unoffending and helpless. It leads by insensible degrees a greater number of wretches to the gallows, than the higher atrocities from which that terminus is seen more plainly. And yet statesmen make it the means of revenue, and kings bestow on it the title of *royal* under the name of lottery. The royal lottery-keeper is both a gambler and a swindler; for in his playing he knows that the stake he lays down is unequal to his opponent's. I keep aloof not only from these pick-pockets, but also aside from the confederate gang who fain would hustle me against them. Moreover I belong to no party.

[1] 2nd ed. reads: " gambler too, and a liar and an impostor, if I would hold the rank my forces entitle me to amongst the whigs."
[2] From " Gambling " to " party " added in 3rd ed.

JOHNSON AND HORNE (TOOKE)

Johnson.[1] That sounds well: and yet he surely is a bad man, sir, who forms no affinities; a solitary sceptic; the blind man in *blind man's buff*, unable to stand a moment on either side, or to fix upon any one about him.

Tooke. All this is true, Doctor. I am a bad man, but exactly in the contrary of the word's original meaning, which I thank you for reminding me of. A *bad* man is a *bade* man, or *bidden* man; a slave in other words; and the same idea was attached to the expression by the Italians and the French (while their language and they had a character) in *cattivo* and *chétif*, and by us in *caitiff*, men in no other condition than that wherein they must do as they are *bid*. We should ourselves have been in no higher condition, if we had not resisted what, in palaces and churches and colleges, was called legitimate power: and indeed we should still be, rather than men, a pliant unsubstantial herbage, springing up from under the smoky, verminous, unconcocted doctrine of passive obedience: to be carted off by our kings amid their carols, and cocked and ricked and cut, and half-devoured, half-trampled and wasted, in the pinfold of our priesthood.

If[2] we take away a letter from the words I have stated, we add one with as little discernment to *therefor* and *wherefor*: we should as reasonably write *thereofe, whereofe, thereine, whereine* : strictly, it would be better to take away one *e* more, and write *therfor*, as was done formerly. I know the origin of the error: the origin may *explain*, but not *excuse*. It is this: the ancients wrote *therforre*. The useless *r* was removed from an infinity of words; and those who removed it in this instance, were little aware that they had better left it, unless they also took away the *e*. We[3] write *solely*, not *soly*, yet we do not write *idlely*, but *idly*: we should about as properly write *barly* for *barely*.

Johnson. I doubt whether you would gain anything by taking this *barly* to market.

Tooke. I should be cried out against as loudly as you were (on another occasion) for your *oats*. If we write *incur* and *recur*, why not *succur* : if *monster*, why not *theater* : if *barometer*, why not *meter* ?

---

[1] 2nd ed. reads: " That sounds well: it comes from a full cup tho a cracked one : and yet you are a bad man, sir, to form no affinities," etc.
[2] From " If " to " took away the *e* " preserved from 1st ed.
[3] From " We " to " *lettre* " added in 3rd ed.

IMAGINARY CONVERSATIONS: ENGLISH

JOHNSON. After all, Mr. Tooke, I must pronounce it as my opinion, that we should do very well in continuing to write as we write at present.

TOOKE. With due submission, I will not pronounce but suggest that nothing is done very well which can be done better. In several words we follow the French without any reason; and we do not follow them where they have seen and abandoned their error. For instance, we follow them in *theatre*, which they spell according to the genius of their language and the exigence of their verse, but contrary to ours: to be consistent we should spell *letter, lettre*. I[1] do not see why *little, able, probable*, &c., should not be written *littil, abil, probabil:* as *civil* forms *civility*, so *abil* forms *ability, probabil* forms *probability:* the others, as we corruptly use them, form *ablety* and *probablety*. There is also another reason: in verse there is an hiatus when they come before a vowel, which hiatus could not exist if we followed what analogy prescribes. I strongly object to *subtle* and *subtlety*, and would propose *subtil* and *subtility*, as *fertil* and *fertility*. From *epistle* and *apostle*, " epistolary " and " apostolical " can not be formed; they may be, and are, from " epist*ol* " and " apost*ol*." It is lucky that " angels " are not as ill-treated as " apostles." If I am to have an *apostle*, I may as well have a *symble*. I would retain, in spelling and in everything else, whatever old manners and old customs are commodious: I would discountenance all the newer which violate propriety or shake consistency. Why should *proceed* and *succeed* be spelt in one way, *precede* and *accede* in another? Why should not the two former be written in the second syllable like the two latter?

JOHNSON. I know not: I think it would be better.

TOOKE. I do not go so far in these matters as your friend Elphinstone; and although I would be a reformer, my reform should be temperate and topical. Many have written *exil* for *banishment:* I would constantly do so, and *exile* for *banished man*.

JOHNSON. The distinction has not been observed by anyone, and would be commodious.

---

[1] In 2nd ed. " took away the *e* " is followed by : " I would write until, til, and still: the latter words, both for analogy and distinction, form the adjective *still*. I mean I would write in this manner if I had any grave authority before me; for without it laws in language are no more to be infringed or modified than laws in politics. I do not see," etc. From " I " to " subtility " preserved from 1st ed.; from " as " to " consistency " added in 3rd ed.

JOHNSON AND HORNE (TOOKE)

TOOKE. You might imagine from the spelling that *complain* and *explain* were of the same origin. To avoid this error, I would follow the authors who have written the latter word *explane;* and the rather, as the substantive is *explanation*, not *explaination*, nor *explaint*. *Passenger* and *messenger* are coarse and barbarous for *passager* and *messager*, and nothing the better for having been adopted into polite society. It [1] may soon admit *sausinges*. Middleton,[2] we have seen, writes *declame*, and elegantly: Milton writes *sovran* and *foren* equally so: for neither the pronunciation nor the etymology authorises the vitiated mode in common use. These writers may be considered as modern; both must be considered as learned, one as eloquent; and until men who are more so write differently, Milton [3] at least shall be my guide. A [4] beautiful adjective in *Paradise Lost* hath ceased to be used in prose, or even in poetry; *alterne*.

> The greater to have rule by day,
> The less by night, *alterne*.

Alternate would serve more properly for the verb.

There is hardly a writer of the Elizabethan age who will not induce us to hesitate on our spelling, or rather who will not suggest some improvement. *Abbot*, from *abbas*, should be spelt *abbat*, as Tanner spells it. Massinger [5] writes *carroch*, from *carozza*: our *carriage* is inelegant. Jonson in his verses to Wroth, says,

> In autumn at the *partrich* mak'st a flight.

I would write the word so, if it were for no other reason than that we write *ostrich* in the same manner.[6]

JOHNSON. I remember two of his verses for a word to be corrected in them.

> When thy latest sand is spent,
> Thou mayest think life a thing but lent.

It would then be too late: *when* should be *ere*.

[1] From "It" to "*sausinges*" added in 3rd ed.
[2] From "Middleton" to "differently" preserved from 1st ed.
[3] 1st ed. reads: "these shall be my guides."
[4] From "A" to "verb" added in 3rd ed.
[5] From "Massinger" to "inelegant" added in 3rd ed.
[6] 2nd ed. reads: "manner. He and Shakespear, I am inclined to think, often wrote *fier* as well as *fire*: we still retain the trace of it in the adjective *fiery*. In those poets it occurs as a dissyllable, altho in the printed copies it is *fire*. I find it in the poem I have quoted, which pleases me better than any other of the same author. I only wish he had omitted the last lines, taken from Juvenal. JOHNSON. I remember them for a word," etc.

IMAGINARY CONVERSATIONS: ENGLISH

TOOKE. True.

JOHNSON. As *fire* and *sire* and *hour* and *four* sometimes are dissyllables in the old poets, so likewise are *year* and *sure;* while *entire* and *desire* are trisyllables; *contrary*, a quadrisyllable. They spelt indifferently and wrote arbitrarily. Shakespeare takes no liberties of this kind unauthorised in fact or analogy by other writers more scholastic.

TOOKE. They favor my proposition of spelling by *il* what we spell by *le;* such as *humbil, dazzil, tickil;* for in whatever way they wrote the word, they often make a trisyllable of *humbled* and *dazzled*.

And [1] that hath dazzled my reason's light

says Shakespeare; and in *Henry VI.* he makes a trisyllable of "*English*."

JOHNSON. I know not what advantages we can obtain from a perception of crudities and barbarisms, unless it be that it enables us to estimate more correctly the great improvements we have made in later times. But [2] I admit that we might have retained a few things to our advantage. Who would read Chaucer and Spenser for their language?

TOOKE. Spenser I would not,[3] delightful as are many parts of his poetry; but Chaucer I would read again and again both for his poetry and his language.

JOHNSON. I suppose, sir, you prefer the dialect of Thomson, a whig, to Spenser's?

TOOKE. No, Doctor; his is worse still; but there are images and feelings in his *Winter*, in comparison with which the liveliest in Spenser are faint.

JOHNSON. And those too, no doubt, on the same subject in the *Georgics!*

TOOKE. Beyond a question. It appears to me that there is more poetry in it than in the whole of that elaborate poem, beautiful as it is in versification and in language; both of which are wanting in almost every place to Thomson.

---

[1] Quotation added in 3rd ed. 2nd ed. reads: "dazzled and tickled. Shakespeare in *Henry VI.* makes," etc.

[2] "But" to "advantage" added in 3rd ed.

[3] 2nd ed. reads: "not; for he is among the most inelegant of our writers in prose or verse, delightful as," etc.

JOHNSON AND HORNE (TOOKE)

JOHNSON. Oh! you do acknowledge then that the versification is elaborate, and the language beautiful!

TOOKE. Doctor, I hate carping. Where much is good in a man or a poem I would always mention it; and where in the same man or poem there is a little bad, I would pass it over.

JOHNSON. What is the bad, sir, in the *Georgics?* Come, I have you now off the ground : your strength, such as it is, has left you.

TOOKE. May all men's strength leave them when they would make invidious objections!

JOHNSON. Rare subterfuge! Virgil is a dead prince, sir; you cannot hurt him.

TOOKE. Far be the wish from me! I would act toward him as the pious ancients did toward the dead : I would wash him first, and afterward perfume him with the most precious unguents.

JOHNSON. Up with your sleeves then, and begin the washing. Here, take the *Georgics;* I usually carry them about me.

TOOKE. Has [1] Ovid, has Lucan, has any other Latin poet, written such balderdash and bombast as the nineteen verses in the beginning, at the close of an invocation already much too prolix? Why all these additions to the modest prayer of Varro, which he has versified? Here let me suggest a new and a necessary reading just above these lines.

Quique novas alitis non *ullo* semine fruges.[2]

It must be *uno*, to avoid nonsense; which is always a benefit, even in poetry; and so represent *wheat, barley, oats,* &c.; that is to say, "not only one kind of grain." The lines of the letter *n* and the double *l*, may have been much alike in manuscript, and may have easily misled transcribers. I will not dwell upon the verses after

Tethys emat omnibus undis; [3]

but really those eight appear to me like an excrescence on the face of a beautiful boy.

JOHNSON. They are puerile, are they? a blemish, a deformity!

TOOKE. In honest truth I think so.

JOHNSON. You have turned over only one leaf: the faults must lie thick.

TOOKE. Somewhat. Beginning again at the eighty-first line, I

[1] From " Has " to " transcribers " added in 3rd ed.
[2] *Georg.*, i. 22.   [3] *Georg.*, i. 31.

IMAGINARY CONVERSATIONS: ENGLISH

find the *earth* ending that and all the five following, with one exception, *agros, arva, terræ, agros,* flammis, *terræ.*

JOHNSON. I do not credit you.

TOOKE. Take the book.

JOHNSON. No, sir, I will not take the book : read on.

TOOKE. In the next page, *arvis, arva, arva,* close the verse within twelve successive lines. In the next beyond *moveri, removit, repressit,* one after the other; and immediately after " extund*eret* artes," " quær*eret* herbam," and " excud*eret* ignem." Three more pages, and the words *convivia curant* are followed in the next verse by " *cura*sque resolvit." May I express my delight at——

JOHNSON. No, sir ! no, sir ! no delight about anything ! Spit your spite.

TOOKE. Since you are so urgent in your commands, I will proceed. Beginning from the 406th verse, there are thirteen which end with spondaic words. In the second book,

> Et gens illa quidem sumptis non tarda pharetris [1]

is another excrescence; and in the following we find *tardumque saporem.*

JOHNSON. Sir, can you construe that line ? I doubt it.

TOOKE. Instruct me then.

JOHNSON. You, being a word-catcher, ought to know that our word *tart,* for *sharp,* corresponds with *tardus.*

TOOKE. I perceive the commentator gives this interpretation ; a very wrong one. *Tart* is not related to *tardus.* Virgil means that the citron ripens late. Before we reach the 300th line, here are together twelve more ending with spondaic words. Now, my dear sir, do let me give utterance to my enthusiasm on " O fortunatos nimium." Permit [2] my raptures at sitting down among the " *saltus et lustra ferarum,*" the feeling is so new. Did I hear one of them ? methought I heard a growl, or something similar.

JOHNSON.[3] Go on, sir, and mind your business.

TOOKE. Well then ; *rura* ends one line, *jura* the next. " Atque alio *patriam* "—then, with one line between—" *hinc patriam.*" " Pascitur in *magna* sylvâ," and just below, " *magnus* Olympus." Doctor, how do you construe " *Odor attulit auras* " *?*

---

[1] *Georg.,* ii. 125. [2] From " Permit " to " new " added in 3rd ed.
[3] From " JOHNSON " to " then " added in 3rd ed.

JOHNSON AND HORNE (TOOKE)

JOHNSON. That is an hypallage, sir.

TOOKE. But construe it.

JOHNSON. One must reverse the sense.

TOOKE. A pretty idea of poetry. His [1] *odor attulit auras* is like Shakespeare's " *The oats have eaten the horses* "; but Shakespeare's was fun, and Virgil's was affectation. In fact the hypallage, of which Virgil is fonder than any other writer, is much the gravest fault in language.

JOHNSON. What, sir ! graver than solecism ?

TOOKE. Yes, Doctor ; in the same degree as nonsense is worse than inelegance. A boy shouts at another boy and holds him in derision, when he finds him putting, as he calls it, the cart before the horse. Onward, if you please : and here we find again, at *currentem ilignis*, fourteen final spondees without one bacchic foot among them. At last we arrive at that passage which provoked you to throw poor Thomson under the triumphal car of Virgil.

> Concrescunt subitæ currenti in flumine crustæ,
> Undaque jam *tergo* ferratos sustinet orbes,
> Puppibus illa prius, patulis nunc hospita plaustris.[2]

These and the four following would make but an indifferent figure in the exercise of an Eton boy ; there is no harmony, no fluency in them ; they are broken pieces of ice. What think you, after " *Æraque dissiliunt vulgo*," of " *vestesque rigescunt* " ? Such an instance of the art of sinking you will not find in the Latin, nor easily in any other poetry. What follows is much better ; but it will bear no comparison with the Miltonian description in Thomson, of the frozen regions visited by the caravan from Cathay.

JOHNSON. Sir, even the description of Orpheus and Eurydice could not stir your cold blood.

TOOKE. Doctor, you have formed your judgment upon it ; let me reflect and hesitate a little before I deliver mine.

JOHNSON. Now I would lay a wager that all this magnificence is not worth your Scotch-Cathay caravan.

TOOKE. I would do the same.

JOHNSON. Then, sir, you have either no sense of shame or no soul for poetry.

---

[1] From " His " to " affectation " added in 3rd ed. [2] *Georg.*, iii. 360.

IMAGINARY CONVERSATIONS: ENGLISH

TOOKE. On *shame* and *soul* the discussion might be unsatisfactory. But let us, my dear sir, survey together the character of Proteus. Nothing can be harder, unless it be myself: he must be chained to make him civil or tractable, to make him render the slightest and easiest service to anyone. He had no affinity or friendship, no community of character or country, with Orpheus and Eurydice. One would think he could have known little about them, and cared less. In a monster, for such he was, and so unfeeling and solitary, the description is far from natural; and even in Virgil himself, who seems to have forgotten that he was not speaking in his own person, it would have been somewhat overcharged. The Homeric simile of the nightingale, and the silly tale of a head speaking when it was cut off and rolling down a river, and speaking so loud too as to make an echo on the banks, is puerile, absurd, and preposterous.

JOHNSON. The verses on the nightingale are inharmonious, no doubt?

TOOKE. I did not say it; but some parts are. Beside, " *mærens, queritur, flet, miserabile, mæstis* " : surely we do not want all at once, nor to express one feeling. *Observans nido implumes detraxit* is as inharmonious as any verse can easily be made. On the whole, how much better would the episode have been if Proteus had said little, and if Cyrene had given the description.

JOHNSON. You know nothing of poetry; but that last remark is true. Who suggested it?

TOOKE. Doctor Johnson; when he favoured me with the volume which I now return to him.

JOHNSON. Sir, you carry your revolutionary and chaotic principles into the fields and groves, into the woods and mountains, and render more fierce and gloomy the winds and tempests and eternal snows. You have no love of order even in works of art.

TOOKE. Doctor, we were talking just now of dissyllables and tri-syllables and Chaucer. He writes,

> With Theseus the squire principal.

JOHNSON. If you quote such metre, you may quote that also which was

> Written by William Prynne esquire, the
> Year of our Lord six hundred thirty-three.

JOHNSON AND HORNE (TOOKE)

TOOKE. Never did the muses sail to their antipodes so expeditiously as under the steerage of their new Tiphys, if you on this occasion will let me call you so.

JOHNSON. Call me anything, sir, rather than call Thomson a writer of English.

TOOKE. Affectation is his greatest fault; and it is a matter of wonder to me that he seldom errs on any other side. I do not remember that he confuses, as the Scotch and Irish do perpetually, *shall* and *will*. We ourselves confound them without knowing it; but idiomatically.

JOHNSON. In what manner? Good writers never do.

TOOKE. For instance, *You will be burnt if you touch the tea-urn. Shall I be burnt if I touch the tea-urn?* Here the action and time are the same, yet the words differ. In fact, "*will I*" can only be used in the rebutment of a question; as when a person asks, *Will you or will you not?* and the reply, instead of affirmation or negative, is angrily, *Will I or will I not?* in which is understood, *Do you ask me thus?* To another we say "*Shall I?*" and he replies "*If you will.*"

These things, Doctor, would appear trifling to trifling men; but not to you, who can not be less curious in the philosophy of a language than in its etymology.

JOHNSON. Let us stop where we are, and while we are innocent. Philosophy in these matters draws us away to analysis: the dry *seta equina* of analysis breaks into pieces, in one or two of which pieces we soon descry the restless heads and wriggling tails of metaphysics. Sir, metaphysics lead to materialism, and materialism to atheism. Those who do not see this see nothing: but there are more who see it than will confess it. Of what value is anything, although it should conduce at first to some truth even less dry and sterile, if in its progression it renders men insincere, and in its termination unhappy? Anatomise words, flay, dissect, eviscerate language, but keep your faith out of the crucible, for the daily use and sustenance of your family.

TOOKE. I began to fear, Doctor, that you would have concluded your sentence in another manner.

JOHNSON. In what manner, sir?

TOOKE. That you would have said, *to go to market with*, for the daily use and sustenance of my family. My faith, I do assure you,

IMAGINARY CONVERSATIONS: ENGLISH

I keep both out of the crucible and out of the *aqua regia;* another great melter and transmuter. My dear sir, I would divert the gathering storm of your anger by any propitiation and concession.

JOHNSON. Rogue!

TOOKE. Excellently and most opportunely introduced. I could say something upon that word too; but I doubt whether it would be quite so agreeable to you as another of which I was thinking. In your reading of our ancient poets, particularly our dramatists, you must have observed that *kind* is frequently used for *nature.* This is a beautiful feature in our language. Our ancestors identified *nature* with *kindness.* I love our old modes of thinking in most things, and of speaking in many. We have several ancient words used at present in a different sense from what they were formerly; *rogue* for instance.

JOHNSON. No sedition, sir! no vague allusions! no contempt of authority! I know who rogues are, as well as you do; but I abstain from throwing a firebrand into their houses, and lighting the populace to pillage and murder.

TOOKE. Well judged: the populace has no right to any such things.

JOHNSON. Strange! marvellous! You enunciate even these sentences, the most detestable, the most impious, the most seditious, uninflamed, unwarmed; like your chemists, who pour from one bottle into another, just as unconcernedly, I know not what pestiferous and heavy air of theirs, if report speaks truly, corking it down until they can find something to set the whole of it in a blaze; and thus teaching us that what is the lowest in its nature is the most destructive in its application.

TOOKE. Doctor, in the asbestine quality of my mind, with the flames and faggots on both sides, you appear to see a miracle: if you could see more clearly, you would discover in it Christianity without one.

JOHNSON (*aside*). I did not imagine that this logical wronghead could balance and swing and dandle me so easily.

I recollect no expression in Chaucer worth retaining and not retained.

TOOKE. What think you of *swough*, the long-continued sound of wind?

                a *swough*
As thof a storme should brasten every bough.
                    Palamon and Arcite.

JOHNSON AND HORNE (TOOKE)

JOHNSON. It sounds grandly : there is something of a melancholy and a lonely wildness in it.

TOOKE. The Scotch retain it still, spelling it *sugh*.

JOHNSON. Let them keep it, sir, to themselves. I would not give a straw for it. We want neither harsh words nor obsolete ones.

TOOKE. Suppose we found in Chaucer some words less harsh in their pronunciation than they appear at present ; and others, if not less so, yet useful for variety or for rhyme ; such are *beforne*, before, *withouten*, without, *somdel*, somewhat, *astonned*, astonished, *brast* and *brasten*, burst or broken, and many more.

JOHNSON. Let our language rest where it is.

TOOKE. Languages, like men, when they have rested long and totally, grow heavy and plethoric : we must renew their juices, and bring them back into their native air.

We have *presently*, but want *futurely*, used by Fletcher in the *Two Noble Kinsmen*. Fashionable [1] people turn nosegays out of doors, and send to France for *bouquets*. Why have we forgotten our more beautiful *posy*, of which Spenser and Swift were not disdainful ? Among the rich furniture of our ancestors which we cast aside, may be reckoned a certain two-handed instrument of great utility and strength. *By* and *of* were employed by them at their option. Shakespeare says

Unwhipt of Justice.

We now abandon altogether the better usage : I would have reserved both. We use the word *bat* for various things ; among the rest, for that animal which partakes the nature of bird and mouse : why not call it, at least in poetry, what Ben Jonson does, *flittermouse ?* The word in all respects is better ; it is more distinguishing, more descriptive, and our language is by one the richer for it.

JOHNSON. The reasons are valid and unobjectionable.

TOOKE. The verb to *beat* is the same in its present tense and in its preterite ; so irregularly and improperly, that you can not but have observed how people avoid the use of it in the latter.

JOHNSON. The Romans did the same in their *ferio*. Instead of taking a preterite from it, they used *percussi*. I think however that I have somewhere seen the preterite, *bate*.

TOOKE. We had our choice either to follow the inflexion of *cheat*

---

[1] From " Fashionable " to " disdainful " added in 3rd ed.

or *eat;* we took the latter; and then would have neither. I am afraid of reminding you where you probably last met with *bate,* which you seem looking after.

JOHNSON. Subdue your blushes, my gentle sir, and conduct me back to the place, be it where it may.

TOOKE. The Irishman in Fielding's *Tom Jones* says, " He *bate* me."

JOHNSON. What we hear from an Irishman we are not overfond of repeating, whether in grammar or fact: but in this case our risibility is excited by the circumstances rather than the language, although the language too has its share in it. The dialect is Hibernian.

TOOKE. We certainly should not either smile at the expression in a vulgar countryman of our own, nor condemn it in a learned discourse from the pulpit.

JOHNSON. I would not hesitate to employ it in graver composition.

TOOKE. Nor I: for authors much richer both in thought and language than any now living or any recently deceased, have done so.

JOHNSON. If we begin to reinstate old words, we shall finish by admitting new ones.

TOOKE. There would be the less danger of that, as there would be the less need. Yet even new words may be introduced with good effect, and particularly when the subject is ludicrous.

JOHNSON. Phrynicus and Julius Pollux animadvert with severity on Menander for inventing new words, and for using such others as were unknown in Attica: and perhaps this is the reason why he was frequently vanquished by Polemon in the contest for the prize of comedy. Gellius tells us, on the authority I think of Apollodorus, that, although he wrote a hundred and five pieces, he was the victor but in eight.

TOOKE. And if we could recover them all, we should find probably those eight the very worst among them, and the only ones that fairly could admit a competition. When Menander asked Polemon whether he did not blush at being his vanquisher, the answer (I can well imagine) was another such suffusion; and not, as would have been the case if there were any room for it, that the inelegance or inexactness of Menander turned the countenance of the judges from him. He was considered by the best critics of succeeding ages as the most Attic of the Athenians; and certainly was not the less so

JOHNSON AND HORNE (TOOKE)

for employing those expressions, novel or foreign, which suited the characters he introduced. A word may be excellent in a dialogue which would deteriorate and deform an oration. Julius Pollux, I remember, disapproves of many words used by Plato and Herodotus. Now although Plato is often flat and insipid, as Dionysius of Halicarnassus demonstrates by examples, yet I can not think he ever used a term improperly or unfitly. In regard to Herodotus, his style I consider as the most proper, the most pure, the most simply and inelaborately harmonious, of any author in any language. His genius, what rarely happens, is well seconded and sustained by his spirit of research and his delight in knowledge. He has been censured for a deficiency of elevation. Many can judge of elevation in phraseology; fewer of that which is attained by an elastic vigour in the mind, keeping up easily a broad continuance of imaginative thought. This is almost as necessary to matter of fact as to poetry, if the matter of fact is worthy to be impressed on the memory or understanding.

How much better is *disherited* than *disinherited*? *innerest* than *innermost*? How much more properly is *tongue* written *tong*, *fruit frute*, *suit sute*, *friend frend*, *atchieve acheve*? We[1] derive *conceive*, *receive*, *perceive*, through the French, who never thrust into them the letter *i*: why then should we? These are not new modes: we find them in the time of Spenser, and most of them in his works. He writes the verbs, *wil* and *shal;* he also writes *til* and *ontil*. He would not do so unless others whom he esteemed as good authors had given him the example; for his rhyme, which he favours at any rate, did not exact it. Anciently[2] *work* was spelt *werke*, as we continue to pronounce it. The final vowel in this word and many others, was retained long after its use had ceased.

JOHNSON. Of what use was it?

TOOKE. It often served to form a dissyllable in the plural, and in the genitive singular, as we find in Chaucer, and it was not only in poetry that it was thus pronounced.

JOHNSON. Raleigh uses the grand word *sumptuosity*, ill exchanged for *costliness* or *expensiveness*.

TOOKE. I have lately heard *illùstrate* for illústrate: we shall

[1] From "We" to "we?" added in 3rd ed.
[2] From "Anciently" to "write another" (in Tooke's speech beginning, "Wonderful, but") added in 3rd ed.

IMAGINARY CONVERSATIONS: ENGLISH

presently come to impèrceptible. We have *aspect, prospect, respect, retrospect;* we formerly had also the substantive *suspect*. Raleigh uses it. " But this was not his manner of reasoning with Hastings, whose fidelity to his master's sons was without *suspect*." We have moreover his authority, and Hooker's, for *possest, exprest, supprest, confest, mockt*. He writes *samplar*, and *begger :* we, very improperly, *sampler* and *beggar*. Milton, the great master of our language and its harmonies, accents on the second syllable, *consùlt* (the substantive), *accèss, procèss, advèrse, aspèct, convèrse, insùlts* (substantive), *contèst* (substantive), *impùlse, pretèxt, blasphèmous, crystàlline, remèdiless, surfàce, triùmphed, contrìte, maritìme, prodùct, prescrìpt, conflàgrant*. You perceive by those accentuations how obtuse are the ears of our fashionable poets in comparison with Milton's. *Prune* and *preen* are the same word, meaning to *trim :* but it would be well to apply *prune* exclusively to the trimming of trees, and *preen* exclusively to the trimming of the feathers by birds. Dryden and Pope use *prune* in the latter sense, misled by what they found printed in Shakespeare, who, rich in the phraseology of the country, wrote (I am confident) *preen*. South writes *an* before *high*. Addison writes *superiour;* Milton, Taylor, Locke, and Swift, *superior*. In many instances the spelling of Chaucer is more easy, more graceful and elegant, than the modern : for example, where he avoids the diphthongs, ea, oa, and the reduplication of the vowel in the following :

> In *cote* and hode of *grene*
> A *shefe* of peacocke armes brighte and *kene*.

This was continued for many centuries, and we find it in Ben Jonson : who also writes *cossen* (cousin), *linage, coles, pen'd, dore, ake, balkt, bewitcht, finde, purchast, hoopt, confest, cloke, nere, borne, onlly, kist, beleeve, sute, cloke, armor, jayle, stript, clensd, reproch, dote, stretcht, stampt, lothe, polisht, iland, accomplisht, starcht, tand, neere, furnisht, crackt, brest, smel, led, wel, stabd, mockt, pluckt, incenst, scepter, theater, theeves, fetcht, supprest, flote, distinguisht, doo* (do), *honor* (both verb and substantive), *profest, deprest, prest*. We have altered every one of those spellings ; can any man tell me which in the whole number is altered for the better ?

JOHNSON. How would you deal with the preterite of such a verb as *notice ?*

TOOKE. It must be *noticed :* and I wish we were obliged to pro-

JOHNSON AND HORNE (TOOKE)

nounce distinctly each of its three syllables. Countrymen in the midland shires have preserved the verb *notize;* like *prize* and *advertize.* I wish we never had rejected it, and had kept *notice* for the substantive only.

JOHNSON. I have remarked the preterite spelt *notic'd*, and by writers of reputation, in the beginning of this century.

TOOKE. Wonderful, but perfectly true. I would rather see Grammar a shrew than a slattern. There are hours and occasions when she needs not be full-dressed; there are none when it is pardonable in her to come down with tangled hair. There are fictions in our laws, and there are fictions also in our language: *notic'd*, *entic'd*, are examples. We have seen them printed; we never have heard or can hear them pronounced. Bottles in print are *corked*, in the cellars they are *corkt:* no human voice ever uttered *cork'd*. Since we have two ways, why take that which leads us wrong? We have both *blest* and *blessed;* but we have not both *prest* and *pressed, carest* and *caressed.* Like the Achilles of Horace, who "jura negat sibi nata," &c., we seize upon what does not belong to us, and cast aside what does: we speak one thing and write another.

We never say *patriarchical*, yet we say *monarchical* and *anarchical*: harsh words! Since the choice is left me by prescription in the one, by analogy in the other, I would constantly write *anarchal* and *monarchal*. It[1] occurs to me now, what I should have mentioned before if I had thought of it at the time when we were speaking on the subject, that Fairfax, instead of writing *embraced*, wrote (as many did) *embrast*.

> Gather the rose of love while yet thou *maist*,
> Loving be loved, embracing be *embrast*.

JOHNSON. Indeed the word "embra*s*e" comes more directly from its origin.

TOOKE. Ménage tells us that he did the contrary of what was done by the Academy. "They fill their dictionary," says he, "with words in use: I take greater care, in my etymologies, of those which are no longer so, that they may not be quite forgotten."

JOHNSON. Both did right. It is interesting to trace the features of a language in every stage of its existence. I wish you would do it,

---
[1] From "It" to "origin" added in 3rd ed.

IMAGINARY CONVERSATIONS: ENGLISH

Mr. Tooke : I have done enough : it must be the exercise of learned leisure, and not of him whose daily bread is dipped in ink.

TOOKE. Doctor, there was a time when I sighed at what raised my admiration : I thought it was over : your last words renew it. I am not the adviser of pensions : I should be happy to see the greater part of them struck off : but more gladly still should I read an act of parliament, in pursuance of which ten were established in perpetuity for our ten best writers. Five of them should enjoy five hundred a year, the others three, closing only when preferment of higher value were given them.

JOHNSON. And pray, sir, would you admit the partisan of rebellion to the advantages of this endowment ?

TOOKE. I would exclude none whatever for his opinions, political or theological. The minister who had granted such an indulgence to his opponent, would indemnify himself by the acquisition of worthier supporters, attached to him by his magnanimity : the partisan of rebellion who accepted it, would render but little service to his cause. The whole sum thus expended is barely what you throw upon the desk of the lowest scribbler, appointed Secretary (we will suppose) to the Board of Admiralty for some smutty song or pious pasquinade ; barely what a vulgar commissary gains in one day's contract for bullocks ; and therefore on neither side of the house would the motion find, consistently, any opponent who can spell and cast accounts. Since the form of our constitution is not such as admits every man of superior abilities to the place he might occupy in one more popular, so slight amends may surely be made for the privation. I venture to assert that it would render our government more respected abroad than it is rendered by our armies and navies, and more beloved at home than it is by our assessments and excise.

JOHNSON. Ay, ay ! among the ten we should find your name, no doubt !

TOOKE. No, sir, my name is not to be where ten are at a time : beside, there is no Minister whose exclusion of me would be unjustifiable. These two considerations make me speak openly and warmly. Few authors could recommend the motion : I dare to do it, excited by the neglected genius of my adversary here, and the glory no less neglected of my country.

JOHNSON. I would hardly be so ministerial on this point as you

JOHNSON AND HORNE (TOOKE)

are: I would increase the value of the pension by making it depend on the vote of parliament.

TOOKE. This is better: we may suppose three names recommended by a committee on every vacancy.

JOHNSON. I perceive that you, in the midst of letters, always turn aside to the political.

TOOKE. I wish, in the midst of the political, our representatives were turned for a moment to the consideration of letters. What I recommend is practicable and uncostly. Hardly one member of the Honourable House is interested in recommending a relative or friend: and I doubt whether, in all the ten to be chosen, more than two or three would be nominated on an unpaid bill, by coach-maker or fishmonger or tailor.

JOHNSON. Ah false suitor! you have unwoven with your own hands Penelope's bright web: you might have left it to Penelope herself: night would have closed again on it in scattered filaments.

TOOKE. No, my dear sir, I have not hurt the web; I have only puffed away a design of it which was never designed to be executed. Cadmus, who found letters, found also the dragon's teeth to be sown among them and to consume them. Now[1] we are in Asia, let us turn it to our purposes, as others do.

The word *Tartar*, we are informed of late, is properly *Tatar* in its own language: be it so: this is no sufficient reason why we also should be *Tatars* or speak *tatar*. The word *Tartar* has been received among us some centuries, and invariably used. *Caractacus, Cassibellaunus*, and *Britannia*, are not exactly the British words: yet a Roman would have been ridiculed who, a hundred years after the reception of them, should rather have inserted the original British in his history. We are become well acquainted with *Mahomet*: but every man who has travelled in the East brings home a new name for the prophet, and trims his turban to his own taste.

JOHNSON. I am reminded of an observation I made the other day, that some recent authors write *Tartarian* as the adjective of *Tartar*: *Tartarian* is that of *Tartarus*: *Tartar* is itself an adjective.

TOOKE. I[2] will pay you down on the nail a substantive for your adjective. We say *poulterer*: we might as well say *ministerer, masterer*, and *maltsterer*. Our language, sir, is losing a little of its

---

[1] From "Now" to "do" added in 3rd ed.
[2] From "I" to "maltsterer" added in 3rd ed.

propriety every year. It becomes more trim by its espaliers; but I wish I could say its fruit is the better for the reduction of its branches. We have *anger* and *wrath* in our old language; *resentment, rage, pique,* the worse and weaker parts of the feeling, come from the French.

JOHNSON. You place too little reliance upon good authorities.

TOOKE. Good writers are authorities for only what is good, and by no means and in no degree for what is bad, which may be found even in them.

JOHNSON. How then decide upon what is really bad or good?

TOOKE. By exercising our ratiocination upon it, and by comparing with it other modes of expression. Many of those who are generally called good writers are afraid of writing as they speak. This is a worse than panic fear; and is the principal reason why our moderns are less rich and less easy than their predecessors. They are reluctant to mount up above the time of Dryden; not indeed a mean writer in prose or poetry, singularly terse in his moral sentences and felicitous in his allusions; but in copiousness and beauty of language no more comparable to Barrow and Taylor and some others, than the canal in St. James's Park is comparable to the Thames. If we wish to breathe freely and largely, and to fill our innermost breasts with the spirit of our language, we must ascend higher.

JOHNSON. The most curious thing I know in it is, that *ever* and *never* should be synonymous. Can you account for this?

TOOKE. The *mai* of the Italians, in like manner, serves both purposes. *Were you never so just* is the same in its meaning as *Were you ever so just*. The one is *were you never in your life so just as upon this occasion*: the other, *howsoever just you were.*

JOHNSON. This satisfies me. I should myself have given the same solution.

TOOKE. It must then, Doctor, be a clear and easy one.

JOHNSON (*aside*). The man's words are ambiguous; although it is plain that he is not aware of it; for nothing was ever so serene as his countenance, so unembarrassed as his manner, so polite as his whole demeanour. Can this fellow now be in his heart almost a republican? Impossible!

TOOKE. We [1] have another odd expression in the verb *help,* when we say, "*I can not help thinking,*" for "I can not *but* think." We

---

[1] From "We" to "spelling-book" added in 3rd ed.

help in assisting and resisting. It is an exercise of power : here the power is on the side of resistance. Again to the spelling-book : *Rind*,[1] *bind, mind, find, wind* (the verb), *kind, blind,* &c., we already have acknowledged, are better written as they were formerly, with a final *e,* as also *child, wild, mild;* that the sound may accord with the spelling, which should always be the case where no very powerful reason interposes its higher authority. *Ache,* why not *ake : height*,[2] why not *highth,* as Milton writes it? Those who polish language, like those who clean pictures, often rub away the colouring. Roughness, you will tell me, is removed by the process of the moderns : I could adduce no few instances to the contrary. Now do you imagine that the fashionable way of writing *empress's son,* if we *could* pronounce it accordingly, would be better than *empresses?*[3] No other language in the world (for though the serpent could once speak he could never write) presents four *esses* in conjunction[4]. The final *es* is more proper, more ancient, more English, than the substitute *his,* which Addison, Dryden (in " Etheridge *his* courtship "), and a crowd of inferiors, have employed. Raleigh himself, greatly more learned and eloquent than either, writes, " He was advised of Asdrubal *his* approach."

JOHNSON. Reverting to the " *empress's son,*" who would not rather say " *son of the empress* " ?

TOOKE. I talk of what exists in the language, not of what is best in it: nor indeed would your alteration be preferable in all contingencies. What for instance think you of this ? " We have heard of the ill state of health of the son of the empress of Russia." The double genitive ought to be avoided as much as possible in all composition : it has however a worse effect in modern languages than in ancient. To ours the ancient termination designating it, is highly advantageous. It has not only two genitives, but let me also remark to you, it has a greater variety of sounds in it than in any other I know.

JOHNSON. Surely not than the Greek.

[1] From " Rind " to " authority " preserved from 1st ed.
[2] 2nd ed. reads : " *Heighth* and *neighbour* should be written *highth* and *nighbour :* the former comes from *high,* not *heigh!* the latter from *nigh,* not *neigh.* Those who," etc. From " Those " to "*facienda* " (p. 92) preserved from 1st ed.
[3] 2nd ed. spells : " empressis." It would appear that Landor mispronounced all plurals in *es,* as well as a few other of the words discussed in this Conversation.
[4] 2nd ed. reads : " conjunction. The final *s* hath nothing to do with what Addison and others have substituted for it, *his*: it is among our few declined cases. JOHNSON. Who would not rather say," etc.

IMAGINARY CONVERSATIONS: ENGLISH

TOOKE. Beyond a question; if you acknowledge that the Greeks, who have never lost their language, know how to pronounce it better than we do. Their diphthongs are almost insensibly so: we give to their *ai* and *oi* our own deep-mouthed tone, our own as exclusively as *i* in *mine*, &c.

Returning to the *s*, although we have one word of nine letters in which it occurs five times, and another of only eight in which it appears as often (*possesses* and *assesses*), yet I once from curiosity examined a hundred verses in Shakespeare and the same number in Sophocles, and found it more frequent in the latter. If I had counted the *xis*, the *zetas*, and the *psis*, which contain it, the difference would have been still greater. It is true, the Greek iambic contains more syllables than ours, but the number of letters is nearly the same in each.

JOHNSON. I am unsatisfied, after all, that the English *is*, whether joined to the word or disjoined from it, whether in full or in contraction, may not be *his*, as our grammarians have supposed.

TOOKE. That it has not relation to *his* may be demonstrated by its being common to both male and female, to both singular and plural: we say not only *Edwin's book*, but *Emma's book*, and, with as little hesitation, *men's minds*. Beside[1], the most part of old authors do not write the possessive case in *is* but in *es*; because *e* was the general termination of substantives.

There are some words which, if we receive them, we cannot spell rightly; they have been so perverted by custom: such are *amaze*, *alarm*, a *newt*; the first of which was a *maze*, the second a *larum*, the last an *evet*. So the French *affaire*, and the Italian *affare*; *à faire*, *a fare*; demonstrable in the latter by the earlier word, still equally in common use, *facenda*, res *facienda*. *Bower* is part of *arbour*, and *cate* is part of *delicate*.

JOHNSON. Is *delicate* then used anywhere as a substantive for *delicacy*?

TOOKE. Marston in one of his plays says *princely delicates*. *Débonnaire* was formerly used in a different sense from the present. "*Il faut être simple, obéissant et débonnaire, pour être propre à recevoir religion*," says Charron, a writer scarcely less shrewd than Bacon and much more elegant. But I have traced the old gentleman pretty often out of Seneca into Plutarch.

[1] From " Beside " to " substantives " added in 3rd ed.

JOHNSON AND HORNE (TOOKE)

Johnson. I do not much read French : that language appears to have been greatly changed in one century.

Tooke. Even since Pascal, Ménage, and Mad. de Sévigné. Formerly to teach Greek was *montrer le Grec :* it would have been thought an Italianism to say *enseigner.* This is remarkable in the French, that it is more figurative in common conversation than in ordinary prose writing, and more so in prose than in verse. A *batterie de cuisine,* a *chapeau abîmé,* an artificial flower *magnifique,* a false curl *superbe,* a kidney-bean ill-boiled *horrible,* an old-fashioned coat *affreux;* a [1] turbot with a wrong sauce an *assassination.*

We [2] see written *mantua*-maker, for *manteau*-maker, a vulgar and ludicrous error : we see also *ameliorate* for *meliorate,* although one would reasonably suppose that it signified the reverse. We write *posthumous,* in the silly opinion that the word is derived from *post* and *humus :* the termination in fact is nowise different from that of *maxumus* and *optumus* in the Latin, although, by one of the chances common in language, it has escaped that change in the middle syllable which the others have undergone.

You would derive a good many words from the Latin which come to us from nearer relatives in the North : and there are some few which really are Latin, and you do not notice as such. What think you for instance of *hocus pocus ?*

Johnson. Sir, those are exclamations of conjurers, as they call themselves.

Tooke. Well, Doctor, let us join them, and try to be conjurers ourselves a little. We know that the common people often use the aspirate unnecessarily, and as often omit the *i:* for instance, they constantly say *ingenous* for *ingenious :* u and i are not only confounded by us, as in *grum* for *grim,* &c., but were equally so by the Romans, as *lacruma* was *lacrima.*

Johnson. You mean rather with *y.*

Tooke. No ; they oftener wrote it with *i:* the conceited and ignorant used *y,* only to make it appear they knew the derivation. For the same reason among us people write *thyme* with the *h,* contrary to the manner of pronouncing it.

Johnson. Pray go on.

[1] 2nd ed. reads : " a kick on the breech, or a turbot," etc.
[2] From " We " to " undergone " preserved from 1st ed.

IMAGINARY CONVERSATIONS: ENGLISH

TOOKE. The preliminaries are acceded to. *Hocus* then is *ocus*, out of use, or *ocius: pocus* is *pocis*.

JOHNSON. What is that?

TOOKE. The ancient Romans, followed in this by the modern Italians, wrote *pocis* for *paucis*, *Clodius* for *Claudius*, *plodite* for *plaudite*. *Ocus pocis*, is, *quickly! at few words!* the conjurer's word of command, as *præsto* is.

JOHNSON. You pronounced *paucis* as if the *c* was *k*.

TOOKE. So did the Romans: we are taught by the Greek biographers and historians. They write Latin proper names according to the pronunciation; *Kikeron* not *Siseron*, *Kaisar* not *Sæsar*; which to their ears would have been as absurd as *Sato* would have been for *Cato*.

There [1] are also some few inaccuracies whereinto our most applauded speakers and our least objectionable writers have fallen. For instance, *I had rather not go: you had better not do it.* This error arises from ambiguity of sound. *I'd* rather, or *I'ou'd* rather: contractions of *would*, and pronounced more like *had*.* [2]

If I am not mistaken, is often prefatory or parenthetical to an affirmative, in our language and most others. Nothing is absurder; for nothing is more self-evident than that a thing is this or that *if there is no mistake*. But by saying for instance, " If I am not *much* mistaken, sir, you are Doctor Johnson," the absurdity in the stranger would be none; for he acknowledges a *great* mistake in taking you for another, or another for you. And the same may be said of anything else on which inquiry or curiosity has been exercised.

JOHNSON. Sir, you mix up so much of compliment with so much of argument, that I know not how I can answer you, unless by saying that your observation on the phrase is perfectly correct, and that I believe it to be no less new.

---

[1] From " There " to " had " preserved from 1st ed.

*   " Poet who hath been building up the rhyme . . .
         When he *had* better far *have* stretched his limbs
         Beside a brook, in mossy forest dell."—COLERIDGE.

A similar instance has been given from Middleton.—W. S. L.

" A poet *had better* borrow anything except money than the thoughts of another." *Note to* DON JUAN, c. v.—W. S. L.

[2] In 2nd ed. footnote reads: " I find this mode of expression in the poetry of a very distinguished scholar and critic: ' Poet,' " etc. " And again in the prose of a celebrated nobleman: ' A poet had better,' " etc.

JOHNSON AND HORNE (TOOKE)

TOOKE. We [1] do many things now which we never thought of doing formerly. We *contemplate* going to a ball and dancing a fandango: we are *installed* in a new lodging: we *place ourselves* in communication: we *take* tea: this is an improvement, we used to *take* physic only: and then we *seek* our pillow: of all things upon earth the most easily found, although sometimes the most unwillingly. We can not bear an *indifferent* judge, or *indifferent* law, or *indifferent* history: we think them the reverse of what they are: in one word, bad. But no wonder: we have been moving in a *high circle*, and beyond the *sphere* of utility, so that we fancy we have been *edified* by a sermon, and mistake a cluster of colleges for what it is most remote from, a *university*.

JOHNSON. It is not we alone who do that.

TOOKE. Answer enough for every objection. There are older peculiarities which require attention and yet have not found it. You would say *two or three times*.

JOHNSON. Why not?

TOOKE. Because you would not say *two times*.[2]

JOHNSON. I should rather say *twice or thrice*. Certainly, as more elegant.

TOOKE. Beside, it saves a word; no inconsiderable thing, when we find a large family of young thoughts springing up about us, and calling on us for decent clothing.

JOHNSON. You, who are fond enough of innovation in politics, are reluctant to admit any new improvement in our modes of composition. Doubtless you think it as elegant to close a member of a sentence, or the sentence itself, with *of, against, in, for*, as to write " with which to contend," " of which to speak," " against which to write," " in which to partake," " for which to be zealous."

TOOKE. Not only as elegant, but much more. It is strictly idiomatical; it avoids an unnecessary word; and it is countenanced by the purest writers of Greece. The iambics of the tragedians (if that be anything) sometimes end with such words as $\dot{\epsilon}\pi\iota$, $\pi\alpha\rho\alpha$, $\pi\epsilon\rho\iota$, $\dot{\upsilon}\pi o$, $\dot{\upsilon}\pi\epsilon\rho$. I would rather close a sentence thus; *there is nobody to con-*

---

[1] From " We " to " objection " added in 3rd ed.
[2] 2nd ed. reads: "*times*; it is anidiomatical. JOHNSON. Anidiomatical! TOOKE. We want the word; take it from me. It is not so, when *or three* comes between. JOHNSON. I should . . . elegant; besides it saves . . . decent and warm clothing. You, who," etc., portion of Johnson's speech being assigned to Tooke.

IMAGINARY CONVERSATIONS : ENGLISH

tend with, than, *there is nobody with whom to contend* : rather with *there is none to fight against*, than *there is none with whom to fight*.[1] Even the French formerly were not shocked at closing a sentence with *avec*, although little accordant with their language. We [2] often hear, *the first among them.*

JOHNSON. Well, why not ?

TOOKE. Because what is *first* or *before* is not *among*.

JOHNSON. You might argue then that what is *before* is not *of*, and that it has ceased to be so when, in a nautical phrase, it has parted company : yet surely you do not object to the expression, " the first of them."

TOOKE. It has not ceased to be *of* by being *before* ; for *of* is *off*, however we may, for obvious reasons, separate them in the parts of speech.[3] We perceive a slight shade of difference between *yet* and *still*. The most remarkable example of it was given by a great foreign linguist, who, conversing with an English prelate on many occasions and at many different times, committed but one mistake, " When this event happened I was not *still* born." *Above* and *over* are not always synonymous. We may say *he wept over me ;* we can not say *he wept above me.* The words *can not* remind me that these should always be separated ; a remark made by Ben Jonson, but never attended to. You are well-*read* and well-*spoken*, have you any objection to be well-*mounted ?*

JOHNSON. Strange inversion of active and passive.

TOOKE. What an outcry would be raised against you or me if we applied a verb in the singular to several nouns !

JOHNSON. And justly.

TOOKE. Yet elegance sometimes requires it, even in our own language. The Italian has not repudiated it : Metastasio says,

> La mia Filli e la mia cetra
> Sempre cara a me sarà :

---

[1] 2nd ed. reads : " *fight*. Whenever we can avoid whom and which, we should ; and above these the relative *that*—the stiff plantain of hard and uncultivated tracts in our literature. Even," etc.

[2] From " We " to " speech " preserved from 1st ed.

[3] 1st ed. reads : " speech. You toss your head about, doctor : is there *fœnum in cornu ?* must I make my escape ? or will you accept my apology for so deep an encroachment on your time and patience ? JOHNSON. If your arguments . . . remark," the Conversation ending there. 2nd ed. reads : " speech . . . heartily," as in concluding part of what is here the first Conversation.

JOHNSON AND HORNE (TOOKE)

And Petrarca,
>Benedetto si*a* il giorno e 'l mese e l' anno.

The best of the French poets and prose-writers have complied with it, and the Athenians cherished it.

JOHNSON. We look rather to the Latin.

TOOKE. Even there, in the most common school-books we find it. Virgil says,
>Voc*a*t ingenti clamore Cytheron
>Taygetique canes domitorque Epidaurus equorum.[1]

The first page of Horace offers also an example.
>Metaque fervidis
>Evitata rotis palmaque nobilis
>Terrarum dominos eveh*i*t ad deos.

And again,
>Dum pudor
>Imbellisque lyræ musa potens vet*a*t.

JOHNSON. These are strong instances; but I would rather you adduced an authority from some great writer in prose.

TOOKE. I will adduce one from the most unquestionable of all Latin grammarians, Quintilian. " Et animantium quoque sermone carentium ira, lætitia, adulatio, et oculis et quibusdam aliis corporis signis deprehend*i*tur."

Milton writes,
>That hill and valley rings. *Par. Lost*, B. 2. v. 496.

And in his prose, " Yet ease and leisure *was*."

We have lately seen such words as *carry out*, and *open up*. Who would not think that *carry out* a measure signifies to reject it, or dismiss it? whereas it is forced to say quite the contrary, *carry into* effect. To " open *up* " is no less wrong than to *examine into: up* is redundant; *into* is inapplicable; for to examine is to *weigh out*. But where we are pleased, improprieties pass by unnoticed. In Shakespeare we have (not of Shakespeare, however, but of the printer),
>I never yet did hear
>That the bruised heart was pierced through the ear.

---

[1] *Georg.*, iii. 44. Thus in every ed., including Crump's. |Read: " domitrixque Epidaurus," etc.

IMAGINARY CONVERSATIONS: ENGLISH

As we read these verses they are nonsense. It should be *pieced* (made whole again), not *pierced* (made sensible). Being " bruised " it could not want this.

JOHNSON. This reading never occurred to me. Have you any more?

TOOKE. Several, and quite as obvious. But let us rather walk back again to the old serviceable words we left behind.

JOHNSON. And now, pray, what more would you antiquate?

TOOKE. Whatever is reasonable. Can it be questioned that *friend* written *frend*, as we pronounce it and as good authors wrote it formerly, is better? If we write, as we do, *diameter* and *thermometer*, should we not also *meter?* Just now we were speaking of *who* and *which*. In the Litany, " Our father *which* art in heaven," is often read by conceited young clergymen, " *who* art."

JOHNSON. I would strip their gowns over their shoulders.

TOOKE. To some purpose, I hope. Waller writes,

> Let those *which* only warble love,
> And gargle in their throat.

JOHNSON. In that poem, addressed to Henry Lawes, Waller's expression is more vigorous and happy than usual, especially in the following words,

> Make a *shrill sally* from the breast.

He wrote as elegantly as South.

TOOKE. No high compliment. South was clever and dexterous. Throw out a flimsy and showy argument to him, and he will bite it to pieces from between his ruffles as a lapdog an embroidered glove. He spells many words rightly: for example, *scepter, counsils, exil, honor, public, proclame, procede, humor, suitable, onely, woolfe;* others wrongly: for example, *doe* (do), *hapned, weakned, heightned, hardned, souldier, publique, daign, supream*. He uses *act* for *actuate*, " Petty tyrants acted by party," " acts the whole man." Then, " What course have we *took* to allure the former? " " The most effectual way to destroy religion is to embase (debase) the teachers and dispensers of it." Worst of all, " Their opinions *wholly* divided." Here the word is first badly spelt, for *whole* must be *wholy* or *wholely*, as *sole* is *soly* or *solely:* the adverb can not have a double *l* if the adjective has a single one. I have before remarked this.

JOHNSON AND HORNE (TOOKE)

JOHNSON. Sir, I would rather you found faults in South than authority in Hume.

TOOKE. Certainly the others were quite sufficient without him. I would only demonstrate by it that the practice has continued down to the present day in an unbroken line of good authors.

JOHNSON. I am not to be guided in my language by a Scotchman.

TOOKE. Then take any of the others you prefer. Archibald Bower is a Scotchman, yet he writes with almost as much purity as Blackstone himself. But, Doctor, why this hostility to writers who never have molested you? It seems wonderful that you should hate the nation as you do, a nation which would have restored the prince you reverenced. If there were any worth in him of any kind whatever, it might have created a desire to see him supersede the occupant of his grandfather's throne, provided we could be sure of his maintaining the religion and liberties of the people. But since no member of that family ever had honour enough to maintain his word, or religion enough to observe his oath, your probity would surely suppress your predilection.

JOHNSON. Kings, good or bad, are not to be roughly handled or irreverently approached.

TOOKE. If the nation looks at them for an example, and finds the example a bad one; if those nearest their persons imitate them; if the imitation goes on in exaggerated lines until in every house and bed-chamber there is a copy of it; the mischief is enormous, and it may continue far beyond our calculation. Never do even the best kings sympathise deeply with the sufferings of the people. Their preachers and courtiers take out the heart and entrails, put strong spices in room of them, stroke the plumage softly down, infix false eyes, and place them in glass cases out of reach.

JOHNSON. Out of reach! So they should be.

TOOKE. Has the practice been successful in the princes you supported? or does it promise any better success in those who supersede them?

JOHNSON. You would have none.

TOOKE. You mistake. Hereditary kings are the only safeguards for us: and theirs is the only station I wish to be hereditary. I have seen a child born to a large fortune, so carefully wrapped up, so protected from a breath of air, that his estate, when he came to possess it, was no enjoyment to him; in like manner is the seclusion

IMAGINARY CONVERSATIONS: ENGLISH

of princes from the people injurious to them, infecting their moral vigour, and contracting the action of the heart. I do not blame any attachment in which pity and generosity are concerned. But if you commiserate the Stuarts, spare at least the nation which rose in arms for their defence, and whose shouts of enthusiasm you might almost have heard at Lichfield.

JOHNSON. I heard them nearer: but no more on that. Prejudices I may have; for what man is without them? but mine, sir, are not such as tend to the relaxation of morals, the throwing down of distinctions, the withholding of tribute to whom tribute is due, honour to whom honour. You and your tribe are no more favourable to liberty than I am. The chief difference is, and the difference is wide indeed, that I would give the larger part of it to the most worthy, you to the most unworthy. I would exact a becoming deference from inferiors to superiors; and I would not remove my neighbour's land-mark, swearing in open court that there never was any but an imaginary line between the two parties. Depend upon it, if the time should come when you gentlemen of the hustings have persuaded the populace that they may hoot down and trample on men of integrity and information, you yourself will lead an uncomfortable life, and they a restless and profitless one. No man is happier than he who, being in a humble station, is treated with affability and kindness by one in a higher. Do you believe that any opposition, any success, against this higher can afford the same pleasure? If you do, little have you lived among the people whose cause you patronise, little know you of their character and nature. We are happy by the interchange of kind offices, and even by the expression of good-will. Heat and animosity, contest and conflict, may sharpen the wits, although they rarely do; they never strengthen the understanding, clear the perspicacity, guide the judgment, or improve the heart.[1]

[1] 2nd ed. has the following note at end:—
"The study of language has become, of late years, greatly more extensive and more profound than formerly; and it would be difficult to point out any English work, excepting certain famous Novels, remarkably defective in that particular. I do not attempt to conjecture who is the author of them; but he is evidently a person who in his youth and early manhood was without the advantages of literary, or polished, or very decorous society. It is remarkable that the most popular works of our age, after Lord Byron's, are certainly less elegant in style than any of any age whatever. I have perused no volume of them, in which there are not, at the lowest computation, twenty gross vulgarisms, or grosser

violations of grammar, and in places where the character did not require or authorize them. Sometimes a sentence holds them, like Fox's placemen, *three in a bed*; and occasionally a single and short member of one contains a couple: for instance,

"' But I *will* doubtless find some English person, *at* whom to make inquiries.'

" Again, a well-educated gentleman talks of ' laughing *consumedly*,' and even the *Dean of Faculty* says in *Redgauntlet*, ' It was as fine a first *appearance* as I ever heard : I should be sorry if your son did not *follow it up* in a reply.' (Vol. ii. p. 45.) Follow up what ? his own *first appearance !* which *appearance* was both heard and followed—by whom ? by the appearer himself ! A few words beyond, 'Having thus *taken his ground* to the Dean of Faculty.'

" I invite the learned to shew me in any volume in any language, the same number of equally great faults within the same space."

XXVI. WINDHAM AND SHERIDAN

(*Wks.*, ii., 1846 ; *Wks.*, iii., 1876.)

WINDHAM. It is seldom, Mr. Sheridan, that we have met anywhere out of the House of Commons these last two years ; and I rejoice in the opportunity of expressing my admiration of your generous conduct, on an occasion in which the country at large, and I particularly as Minister, was deeply interested.

SHERIDAN. I am happy, sir, to be countenanced by your favourable opinion on any : but I presume you now refer to my speech on the mutiny at the Nore.

WINDHAM. Indeed I do : you stood nobly forth from your party. Never was behaviour more ignominious than the behaviour of the Whigs has been, systematically, since the commencement of the war. Whatever they could do or suggest to the detriment of their country, or to the advancement of France, they seized on with avidity. But you manfully came forward and apart from those traitors, declaring that insubordination should be reduced, and that rebellion should be crushed. I heartily wish, and confidently hope, that you will display the same energy and decision in the great measure of the Union now projected with Ireland.

SHERIDAN. I have heard nothing about it, as likely to be carried speedily into execution. But the vast number of indigent and worthless people who have lately been made Irish peers, might excite a suspicion that something of moment was in agitation. Many must be bought over again. Such men, for instance, as Hely Hutchinson[1], Lord Clonmel, Lord Clare, and other exhalations of the bog and dunghill, who have always in readiness for the service of any Administration a menace, a defiance, and a pistol ; such men will never be contented with the few thousands of income they have in various ways obtained : their demands will rise with their services ; and unless the demands are satisfied, the petitioners will turn into

[1] Hely Hutchinson, notoriously an opportunist ; Clonmel, Lord Chief Justice of Ireland ; Clare, Chancellor of Ireland.

patriots. In such a course is usually the beginning or the termination of public men : seldom both. The Irish have begun to learn arithmetic in the English school. Fortunes in this country have risen so high and so suddenly on the base of politics, as to have attracted the gaze and to have excited the aspiration of Ireland. She sees how the Grenvilles and Temples have always speculated on this grand Exchange. They have bought in and sold out with singular discretion. Hence a family of small pretensions to antiquity, far from affluent until recently, has been somewhat enriched at every generation. Lord Grenville, who receives forty thousand a year from his tellership of the Exchequer, which in time of peace brought him scarcely a tenth, was strenuous for war ; while Pitt hung back, in suspense for a moment whether he should comply with the king's wishes or retire from office. The Duke of Portland, as you know, stipulated for a renewal of the lease of Marybone Park, before he would join the ministry with his adherents. The value of this lease is calculated at two hundred thousand. The Irish peers may fairly demand something handsome for the surrender of their power and patronage ; I should have added their *dignities*, had I not been aware that either to laugh or to excite laughter, is, at times, unseasonable.

WINDHAM. The terms are not exactly known at present ; and indeed the business is so complicated, that doubts are beginning to arise whether the scheme will be practicable in the present year.

SHERIDAN. Much depends on the amount of secret-service money the Parliament will consent to vote.

This union might be the greatest blessing that ever was conferred on Ireland. But when I consider how unjustly, how harshly, how treacherously, she has been treated by all administrations, my suspicions rise far above my hopes. It is rumoured that the conditions (which however there will be time enough to reconsider and to modify) are less favourable than were granted to Scotland : and that what is, and always has been in every country under heaven, the main object, is not to be conceded : I mean the religion of the majority. On the abolition of episcopacy in Scotland, its revenues were applied to the religious and moral education of the people, who renounced the old religion, rejected the formulary of the English, and chose another. Surely then in common justice, to say nothing of policy, nothing of conciliation, those from whom churches and church-lands were taken away, having at least as fair a claim to such things as those who never were in possession of them, should receive the plunder back. In doing this to the full extent, you would still do less for Ireland than was done for Scotland.

WINDHAM. We have always been tender in touching vested rights.

SHERIDAN. To my apprehension you were not very tender in your touch on the vestment of the Irish Catholic Church. The vestment had indeed too many folds and flounces about it, and, instead of covering the brawny shoulders of twenty or thirty fathers, might have been conveniently cut up for the shirts and shifts of as many hundred children. But you never drew out scissors or measure for that purpose: you only stripped the vesture off one fat fellow to clap it on another fatter.

WINDHAM. True enough. The bishop of Derry's landed property extends, I hear, over a hundred and fifty thousand acres; and cottagers pay thirty shillings a year for half acres, not the best, of this very land. Suppose that at the termination of the war, after hard cruises, hard battles, and harder blockades, all our admirals return home, many with amputated limbs, many with incurable wounds, many (indeed most) with broken or impaired constitutions; raise the number of them to half a hundred; and the consolidated pay of these half hundred great and glorious defenders of their country, will be less than the pay of one churchman.

SHERIDAN. And it is painful to think of how much shorter date.

WINDHAM. Have they no reason to complain of such inequality? have they no right to check and correct it?

All of what are called church-lands belong to the State, as the church itself does; and bishoprics have, since the Reformation, not only been curtailed, but abolished. If Parliament can take away a whole bishopric, it surely can take away a moiety, especially that moiety which bishops care least about, the temporalities. Grievous responsibility would be thus removed from them. No longer a necessity to rise early and to sit down late, for the purpose of supplying the indigent and afflicted: no longer a solicitude in seeking out the faithful, merciful, discreet, and active almoner: no longer the worldly care of laying aside the larger part of their revenues, in just and exact proportions, for families more or less numerous, for curates more or less laborious, " for sick widows and young children."

WINDHAM AND SHERIDAN

SHERIDAN.[1] In other parts of Europe to which the Reformation has extended, not only the religion but also its emoluments have been revised and corrected. Government in England should exercise this authority where required. Where there are no, or only few, communicants of the Anglican Church in Ireland, it is expedient for them to remove to places where there are many. At all events I would maintain no church establishment for a less number than a hundred adults.

WINDHAM. There are gentlemen in the House of Commons who insist that where a single man, woman, or child, exists in any parish, that parish should enjoy its parson, if Protestant.

SHERIDAN. But there are many parishes in which there is not a single Protestant, man, woman, or child: however, as there is a steeple, and not only a steeple, but a pulpit, no doubt there should also be a minister of religion for their benefit. If towns which contain several thousand inhabitants have no representative at all, there would be no worse hardship in fewer than one hundred having no established pastor. But this hardship might not befall them: for they might elect one; and they might themselves pay him proportionally to the service he renders; or they might remove into a more convenient and less contracted fellowship. The most pious and serious of the English people are taught the doctrines of the English Church by unendowed ministers. The followers of Wesley do not hanker after gowns and surplices; at least such gowns and surplices as mount the pulpit. Well-educated young men of his persuasion are always in readiness to accept the cure of souls. It is only the earnest and patient who are likely to file the old rust and new paint off the crucifix. The Wesleyans may be too impetuous, heady, and frothy; but a gutter that runs with rapidity is less unwholesome than a stagnant ditch. I feel that I lie open to a charge of partiality in this recommendation of the Methodists; but I do assure you I am not about to join them: and I venture to hope that your smile is not a smile of incredulity.

WINDHAM. Be perfectly at ease. But seriously; in turning out this acid on such putridity, there would be a violent fermentation: there would be animosities and conflicts. However, what harm, if there should be? Turn out the weasel against the rat, and, at least while they are fighting, neither of them can corrode the rafters or

---

[1] By error, *Wks.*, 1876, assigns this speech to Windham.

infest the larder. Your countrymen are a joyous and light-hearted people, and run with alacrity to festivals and fairs. They would not so readily fall in with Calvinism; they are more disposed to fighting, frolic, and pardon.

SHERIDAN. Frolic and pardon they would never find among the Calvinists, who however in strict justice would amply make out the difference, with fighting.

WINDHAM. We will revert to the right which all governments possess, of curtailing or abolishing the hire of their servants: I admit it. The question at last resolves itself into mere expediency. If our government, after a war, reduces the pay of its soldiers, and abolishes altogether the pay of its sailors, it may consistently, justly, and legally, do the same in regard to the Church militant. Whether the pay arises from a turf or from a counter, no matter.

SHERIDAN. Apply the principle more especially to Ireland. A nation has been misruled for above six centuries by its conqueror. The conqueror has derived the most powerful and efficient aid from it, against all his enemies, and wishes to derive more. To accomplish which, a sudden thought strikes him, which never entered his head until now; that by rendering it more flourishing, he renders it more effectual in his defence. Another sudden thought strikes him. He remembers that, a century ago, he made a compact of Union with another out-lying country, and that both grew richer and happier instantaneously. The out-lying country had fought, and would fight again, for the establishment and maintenance of its religion. The conqueror cares little about the matter, as far as God and conscience are concerned, but very much about the interests of some riotous idlers and rich absentees.

Ireland would be contented with a less measure of justice than was meted out to Scotland: and you may gain ten-fold as much by it. Scotland has no important bays and harbours: Ireland has more than any country of the same extent.

WINDHAM. More than Norway?

SHERIDAN. Those of Norway are unimportant, although capacious. Surrounded by barren rocks, affording no anchorage, there is neither traffic nor population. Ireland has better and more than all France. What wars would not England engage in to wrest them from an enemy! What a bustle in the last century about Dunkirk! and in the century before about such a pitiful hole as Calais! A single act of beneficence, of justice, of policy, of policy the most advantageous to ourselves, would render these noble bays and harbours ours for ever, guarded at no expense to us, by as brave and loyal a nation as any upon earth. Can stubbornness and stupidity be imagined grosser, than in refusing to curtail the superfluity of about eight hundred inefficient drones, detested in general by the majority of their neighbours, when it would conciliate eight millions, and save the perpetual expenditure of a standing army to control them?

WINDHAM. His Majesty is averse to concession.

SHERIDAN. His Majesty was averse to concession to America; and into what disasters and disgraces, unexperienced, unapprehended, unheard of among us until his Majesty's reign, did this pigheadedness of his Majesty thrust us down!

WINDHAM. By what I hear, there is also another thing which may disincline the Irish from the Union. Not only will the property of the Irish Catholic Church be withholden from its first destination, from which destination, I acknowledge, it was forcibly and violently torn away, but a certain part of our own national debt will be saddled on that people.

SHERIDAN. What! when we lie on the debtor's side, and they on the creditor's? If Ireland were paid for her soldiers, in the same proportion as we pay for the Hanoverians and Hessians and other Germans, what a balance would she strike against us!

By reducing the English Church in Ireland to the same condition of wealth as the reformed churches of Germany; by selling all church-lands there, and by devoting to the religious and moral education of the people the whole proceeds, in just proportion to the Papal and Protestant communicants, you would conciliate all farsighted, all humane, all equitable men throughout the island. The lands held under the Crown might also be added.

WINDHAM. Now indeed you are a visionary, Mr. Sheridan! You could sooner uproot the whole island from the Atlantic, than tear from his Majesty an acre of the worst land in it.

SHERIDAN. I do believe in my conscience he would rather lose the affection of half his subjects than the carcase of one fat sheep. I am informed that all his possessions in Ireland never yielded him five thousand a year. Give him ten; and he will chuckle at overreaching you; and not you only, but his own heirs for ever; as he chuckled when he cheated his eldest son of what he pocketed in twenty years from Cornwall, Lancashire, and Wales. The crown lands in Ireland, unprofitable at present, are large enough to support half a million subjects, reduced to poverty and starvation by his oppressive policy and unjust wars.

WINDHAM. You have been suggesting two impracticabilities, however desirable.

SHERIDAN. Ministers then have been suggesting another, the Union. They may bring about an Act of Parliament called an Act of Union: but they will be necessitated to piece out their parchment with cartridge paper.

WINDHAM. We can have fighting enough on easier terms elsewhere. If the framers of the Union are equitable and indulgent, Ireland in half a century from its commencement may contribute ten millions a year to the national revenue. If they are unjust, not only will she contribute less than half that amount, but she will oblige the Government to keep up a standing army to coerce her. Instead of furnishing us with a third of our forces, she will paralyze a third of them and keep them sedentary.

SHERIDAN. Beside, she will become a temptation to France, and even to inferior Powers, to provoke us with aggression and insult, showing them that one hand is tied up behind us. What a farce in the meanwhile is the diversionary talk about the abolition of the slave-trade! What insanity to think of throwing down fifteen or twenty millions to compass an impracticability, to consolidate a dream! Half the money laid out upon Ireland, not in an unmanageable mass all at once, but million by million, year after year, would within ten years render that country prosperous and contented: not however if you resolve to proscribe her religion, to strip its ministers to the skin, and to parade before them and their communicants, on their own ground, your greasy pastors; mere boils and blotches covered with the vestments purloined from their Church.

WINDHAM. Indeed it would be well, and certainly is expedient, to conciliate so brave a people. When we are richer we may encourage their agriculture and their fisheries.

SHERIDAN. They want no other encouragement from you than equity and security. Let the people be contented; and tranquillity is necessarily the result. Let tranquillity be established, and speculators will cover land and sea with English capital.

WINDHAM AND SHERIDAN

WINDHAM. As politicians we may rejoice in a religion which, were the natives in easy circumstances, would be favourable to the fisheries.

SHERIDAN. At the present time there are millions of Roman Catholics in the country who never tasted fish.

WINDHAM. It must be acknowledged that little has been hitherto effected for the comforts of the people. The first man that ever made a movement to assist them was Lord Bacon. He would have given to them the same advantages of every kind as we ourselves enjoy. Humanity was never very urgent with him; but his consummate wisdom prompted to this counsel. I am afraid we must wait until we have men equally wise among us before the counsel is taken.

SHERIDAN. What hope then? No nation in Europe has treated the conquered so iniquitously as the English have treated the Irish. We must go back to Sparta and the Helots for a parallel. But Sparta did not send out missionaries to establish her pure faith in other lands: Sparta did not piously curse her poorer citizens if they happened to enjoy one day in seven. We, having such advantages over her, may feel somewhat too confident of God's countenance and blessing, and we may at last encroach and push his patience until he loudly cries out and curses us.

WINDHAM. I indulge in few golden dreams about the green island; but certainly no country is capable of such improvement so easily effected.

SHERIDAN. Henry IV. expressed a wish and indulged a hope to see the day when every householder in France should have a pullet for dinner once a week: I only wish that every poor Irishman could add a duck annually to his household. Pig and duck (as Lord Castlereagh would express it, if he knew anything or cared anything about the matter) play into one another's hands very nicely. Even this addition to the comforts of an Irish family is little to be expected from the framers of the Union.

XXVII. MR. PITT AND MR. CANNING

(*Imag. Convers.*, iv., 1829 ; *Wks.*, i., 1846 ; *Wks.*, iii., 1876.)

PITT. Dear Canning, my constitution is falling to pieces, as fast as, your old friend Sheridan would tell you, the constitution of the country is, under my management. Of all men living, you are the person I am most desirous to appoint my successor. My ambition is unsatisfied, while any doubt of my ability to accomplish it remains upon my mind. Nature has withholden from me the faculty of propagating my species : nor do I at all repine at it, as many would do : since every great man must have some imbecile one very near him, if not next to him, in descent.

CANNING. I am much flattered, sir, by your choice of me, there being so many among your relatives who might expect it for themselves. However, this is only another instance of your great disinterestedness.

PITT. You may consider it in that light if you will : but you must remember that those who have exercised power long together, and without control, seldom care much about affinities. The Mamelukes do not look out for brothers and cousins : they have favourite slaves who leap into their saddles when vacant.

CANNING. Among the rich families, or the ancient aristocracy of the kingdom——

PITT. Hold your tongue ! prythee hold your tongue ! I hate and always hated these. I do not mean the rich : they served me. I mean the old houses : they overshadowed me. There is hardly one however that I have not disgraced or degraded ; and I have filled them with smoke and sore eyes by raising a [1] vassal's hut over them.

I desire to be remembered as the founder of a new system in England : I desire to bequeath my office by will, a verbal one : and I intend that you, and those who come after you, shall do the same !

As you are rather more rash than I could wish, and allow your words to betray your intentions ; and as sometimes you run counter

---

[1] 1st ed. reads : " their neighbour's hut," etc.

MR. PITT AND MR. CANNING

to them in your hurry to escape from them, having thrown them out foolishly where there was no occasion nor room [1]; I would advise you never to speak until you have thoroughly learnt your sentences. Do not imagine that, because I have the gift of extemporary eloquence, you have the same. No man ever possessed it in the same degree, excepting the two fanatics, Wesley and Whitfield.

CANNING. In the same degree certainly not; but many in some measure.

PITT. Some measure is not enough.

CANNING. Excuse me: Mr. Fox possessed it greatly, though not equally with you [2], and found it enough for his purpose.

PITT. Fox foresaw, as any man of acuteness may do, the weaker parts of the argument that would be opposed to him, and he always learnt his replies [3]: I had not time for it. I owe everything to the facility and fluency of my speech, excepting the name bequeathed me by my father: and, although I have failed in everything I undertook, and have cast in solid gold the clay colossus of France, people will consider me after my death as the most extraordinary man of my age.

CANNING. Do you groan at this? or does the pain in your bowels grow worse? Shall I lift up the cushion of your other chair yonder?

PITT. Oh! oh!

CANNING. I will make haste, and then soften by manipulation those two or three letters of condolence.

PITT. Oh! oh!—— next to that cursed fellow who foiled me with his broken weapon, and befooled me with his half-wit, Bonaparte.

CANNING. Be calmer, sir! be calmer.

PITT. The gout and stone be in him! Port wine and Cheltenham-water! An Austrian wife, Italian jealousy, his country's ingratitude, and his own ambition, dwell with him everlastingly.

CANNING. Amen! let us pray!

PITT. Upon my soul, we have little else to do. I hardly know where we can turn ourselves.

CANNING. Hard indeed! when we can not do that!
Be comforted, sir! The worse the condition of the country, the

---

[1] 1st ed. reads: " room for them, I," etc.
[2] 1st ed. reads: " with you. PITT. Fox foresaw, as any man of prudence," etc.
[3] 1st ed. reads: " his replies more studiously than anything else. I," etc.

greater is the want of us; the more power we shall possess, the more places we shall occupy and distribute.

PITT. Statesmanlike reflection.

CANNING. Those who have brought us into danger can alone bring us out, has become a maxim of the English people.

PITT. If they should ever be strong again, they would crush us.

CANNING. We have lightened them; and, having less ballast, they sail before the wind at the good pleasure of the pilot.

PITT. A little while ago I would have made you Chancellor or Speaker, for composing and singing that capital song of the *Pilot :* so I thought it : at present I never hear the word but it gives me the sea-sickness, as surely as would a fishing-boat in the Channel. It sounds like ridicule.

CANNING. *We* have weathered the storm.

PITT. I have not. I never believed in any future state; but I have made a very damnable one of the present, both for myself and others. We never were in such danger from without or from within. Money-lenders and money-voters are satisfied : the devil must be in them if they are not : but we have taken the younger children's fortunes from every private gentleman in Great Britain.

CANNING. Never think about it.

PITT. I have formerly been in their houses : I have relatives and connections among them : if you had, you would sympathise. I feel as little as any man can feel for others, you excepted. And this utter indifference, this concentration, which inelegant men call selfishness, is among the reasons why I am disposed to appoint you my successor. You are aware that, should the people recover their senses, they would drive us in a dung-cart to the scaffold : *me* they can not : I shall be gone.

CANNING. We must prevent the possibility : we must go on weakening them. The viper that has bitten escapes : the viper that lies quiet in the road, is cut asunder.

PITT. Why! Canning! I find in you both more reasoning and more poetry than I ever found before. Go on in this manner, and your glory as a poet will not rest on *pilots* and *pebbles*, nor on a ditch-side nettle or two of neglected satire. If you exhibit[1] too much reflection, I may change my mind. You will do for my successor : you must not more than do.

[1] 1st ed. reads : " show."

MR. PITT AND MR. CANNING

CANNING. On the contrary, sir, I feel in your presence my deep [1] inferiority.

PITT. That of course.

CANNING. Condescend to give me some precepts, which, if your disease should continue, it might be painfuller to deliver at any other time. Do not, however, think that your life is at all in danger, or that the supreme power can remain long together in any hands but yours.

PITT. Attempt not to flatter me, Canning, with the prospect of much longer life. The doctors of physic have hinted that it is time I should divert my attention from the affairs of Europe to my own: and the doctors of divinity drive oftener to the Chancellor's door than to mine. The flight of these sable birds portends a change of season and a fall of bones.

I have warned you against some imprudences of yours: now let me warn you against some of mine. You are soberer than I am: but when you are rather warm over claret, you prattle childishly. For a successful Minister three things are requisite on occasion; to speak like an honest man, to act like a dishonest one, and to be indifferent which you are called. Talk of God as gravely as if you believed in him. Unless you do this, I will not say what our Church does, you will be damned; but, what indeed is a politician's true damnation, you will be dismissed. Most very good men are stout partisans of some religion, and nearly all very bad ones [2]. The old women about the prince are as notorious for praying as for prostitution; and if you lose the old women, you lose him. He is their prophet, he is their champion, and they are his Houris.

CANNING. I shall experience no difficulty in observing this commandment. In our days, only men who have some unsoundness of conscience and some latent fear, reason against religion; and those only scoff at it who are pushed back and hurt by it.

PITT. Canning! you must have brought this with you from Oxford: the sentiment is not yours even by adoption: it is too profound for you, and too well expressed. You are brilliant by the multitude of flaws, and not by the clearness or the quantity of light.

---

[1] 1st ed. reads: "incalculable."
[2] 1st ed. reads: "bad ones. Besides, if you lose the old women you lose the Heir Apparent. He is their champion," etc.

IMAGINARY CONVERSATIONS: ENGLISH

CANNING. On second thoughts, I am not quite sure, not perfectly satisfied, that it is, as one may say, altogether mine.

PITT. This avowal suggests another counsel.

Prevaricate as often as you can defend the prevarication, being close pressed : but, my dear Canning ! never—I would say—come, come, let me speak it plainly : my dear fellow, never lie.

CANNING. How, sir ! what, sir ! pardon me, sir ! But, sir ! do you imagine I ever lied in my lifetime ?

PITT. The certainty that you never did, makes me apprehensive that you would do it awkwardly, if the salvation of the country (the only case in question) should require it.

CANNING. I ought to be satisfied : and yet my feelings—— If you profess that you believe me incapable——

PITT. What is my profession ? what is my belief ? If a man believes a thing of me, how can I [1] prevent or alter his belief? or what right have I to be angry at it ? Do not play the fool before me. I sent for you to give you good advice. If you apprehend any danger of being thought, what it is impossible any man alive should ever think you, I am ready to swear in your favour as solemnly as I swore at Tooke's trial. I am presuming that you will become Prime Minister ; you will then have plenty of folks ready to lie for you ; and it would be as ungentlemanly to lie yourself as to powder your own hair or tie your own shoe-string. I usually had Dundas [2] at my elbow, who never lied but upon his honour, or supported the lie but upon his God. As for the more delicate duty of prevarication, take up those letters of inquiry and condolence, whether you have rubbed the seals off or not in your promptitude to serve me, and lay them carefully by ; and some years hence, when anyone exclaims, " What would Mr. Pitt have said ! " bring out one from your pocket, and cry, " This is the last letter his hand, stricken by death, could trace." Another time you may open one from Burke, some thirty years after the supposed receipt of it, and say modestly, " Never but on this momentous occasion did that great man write to me. He foretold, in the true spirit of prophecy, all our difficulties." But remember ; do not quote him upon finance; else the House will laugh at you. For Burke was as unable to cast up a tailor's bill, as Sheridan is to pay it.

I was about to give you another piece of advice, which on recol-

---

[1] 1st ed. reads : " can I alter," etc., and : " What right," etc.
[2] 1st ed. reads : " D——."

MR. PITT AND MR. CANNING

lection I find to be superfluous. Surely my head sympathizes very powerfully with my stomach, which the physicians tell me is always the case, though not so much with us in office as with the honourable gentlemen out. I was on the point of advising you never to neglect the delivery of long speeches : the Minister who makes short speeches enjoys short power. Now, although I have constantly been in the habit of saying a great deal more than was requisite to the elucidation of my subject, for the same reason as hares, when pursued, run over more ground than would bring them into their thickets, I would have avoided it with you, principally to save my breath. You can no more stop when you are speaking, than a ball can stop on an inclined plane. You bounce at every impediment, and run on ; often with the very thing in your mouth that the most malicious of your adversaries would cast against you ; and showing what you would conceal, and concealing what you would show [1]. This is of no ill consequence to a Minister : it goes for sincerity and plain dealing. It would never have done at Christ-Church or Eton : for boys dare detect anything, and laugh with all their hearts. I think it was my father who told me (if it was not my father I forget who it was) that a Minister must have two gifts ; the gift of places and the gift of the gab. Perfectly well do I remember his defence of this last expression, which somebody at table, on another occasion, called a vulgarism. At the end of the debate on it, he asked the gentleman whether all things ought not to have names ; whether there was any better for this ; and whether the learning and ingenuity of the company could invent one. The importance of the faculty was admirably exhibited, he remarked, by the word *gift :* he then added, with a smile, " The alliteration itself has its merit : these short sayings are always the better for it : a pop-gun must have a pellet at both ends."

Ah, Canning ! why have I not remembered my father as perfectly in better things ? I have none of his wit, little of his wisdom : but all his experience, all his conduct, were before me and within my reach. I will not think about him now, when it would vex and plague me.

CANNING. It is better to think of ourselves than of others ; to consider the present as everything, the past and future as nothing.

[1] 1st ed. reads : " show, as Lady D. did at Lady A.'s, while she was arranging the flowers in her bosom, talking to an admirer and forgetting she was on the stairs, until she fell down them. This is," etc.

PITT. In fact, they are nothing: they do not exist: what does not exist, is nothing.

CANNING. Supposing me to be Prime Minister—I am delighted at finding that the very idea has given a fresh serenity to your countenance.

PITT. Because it makes me feel my power more intensely than ever; or at least makes me fancy I feel it. By my means, by my authority, you are to become the successor of a Shelburne, of a Rockingham, and a Chatham.

CANNING. Sir, I request you to consider——

PITT. Whether I have the right of alluding to what all have the right of recollecting, and which right all will exercise. I wish you as well as if, by some miracle in my favour, I had been enabled to beget you: that which I hope to do is hardly less miraculous; and, if I did not bring to my mind what you are, I should not feel what I am. Do not you partake of the sentiment? Would it be any great marvel or great matter, if the descendant of some ancient family stepped up to the summit of power; even with clean boots on? You must take many steps, and some very indirect ones; all which will only raise you in your own esteem, if you think like a politician.

You are prone to be confident and overweening. Be cautious not to treat Parliament as you may fancy it deserves, and not to believe that you have bought votes when you have paid the money for them.

CANNING. Why, sir?

PITT. Because it will be expected of you in addition to speak for a given space of time. The people must be made to believe that their representatives are *persuaded:* and a few plain words are never thought capable of effecting this. Your zeal and anxiety to leave no scruple on the mind of any reasonable man, must be demonstrated by protestations and explanations; and your hatred of those who obscure the glory of England, in their attempts to throw impediments in your way, must burst forth vehemently, and stalk abroad, and now and then put on a suit that smells of gunpowder.

CANNING. I have no objection to that.

PITT. It saves many arguments, and stops more; and in short is the only comprehensible kind of *political economy.*

Whenever the liberty or restriction of the Press is in debate, you will do wisely to sport a few touches of wit, or to draw out a few

MR. PITT AND MR. CANNING

sentences of declamation on blasphemy and blasphemers. I have observed by the countenances of country gentlemen, that there is something horrifying in the sound of the word, something that commands silence.

CANNING. I do not well understand the meaning of it.

PITT. Why should you ? Are you to understand the meaning of everything you talk about ? If you do, you will not be thought deep. Be fluent, and your audience will be over head and ears in love with you. Never stop short, and you will never be doubted. To be out of breath is the only sign of weakness that is generally understood in a Chancellor of the Exchequer. The bets, in that case, are instantly against him, and the sounder in wind carries off the King's plate.

CANNING. I am aware that to talk solemnly of blasphemy, gives a man great weight at the time, and leaves it with him. But if a dissenter or a lawyer should ask me for a definition of a blasphemer ?

PITT. Wish the lawyer more prudence, and the dissenter more grace. Appeal to our forefathers.

CANNING. To which of them ? The elder would call the younger so, and the younger the elder.

PITT. Idiots ! but go on.

CANNING. In our own days the Lutheran denounces the Unitarian for it : *he* retorts the denunciation. The Catholic comes between, to reconcile and reclaim them. At first he simmers ; then he bubbles and boils ; at last, inflamed with charity, he damns them both. " To you, adopted heir of the Devil and Perdition," says he to the believer in God's unity, " it would be folly and impiety to listen a moment longer. And you, idle hair-splitter, are ignorant, or pretend to be, that transubstantiation rests upon the same authority as trinitarianism. The one doctrine shocks the senses, the other shocks the reason : both require to be shocked, that faith may be settled."

" Very like your Saint Augustin," interposes the Unitarian : " he should have written this. When Faith enters the school-room, Reason must not whisper : if she might, she would say perhaps, the question is, whether the senses or arithmetic be the most liable to error."

" Sir ! sir ! " cries again the Catholic, " you have no right to bring any question into the house of God without his leave, nor to push your sharp stick against the bellies of his sheep, making them shove one another and break the fold."

PITT. Do not run wild in this way, retailing the merriment of your Oxford doctors in their snug parties. Such, I am sure, it must be: for you have not had time to read anything since you left Eton: you think but little, and that little but upon yourself: nor has indeed the wing of your wit either such a strength of bone in it or such a vividness of plumage.

CANNING. I don't know that. I must confess, however, I drew [1] a good deal both of my wit and my divinity from our doctors, when they had risen twice or thrice from the bottle, and turned their backs on us from the corner of the room.

PITT. I hope you will be rather more retentive; and remember at what time you are to lament, as well as at what time you are to joke and banter. On these occasions, lower your voice, assume an air of disdain or pity, bless God that such is the peculiar happiness of our most favoured country, every man may enjoy his opinion in security and peace.

CANNING. But some, I shall be reminded, have been forced to enjoy it in solitude and prison.

PITT. Never push an argument or a remark too far: and take care to have a fellow behind you who knows when to cry *question! question!* As for reminding, those only whom you forget will remind you of anything. Others will give you full credit for the wisdom of all your plans, the aptness of all your replies, the vivacity of all your witticisms, and the rectitude of all your intentions.

CANNING. Unless it should fatigue you, sir, will you open your views of domestic polity a little wider before me?

PITT. Willingly. Never choose colleagues for friendship or wisdom. If friends, they will be importunate: if wise, they may be rivals. Choose them for two other things quite different; for tractability and connexions. A few men of business, quite enough for you, may be picked up anywhere on the road-side. Be particular in selecting for all places and employments the handsomest young men, and those who have the handsomest wives, mothers, and sisters. Every one of these brings a large party with him; and it rarely happens that any such is formidable for mental prowess. The man who can bring you three votes, is preferable to him who can bring

[1] 1st ed. reads: "drew all from our," etc.

MR. PITT AND MR. CANNING

you thrice your own quantity of wisdom. For, although in private life we may profit much by the acquisition of so much more of it than we had ourselves, yet in public we know not what to do with it. Often it stands in our way; often it hides us; sometimes we are oppressed by it. Oppose in all elections the man, whatever may be his party or principles, who is superior to yourself in attainments, particularly in ratiocination and eloquence. Bring forward, when places are found for all the men of rank who present themselves, those who believe they resemble you; young declaimers, young poets, young critics, young satirists, young journalists, young magazine-men, and young lampooners and libellers: that is, those among them who have never been more than ducked and cudgelled. Every soul of them will hope to succeed you by adoption.

My father made this remark *, in his florid way. When an insect dips into the surface of a stream, it forms a circle round it, which catches a quick radiance from the sun or moon, while the stiller water on every side flows without any; in like manner a small politician may attract the notice of the King or people, by putting into motion the pliant element about him; while quieter men pass utterly away, leaving not even this weak impression, this momentary sparkle. On which principle Dundas [1] used to say, " Keep shoving, keep shoving ! " I do not know whether the injunction was taken by all his acquaintance in the manner and in the direction he intended.

A great deal has been spoken, in the House and out of the House, on Parliamentary reform.

CANNING. I have repeatedly said that without it there is no salvation for the country: this is embarrassing.

PITT. Not at all: oppose it: say you have changed your mind: let that serve for your reason; and do not stumble upon worse by running against an adversary. You will find the country going on just as it has gone on.

CANNING. Bad enough; God knows !

PITT. But only for the country. People will see that the fields and the cattle, the streets and the inhabitants, look as usual. The houses stand, the chimneys smoke, the pavements hold together:

---

* Pitt's father never made it; but it was necessary to attribute it to some other person than Pitt himself.—W. S. L. [1st ed. adds: " a thing so much above his capacity or imagination."]

[1] 1st ed. reads: " Melville used," etc.

this will make them wonder at your genius in keeping them up, after all the prophecies they have heard about their going down. Men draw their ideas from sight and hearing. They do not know that the ruin of a nation is in its probity, its confidence, its comforts. While they see every day the magnificent equipages of contractors and brokers, read of sumptuous dinners given by cabinet-ministers and army agents, and are invited to golden speculations in the East and in the West, they fancy there is an abundance of prosperity and wealth; whereas, in fact, it is in these very places that wealth and prosperity are shut up, accumulated, and devoured.

I deferred from session to session a reform in Parliament; because, having sworn to promote it by all the means in my power, I did not wish to seem perjured to the people. In the affair of Maidstone nobody could prove me so: I only swore I had forgotten what nobody but myself could swear that I remembered[1]. It was evident to the whole world that I was a perjured man; it was equally that I was a powerful one: and the same nation which would have sent another to the pillory, sent me to the Privy Council. It is inconceivable to you what pleasure I felt in committing it, when I reflected on the difference it proved between me and people in general. But beware of fancying you resemble me. My father's crutch was my sceptre, and it will fall into the grave with me. There is no bequeathing or devising this part of the inheritance. I improved it not a little. My adherents at Maidstone thought my father would have hesitated to forget so bravely. Appearances were against me. The main object of my early life, what I had repeated every day, what brought me into credit and into power, was unlikely to escape my memory in an instant; and in the midst of those who at that time had surrounded me, applauded me, and followed me. Yet Bishops and Chancellors will drink to me after my death, as the most honest man that ever lived.

CANNING. What! even when they can get nothing and want nothing from you?

PITT. They want from me more than you are aware of: they want my example to stand upon. They will take their aim against our country from behind my statue.

CANNING. She has fleshier parts about her than the heel, and their old snags will stick tight in them till they rattle in the coffin.

[1] 1st ed. reads: " remembered; certainly all appearances were," etc.

MR. PITT AND MR. CANNING

PITT. Do not disturb them. You may give over your dalliance with reform whenever you are tired of it. You did not begin as a states-*man* but as a states-*boy:* you were under me: and you can not act more wisely than by telling folks that I had seen my error in the latter part of my life.

CANNING. Perhaps they will not believe me.

PITT. Likely enough! but courtesy and interest will require their acquiescence, and they will act as if they did. The noisiest of the opposition are the lawyers; partly from rudeness, partly from rapacity. Lay it down as a rule for your conduct, that the most honest one in Parliament is as indifferent about his party as about his brief: whoever offers him his fee has him. Of these there is hardly an individual who had any more of a qualification than you or I had: yet they assume it, as well as we. Is there in this no fallacy, no fraud? Some of them were so wretchedly poor, that a borrowed watch-key hung from a broken shoe-string at their tattered fob; and when they could obtain on credit a yard of damaged muslin for their noses, they begged a pinch of snuff at the next box they saw open, and sneezed that they might reasonably display their acquisition.

CANNING. I wonder that these people should cry out so loudly for a fairer representation.

PITT. Some have really the vanity to believe that they would be chosen, and might choose their colleagues; others follow orders; the greater part wish no such thing; and, if they thought it likely to succeed, would never call for it. The fact is this: the most honest and independent members of Parliament are elected by the rotten boroughs. They pay down their own money, and give their own votes: they are not subservient to the aristocracy nor to the treasury. The same can not be said on any other description of members. I never ventured to make such a remark in Parliament. The people would be alarmed and struck with horror, if you clearly showed that the very best part of their representation is founded on nothing sounder than on rank corruption.[1] Perhaps I am imprudent in suggesting the fact to you, knowing your *diabetes* of mind, and having found that your tongue is as easily set in motion, and as unconsciously, as the head of a mandarin on the chimney-piece at an inn.

[1] 1st ed. inserts following footnote: " It was said to be so in the time of Pitt."

IMAGINARY CONVERSATIONS: ENGLISH

Cease to be speculative.

CANNING. We cease to be speculative when we touch the object.

PITT. It is then unnecessary to remind you that you want only a numerical majority. Talents count for talents; respectability for respectability. The veriest fag that Dundas [1] ever breeched for the South gives as efficient a vote as a Romilly or a Newport.

In the beginning of my career as Minister, I sometimes wished that I could have become so and have been consistent. I have since found that inconsistency is taken for a proof of greatness in a politician. " He knows how to manage men; he sees what the times require: his great mind bends majestically to the impulse of the world." These things are said, or will be. Certain it is, when a robe is blown out by the wind, showing now the outer side, now the inner, then one colour, then another, it seems the more capacious[2], and the richer.

If at any time you are induced by policy, or impelled by nature, to commit an action more ungenerous or more dishonest than usual; if at any time you shall have brought the country into worse disgrace or under more imminent danger; talk and look bravely: swear, threaten, bluster: be witty, be pious: sneer, scoff: look infirm, look gouty: appeal to immortal God that you desire to remain in office so long only as you can be beneficial to your King and country: that however, at such a time as the present, you should be reluctant to leave the most flourishing of nations a prey to the wild passions of insatiate demagogues: and that nothing but the commands of your venerable sovereign, and the unequivocal voice of the people that recommended you to his notice, shall ever make you desert the station to which the hand of Providence conducted you. They have keen eyes who can see through all these words: I have never found any such, and have tried thousands. The man who possesses them may read [3] Swedenborg and Kant while he is being tossed in a blanket.

Above all things keep your friends and dependants in good humour and good condition. If they lose flesh, you lose people's confidence. My cook, two summers ago, led me to this reflection at Walmer. Finding him in the court-yard, and observing that,

---

[1] 1st ed. reads: " Melville ever," etc.
[2] 1st ed. reads: " capacious, the more flowing, and," etc.
[3] 1st ed. reads: " read Adam Smith and Emmanuel Kant," etc.

MR. PITT AND MR. CANNING

however round and rosy, he looked melancholy, and struck his hips with his fists very frequently as he walked along, I called to him, and when he turned round, inquired of him what had happened to discompose him. He answered that Sam Spack the butcher had failed.

"Well, what then?" said I, "unless you mean that his creditors may come upon me for the last two years' bill?" He shook his head, and told me that he had lent Sam Spack all he was worth, a good five hundred pounds. "The greater fool you!" replied I. "Why, sir!" said he, opening his hand to show the clearness of his demonstration, "who would not have lent him anything, when he swore and ate like the devil, and drank as if he was in hell, and his dog was fatter than the best calf in Kent?"

It occurs to me that I owe this unfortunate cook several years' wages. Write down his name, William Ruffhead. You must do something to help him: a diversion on the coast of France would be sufficient: order one for him: in six months he may fairly pocket his quiet twenty thousands, and have his paltry three guineas a day for life. Write above the name, "deputy commissary." Ruffhead is so honest a creature, he will only be a dogfish in a shoal of sharks.

Never consent to any reduction in the national expenditure. Consider what is voted by Parliament for public services as your own property. The largest estate in England would go but a little way in procuring you partisans and adherents: these loosely counted millions purchase them. I have smiled when people in the simplicity of their hearts applauded me for neglecting the aggrandizement of my fortune. Every rood of land in the British dominions has a mine beneath it, out of which, by a vote of Parliament, I oblige the proprietor to extract as much as I want, as often as I will. From every tobacco-pipe in England a dependant of mine takes a whiff; from every salt-vase a spoonful. I have given more to my family than is possessed by those of Tamerlane and Aurungzebe; and I distribute to the amount of fifty millions a-year in the manner I deem convenient. What is any man's private purse other than that into which he can put his hand at his option? Neither my pocket nor my house, neither the bank nor the treasury, neither London nor Westminster, neither England nor Europe, are capacious enough for mine: it swings between the Indies, and sweeps the whole ocean.

CANNING. I am aware of it. You spend only what you have time

IMAGINARY CONVERSATIONS : ENGLISH

and opportunity for spending. No man gives better dinners : few better wine——

PITT. Canning! Canning! Canning! always blundering into some coarse compliment!

Reminding me of wine, you remind me of my death, and the cause of it. To spite the French and Bonaparte, I would not drink claret : Madeira was too heating : hock was too light and acid for me.

CANNING. Seltzer water takes off this effect, the Dean of Christ-church tells me.

PITT. It might have made my speeches windier than was expedient ; and I declined to bring into action a steam-engine of such power, with Mr. Speaker in front and the treasury-bench in rear of me. The detestable beverage of Oporto is now burning my entrails.

CANNING. Beverage fit for the condemned.

PITT. If condemned for poisoning.

As you must return to London in the morning, and as I may not be disposed or able to talk much at another time, what remains to be said I will say now.

Never be persuaded to compose a mixed administration of whigs and tories : for, as you can not please them equally, each will plot eternally to supplant you by some leader of its party.

Employ[1] men of less knowledge and perspicacity than yourself, if you can find them. Do not let any stand too close or too much above ; because in both positions they may look down into your shallows and see the weeds at the bottom. Authors may be engaged by you ; but never pamper them ; keep them in wind and tractability by hard work. Many of them are trusty while they are needy :

---

[1] From " Employ " to " author " inserted in 2nd ed. to replace the following :—
" Wellesley has a great deal more acuteness, a great deal more perspicuity than you. Employ him at a distance, and gratify his inclination for pleasure and expense. Among the whigs Lord Henry Petty has conciliated many friends by his good manners, his variety of information, his facility of communicating it, and his sincerity. He speaks well ; and though you have the credit of being a good scholar, he is known to be a better. These are the only men in both houses worth noticing ; beware of them. Lord Henry would be the worse neighbour to you from the memory of his father, who was liberal in his encouragement to the learned, and indeed to men of genius and science in every department. I am afraid the son partakes of this feeling, which will draw many about him, and obtain him friends and supporters even among those who have no literary claims and no want of patronage. For my part I have no respect for any living author or living genius. The only one," etc.

MR. PITT AND MR. CANNING

enrich them only with promised lands, enjoying the most extensive prospect and most favourable exposure. For my part, I little respect any living author[1]. The only one, ancient or modern, I ever read with attention is Bolingbroke, who was recommended to me for a model. His principles, his heart, his style, have formed mine exclusively: everything sits easy upon him: mostly I like him because he supersedes inquiry: the thing best to do and to inculcate. We should have been exterminated long ago, if the House of Commons had not thought so, and had not voted us a Bill of Indemnity: which I was certain I could obtain as often as I should find it necessary, be the occasion what it might. Neither free governments nor arbitrary have such security: ours is constituted for evasion. I hope nobody may ever call me the *Pilot of the Escape-boat*. In Turkey I should have been strangled; in Algiers I should have been impaled; in America I should have mounted the gallows in the market-place; in Sweden I should have been pistolled at a public dinner or court-ball: in England I am extolled above my father.

Ah Canning! how delighted, how exultant was I, when I first heard this acclamation! When I last heard it, how sorrowful! how depressed! He was always thwarted, and always succeeded: I was always seconded, and always failed. He left the country flourishing: I leave it impoverished, exhausted, ruined. He left many able statesmen; I leave *you*.

Excuse me: dying men are destined to feel and privileged to say unpleasant things.

Good night! I retire to rest.

[1] 1st ed. reads: " author or living genius," etc.

XXVIII. ROMILLY AND WILBERFORCE

(*Wks.*, ii., 1846; *Wks.*, iii., 1876.)

ROMILLY. Indeed, sir, I cannot but suspect that the agitation of this question on the abolition of the slave-trade, is countenanced by Mr. Pitt chiefly to divert the attention of the people from crying grievances nearer home. Our paupers are increasing daily both in number and in wretchedness; our workhouses, our hospitals, and our jails, are crowded and overflowing; our manufactories are almost as stifling as slave-ships, and more immoral; apprentices, milliners, dressmakers, work throughout the greater part of the night, and, at last disabled by toil, take the sorrowful refuge of the street. After so many have coldly repeated that vice leads to misery, is there no generous man who will proclaim aloud that misery leads to vice? We all see it every day: we warn the wretched too late: we are afraid of warning the affluent too soon: we are prodigal of reproaches that make the crushed heart bleed afresh: we think it indecorous to approach the obdurate one, and unsafe to touch it —barbarous and dastardly as we are.

WILBERFORCE. Postponing all these considerations, not immediately applicable to the subject on which, Mr. Romilly, I have taken the liberty to knock at your door, I must assure you that my friend Mr. Pitt[1] is not only the most unbending and unchanging, but also the most sincere man living.

ROMILLY. It is happy when we can think so of any, especially of one in power.

WILBERFORCE. Do you doubt it?

ROMILLY. I never oppose, without reluctance, opinion to sentiment; or, when I can help it, a bad opinion to a good one.

WILBERFORCE. O! if you knew him as I do!

ROMILLY. The thing is impossible.

WILBERFORCE. Why so? I should be proud to introduce you.

---

[1] One of Landor's anachronisms: Pitt died three months before Romilly entered the House of Commons.

ROMILLY AND WILBERFORCE

ROMILLY. The pride would rest entirely apart from me. It may be that coarse metals are less flexible than finer; certain it is that they do not well cohere.

WILBERFORCE. But on this occasion you invariably vote together.

ROMILLY. In the House of Commons.

WILBERFORCE. It is there we must draw up our forces.

ROMILLY. Do you never doubt, however slightly, and only on one occasion, the fidelity of your leader?

WILBERFORCE. Leader! Mr. Romilly! leader! Humble as I am, the humblest indeed of that august assembly, on this question, on this alone perhaps, yes, certainly on this alone, I am acknowledged, universally acknowledged, I know too well how unworthily, yet I do know, and God has given me strength and grace to declare it before men, that I, the weakest of his creatures, *there* am leader. It is I, a band of withy, who bind giants: it is I who keep together on this ground the two rival parties: it is I, a potter's vessel, who hold out across the Atlantic the cup of freedom and of fellowship.

ROMILLY. Certainly you have seconded with admirable zeal the indefatigable Clarkson. Those who run with spirit and celerity have no breath for words: the whole is expended in action.

WILBERFORCE. Just so with me. However, I can spare a speech of a few hours every session, in expounding the vexations and evils of slavery, and in showing how opposite it is to Christianity.

ROMILLY. I am almost a believer in that doctrine.

WILBERFORCE. Almost?

ROMILLY. I should be entirely, if many of the most orthodox men in both Houses, including a great part of the bishops, had been assenters.

WILBERFORCE. Are they not?

ROMILLY. Apparently no. Otherwise they would never be absent when the question is discussed, nor would they abstain from a petition to the Crown, that a practice so dangerous to salvation, so certain to bring down a curse on the country, be, with all expedient speed, abolished.

WILBERFORCE. It is unnecessary for me to defend the conduct of my Right Reverend friends; men of such piety as no other country hath exhibited; but permit me to remark, Mr. Romilly, that you yourself betray a lukewarmness in the cause, when you talk of expedient speed. Expedient indeed! Gracious Jesu! Ought such a crime to be tolerated for one hour? Are there no lightnings in heaven——

ROMILLY. Probably there are: there were last summer. But I would rather see them purifying the air than scorching the earth before me. My good Mr. Wilberforce! abstain, I beseech you, from a species of eloquence in which Mr. Sheridan and Mr. Pitt excell you, especially when it is late in the evening: at that season such men are usually the most pious. The lightnings of heaven fall as frequently on granaries as on slave-ships. It is better at all times to abstain from expostulating with God; and more especially on the righteousness of his judgments and the delay of his vengeance.

WILBERFORCE. Mr. Romilly! Mr. Romilly! the royal psalmist——

ROMILLY. Was too often like other royal personages, and, with much power of doing evil, was desirous of much more. Whenever we are conscious of such propensities, it would be wiser and more religious to implore of God to pardon than to promote them.

WILBERFORCE. We must bow to authority in all things.

ROMILLY. So we hear: but we may be so much in the habit of bowing as at last to be unable to stand upright. Before we begin at all, it is useful to inquire what is authority. We are accustomed to mistake place and power for it. Now the Devil, on this earth at least, possesses as much power as the Deity, and more place. Unless he did, we tell a manifest lie in every prayer and supplication. For we declare that we are, and always have been, miserable sinners, and that there is no truth in us.

WILBERFORCE. Ah, my dear sir! you are no theologian, I see. Some of us, by the blessing of God, are under grace; and, once under grace, we are safe. But it is not on this business I visit you. Here we may differ; but on the Abolition we think alike.

ROMILLY. I am not quite sure of that.

WILBERFORCE. Indeed! Then, pray, my dear sir, correct your judgment.

ROMILLY. I have been doing it, to the best of my ability, all my life.

WILBERFORCE. If you had only clung to the Cross, you would have been sure and stedfast from your very childhood.

ROMILLY. Alas! I see but one cross remaining on earth, and it is that of the unrepentant thief. What thousands of the most venomous wasps and hornets swarm about it, and fight for its

ROMILLY AND WILBERFORCE

putrescences! The blessed one was pulled down long ago, indeed soon after its erection, in the scuffle of those who would sell the splinters. Great fortunes are daily made by it, and it maintains as many clerks and treasurers as the South-sea. The money-changers in the Temple of old did at least give change: ours bag the money and say *call to-morrow*.

WILBERFORCE. Unholy as the gains may be, we must not meddle with vested rights and ancient institutions.

ROMILLY. Then, worthy Mr. Wilberforce, let slavery continue; for certainly no institution is more ancient. In this also am I to correct my judgment?

WILBERFORCE. The fact is too true. You were erroneous there only where you differed from me on that subject, which I had examined attentively and minutely.

ROMILLY. Namely, the Abolition.

WILBERFORCE. Exactly so.

ROMILLY. The clearers of ground in the forests of America clear first the places round about the homestead. On this principle I would begin to emancipate and enlighten the suffering labourers in my own vicinity. Look at the draught-horses now passing under the window. The first quarter of their lives was given to their growth: plentiful food came before painful service. They are ignorant of our vices, insensible of our affections: ease is all in all to them; and while they want it most, and while it is most profitable or promissory to the master, they enjoy it.

WILBERFORCE. We then put blinkers before their eyes, that nothing may make them swerve on the road. Here is another act of humanity.

ROMILLY. If you attempt to put blinkers before the intellectual eye, you only increase its obliquity. Give as much clear-sightedness as possible, give reasonable leisure, or you never will conciliate affection to your institutions. Inflict on men the labour and privations of brutes, and you impress on them the brutal character: render them rationally happy, and they are already on the highway to heaven. No man rationally happy will barter the possession he enjoys for the most brilliant theory: but the unhappy will dream of daggers until he clutches them. If your friend Mr. Pitt wishes to retard the revolutionary movement, he will not attempt to put the fetter on the white man while you are taking it off the black:

he will not bring forward a flogged soldiery to confront an enthusiastical one: he will not display to the vigorous sons of starving yeomen the sight of twenty farm-houses rising up from the ruins of one *château*. Peace is easier to retain than to recall.

WILBERFORCE. Well, Mr. Romilly! we are departing a little from the object of my visit: and, if we continue to digress, I am afraid you may not be so entirely at leisure to hear me repeat the speech I have prepared on the Abolition. Your room appears to be well adapted to my voice.

ROMILLY. Already I have had the benefit of your observations the three last sessions.

WILBERFORCE. You will hear me again, I confidently hope, with the same pleasure in a very crowded House.

ROMILLY. You represent a Riding in the county of York.

WILBERFORCE. I have that honour.

ROMILLY. To represent a county is not in itself an honour; but it offers opportunities of earning many. Inform your constituents that the slavery in the West Indies is less cruel and pernicious than the slavery in their own parishes: that the condition of the Black is better on the whole than the condition of the pauper in England, and that his children are incomparably more comfortable and happy.

WILBERFORCE. Lord of mercy! do I hear this from a philanthropist?

ROMILLY. I venture to assert, you do, however deficient I may be in the means of showing it. You might, in any Session of Parliament, obtain a majority of votes in favour of a Bill to diminish the hours of a child's labour in factories. Every country gentleman, every peer, would vote that none under his eighth year should be incarcerated in these pesthouses.

WILBERFORCE. O Sir! is such a word applicable?

ROMILLY. Precisely: although a pesthouse is usually the appellation of that building which excludes the malady and receives the endangered. From eight years to twelve, I would prohibit a longer daily work than of six hours, with two hours between each three, for food and exercise. After the twelfth year the sexes should not be confounded.

WILBERFORCE. The first regulation would create much discontent among our wealthiest supporters; and even the parents would object to them.

ROMILLY AND WILBERFORCE

ROMILLY. Two signal and sorrowful truths! There are also two additional. They who feel the least for others feel the most for themselves: and the parents who waste away their own strength in gin-shops are ready to waste their children's in factories. If our inconsiderate war and our prodigal expenditure permitted the exercise of policy, we should bethink ourselves that manly hearts and sound bodies are the support of states, not creaking looms nor over-pressed cotton-bags in human shape. We have no right to break down the sinews of the rising generation: we have no right to devote the children of the poor either to Belial or to Moloch. I do care about the Blacks; I do care greatly and anxiously about them; but I would rather that slavery should exist for seven centuries longer in the West Indies, than for seven years longer in Lancashire and Yorkshire. If there be any sincerity in the heart of Mr. Pitt, why does he not order his dependants in both Houses (and nearly all are his dependants in both alike) to vote for your motion?

WILBERFORCE. He wishes us well: but he is aware that a compensation must be made to the masters of the slaves; and he has not money for it.

ROMILLY. Whose fault is that? He always has found money enough for extending the miseries of other nations and the corruption of his own. By his extravagance and the excess of taxation he is leading to that catastrophe which he avowed it was his object to prevent.

WILBERFORCE. God forbid!

ROMILLY. God has forbidden; but he does not mind that.

WILBERFORCE. You force me to say, Mr. Romilly, what I hope you will not think a personality. The French Revolution was brought about in great measure by the gentlemen of your profession.

ROMILLY. The people were rendered so extremely poor by the imposts, that there were few litigations in the courts of law. Hence the lawyers, who starved others until now, began to be starved in turn, and incited the people to revolution, that there might be crime and change of property. England has now taken the sins of the world upon her, and pays for all.

WILBERFORCE. Awful expression! Let us return to the Blacks. It is calculated that twenty millions are requisite to indemnify the slave-holders.

IMAGINARY CONVERSATIONS: ENGLISH

ROMILLY. Do you wonder then that he is evasive?

WILBERFORCE. I should wonder if a man of his integrity were so upon any occasion. But he has frankly told me that he does not see clearly at what time the measure may be expedient.

ROMILLY. Everything can be calculated, except the hour for the abolition of injustice. It is not always in our power to retrace our steps when we have committed it. Nay, sometimes is it requisite not only to go on with it, but even to add fresh. We waged a most unnecessary, a most impolitic, a most unjust war against France. Nothing else could have united her people: nothing else could have endangered or have interrupted our commerce. Having taken the American islands from our enemy, we should have exported from them the younger slaves into our own, taking care that the number of females be proportional to the number of males. We should have granted our protection to Brazil and Cuba, on condition that the traffic in African slaves immediately cease, and that every one belonging to Spaniard or Portuguese, who had served fourteen years, should be free. Unhappily we ourselves can do little more at present for our own, without a grievous injustice to a large body of our fellow-subjects. We can however place adequate power in the hands of the civil and military governors, authorising them to grant any slave his freedom who shall be proved to have been cruelly treated by his master. What a curse is it upon us, that at present we neither can make peace nor abolish slavery! We can decree, and we ought instantly, that the importation and sale of slaves do cease at this very hour throughout the world. We can decree, and we ought instantly, that husband and wife be united, and separated no more. We can decree, and ought instantly, that children from seven to ten years of age be instructed one hour daily. But, as things are now constituted, I think I have no right to deprive a proprietor of his property, unless he has forfeited it by a violation of law. To repay me for my protection, and for granting him a monopoly during the war, I would stipulate with him, that whoever had served him fourteen years should be emancipated. He should also be obliged to maintain as many females as males, or nearly, and to set apart a plot of ground for every emancipated slave, enough for his support, on lease for life, at such a rent as those deputed by the governor may think reasonable. The proposition of granting twenty, or ten, or five millions to carry into execution the abolition

ROMILLY AND WILBERFORCE

of slavery, by way of indemnity to the slave-holders, is absurd. Abolish all duties of importation and exportation; that will be sufficient. The abolition of the slave-trade is greatly more important than the abolition of slavery in our islands. The traffic can be terminated at once; the servitude but gradually. It is in politics as in diet. They who have committed excesses can not become quite temperate at the first perception of their perilous situation. The consequences of a sudden change might be fatal.

WILBERFORCE. Religion teaches us that we should consent to no truce with Sin.

ROMILLY. We should enter into no engagements with her: but the union is easier than the divorce. There are materials which, being warped, are not to be set right again by a stroke of the hammer, but by temperance and time. Our system of slavery is in this condition. We have done wrong with impunity; we can not with impunity do right. We wound the state in stripping the individual.

WILBERFORCE. I would not strip him; I would grant him a fair and full indemnity.

ROMILLY. What! when all your property is mortgaged? When you are without a hope of redeeming it, and can hardly find wherewithal to pay the interest? If ever you attempt the undertaking, it can be only at the peace.

WILBERFORCE. I am sorry to find you so despondent.

ROMILLY. I am more despondent than I have yet appeared to be.

WILBERFORCE. With what reason?

ROMILLY. Hostilities having ceased, the people will be clamorous for the removal of many taxes; and some of the most productive will be remitted the first. In my opinion, unwise as was the war, and entered into for the gratification of an old madman, who never knew the difference between a battle and a review, and who chuckled at the idea of his subjects being *peppered* when they were *shot;* a war conducted by grasping men, outrageous at the extortion of their compliance, and at the alternative that either their places or their principles must be surrendered; we nevertheless ought to discharge the debt we contracted, and not to leave the burden for our children. If our affairs are as ill conducted in peace as they are in war, it is greatly to be feared that we may injure the colonist more than we benefit the slave. We may even carry our imprudence so far as to restore to our enemies the lands we have conquered from them, cultivated by blacks.

WILBERFORCE. Impossible. Mr. Pitt has declared that peace is never to be signed without indemnity for the past, and security for the future. These are his very words.

ROMILLY. Not as a politician, but as an arithmetician, he knew when he uttered these words that they never could be accomplished. War is alike the parent and the child of evil. It would surpass your ingenuity, or Mr. Pitt's, to discover any whatsoever which does not arise from war, or follow war, or romp and revel in the midst of war. It begins in pride and malice, it continues in cruelty and rapine, it terminates in poverty and oppression. Our bishops, who pray for success in it, are much bolder men than our soldiers who engage in it bayonet to bayonet. For the soldier fights only against man, and under the command of man: the bishop fights against the command of God, and against God himself. Every hand lifted up in prayer for homicide, strikes him in the face.

WILBERFORCE. Mr. Romilly! I entertain a due respect for you, as being eminent in your profession, a member of Parliament, a virtuous and (I hope) a religious man: you would however rise higher in my estimation if you reverenced your superiors.

ROMILLY. It must be a man immeasurably above me, both in virtue and intellect, whom, knowing my own deficiency, I could reverence. Seldom is it that I quote a verse or a sentiment, but there is in a poet not very original a thought so original that nobody seems ever to have applied it to himself or others:

Below the good how far! how far above the great!

WILBERFORCE. There is only one half of it I would hear willingly. When men begin to think themselves above the great, social order is wofully deranged. I deplore the absence of that self-abasement on which is laid the foundation of all Christian virtues.

ROMILLY. Unless we respect ourselves, our respect for superiors is prone to servility. No man can be thrown by another from such a height as he can throw himself from. I never have observed that a tendency toward the powerful was a sufficient check to spiritual pride: and extremely few have I known, or heard of, who, tossing up their nostrils into the air and giving tongue that they have hit upon the trail to heaven, could distinguish humility from baseness.

ROMILLY AND WILBERFORCE

Mostly they dirty those they fawn on, and get kicked before they get fed.

WILBERFORCE. Christianity makes allowances for human infirmity.

ROMILLY. Christianity, as now practised by the highest of its professors, makes more infirmities than allowances. Can we believe in *their* belief who wallow in wealth and war? in theirs who vote subsidies for slaughter? who speed the slave-ship with their prayers? who bind and lacerate and stifle the helpless wretches they call men and brethren?

WILBERFORCE. Parliamentary steps must be taken before you can expect to mitigate the curses of war and slavery.

ROMILLY. By whom first should the steps be taken? Persuade the bishops, if you can, to raise their voices for the double abolition. Let them at least unite and join you in that which, apparently, you have most at heart. In order to effect it gradually, I am ready to subscribe my name to any society, of which the main object shall be the conversion of our spiritual lords to Christianity. The waters of Jordan, which were formerly used for bleaching, serve at present no other purpose than the setting of scarlet and purple.

WILBERFORCE. There is danger in touching the altar. We may overturn the table and bruise the chalice in attempting any restoration of the structure.

ROMILLY. Christianity is a plant which grows well from seed, but ill from cuttings: they who have grafted it on a wilding have sometimes succeeded; never they who (as we have) inoculated it on one cracked in the stem and oozing over with foul luxuriance. I do not deny that families and small communities have profited by secession from more corrupt religions: but as soon as ever cities and provinces have embraced the purer creed, ambitious men have always been ready to materialize the word of God and to raise houses and estates upon it.

WILBERFORCE. The prosperity of the labourers in Christ's vineyard has excited the envy of the ill-disposed.

ROMILLY. What prosperity? Success in improving it?

WILBERFORCE. No indeed, but their honest earnings.

ROMILLY. Did the master pay such earnings to those whose work was harder? or did he command, or will, that such should be paid on any future day?

WILBERFORCE. I am sorry, Mr. Romilly, that you question and

quibble (pardon me the expression) just like those unhappy men, miscalled philosophers, who have brought down the vengeance of Heaven on France, Voltaire at the head of them.

ROMILLY. No indeed; I never have sunned myself on the trim and short grass bordered by the papered pinks and powdered ranunculuses of Voltaire. His pertness is amusing: but I thought it pleasanter to bathe in the deep wisdom of wit running up to its banks through the romantic scenery of Cervantes.

WILBERFORCE. Little better than infidelity.

ROMILLY. But not, as infidelity generally is, sterile and flimsy. Christians themselves are all infidels in the sight of some other Christians; and they who come nearest to them are the most obnoxious. Strange interpretation of " Love your neighbour ! " If there are grades of belief, there must also be grades of unbelief. The worst of unbelief is that which regrets the goodness of our heavenly Father, and from which there springs in us a desire of breaking what we can not bend, and of twisting wire after wire and tying knot after knot in his scourge. Christianity, as I understand it, lies not in belief but in action. That servant is a good servant who obeys the just orders of his master; not he who repeats his words, measures his stature, or traces his pedigree ! On all occasions it is well to be a little more than tolerant; especially when a wiser and better man than ourselves thinks differently from us. Religious minds will find an additional reason for their humility, when they observe such excellent men as Borromeo and Fénelon adhering to the religion they were born in, amidst the discussions and commotions of every land around.

WILBERFORCE. My opinion is, that religion should be mixed up in all our institutions, and that it not only should be a part, but the main part of the state.

ROMILLY. I am unwilling to obtrude my sentiments on this question, and even to answer any. For I always have observed that the most religious men become the most impatient in the course of discussion, calling their opponents weak wavering sceptics, or obstinate reckless unbelievers. But since the constitution of our country is involved in it, together with its present defects and future meliorations, I must declare to you my conviction that even the best government and the best religion should be kept apart in their ministries.

ROMILLY AND WILBERFORCE

In building a house, brick and lime are ingredients. Let the brick be imbedded in the lime reduced to mortar: but if you mix it in the composition of the brick, it swells and cracks and falls to pieces in the kiln.

WILBERFORCE. That is no argument.

ROMILLY.* Arguments cease to be arguments the moment they come home. But this, I acknowledge, is only an illustration. To detain you no longer, Mr. Wilberforce, I give you my promise I will attend at the debate, and vote with you. Neither of us can live long enough to see the Africans secure from bondage, or from the violence of tribe against tribe, and from the myriads of other calamities that precede it. Europe is semi-barbarous at the present hour; and, even among the more civilized, one state is as suspicious of another as one Black is of another in the belligerents of Senegal and Gambia. For many years to come, no nation will unite with us in any work or project for the furtherance of our mutual well-being: little then can we expect that Honour, now totally lost sight of on the Continent, will be recognised in a character so novel as the Knight-errant of Humanity.

One more remark at parting; the only one by which in this business I can hope to serve you materially. Permit me to advise you, Mr. Wilberforce, to display as small a portion of historical research as you possibly can, consistently with your eloquence and enthusiasm.

WILBERFORCE. Why so, Mr. Romilly?

ROMILLY. Because it may counteract your benevolent intentions.

WILBERFORCE. Nothing shall counteract them.

ROMILLY. Are you aware to which of our sovereigns we must attribute the deadly curse of African slavery, inasmuch as our country is concerned in it?

WILBERFORCE. Certainly to none of our justly revered kings can so horrible a crime be imputed, although the royal power, according

---

* Parliament has been proved in our times, and indeed in most others, a slippery foundation for names, although a commodious one for fortunes. But Romilly went into public life with temperate and healthy aspirations. Providence, having blessed him with domestic peace, withheld him from political animosities. He knew that the sweetest fruits grow nearest the ground, and he waited for the higher to fall into his bosom, without an effort or a wish to seize on them. No man whosoever in our Parliamentary history has united in more perfect accordance and constancy pure virtue and lofty wisdom.—W. S. L.

to the limitations of our constitution, may have been insufficient to repress it effectively.

ROMILLY. Queen Elizabeth [1] equipped two vessels for her own sole profit, in which two vessels, escorted by the fleet under the command of Hawkins, were the first unhappy Blacks inveigled from their shores by Englishmen, and doomed to end their lives in servitude. Elizabeth was avaricious and cruel; but a small segment of her heart had a brief sunshine on it, darting obliquely. We are under a king notoriously more avaricious; one who passes without a shudder the gibbets his sign-manual has garnished; one who sees on the field of the most disastrous battles, battles in which he ordered his people to fight his people, nothing else to be regretted than the loss of horses and saddles, of haversacs and jackets. If this insensate and insatiable man even hears that Queen Elizabeth was a slave-dealer, he will assert the inalienable rights of the Crown, and swamp your motion.

[1] Hawkins having, in 1562, entered on the slave-trade without official countenance, was condemned by Elizabeth, who predicted the vengeance of Heaven on such undertakings. But in 1564 she lent Hawkins one of her own ships for a slaving voyage. Mr. Stephen Wheeler provides me with references to Claridge's *History of the Gold Coast* and Hill's *Naval History*.

XXIX. SOUTHEY AND PORSON

(*London Magazine*, July 1823; *Imag. Convers.*, i., 1824; i., 1826; *Wks.*, i., 1846; *Wks.*, iv., 1876.)

PORSON. I suspect, Mr. Southey, you are angry with me for the freedom with which I have spoken of your poetry and Wordsworth's.

SOUTHEY. What could have induced you to imagine it, Mr. Professor? You have indeed bent your eyes upon me, since we have been together, with somewhat of fierceness and defiance; I presume you fancied me to be a commentator.[1] You wrong me, in your belief that any opinion on my poetical works hath molested me; but you afford me more than compensation in supposing me acutely sensible of injustice done to Wordsworth. If we must converse [2] on these topics, we will converse on him. What man ever existed who spent a more inoffensive [3] life, or adorned it with nobler studies?

PORSON. None,[4] and they who attack him with virulence are men of as little morality as reflection. I have demonstrated that one of them, he who wrote the *Pursuits of Literature*, could not construe a Greek sentence or scan a verse; and I have fallen on the very *Index* from which he drew out his forlorn hope on the parade. This is incomparably the most impudent fellow I have met with in the course of my reading, which has lain, you know, in a province where impudence is no rarity [5]. I [6] am sorry to say that we critics who write for the learned, have sometimes set a bad example to our younger brothers, the critics who write for the public: but if they were

---

[1] 1st, 2nd, and 3rd eds. read: "commentator; and I am not irritated at a mistake. You," etc.

[2] 1st three eds. read: "converse at all," etc.

[3] 1st three eds. read: "a more inoffensive, a more virtuous," etc.

[4] 1st three eds. read: "I believe so; I have always heard it; and those who attack him with virulence or with levity are men of no morality and no reflection."

[5] 1st and 2nd eds. read: "rarity. He has little more merit in having stolen, than he would have had if he had never stolen at all. Those who have failed as painters," etc.

[6] From "I" to "celebration," p. 144, added in 3rd ed.

considerate and prudent, they would find out that a deficiency in weight and authority might in some measure be compensated by deference and decorum. Not to mention the refuse of the literary world, the sweeping of booksellers' shops, the dust thrown up by them in a corner to blow by pinches on new publications; not to tread upon or disturb this filth, the greatest of our critics now living are only great [1] comparatively. They betray their inconsiderateness when they look disdainfully on the humbler in acquirements and intellect. A little wit, or, as that is not always at hand, a little impudence instead of it, throws its rampant briar over dry lacunes: a drop [2] of oil, sweet or rancid, covers a great quantity of poor broth. Instead of anything in this way, I would seriously recommend to the employer of our critics, young and old, that he oblige them to pursue a course of study such as this: that under the superintendence of some respectable student from the university, they first read and examine the contents of the book; a thing greatly more useful in criticism than is generally thought; secondly, that they carefully write them down, number them, and range them under their several heads; thirdly, that they mark every beautiful, every faulty, every ambiguous, every uncommon expression. Which being completed, that they inquire what author, ancient or modern, has treated the same subject; that they compare them, first in smaller, afterward in larger portions, noting every defect in precision and its causes, every excellence and its nature; that they graduate these, fixing *plus* and *minus*, and designating them more accurately and discriminately by means of colours, stronger or paler. For instance, purple might express grandeur and majesty of thought; scarlet, vigour of expression; pink, liveliness; green, elegant and equable composition: these however and others, as might best attract their notice and serve their memory. The same process may be used where authors have not written on the same subject, when those who have are wanting, or have touched it but incidentally. Thus Addison and Fontenelle, not very like, may be compared in the graces of style, in the number and degree of just thoughts and lively fancies: thus the dialogues of Cicero with those of Plato, his ethics with those of Aris-

---

[1] 3rd ed. reads: " only great men comparatively; which they betray when they look disdainfully on the humbler in judgment and intellect: for if these were not humbler what would they themselves be ? A little wit," etc.

[2] 3rd ed. reads: " a little grease covers," etc.

SOUTHEY AND PORSON

toteles, his orations with those of Demosthenes. It matters not if one be found superior to the other in this thing, and inferior in that; the exercise is taken; the qualities of two authors are explored and understood, and their distances laid down, as geographers speak, from accurate survey. The *plus* and *minus* of good and bad and ordinary, will have something of a scale to rest upon; and after a time the degrees of the higher parts in intellectual dynamics may be more nearly attained, though never quite exactly.

SOUTHEY. Nothing is easier than to mark and number the striking parts of Homer: it is little more difficult to demonstrate why they are so: the same thing may then be done in Milton: these pieces in each poet may afterward be collated and summed up. Every man will be capable or incapable of it in proportion as his mind is poetical: few indeed will ever write anything on the subject worth reading; but they will acquire strength and practice. The critic of the trade will gain a more certain livelihood and a more reputable one than before, and no great matter will be spent upon his education.

PORSON. Which however must be entered on in an opposite way from the statuary's: the latter begins with dirt and ends with marble; the former begins with marble and ends with dirt. This, nevertheless, he may so manage as neither to be ridiculed nor starved.

SOUTHEY. For my own part, I should be well contented with that share of reputation which might come meted out and delivered to me after the analytical and close comparison you propose. Its accomplishment can hardly be expected in an age when everything must be done quickly. To run with oars and sails, was formerly the expression of orators for velocity: it would now express slowness. Our hats, our shoes, our whole habiliments, are made at one stroke; our fortunes the same, and the same our criticisms. Under my fellow-labourers in this vineyard, many vines have bled and few have blossomed. The proprietors seem to keep their stock as agriculturists keep lean sheep, to profit by their hoof and ordure.

PORSON. You were speaking this moment of the changes among us. Dwarfs are in fashion still; but they are the dwarfs of literature. These little zanies are invited to the assemblies of the gay world, and admitted to the dinners of the political. Limbs of the law, paralysed and laid up professionally, enter into association with printers, and take retaining fees from some authors, to harangue against others out of any brief before them.

SOUTHEY. And they meet with encouragement and success! We stigmatise any lie but a malignant one, and we repel any attack but against fame, virtue, and genius. Fond of trying experiments on poison, we find that the strongest may be extracted from blood; and this itself is rejected as unworthy of our laboratory, unless it be drawn from a generous and a capacious [1] heart.

PORSON. No other country hath [2] ever been so abundant in speculation as ours; but it would be incredible if we did not see it, that ten or fifteen men, of the humblest attainments, gain a comfortable [3] livelihood by periodical attacks on its best writers. Adverse as I have declared myself to the style and manner of Wordsworth, I never thought that all his reviewers put together could compose anything equal to the worst paragraph in his volumes. I have spoken vehemently against him, and mildly against them; because he could do better, they never could.[4] The same people would treat me with as little reverence as they treat him with, if anything I write were popular, or would [5] become so. It is by fixing on such works that they are carried with them into the doorway. The porter of Cleopatra would not have admitted the asps if they had not been under the figs. Show me, if you can, Mr. Southey, a temperate, accurate, solid exposition, of any English work whatever, in any English review.

SOUTHEY. Not having at hand so many numbers as it would be requisite to turn over, I must decline the challenge.

PORSON. I have observed the same man extol [6] in private the very book on whose ruin he dined the day before.

SOUTHEY. His judgment then may be ambiguous, but you must not deny him the merit of gratitude. If you blame the poor and vicious for abusing the solaces of poverty and vice, how much more should you censure those who administer to them the means of such indulgence.

PORSON. The publications which excite the most bustle and biting

---

[1] 3rd ed. reads: " gifted heart."   [2] 3rd ed. reads: " has ever," etc.
[3] 3rd ed. reads: " gain a livelihood," etc.
[4] 3rd ed. reads: " could. If he thinks me his enemy it is through modesty: if they think me their friend it is through impudence. The same," etc.
[5] 3rd ed. reads: " could become," etc.
[6] 3rd ed. reads: " extoll," etc.

SOUTHEY AND PORSON

from these fellows, are always the best, as the fruit on which the flies gather is the ripest. Periodical critics were never so plentiful as they now are. There is hardly a young author who does not make his first attempt in some review; showing his teeth, hanging by his tail, pleased and pleasing by the volubility of his chatter, and doing his best to get a penny for his exhibitor and a nut for his own pouch, by the facetiousness of the tricks he performs upon our heads and shoulders. From all I can recollect of what I noticed when I turned over such matters, a wellsized and useful volume might be compiled and published annually, containing the incorrect expressions, and omitting the opinions, of our booksellers' boys, the reviewers. Looking the other day by accident at two pages of *judgments*, recommendatory of new publications, I found, face to face, the following words, from not the worst of the species. *Scattering so considerable a degree of interest over the contemplation, &c.* . . . *The dazzling glitter of intellect, &c.*[1] Now in what manner can we *scatter a degree?*

[1] 3rd ed. contains the following footnote :—

" Altho the expressions of Reviews are nearly the same, it would be curious if Porson should have stumbled on these two together. I find them appended to my first volume, as extracts from the *Monthly Review* of June 1823 and May 1820. One of these extracts is from a criticism on a publication of Hazlitt, in which publication there are strokes as vivid and vigorous as in any work edited these hundred years. I regrett all enmities in the literary world, and particularly when they are exercised against the ornaments and glories of our country, against a Wordsworth and a Southey. It has been my fortune to love in general those men most who have thought most differently from me, on subjects wherein others pardon no discordance. I think I have no more right to be angry with a man, whose reason has followed up a process different from what mine has, and is satisfied with the result, than with one who has gone to Venice while I am at Sienna, and who writes to me that he likes the place, and that, altho he said once he should settle elsewhere, he shall reside in that city. My political opinions are my only ones, beyond square demonstration, that I am certain will never change. If my muscles have hardened in them and are fit for no other, I have not on this account the right or inclination to consider a friend untrue or insincere, who declares that he sees more of practical good in an opposite quarter, to that where we agreed to fix the speculative; and that he abandons the dim astounding majesty of mountain scenery, for the refreshing greenness and easy paths of the plain. I have walked always where I must breathe hard, and where such breathing was my luxury : I now sit somewhat stiller and have fewer aspirations, but I inhale the same atmosphere yet.

" Now to others—— We have amongst us seven or eight great men; a number we never had in former times: why should they act like children ! snatching at the coach and horses, or bread and butter, across the table, and breaking them and trampling them underfoot; rejoicing at the wry faces and loud cries they occasion, and ready to hug and kiss only at the moment when they are called away. For myself I neither ask nor deprecate: no compacts, no

IMAGINARY CONVERSATIONS : ENGLISH

unless it be one of those degrees which are scattered at Edinburgh and Glasgow. Such an expression as *dazzling glitter* may often be applied to fancy, but never to intellect.[1] These gentlemen might do somewhat better, if they would read us for the sake of improvement, and not for the sake of showing off a somewhat light familiarity, which never can appertain to them. The time however, I am inclined to believe, is not far distant, when the fashionable will be as much ashamed of purchasing such wayside publications, as the learned would be of reading them. Come, let us away from these criers of cat's-meat and dog's-meat, who excite so many yelpings and mewings as they pass : the vicinity [2] is none of the sweetest.

You will do me the favour, Mr. Southey, not to mention to those who may be kept under the regimen, what I have been proposing here for the benefit of literature [3] : since, although [4] in the street and at college I have had quarrels, lighter or graver, with most other conditions, I have avoided both conflict and contact with writers for reviews and almanacks. Once indeed, I confess it, I was very near falling as low : words passed between me and the more favoured man of letters, who announces to the world the *works and days* of Newmarket, the competitors at its games, their horses, their equisons and colours, and the attendant votaries of that goddess who readily leaves Paphos or Amathus for this annual celebration.

Those who have failed as painters turn picture-cleaners, those who have failed as writers turn reviewers. Orator Henley taught in the last century, that the readiest-made shoes are boots cut down :

conventions, no confraternities, for me. Let them consider me as a cloud if they will : could they break and dissipate this cloud, which they cannot, it would form again upon some other day. The breath of the universe, directed at once against me, could detach from me but some loose atoms, and such only as ought to fall of themselves. Literature is not the mother who should talk so frequently to her children about chastisement ; the most favorite word with her ever since her re-appearance amongst us. If chastisement is to be inflicted, let it fall upon the felon, who has no forbearance, no shame, no pity ; who attacks the timid and modest, the partner once of his freshest and best assorted opinions, and, holding him by the throat, exults and laughs, and chaunts to young templars and benchers, in a loud clear voice, the ritual of apostacy, as by law established. No ; even him let us rather pass quietly ; and with patience let us hear others recommend him, for his decorum to be a gentleman of the bed-chamber, for his accuracy a lord of the treasury, for his dexterity a parliamentary leader, or for his equity a judge."—W. S. L.

[1] 3rd ed. reads : " to *judgement*."
[2] 3rd ed. reads : " neighbourhood," etc.
[3] 3rd ed. reads : " of letters," etc.   [4] 3rd ed. reads : " altho," etc.

SOUTHEY AND PORSON

there are those who abundantly teach us now, that the readiest-made critics are cut-down poets. Their assurance is however by no means diminished from their ill success.[1]

SOUTHEY.[1] Puffy fingers have pelted me long enough with snow-balls, and I should not wonder if some of them reached the skirts of my greatcoat; but I never turned round to look.

PORSON. The little man who followed you in the *Critical Review*, and whose pretensions widen every smile his imbecility excited, would, I am persuaded, if Homer were living, pat him in a fatherly way upon the cheek, and tell him that, by moderating his fire and contracting his prolixity, the public might ere long expect something from him worth reading.

I had visited a friend in *King's Road* when he [2] entered.

" Have you seen the Review ? " cried he. " Worse than ever ! I am resolved to insert a paragraph in the papers, declaring that I had no concern in the last number."

" Is it so very bad ? " said I quietly.

" Infamous! detestable! " exclaimed he.

" Sit down then: nobody will believe you " : was my answer.

Since that morning he has discovered that I drink harder than usual, that my faculties are wearing fast away, that once indeed I had some Greek in my head, but—he then claps the forefinger to the side of his nose, turns his eye slowly upward, and looks compassionately and calmly.

SOUTHEY. Come, Mr. Porson, grant him his merits: no critic is better contrived to make any work a monthly [3] one, no writer more dexterous in giving a finishing touch,

PORSON. Let [4] him take his due and be gone: now to the rest. The plagiary has a greater latitude of choice than we: and if he brings home a parsnip [5] or turnip-top, when he could as easily have pocketted [5] a nectarine or a pine-apple, he must be a blockhead. I never heard the name of the [6] *pursuer of literature*, who has little more merit in having stolen, than he would have had if he had never

---

[1] From " SOUTHEY " to " look " added in 4th ed. First three eds. read : " ill success. Even the little . . . *Review*, poor Robin Fellowes, whose," etc.

[2] First three eds. read : " Robin entered."

[3] 1st two eds. read : " a very periodical one," etc.

[4] From " Let " to " rest " added in 3rd ed.

[5] 1st three eds. read : " parsnip . . . pocketed." Spelling changed 4th ed.

[6] 1st two eds. read : " that pursuer," etc.—[T. J. Mathias.]

IMAGINARY CONVERSATIONS: ENGLISH

stolen at all; and I have forgotten that other man's, who evinced his fitness to be the censor of our age, by a translation of the most naked and impure satires of antiquity, those of Juvenal, which owe their preservation to the partiality of the friars.[1] I shall entertain an unfavourable opinion of him if he has translated them well: pray has he?

SOUTHEY. Indeed I do not know. I read poets for their poetry, and to extract that nutriment of the intellect and of the heart which poetry should contain. I never listen to the swans of the cesspool, and must declare that nothing is heavier to me than rottenness and corruption.

PORSON. You are right, sir, perfectly right. A translator of Juvenal would open a public drain to look for a needle, and may miss it. My nose is not easily offended; but I must have something to fill my belly. Come, we will lay aside the scrip of the transpositor and the pouch of the pursuer, in reserve for the days of unleavened bread: and again, if you please, to the lakes and mountains. Now we are both in better humour, I must bring you to a confession that in your friend Wordsworth there is occasionally a little trash.

SOUTHEY. A haunch of venison would be trash to a Brahmin, a bottle of burgundy[2] to the xerif of Mecca.

PORSON.[3] I will not be anticipated by you. Trash, I confess, is no proof that nothing good can lie above it and about it. The roughest and least manageable soil surrounds gold and diamonds. Homer and Dante and Shakespeare and Milton have each many hundred lines worth little; lines without force, without feeling, without fancy; in short, without beauty of any kind. But it is the character of modern poetry, as it is of modern arms and equipments, to be more uniformly trim and polished. The ancients in both had more strength and splendour; they had also more inequality and rudeness.

SOUTHEY. We are guided[4] by precept, by habit, by taste, by constitution. Hitherto[5] our sentiments on poetry have been delivered down to us from authority; and if it can be demonstrated, as I

---

[1] 1st two eds. insert: "friars; but indeed they are so impregnated and incrusted with bay-salt and alum that they would not burn. I shall," etc.
[2] 1st three eds. read: "burgundy or tokay," etc.
[3] From "PORSON" to "SOUTHEY" added in 3rd ed.
[4] 1st two eds. read: "guided in our choice," etc.
[5] 1st three eds. read: "Hitherto all our sentiments," etc.

think it may be, that the authority is inadequate, and that the dictates are often inapplicable and often misinterpreted, you will allow me to remove the cause out of court. Every man can see what is very bad in a poem, almost every one can see what is very good; but you, Mr. Porson, who have turned over all the volumes of all the commentators, will inform me whether I am right or wrong in asserting, that no critic hath yet appeared who hath been able to fix or to discern the exact degrees of excellence above a certain point.

PORSON. None.

SOUTHEY. The reason is, because the eyes of no one have been upon a level with it. Supposing, for the sake of argument, the contest of Hesiod and Homer to have taken place: the judges, who decided in favour of the worse [1], and he indeed in the poetry has little merit, may have been elegant, wise, and conscientious men. Their decision was in favour of that [2] to the species of which they had been the most accustomed. Corinna was preferred to Pindar no fewer than five times; and the best judges in Greece gave her the preference; yet whatever were her powers, and beyond a question they were extraordinary, we may assure ourselves that she stood many degrees below Pindar. Nothing is more absurd than the report that the judges were prepossessed by her beauty. Plutarch tells us that she was much older than her competitor, who consulted her judgment in his earlier odes. Now, granting their first competition to have been when Pindar was twenty years old, and that the others were in the years succeeding, her beauty must have been somewhat on [3] the decline; for in Greece there are few women who retain the graces, none who retain the bloom of youth, beyond the twenty-third year. Her countenance, I doubt not, was expressive: but expression, although it gives beauty to men, makes women pay dearly for its stamp, and pay soon. Nature seems, in protection to their loveliness, to have ordered that they who are our superiors in quickness and sensibility, should [4] be little disposed to laborious thought or to long excursions in the labyrinth of fancy. We may be convinced that the verdict of the judges was biassed by

---

[1] 1st two eds. read: " worse, who indeed has little merit, may," etc.
[2] 1st two eds. read: " of that poetry to the species of which," etc.
[3] 1st two eds. read: " somewhat in," etc.
[4] 1st two eds. read: " should in general be," etc.

nothing else than their habitudes of thinking : we may be convinced too that, living in an age when poetry was cultivated [1] highly, and selected from the most acute and the most dispassionate, they were subject to no greater errors of opinion than are the learned messmates of our English colleges.

PORSON. You are more liberal in your largesses to the fair Greeks than a friend of mine was, who resided in Athens to acquire the language. He assured me that beauty there was in bud at thirteen, in full blossom at fifteen, losing a leaf or two every day at seventeen, trembling on the thorn at nineteen, and under the tree at twenty.[2]

Returning [3], Mr. Southey, to the difficulty, or rather to the rarity, of an accurate and just survey of poetical and other literary works, I do not see why we should not borrow an idea from geometricians and astronomers, why we should not have our triangles and quadrants, why, in short, we should not measure out writings by small portions at a time, and compare the brighter parts of two authors page by page. The minor beauties, the complection and contexture, may be considered at last, and more at large. Daring geniusses, ensigns and undergraduates, members of Anacreontic and Pindaric clubs, will scoff at me. Painters who can draw nothing correctly, hold Raffael in contempt, and appeal to the sublimity of Michael-Angelo and the splendour of Titian: ignorant that these great men were great by science first, and employed in painting [4] the means I propose for criticism. Venus and the damned submitted to the same squaring.

Such a method would be useful to critics in general, and even the wisest and most impartial would be much improved by it; although few, either by these means or any, are likely to be quite correct or quite unanimous on the merits of any two authors whatsoever.

SOUTHEY. Those who are learners would be teachers; while those who have learnt much would procure them at any price. It is only when we have mounted high, that we are sensible of wanting a hand.

---

[1] 1st two eds. read : " cultivated so highly," etc.
[2] 1st three eds. read : " twenty. He would have been but an indifferent courtier in the palace of a certain prince, whose exclamation was,
        O could a girl of sixty breed,
        Then, marriage, thou wert bliss indeed ! "
[3] From " Returning " to " genius," p. 150, added in 3rd ed.
[4] 3rd ed. reads : " painting, at all times, the very means," etc.

SOUTHEY AND PORSON

PORSON. On the subject of poetry in particular, there are some questions not yet sufficiently discussed: I will propose two. First, admitting that in the tragedies of Sophocles there was (which I believe) twice as much of good poetry as in the *Iliad*, does it follow that he was as admirable a poet as Homer?

SOUTHEY. No, indeed [1]: so much I do attribute to the conception and formation of a novel and vast design, and so wide is the difference I see between the completion of one very great, and the perfection of many smaller. Would even these have existed without Homer? I think not.

PORSON. My next question is, whether a poet is to be judged from the quantity of his bad poetry, or from the quality of his best?

SOUTHEY. I should certainly say from the latter: because it must be in poetry as in sculpture and painting: he who arrives at a high degree of excellence in these arts, will have made more models, more sketches and designs, than he who has reached but a lower; and the conservation of them, whether by accident or by choice, can injure and affect in no manner his more perfect and elaborate works. A drop of sealing-wax, falling by chance or negligence, may efface a fine impression: but what is well done in poetry is never to be effaced by what is ill done afterward. Even the bad poetry of a good poet hath something in it which renders it more valuable, to a judge of these matters, than what passes for much better, and what in many essential points is truly so. I will however keep to the argument, not having lost sight of my illustration in alluding to design and sketches. Many men would leave themselves penniless [2] to purchase an early and rude drawing by Raffael; some arabesque, some nose upon a gryphon [3] or gryphon upon a nose; and never would inquire whether the painter had kept it in his portfolio or had cast it away. The same persons, and others whom we call much wiser, exclaim [4] loudly against any literary sketch unworthy of a leaf among the productions of its author. No ideas are so trivial, so incorrect, so incoherent, but they may have entered the idle fancy, and have taken a higher place than they ought in the warm imagination, of the best poets. We find in Dante, as you just now remarked,

---

[1] 3rd ed. reads: "SOUTHEY. I doubt it; so much do I attribute," etc.
[2] 3rd ed. reads: "pennyless," etc.
[3] 3rd ed. reads: "gryphen," etc.
[4] 3rd ed. reads: "exclame," etc.

IMAGINARY CONVERSATIONS: ENGLISH

a prodigious quantity of them; and indeed not a few in Virgil, grave as he is and stately. Infantine and petty there is hardly anything in the *Iliad*, but the dull and drowthy stop us unexpectedly now and then. The boundaries of mind lie beyond these writers, although [1] their splendour lets us see nothing on the farther side. In so wide and untrodden a creation as that of Shakspeare's [2], can we wonder or complain that sometimes we are bewildered and entangled in the exuberance of fertility? Dry-brained men upon the Continent, the trifling wits of the theatre, accurate however and expert calculators, tell us that his beauties are balanced by his faults. The poetical opposition, puffing for popularity, cry cheerily against them, *his faults are balanced by his beauties;* when, in reality, all the faults that ever were committed in poetry would be but as air to earth, if we could weigh them against one single thought or image, such as almost every scene exhibits in every drama of this unrivalled genius. Do [3] you hear me with patience?

PORSON. With more; although at Cambridge we rather discourse on Bacon, for we know him better. He was immeasurably a less wise man than Shakspeare, and not a wiser writer: for he knew his fellow-man only as he saw him in the street and in the court, which indeed is but a dirtier street and a narrower: Shakspeare, who also knew him there, knew him everywhere else, both as he was and as he might be.

SOUTHEY. There is as great a difference between Shakspeare and Bacon as between an American forest and a London timber-yard. In the timber-yard the materials are sawed and squared and set across: in the forest we have the natural form of the tree, all its growth, all its branches, all its leaves, all the mosses that grow about it, all the birds and insects that inhabit it; now deep shadows absorbing the whole wilderness; now bright bursting glades, with exuberant grass and flowers and fruitage; now untroubled skies; now terrific thunderstorms; everywhere multiformity, everywhere immensity [4].

PORSON.[5] If after this ramble in the heat you are not thirsty, I would ask another question. What is the reason why, when not only

---

[1] 3rd ed. reads: " altho," etc.
[2] 3rd ed. reads: " that of Shakespeare," etc.
[3] From " Do " to " immensity " added in 4th ed.
[4] From " immensity " to " severely " added in 3rd ed.
[5] 3rd ed. reads: " genius. PORSON. A third question. . . . What is," etc.

the glory of great kings and statesmen, but even of great philosophers, is much enhanced by two or three good apophthegms, that of a great poet is lowered by them, even if he should invest them with good verse? For certainly the dignity of a great poet is thought to be lowered by the writing of epigrams.

SOUTHEY. As [1] you said of Wordsworth, the great poet could accomplish better things; the others could not. People in this apparent act of injustice do real justice [2], without intending or knowing it. All writers have afforded some information, or have excited some sentiment or idea, somewhere. This alone should exempt the humblest of them from revilings, unless it appear that he hath misapplied his powers through insolence or malice. In that case, whatever sentence may be passed upon him, I consider it no honour to be the executioner. What must we think of those who travel far and wide that, before they go to rest, they may burst into the arbour of a recluse, whose weakest thoughts are benevolence, whose worst are purity? On his poetry I shall say nothing, unless you lead me to it, wishing you however to examine it analytically and severely.

PORSON. There [3] are folks who, when they read my criticism, say, "*I do not think so.*" It is because they do not think so, that I write. Men entertain some opinions which it is indeed our duty to confirm, but many also which it is expedient to eradicate, and more which it is important to correct. They read less willingly what may improve their understanding and enlarge their capacity, than what corroborates their prejudices and establishes their prepossessions. I never bear malice toward those who try to reduce me to their own dimensions. A narrow mind cannot be enlarged, nor can a capacious one be contracted. Are we angry with a phial for not being a flask? or do we wonder that the skin of an elephant sits unwieldily on a squirrel?

SOUTHEY. Great men will always pay deference to greater: little men will not: because the little are fractious; and the weaker they are, the more obstinate and crooked.

PORSON. To proceed on our inquiry. I will not [4] deny that to

---

[1] From "As" to "Wordsworth" added in 4th ed.
[2] 3rd ed. reads: " justice, and conferr high honour where it is due, without," etc.
[3] From "There" to "inquiry" added in 4th ed.
[4] 1st three eds. read: " not dissemble or deny," etc.

IMAGINARY CONVERSATIONS: ENGLISH

compositions of a new kind, like Wordsworth's, we come without scales and weights, and without the means of making an assay.

SOUTHEY. Mr. Porson, it does not appear to me that anything more is necessary in the first instance, than to interrogate our hearts in what manner they have been affected. If the ear is satisfied; if at one moment a tumult is aroused in the breast, and tranquillised at another, with a perfect consciousness of equal power exerted in both cases; if we rise up from the perusal of the work with a strong excitement to thought, to imagination, to sensibility; above all, if we sat down with some propensities toward evil and walk away with much stronger toward good, in the midst of a world which we never had entered and of which we never had dreamed before, shall we perversely put on again the *old man* of criticism, and dissemble that we have been conducted by a most beneficent and most potent genius? Nothing proves to me so manifestly in what a pestiferous condition are its lazarettos, as when I observe how little hath been objected against those who have substituted words for things, and how much against those who have reinstated things for words.

PORSON.[1] I find, however, much to censure in our modern poets; I mean those who have written since Milton. But praise is due to such as threw aside the French models. Percy was the first: then came the Wartons, and then Cowper; more diversified in his poetry and more classical than any since.

SOUTHEY. I wonder you admire an author so near your own times, indeed contemporary.

PORSON. There is reason for wonder. Men in general do so in regard both to liberty and poetry.

SOUTHEY. I know not whether the Gauls had this latter gift before they assaulted the temple of Apollo at Delphi; certainly from that time downward the god hath owed them a grudge, and hath been as unrelenting as he was with the dogs and mules before Troy. The succeeding race, nevertheless, has tightened and gilded and gallantly tagged the drum of tragic declamation. Surely not Cowper nor any other is farther from it than Wordsworth.

PORSON. But his drum is damp; and his tags are none the better for being of hemp, with the broken stalks in.

SOUTHEY. Let Wordsworth prove to the world that there may be animation without blood and broken bones, and tenderness remote

---

[1] From "PORSON" to "stalks in. SOUTHEY" added in 4th ed.

SOUTHEY AND PORSON

from the stews. Some will doubt it; for even things the most evident are often but little perceived and strangely estimated. Swift ridiculed the music of Handel and the generalship of Marlborough, Pope[1] the perspicacity and the scholarship of Bentley, Gray the abilities of Shaftesbury and the eloquence of Rousseau. Shakespeare hardly found those who would collect his tragedies; Milton was read from godliness; Virgil was antiquated and rustic; Cicero Asiatic.[2] What a rabble has persecuted my friend[3]! An elephant is born to be consumed by ants in the midst of his unapproachable solitudes: Wordsworth is the prey of Jeffrey. Why repine? Let us rather amuse ourselves with allegories, and recollect that God in the creation left his noblest creature at the mercy of a serpent.

PORSON. In our[4] authors of the present day I would recommend principally, to reduce the expenditure of words to the means of support, and to be severe in style without the appearance of severity. But this advice is more easily given than taken. Your friend is verbose; not indeed without something for his words to rest upon, but from a resolution to gratify and indulge his capacity. He pursues his thoughts too far; and considers more how he may show them entirely than how he may show them advantageously. Good men may utter whatever comes uppermost, good poets may not. It is better, but it is also more difficult, to make a selection of thoughts than to accumulate them. He who has a splendid sideboard, should have an iron chest with a double lock upon it, and should hold in reserve a greater part than he displays.

I[5] know not why two poets so utterly dissimilar as your author and Coleridge should be constantly mentioned together. In the one I find diffuseness, monotony, not indistinctness, but uninteresting expanse, and such figures and such colouring as Morland's; in

---

[1] 1st three eds. read: "Pope the style of Middleton and the scholarship of Bentley," etc.

[2] 3rd ed. here inserts following footnote:—
"An admirable scholar and elegant French writer says: *La prose de Molière vaut beaucoup mieux que ses vers.* He would have spoken nearer the truth, if he had said that the prose of Molière is among the most detestable in the whole language."—W. S. L.

[3] 1st three eds. read: "my friend, in these latter times the glory of our country! An elephant," etc.

[4] From "our" to "taken" added in 4th ed. 1st three eds. read: "In my opinion your friend is verbose," etc.

[5] From "I" to "me" added in 4th ed.

the other, bright colours without form, sublimely void. In his prose he talks like a madman when he calls Saint Paul's Epistle to the Ephesians " the sublimest composition of man."

SOUTHEY. This indeed he hath spoken, but he has not yet published it in his writings: it will appear in his *Table Talk*, perhaps.

PORSON. Such table-talk may be expected to come forth very late in the evening, when the wine and candles are out, and the body lies horizontally underneath. He believes he is a believer; but why does he believe that the Scriptures are best reverenced by bearing false witness to them? Is it an act of piety to play the little child in the *go-cart* of Religion, or to beslaver the pretty dress he has just put on,

> Porrigens teneras manus
> Matris e gremio suæ
> Semihiante labello.[1]

Pardon a quotation: I hate it: I wonder how it escaped me.

Wordsworth goes out of his way to be attacked: he picks up a piece of dirt, throws it on the carpet in the midst of the company, and cries *This is a better man than any of you.* He does indeed mould the base material into what form he chooses; but why not rather invite us to contemplate it than challenge us to condemn it? Here [2] surely is false taste.

SOUTHEY. The principal and the most general accusation against him is, that the vehicle of his thoughts is unequal to them. Now did ever the judges at the Olympic games say, " We would have awarded to you the meed of victory, if your chariot had been equal to your horses: it is true they have won; but the people is displeased at a car neither new nor richly gilt, and without a gryphon or sphynx engraved on the axle "? You admire simplicity in Euripides; you censure it in Wordsworth; believe me, sir, it arises in neither from penury of thought, which seldom has produced it, but from the strength of temperance, and at the suggestion of principle. Some [3] of his critics are sincere in their censure, and are neither invidious nor unlearned; but their optics have been exercised on other objects, altogether dissimilar, and they are (permit me an expression not the worse for daily use) entirely out of their element. His very clearness puzzles and perplexes them, and they

---

[1] Catullus.   [2] 1st three eds. read: " This surely," etc.
[3] From " Some " to " indiscriminately " added in 3rd ed.

imagine that straightness is distortion, as children on seeing a wand dipped in limpid and still water. Clear [1] writers, like clear fountains, do not seem so deep as they are : the turbid look the most profound.

PORSON. Fleas know not whether they are upon the body of a giant or upon one of ordinary size, and bite both indiscriminately.

SOUTHEY. Our [2] critics are onion-eaters by the Pyramids of Poetry. They sprawl along the sands, without an idea how high and wonderful are the edifices above, whose base is solid as the earth itself, and whose summits are visible over a hundred ages.

Ignorance [3] has not been single-handed the enemy of Wordsworth; but Petulance and Malignity have accompanied her, and have been unremittent in their attacks. Small poets, small critics, lawyers who have much time on their hands and hanging heavily, come forward unfeed against him; such is the spirit of patriotism, rushing everywhere for the public good. Most of these have tried their fortune at some little lottery-office of literature, and, receiving a blank, have chewed upon it harshly and wryly. We, like jackdaws, are amicable creatures while we are together in the dust; but let any gain a battlement or steeple, and behold! the rest fly about him at once, and beat him down.

Take up a poem of Wordsworth's and read it; I would rather say, read them all; and, knowing that a mind like yours must grasp closely what comes within it, I will then appeal to you whether any poet of our country, since Milton,[4] hath exerted greater powers with less of strain and less of ostentation. I would however, by his permission, lay before you for this purpose a poem which is yet unpublished and incomplete.

PORSON. Pity, with such abilities, he does not imitate the ancients somewhat more.

SOUTHEY. Whom did they imitate? If his genius is equal to theirs he has no need of a guide. He also will be an ancient; and the very counterparts of those who now decry him, will extol him a thousand years hence in malignity to the moderns. The [5] ancients have always been opposed to them; just as, at routs and dances,

---

[1] From " Clear " to " profound " in 3rd ed. follows " indiscriminately " as part of Porson's speech.
[2] From " Our " to " ages " added in 4th ed.
[3] From " Ignorance " to " down " added in 3rd ed.
[4] 1st three eds. read: " since Shakespear." (1st two eds.: " Shakspeare.")
[5] From " The " to " inattention," p. 157, added in 3rd ed.

elderly beauties to younger. It would be wise to contract the scene of action, and to decide the business in both cases by couples.

Why do you repeat the word *rout* so often?

PORSON. Not because the expression is novel and barbarous, I do assure you, nor because the thing itself is equally the bane of domestic, of convivial, and of polite society. I was once at one by mistake, and really I saw there what you describe; and this made me (as you tell me I did, though I was not aware of it) repeat the word, and smile. You seem curious.

SOUTHEY. Rather indeed.

PORSON. I had been dining out: there were some who smoked after dinner; within a few hours the fumes of their pipes produced such an effect on my head, that I was willing to go into the air a little. Still I continued hot and thirsty; and an undergraduate, whose tutor was my old acquaintance, proposed that we should turn into an oyster-cellar, and refresh ourselves with oysters and porter. The rogue, instead of this, conducted me to a fashionable house in the neighbourhood of Saint James's; and although I expostulated with him, and insisted that we were going upstairs and not down, he appeared to me so ingenuous and so sincere in his protestations to the contrary, that I could well disbelieve him no longer. Nevertheless, receiving on the stairs many shoves and elbowings, I could not help telling him plainly, that, if indeed it was the oyster-cellar in Fleet-street, the company was much altered for the worse, and that in future I should frequent another. When the fumes of the pipes had left me, I discovered the deceit by the brilliancy and indecency of the dresses, and was resolved not to fall into temptation. Although, to my great satisfaction and surprise, no immodest proposal was directly made to me, I looked about, anxious that no other man in company should know me, beside those whose wantonness had conducted me thither; and I would have escaped if I could have found the door, from which every effort I made appeared to remove me farther and farther.

A pretty woman said loudly, " He has no gloves on ! "

" What nails the creature has ! " replied an elder one. " Pianoforte keys wanting the white ! " I tried to conceal my hands as well as might be; when suddenly there was a titter from the middle-aged and young, and a grave look and much erectness from the rest. So serious and stern did they appear to me, I never saw the like but once; which was in a file of soldiers, ordered out to shoot a deserter at St. Ives. I was the only person, young or old, male or female, that blushed; and I had not done so before for thirty years, to the best of my recollection. I now understood that blushing is a sign of half-breeding, and that an elevation of the eyebrow, and the opening of the lips a straw's breadth, are the most violent expressions of feeling permitted in such places. The gentlemen were neutral; unless the neutrality may be said to have been broken by two or three words, which I suspect to have been meant for English; a *token-coinage*, fit only for the district. One, however, more polite and more attentive, bowed to me. I did not recollect his features, which he divined by mine, and said, "Sir, I once recovered your watch for you, and wish I could now as easily recover its neighbour the button." I looked down, and perceived that the place of concealment, the refuge of my hand, had, like my conductor, been false to me. The gentleman was a thief-taker: three others of the fraternity had likewise been invited, on suspicion that there were several pickpockets; I mean beside the legitimate, and supernumerary to those who had been seated by the lady of the house at the card-tables. The thief-takers were recognised by the company: the higher and more respectable spoke familiarly with them; persons of inferior rank saluted them more distantly and coldly: and there were some few who slank obliquely from them as they passed, like landsmen walking on deck in a breeze. This shyness was far from mutual; and the gentlemen, who presided here as the good genii or tutelary deities of the place, awakened with winks one another's smiles, and pardoned the inattention.

SOUTHEY.[1] Those are fortunate who lose nothing in such places, and more fortunate who acquire nothing. You yourself remain quite unchanged: not a tone of your voice, not an article of your dress——

PORSON. If this appears strange to you, it will appear stranger that I was an object of imitation. What the thief-taker saw with apprehension, the young gentlemen have copied with sedulity, though they carry gloves. Their hands take that turn.

I [2] little thought that any of the company could have known me, or that my treacherous friend would have mentioned my name;

[1] From "SOUTHEY" to "turn" added in 4th ed.
[2] From "I" to "*daughters*," p. 159, added in 3rd ed.

and still less should I have prognosticated that I must, in an unguarded moment, set a fashion to the dandies, such as the dress of the ancients and the decency of the moderns had hitherto precluded.

I now come to your remark, confirmed to me by my own observation, upon the hostilities at such parties. A beldame with prominent eyes, painted mole-hairs, and abundantly rich in the extensive bleaching-ground of cheeks and shoulders, a German as I imagine, was speaking all manner of spiteful things against a young person called pretty; and after a long discussion, not only on her defects, but also on those of her family and parchments, *Who is she? I should like to know*, terminated the effusion. My betrayer had absconded, not without engaging another to find me and conduct me home. As we were passing through the folding-doors, I saw the baroness (for such he called her) with her arm upon the neck of the girl, and looking softly and benignly, and styling her *my young friend here*, in such a sweet guttural accent, so long in drawing up, you would have thought it must have come from the heart, at the very least. I mentioned my surprise.

" She was so strongly the fashion at the close of the evening," said my Mentor, " that it would never do (for the remainder of the night) not to know her; and, as proper time was wanting to get up a decent enmity, nothing was left for it but sworn friendship. To-morrow the baroness will call her my *protégée*, and the day after ask again, who is she? unless she happens to hear that the girl has a person of high rank among her connexions, which I understand she has; then the baroness will press her to the heart, or to that pound of flesh which lies next it."

Trifling people are often useful, unintentionally and unconsciously: illustrations may be made out of them even for scholars and sages. A hangman sells to a ragman the materials on which a Homer is printed. Would you imagine that in places like these it was likely for me to gain a new insight into language?

SOUTHEY. I should not indeed. Children make us reflect on it occasionally, by an unusual and just expression; but in such society everything is trite and trivial.

PORSON. Yet so it was. A friend who happened to be there, although I did not see him, asked me afterward what I thought of the naked necks of the ladies.

SOUTHEY AND PORSON

"To tell you the truth," replied I, "the women of all countries, and the men in most, have usually kept their necks naked."

"You appear not to understand me, or you quibble," said he; "I mean their bosoms."

I then understood for the first time that *neck* signifies *bosom* when we speak of women, though not so when we speak of men or other creatures. But if *bosom* is *neck*, what, according to the same scale of progression, ought to be *bosom?* The usurped dominion of neck extends from the ear downward to where mermaids become fish. This conversation led me to reflect that I was born in the time when people had *thighs;* before your memory, I imagine. At present there is nothing but leg from the hip to the instep. My friend Mr. Small of Peter-house, a very decent and regular man, and fond of fugitive pieces [1], read before a lady and her family, from under the head of *descriptive*, some verses about the spring and the bees. Unluckily the *honied thighs* of our little European sugar-slaves caught the attention of the mother, who coloured excessively at the words, and said with much gravity of reproof, *Indeed, Mr. Small, I never could have thought it of you*, and added, waving her hand with matronly [2] dignity toward the remainder of the audience, *Sir, I have daughters*. And [3] I know not what offence the Great Toe can have committed, that he never should be mentioned by the graver and more stately members of the family, or, if mentioned, be denounced with all his adherents; when many of these graver and statelier walk less humbly, and with much less heed against offending. In Italy, if any extremity of the human body is mentioned, it is preceded by the words, "*with respect*," so that most respect is shown to the parts, as to the characters, that least deserve it.

SOUTHEY. Pray tell me what else appeared to you remarkable at the rout: for when a person of your age and with your powers of observation is present at one for the first time, many things must strike him which another sees without reflection.

PORSON. I [4] saw among the rest two or three strangers of distinction, as I understood by their dresses and decorations: and, observing that nobody noticed them, except the lady of the house, who

[1] 3rd ed. reads: "fugitive pieces, such as are collected or written by our Pratts and Maras and Valpys, read," etc.
[2] 3rd ed. reads: "matronal dignity," etc.
[3] From "And" to "PORSON" added in 4th ed.
[4] From "I" to "paradox, that" added in 3rd ed.

smiled and dropped a few syllables as she passed, I inquired the next day whether they were discreditable or suspicious. "On the contrary," said my informant, "they are of the highest character as well as of the highest rank, and, above all, of well-proved loyalty: but we Englishmen lose our facility of conversation in the presence of strangers; added to which, we consider it an indecorous thing to pay the least attention to persons to whom we never were introduced. Strangers act otherwise. Every man of education, and of a certain rank, does the honours, not of the house, but of society at large. In no company at Paris, or any other capital in the world, would a foreigner [1] stand five minutes without receiving some [2] attention and courtesy. Abroad all gentlemen are equal, from the *duc et pair* to the Gascon who dines on chestnuts; and all feel that they are. The Englishman of ancient but private name is indignant and sullen that his rights at home are denied him; and his wounded pride renders him unsocial and uncivil. Pride of another kind acts on our society in the same manner. I have seen Irish peers, issuing from the shop and the desk, push rudely and scornfully by the most ancient of the French nobility; the cadets of whose families founded the oldest of ours, and waved the sword of knighthood over our Plantagenets. For which reason, whenever I sit down at table in [3] any public place with an Irish or [4] even an English peer of recent creation, I select the sturdiest of my servants to stand behind my chair, with orders to conduct him by the ears out of the room, should I lift up a finger to indicate the command."

I ought not to have interrupted you so long, in your attempt to prove Wordsworth shall I say the rival or the resembler of the ancients?

SOUTHEY. Such excursions are not unseasonable in such discussions, and lay in a store of good humour for them. Your narrative has amused me exceedingly. As you call upon me to return with you to the point we set out from, I hope I may assert without a charge of paradox, that whatever is good in poetry is common to all good poets, however wide may be the diversity of manner. Nothing can be more dissimilar than the three Greek tragedians: but would

---

[1] 3rd ed. reads: "forener," etc.

[2] 3rd ed. reads: "some mark of attention; a compliment, an inquiry, a congratulation, accompanied by a smile at least, or other act of exterior courtesy. Abroad," etc.

[3] and [4] From "in" to "place" and "or" to "English" added in 4th ed.

SOUTHEY AND PORSON

you prefer [1] the closest and best copier of Homer to the worst (whichever he be) among them ? Let us avoid what is indifferent or doubtful, and embrace what is good, whether we see it in another or not ; and if we have contracted any peculiarity while our muscles and bones were softer, let us hope finally to outgrow it. Our feelings and modes of thinking forbid and exclude a very frequent imitation of the old classics, not to mention our manners, which have a nearer connection than is generally known to exist with the higher poetry. When the occasion permitted it, Wordsworth has not declined to treat a subject as an ancient poet of equal vigour would have treated it. Let me repeat to you his *Laodamia*.

PORSON. After your animated recital of this classic poem, I begin to think more highly of you both. It is pleasant to find two poets living as brothers, and particularly when the palm lies between them, with hardly a third in sight. Those who have ascended to the summit of the mountain, sit quietly and familiarly side by side ; it is only those who are climbing with briers [2] about their legs, that kick and scramble. Yours [3] is a temper found less frequently in our country than in others. The French poets indeed must stick together to keep themselves warm. By employing courteous expressions mutually, they indulge their vanity rather than their benevolence, and bring the spirit of contest into action gaily and safely. Among the Romans we find Virgil, Horace, and several of their contemporaries, intimately united and profuse of reciprocal praise. Ovid, Cicero, and Pliny are authors the least addicted to censure, and the most ready to offer their testimony in favour of abilities in Greek or countryman. These are the three Romans, the least amiable of nations, and (one excepted) the least sincere, with whom I should have liked best to spend an evening.

SOUTHEY. Ennius and old Cato, I am afraid, would have run away with your first affections.

PORSON. Old Cato ! he, like a wafer, must have been well wetted to be good for anything. Such gentlemen as old Cato we meet every day in St. Mary Axe, and wholesomer wine than his wherever there are sloes and turnips. Ennius could converse without ignorance about Scipio, and without jealousy about Homer.

---

[1] 3rd ed. reads : " preferr."
[2] 1st two eds. read: " with gravel in their shoes, that scramble, kick, and jostle."
[3] From " Yours " to " reading *Laodamia*. PORSON " added in 3rd ed.

IMAGINARY CONVERSATIONS: ENGLISH

Southey. And I think he would not have disdained to nod his head on reading *Laodamia*.

Porson. You have recited a most spirited thing indeed [1]: and now to give you a proof that I have been attentive, I will remark two passages that offend me.[2] In the first stanza,

> With sacrifice before the rising morn
> *Performed*, my slaughtered lord *have I required*;
> And in thick darkness, amid shades forlorn,
> Him of the infernal Gods *have I desired*.[3]

I [4] do not see the necessity of *Performed*, which is dull and cumbersome. The second line and the fourth terminate too much alike, and [5] express to a tittle the same meaning: *have I required* and *have I desired* are worse than prosaic; beside [6] which there are four words together of equal length in each.

Southey. I [7] have seen a couplet oftener than once in which every word of the second verse corresponds in measure to every one above it.

Porson. The Scotch have a scabby and a frost-bitten ear for harmony, both in verse and prose: and I remember in *Douglas* two such as you describe.

> This is the place—the centre of the grove,
> Here stands the oak—the monarch of the wood.

After this whiff of vapour I must refresh myself with a draught of pure poetry, at the bottom of which is the flake of tartar I wish away.

> He spake of love, such love as spirits feel
> In worlds whose course is equable and pure;
> No fears to beat away, no strife to heal,
> The past unsighed for, and the future sure;

---

[1] 1st three eds. read: "indeed. I never had read it. Now to," etc.

[2] 3rd ed. here inserts following footnote:—
"The memory of Porson was extraordinary, and quite capable of this repetition."—W. S. L.

[3] In deference to this criticism Wordsworth altered these stanzas in 1827. For Wordsworth's letter on this, and the further criticism of the last lines of the second quotation from *Laodamia*, see Knight's *Wordsworth*, vol. vi.

[4] From "I" to "cumbersome" added in 4th ed.

[5] From "and" to "meaning" added in 4th ed.

[6] From "beside" to "each" added in 3rd ed. The 1st two eds. read: "prosaic. In another,
He spake of love," etc.

[7] From "I" to "away" added in 4th ed.

SOUTHEY AND PORSON

Spake, as a witness, of a second birth [1]
For all that is most perfect [2] upon earth.

How unseasonable is the allusion to *witness* and *second birth!* which things, however holy and venerable in themselves, come stinking and reeking to us from the conventicle. I desire to find [3] Laodamia in the silent and gloomy mansion of her beloved Protesilaus; not elbowed by the godly butchers in Tottenham-court Road, nor smelling devoutly of ratafia among the sugar-bakers' wives [4] at Blackfriars.

Mythologies should be kept distinct: the fire-place of one should never be subject to the smoke of another. The Gods of different countries, when they come together unexpectedly, are jealous Gods, and, as our old women say, *turn the house out of windows.*

SOUTHEY.[5] A current of rich and bright thoughts runs through the poem. Pindar himself would not on that subject have braced one to [6] more vigour, nor Euripides have breathed [7] into it more tenderness and [8] passion. The first part of the stanza you have just now quoted might have been heard with shouts of rapture in the regions it describes.

PORSON. I am not insensible to the warmly chaste morality which is the soul of it, nor indifferent to the benefits that literature on many occasions has derived from Christianity. But poetry is a luxury to which, if she tolerates and permits it, she accepts no invitation: she beats down your gates and citadels, levels your high places, and eradicates your groves. For which reason I dwell more willingly with those authors who cannot mix and confound the manners they represent. The hope that we may rescue at Herculaneum a great number of them, hath, I firmly believe, kept me

---

[1] These last two lines were altered by Wordsworth in 1827 in deference to this criticism.
[2] 1st two eds. read: " perfect upon earth.
" In a composition such as Sophocles might have exulted to own, and in a stanza the former part of which might have been heard with shouts of rapture in the regions he describes, how unseasonable," etc.
[3] 1st three eds. read: " to see Laodamia," etc.
[4] " wives " added in 3rd ed.
[5] In 1st three eds. this speech is part of Porson's.
[6] 1st two eds. read: " one into more nerve and freshness," etc. 3rd ed. reads: " one to more vigour and freshness," etc.
[7] 1st three eds. read: " inspired into," etc.
[8] 1st two eds. read: " and more passion."

alive. Reasonably may the best be imagined to exist in a library of some thousands. It will be recorded to the infamy of the kings and princes now reigning, or rather of those whose feet put into motion their rocking-horses, that they never have made a common cause in behalf of learning, but, on the contrary, have made a common cause against it. The Earth opened her bosom [1] before them, conjuring them to receive again, while it was possible, the glories of their species; and they turned their backs. They pretended [2] that it is not their business or their duty to interfere in the internal affairs of other nations [3]. This is not an internal affair of any [4] : it interests all; it belongs to all: and these scrupulous men have no scruple to interfere in giving their countenance and assistance when a province is to be invaded [5] or a people to be enslaved. [6]

SOUTHEY.[7] To neglect what is recoverable in the authors of antiquity, is like rowing away from a crew that is making its escape from shipwreck.

PORSON. The most contemptible of the Medicean family did more for the advancement of letters than the whole body of existing potentates. If their delicacy is shocked or alarmed at the idea of a [8] proposal to send scientific and learned men to Naples, let them send a brace of pointers as internuncios,[9] and the property is their own. Twenty scholars [10] in seven years might retrieve the worst [11] losses we experience from the bigotry of popes and califs. I do not intend to assert that every Herculanean manuscript might within that period be unfolded; but the three first legible [12] sentences might be; which is quite sufficient to inform the intelligent reader [13] whether a farther [14] attempt on the scroll would repay his trouble. There are fewer than thirty Greek authors worth inquiring for;

[1] 1st three eds. read: " entrails before them, conjured," etc.
[2] 1st three eds. read: " pretend," etc.
[3] 1st two eds. read: " states."
[4] 1st two eds. read: " any state whatever," etc.
[5] 1st two eds. read: " province is to be torn away," etc.
[6] 3rd ed. reads: " people to be invaded."
[7] From " SOUTHEY " to " shipwreck " added in 3rd ed.
[8] 1st three eds. read: " of making a proposal," etc.
[9] " as internuncios " added in 3rd ed.
[10] 1st three eds. read: " Twenty men," etc.
[11] 1st two eds. read: " retrieve all the losses we have experienced," etc.
[12] 1st two eds read: " the three first sentences of the larger part," etc.
[13] 1st three eds. read: " inform the scholar," etc.
[14] 1st three eds. read: " further," etc.

SOUTHEY AND PORSON

they exist beyond doubt, and beyond doubt they may, by [1] attention, patience, and skill, be brought to light.

SOUTHEY.[2] You and I, Mr. Porson, are truly and sincerely concerned in the loss of such treasures: but how often have we heard much louder lamentations than ours, from gentlemen who, if they were brought again to light, would never cast their eyes over them, even in the bookseller's window. I have been present at homilies on the corruption and incredulity of the age, and principally on the violation of the sabbath, from sleek clergymen, canons of cathedrals, who were at the gaming-table the two first hours of that very day; and I have listened to others on the loss of the classics, from men who never took the trouble to turn over half that is remaining to us of Cicero and Livius.

PORSON. The Greek language is almost unknown out of England and northern Germany: in the rest [3] of the world, exclusive of Greece, I doubt whether fifty scholars ever read one page of it without a version.

SOUTHEY. Give fifteen to Italy, twelve to the Netherlands, as many [4] to France; the remainder will hardly be collected in Sweden, Denmark,[5] Russia, Austria. In regard to [6] Spain and Portugal, we might as well look for them among the Moors and Negroes.

PORSON.[7] You are too prodigal to Italy and France. Matthiæ, in his preface to the Greek grammar, speaks of Germany, of England, of Holland; not a word of France; the country of Stephanus, Budæus, and the Scaligers. Latterly we have seen only Villoison and Larcher fairly escape from the barbarous ignorance around them. Catholic nations in general seem as averse to the Greek language as to the Greek ritual.

SOUTHEY.[8] The knowledge of books written in our own [9] is extending daily.

[1] 1st two eds. read: " with attention," etc.
[2] From " SOUTHEY " to " Negroes " added in 3rd ed. as entirely spoken by Southey.   [3] 3rd ed. reads: " remainder of the world," etc.
[4] 3rd ed. reads: " five to France," etc.
[5] " Denmark " inserted in 4th ed.
[6] 3rd ed. reads: " Austria: as for Spain," etc.
[7] From " PORSON " to " ritual " added in 4th ed.
[8] From " SOUTHEY " to " condition " added in 3rd ed.
[9] 3rd ed. reads: " in our own language is extending daily in our country, which, whatever dissatisfaction or disgust its rulers may occasion in you, contains four-fifths of the learned and scientific men now on earth."

IMAGINARY CONVERSATIONS: ENGLISH

PORSON.[1] Although the knowledge too of Greek is extending in England, I doubt whether it is to be found in such large masses as formerly. Schools and universities, like rills and torrents, roll down some grains of it every season; but the lumps have been long stored up in cabinets. I delight in the diffusion of learning; yet, I must confess it, I am most gratified and transported at finding a large quantity of it in one place: just as I would rather have a solid pat of butter at breakfast than a splash of grease upon the tablecloth that covers half of it. Do not attempt to defend the idle and inconsiderate knaves who manage our affairs for us; or defend them on some other ground. Prove, if you please, that they have, one after another, been incessantly occupied in rendering us more moral, more prosperous, more free; but abstain, sir, from any allusion to their solicitude on the improvement of our literary condition. With a smaller sum than is annually expended on the appointment of some silly and impertinent young envoy, we might restore[2] all or nearly all those writers of immortal name, whose disappearance has been the regret of Genius for four entire centuries. In my opinion a few thousand pounds laid out on such an undertaking, would be laid out as creditably as on a Persian carpet or a Turkish tent; as creditably as on a collar of rubies and a ball-dress of Brussels lace for our Lady in the manger, or as on gilding for the adoration of princesses and their capuchins, the posteriors and anteriors of Saint Januarius.

SECOND CONVERSATION

(*Blackwood*, Dec. 1842; *Wks.*, ii., 1846; *Wks.*, iv., 1876.)

PORSON. Many thanks, Mr. Southey, for this visit in my confinement. I do believe you see me on my last legs; and perhaps you expected it.

SOUTHEY. Indeed, Mr. Professor, I expected to find you unwell, according to report; but as your legs have occasionally failed you, both in Cambridge and in London, the same event may happen again

---

[1] 3rd ed. reads: "PORSON. This position is, I think, incontrovertible: but although," etc.

[2] 1st two eds. read: "might recall into existence all, or nearly all, those men of immortal name. . . . Genius for three hundred years. In," etc.

SOUTHEY AND PORSON

many times before the last. The cheerfulness of your countenance encourages me to make this remark.

PORSON. There is that soft and quiet and genial humour about you, which raises my spirits and tranquillises my infirmity. Why (I wonder) have we not always been friends?

SOUTHEY. Alas, my good Mr. Professor! how often have the worthiest men asked the same question, not indeed of each other, but of their own hearts, when age and sickness have worn down their asperities, when rivalships have grown languid, animosities tame, inert, and inexcitable, and when they have become aware of approaching more nearly the supreme perennial fountain of benevolence and truth?

PORSON. Am I listening to the language and to the sentiments of a poet? I ask the question with this distinction; for I have often found a wide difference between the sentiments and the language. Generally nothing can be purer or more humane than what is exhibited in modern poetry; but I may mention to you, who are known to be exempt from the vice, that the nearest neighbours in the most romantic scenery, where everything seems peace, repose, and harmony, are captious and carping one at another. When I hear the song of the nightingale, I neglect the naturalist; and in vain does he remind me that its aliment is composed of grubs and worms. Let poets be crop-full of jealousy; let them only sing well; that is enough for me.

SOUTHEY. I think you are wrong in your supposition, that the poet and the man are usually dissimilar.

PORSON. There is a race of poets; not however the race of Homer and Dante, Milton and Shakespeare; but a race of poets there is, which nature has condemned to a Siamese twinship. Wherever the poet is, there also must the man obtrude obliquely his ill-favoured visage. From a drunken connexion with Vanity this surplus offspring may always be expected. In no two poets that ever lived do we find the fact so remarkably exemplified as in Byron and Wordsworth. But higher power produces an intimate consciousness of itself; and this consciousness is the parent of tranquillity and repose. Small poets (observe, I do not call Wordsworth and Byron small poets) are as unquiet as grubs, which in their boneless and bloodless flaccidity, struggle and wriggle and die, the moment they tumble out of the nutshell and its comfortable drouth. Shakespeare was assailed on every side by rude and beggarly rivals, but he never kicked them out of his way.

SOUTHEY. Milton was less tolerant; he shrivelled up the lips of his revilers by the austerity of his scorn. In our last conversation, I remember, I had to defend against you the weaker of the two poets you just now cited, before we came to Milton and Shakespeare. I am always ready to undertake the task. Byron wants no support or setting off, so many workmen have been employed in the construction of his throne, and so many fair hands in the adaptation of his cushion and canopy. But Wordsworth, in his poetry at least, always aimed at——

PORSON. My dear Mr. Southey! there are two quarters in which you can not expect the will to be taken for the deed : I mean the women and the critics. Your friend inserts parenthesis in parenthesis, and adds clause to clause, codicil to codicil, with all the circumspection, circuition, wariness, and strictness, of an indenture. His client has it hard and fast. But what is an axiom in law is none in poetry. You can not say in your profession, *plus non vitiat ; plus* is the worst vitiator and violator of the Muses and the Graces.

Be sparing of your animadversions on Byron. He will always have more partisans and admirers than any other in your confraternity. He will always be an especial favourite with the ladies, and with all who, like them, have no opportunity of comparing him with the models of antiquity. He possesses the soul of poetry, which is energy ; but he wants that ideal beauty, which is the sublimer emanation, I will not say of the real, for this is the more real of the two, but of that which is ordinarily subject to the senses. With much that is admirable, he has nearly all that is vicious ; a large grasp of small things, without selection and without cohesion. This likewise is the case with the other, without the long hand and the strong fist.

SOUTHEY. I have heard that you prefer Crabbe to either.

PORSON. Crabbe wrote with a twopenny nail, and scratched rough truths and rogues' facts on mud walls. There is, however, much in his poetry, and more in his moral character, to admire. Comparing the smartnesses of Crabbe with Young's, I can not help thinking that the reverend doctor must have wandered in his Night Thoughts rather too near the future vicar's future mother, so striking is the resemblance. But the vicar, if he was fonder of low company, has greatly more nature and sympathy, greatly more vigour and compression. Young moralised at a distance on some external appearances of the human heart ; Crabbe entered it *on all fours,* and told the people what an ugly thing it is inside.

SOUTHEY. This simple-minded man is totally free from malice and animosity.

PORSON. Rightly in the use of these two powers have you discriminated. Byron is profuse of animosity ; but I do believe him to be quite without malice. You have lived among men about the Lakes, who want the vigour necessary for the expansion of animosity ; but whose dunghills are warm enough to hatch long egg-strings of malice, after a season.

SOUTHEY. It may be so ; but why advert to them ? In speaking of vigour, surely you can not mean vigour of intellect ? An animal that has been held with lowered nostrils in the Grotto del Cane, recovers his senses when he is thrown into the Agnano ; but there is no such resuscitation for the writer whose head has been bent over that poetry, which, while it intoxicates the brain, deadens or perverts the energies of the heart. In vain do pure waters reflect the heavens to him : his respiration is on the earth and earthly things : and it is not the whispers of wisdom, or the touches of affection, it is only the shout of the multitude, that can excite him. It soon falls, and he with it.

PORSON. Do not talk in this manner with the ladies, young or old ; a little profligacy is very endearing to them.

SOUTHEY. Not to those with whom I am likely to talk.

PORSON. Before we continue our discussion on the merits of Mr. Wordsworth, and there are many great ones, I must show my inclination to impartiality, by adducing a few instances of faultiness in Byron. For you must bear in mind that I am counsel for the crown against your friend, and that it is not my business in this place to call witnesses to his good character.

SOUTHEY. You leave me no doubt of that. But do not speak in generalities when you speak of him. Lay your finger on those places in particular which most displease you.

PORSON. It would benumb it ; nevertheless, I will do as you bid me ; and, if ever I am unjust in a single tittle, reprehend me instantly. But at present, to Byron as I proposed. Give me the volume. Ay, that is it.

IMAGINARY CONVERSATIONS : ENGLISH

SOUTHEY. Methinks it smells of his own favourite beverage, gin-and-water.

PORSON. No bad perfume after all.

> Nought of life left, save a quivering
> When his limbs were slightly shivering.

Pray, what does the second line add to the first, beside empty words?

> Around a slaughter'd army lay.

What follows?

> No more to combat or to bleed.

Verily! Well; more the pity than the wonder. According to historians (if you doubt my fidelity I will quote them), slaughtered armies have often been in this condition.

> We sat down and wept by the waters
> Of Babel, and thought of the day,
> When our foe, in the hue of his slaughters,
> Made Salem's high places his prey.

A prey " in the hue of his slaughters." This is very pathetic; but not more so than the thought it suggested to me, which is plainer:

> We sat down and wept by the waters
> Of Camus, and thought of the day,
> When damsels would show their red garters
> In their hurry to scamper away.

Let us see what we can find where this other slip of paper divides the pages.

> Let he who made thee.

Some of us at Cambridge continue to say, " Let *him* go." Is this grammatical form grown obsolete? Pray, let *I* know. Some of us are also much in the habit of pronouncing *real* as if it were a dissyllable, and *ideal* as if it were a trisyllable. All the Scotch deduct a syllable from each of these words, and Byron's mother was Scotch.

What have we here?

> And spoil'd her goodly lands to gild his waste.

I profess my abhorrence at *gilding* even a few square leagues of waste.

> Thy fanes, thy temples,

SOUTHEY AND PORSON

What is the difference?
>Rustic plough.

There are more of these than of city ploughs or court ploughs.
>Have flung a desolate cloud o'er Venice' lovely walls.

What think you of a desolate cloud?
>O'er Venice' lovely walls?

Where poets have omitted, as in this instance, the possessive *s*, denoting the genitive case, as we are accustomed to call it, they are very censurable. Few blemishes in style are greater. But here, where no letter *s* precedes it, the fault is the worst. In the next line we find
>Athens' armies.

Further on, he makes Petrarca say that his passion for Laura was a guilty one. If it was, Petrarca did not think it so, and still less would he have said it.

SOUTHEY. This arises from his ignorance, that *reo* in Italian poetry means not only *guilty*, but *cruel* and *sorrowful*.

PORSON. He fancies that Shakespeare's Forest of Arden is the Belgian Forest of the same name, differently spelt, Ardennes; whereas it began near Stratford-upon-Avon, and extended to Red-ditch and the Ridgeway, the boundary of Warwickshire and Worcestershire, having for its centre the little town Henley, called to this day Henley in Arden.

SOUTHEY. You will never find in Wordsworth such faults as these.

PORSON. Perhaps not; but let us see. I am apprehensive that we may find graver, and without the excuse of flightiness or incitation. We will follow him, if you please, where you attempted (as coopers do in their business more successfully) to draw together the staves of his quarter-cask, by putting a little fire of your own chips in it. Yet they start and stare widely; and even your practised hand will scarcely bring it into such condition as to render it a sound or saleable commodity. You are annoyed, I perceive, at this remark. I honour your sensibility. There are, indeed, base souls which genius may illuminate, but cannot elevate.

>Struck with an ear-ache by all stronger lays,
>They writhe with anguish at another's praise.

IMAGINARY CONVERSATIONS: ENGLISH

Meantime, what exquisite pleasure must you have felt, in being the only critic of our age and country, labouring for the advancement of those who might be thought your rivals! No other ventured to utter a syllable in behalf of your friend's poetry. While he " wheeled his drony flight," it lay among the thread-papers and patch-work of the sedater housewifes, and was applied by them to the younger part of the family, as an antidote against all levity of behaviour. The last time we met, you not only defended your fellow-soldier while he was lying on the ground, trodden and wounded and crying out aloud, but you lifted him up on your shoulders in the middle of the fight. Presently we must try our strength again, if you persist in opposing him to the dramatists of Athens.

SOUTHEY. You mistake me widely in imagining me to have ranked him with the Greek tragedians, or any great tragedians whatsoever. I only said that, in one single poem, Sophocles or Euripides would probably have succeeded no better.

PORSON. This was going far enough. But I will not oppose my unbelief to your belief, which is at all times the pleasanter. Poets, I find, are beginning to hold critics cheap, and are drilling a company out of their own body. At present, in marching they lift up their legs too high, and in firing they shut their eyes.

SOUTHEY. There is little use in arguing with the conceited and inexperienced, who, immersed in the slough of ignorance, cry out, " There you are wrong; there we differ," &c. Wry necks are always stiff, and hot heads are still worse when they grow cool.

PORSON. Let me ask you, who, being both a poet and a critic, are likely to be impartial, whether we, who restore the noble forms which time and barbarism have disfigured, are not more estimable than those artisans who mould in coarse clay, and cover with plashy chalk, their shepherds and shepherdesses for Bagnigge-Wells?

SOUTHEY. I do not deny nor dispute it; but, awarding due praise to such critics, of whom the number in our own country is extremely small (bishoprics having absorbed and suffocated half the crew), I must, in defence of those particularly whom they have criticised too severely, profess my opinion that our poetry, of late years, hath gained to the full as much as it hath lost.

PORSON. The sea also, of late years, and all other years too, has followed the same law. We have gained by it empty cockle-shells, dead jelly-fish, sand, shingle, and voluminous weeds. On the other

SOUTHEY AND PORSON

hand, we have lost our exuberant meadow-ground, slowly abraded, stealthily bitten off, morsel after morsel; we have lost our fat salt-marshes; we have lost our solid turf, besprinkled with close flowers; we have lost our broad umbrageous fences, and their trees and shrubs and foliage of plants innumerably various; we have lost, in short, everything that delighted us with its inexhaustible richness, and aroused our admiration at its irregular and unrepressed luxuriance.

SOUTHEY. I would detract and derogate from no man; but pardon me if I am more inclined toward him who improves our own literature, than toward him who elucidates any other.

PORSON. Our own is best improved by the elucidation of others. Among all the bran in the little bins of Mr. Wordsworth's beer-cellar, there is not a legal quart of that stout old English beverage with which the good Bishop of Dromore regaled us. The buff jerkins we saw in Chevy Chase, please me better than the linsywoolsy which enwraps the puffy limbs of our worthy host at Grasmere.

SOUTHEY. Really this, if not random malice, is ill-directed levity. Already you have acquired that fame and station to which nobody could oppose your progress: why not let him have his?

PORSON. So he shall; this is the mark I aim at. It is a difficult thing to set a weak man right, and it is seldom worth the trouble; but it is infinitely more difficult, when a man is intoxicated by applauses, to persuade him that he is going astray. The more tender and coaxing we are, the oftener is the elbow jerked into our sides. There are three classes of sufferers under criticism: the querulous, the acquiescent, and the contemptuous. In the two latter, there is usually something of magnanimity; but in the querulous we always find the imbecile, the vain, and the mean-spirited. I do not hear that you ever have condescended to notice any attack on your poetical works, either in note or preface. Meanwhile, your neighbour would allure us into his cottage by setting his sheep-dog at us; which guardian of the premises runs after and snaps at every pebble thrown to irritate him.

SOUTHEY. Pray, leave these tropes and metaphors, and acknowledge that Wordsworth has been scornfully treated.

PORSON. Those always will be who show one weakness at having been attacked on another. I admire your suavity of temper, and your consciousness of worth; your disdain of obloquy, and your resignation to the destinies of authorship. Never did either poet or lover gain anything by complaining.

SOUTHEY. Such sparks as our critics are in general, give neither warmth nor light, and only make people stare and stand out of the way, lest they should fall on them.

PORSON. Those who have assaulted you and Mr. Wordsworth are perhaps less malicious than unprincipled ; the pursuivants of power, or the running footmen of faction. Your patience is admirable ; his impatience is laughable. Nothing is more amusing than to see him raise his bristles and expose his tusk at every invader of his brushwood, every marauder of his hips and haws.

SOUTHEY. Among all the races of men, we English are at once the most generous and the most ill-tempered. We all carry sticks in our hands to cut down the heads of the higher poppies.

PORSON. A very high poppy, and surcharged with Lethean dew, is that before us. But continue.

SOUTHEY. I would have added, that each resents in another any injustice ; and resents it indeed so violently, as to turn unjust on the opposite side. Wordsworth, in whose poetry you yourself admit there are many and great beauties, will, I am afraid, be tossed out of his balance by a sudden jerk in raising him.

PORSON. Nothing more likely. The reaction may be as precipitate as the pull is now violent against him. Injudicious friends will cause him less uneasiness, but will do him greater mischief, than intemperate opponents.

SOUTHEY. You can not be accused of either fault : but you demand too much, and pardon no remissness. However, you have at no time abetted by your example the paltry pelters of golden fruit paled out from them.

PORSON. Removed alike from the crowd and the *coterie*, I have always avoided, with timid prudence, the bird-cage walk of literature. I have withholden from Herman and some others a part of what is due to them ; and I regret it. Sometimes I have been arrogant, never have I been malicious. Unhappily, I was educated in a school of criticism where the exercises were too gladiatorial. Looking at my elders in it, they appeared to me so ugly, in part from their contortions, and in part from their scars, that I suspected it must be a dangerous thing to wield a scourge of vipers ; and I thought it no very creditable appointment to be linkboy or pander at an alley leading down to the Furies. Age and infirmity have rendered me milder than I was. I am loth to fire off my gun in the warren which lies before us; loth to startle the snug little creatures, each looking so comfortable at the mouth of its burrow, or skipping about at short distances, or frisking and kicking up the sand along the thriftless heath. You have shown me some very good poetry in your author; I have some very bad in him to show you. Each of our actions is an incitement to improve him. But what we cannot improve or alter, lies in the constitution of the man: the determination to hold you in one spot until you have heard him through; the reluctance that anything should be lost; the unconsciousness that the paring is less nutritious and less savoury than the core; in short, the prolix, the prosaic; a sickly sameness of colour; a sad deficiency of vital heat.

SOUTHEY. Where the language is subdued and somewhat cold, there may nevertheless be internal warmth and spirit. There is a paleness in intense fires; they do not flame out nor sparkle. As you know, Mr. Professor, it is only a weak wine that sends the cork up to the ceiling.

PORSON. I never was fond of the florid: but I would readily pardon the weak wine you allude to, for committing this misdemeanour. Upon my word, I have no such complaint to make against it. I said little at the time about these poems, and usually say little more on better. In our praises and censures, we should see before us one sole object: instruction. A single well-set post, with a few plain letters upon it, directs us better than fifty that turn about and totter, covered as they may be from top to bottom with coronals and garlands.

SOUTHEY. We have about a million critics in Great Britain; not a soul of which critics entertains the slightest doubt of his own infallibility. You, with all your learning and all your canons of criticism, will never make them waver.

PORSON. We will not waste our breath on the best of them. Rather let me turn toward you, so zealous, so ardent, so indefatigable a friend, and, if reports are true, so ill-requited. When your client was the ridicule of all the wits in England, of whom Canning and Frere were foremost, by your indignation at injustice he was righted, and more than righted. For although you attributed to him what perhaps was not greatly above his due, yet they who acknowledge

IMAGINARY CONVERSATIONS : ENGLISH

your authority, and contend under your banner, have carried him much further; nay, further, I apprehend, than is expedient or safe; and they will drop him before the day closes, where there is nobody to show the way home.

SOUTHEY. Could not you, Mr. Professor, do that good service to him, which others in another province have so often done to you?

PORSON. Nobody better, nobody with less danger from interruptions. But I must be even more enthusiastic than you are, if I prefer this excursion to your conversation. My memory, although the strongest part of me, is apt to stagger and swerve under verses piled incompactly. In our last meeting, you had him mostly to yourself, and you gave me abundantly of the best; at present, while my gruel is before me, it appears no unseasonable time to throw a little salt into both occasionally, as may suit my palate. You will not be displeased?

SOUTHEY. Certainly not, unless you are unjust; nor even then, unless I find the injustice to be founded on ill-will.

PORSON. That can not be. I stand

> Despicere unde queam tales, passimque videre
> Errare.[1]

Beside, knowing that my verdicts will be registered and recorded, I dare not utter a hasty or an inconsiderate one.[2] I lay it down as an axiom, that languor is the cause or the effect of most disorders, and is itself the very worst in poetry. Wordsworth's is an instrument which has no trumpet-stop.

SOUTHEY. But, such as it is, he blows it well. Surely it is something to have accompanied sound sense with pleasing harmony, whether in verse or prose.

PORSON. What is the worth of a musical instrument which has no

---

[1] Lucret., *De Nat.*, ii. 9.
[2] 1st ed. reads : " one. On this ground the small critics of the *Edinburgh Review* have incalculably the advantage over us. I lay it down . . . trumpet-stop.
" SOUTHEY. But . . . well.
" PORSON. To continue the metaphor, it seems to me, on the contrary, that a good deal of his breath is wiffed on the outside of the pipe, and goes for nothing. He wants absolutely all the four great requisites—creativeness, constructiveness, the sublime and the pathetic—and I see no reason to believe that he is capable or even sensible of the facetious, as Cowper and you have proved yourselves to be on many occasions.
" SOUTHEY. Among the opinions we form of our faculties, this is the one in which we are all the most liable to err. How many are suspicious that they are witty

high key? Even Pan's pipe rises above the baritones; yet I never should mistake it for an organ.

SOUTHEY. It is evident that you are ill-disposed to countenance the moderns; I mean principally the living.

PORSON. They are less disposed to countenance one another.

SOUTHEY. Where there is genius there should be geniality. The curse of quarrelsomeness, of hand against every man, was inflicted on the children of the desert; not on those who pastured their flocks on the fertile banks of the Euphrates, or contemplated the heavens from the elevated ranges of Chaldea.

PORSON. Let none be cast down by the malice of their contemporaries, or surprised at the defection of their associates, when he himself who has tended more than any man living to purify the poetry and to liberalize the criticism of his nation, is represented, by one whom he has called " inoffensive and virtuous," as an author all whose poetry is " not worth five shillings," and of whom another has said that " his verses sound like dumb-bells." Such are the expressions of two among your friends and familiars, both under obligations to you for the earliest and weightiest testimony in their favour. It would appear as if the exercise of the poetical faculty left irritation and weakness behind it, depriving its possessor at once of love and modesty, and making him resemble a spoilt child, who most indulges in its frowardness when you exclaim " what a spoilt child it is ! " and carry it crying and kicking out of the room. Your poetical neighbours, I hear, complain bitterly that you never have lauded them at large in your *Critical Reviews*.

SOUTHEY. I never have; because one grain of commendation more to the one than the other would make them enemies; and no language of mine would be thought adequate by either to his deserts. who raise no such suspicion in anyone else ? Wit appears to require a certain degree of unsteadiness in the character. Diamonds sparkle the most brilliantly on heads stricken by palsy.[1]

PORSON. Yes; but it is not every palsied head that has diamonds, nor every unsteady character that has wit. I am little complimentary; I must, however, say plainly, that you have indulged in it without any detriment to your fame. But where all these higher qualities of the poet are deficient, if we cannot get wit and humour, there ought at least to be abstinence from prolixity and dilation.

SOUTHEY. Surely it is something," etc.

---

[1] Diamonds dart their brightest lustre
From a palsy-shaken head.
    Wordsworth's " Inscriptions supposed to be found in
        and near a Hermit's Cell."

IMAGINARY CONVERSATIONS: ENGLISH

Each could not be called the greatest poet of the age; and by such compliance I should have been for ever divested of my authority as a critic. I lost, however, no opportunity of commending heartily what is best in them; and I have never obtruded on anyone's notice what is amiss, but carefully concealed it. I wish you were equally charitable.

PORSON. I will be; and generous too. There are several things in these volumes, beside that which you recited, containing just thoughts poetically expressed. Few, however, are there which do not contain much of the superfluous, and more of the prosaic. For one nod of approbation, I therefore give two of drowsiness. You accuse me of injustice, not only to this author, but to all the living. Now Byron is living; there is more spirit in Byron: Scott is living; there is more vivacity and variety in Scott. Byron exhibits *disjecti membra poetæ;* and strong muscles quiver throughout; but rather like galvanism than healthy life. There is a freshness in all Scott's scenery; a vigour and distinctness in all his characters. He seems the brother-in-arms of Froissart. I admire his *Marmion* in particular. Give me his massy claymore, and keep in the cabinet or the boudoir the jewelled hilt of the oriental dirk. The pages which my forefinger keeps open for you, contain a thing in the form of a sonnet; a thing to which, for insipidity, *tripe au naturel* is a dainty.

> Great men have been among us, hands that penned
> And tongues that uttered wisdom; better none.
> The later Sydney, Marvel, Harrington,
> Young Vane, and others who called Milton friend.[1]

When he potted these fat lampreys, he forgot the condiments, which the finest lampreys want; but how close and flat he has laid them! I see nothing in poetry since

> Four-and-twenty fiddlers all in a row,

fit to compare with it. How the good men and true stand, shoulder to shoulder, and keep one another up!

SOUTHEY. In these censures and sarcasms you forget

> Alcandrumque Haliumque Noemonaque Prytanimque.

From the Spanish I could bring forward many such.

PORSON. But here is a sonnet; and the sonnet admits not that approach to the prosaic which is allowable in the ballad, particularly

---

[1] *Sonnets dedicated to Liberty.*

SOUTHEY AND PORSON

in the ballad of action. For which reason I never laughed, as many did, at

> Lord Lion King at Arms.

Scott knew what he was about. In his chivalry, and in all the true, gaiety is mingled with strength, and facility with majesty. Lord Lion may be defended by the practice of the older poets who describe the like scenes and adventures. There is much resembling it, for instance, in *Chevy Chase*. *Marmion* is a poem of chivalry, partaking (in some measure) of the ballad, but rising in sundry places to the epic, and closing with a battle worthy of the *Iliad*. Ariosto has demonstrated that a romance may be so adorned by the apparatus, and so elevated by the spirit of poetry, as to be taken for an epic; but it has a wider field of its own, with outlying forests and chases. Spanish and Italian poetry often seems to run in extremely slender veins through a vast extent of barren ground.

SOUTHEY. But often, too, it is pure and plastic. The republicans, whose compact phalanx you have unsparingly ridiculed in Wordsworth's sonnet, make surely no sorrier a figure than

> A Don Alvaro de Luna
> Condestable de Castilla
> El Re Don Juan el Segundo.

PORSON. What an admirable Spanish scholar must Mr. Wordsworth be! How completely has he transfused into his own compositions all the spirit of those verses! Nevertheless, it is much to be regretted that, in resolving on simplicity, he did not place himself under the tuition of Burns; which quality Burns could have taught him in perfection; but others he never could have imparted to such an auditor. He would have sung in vain to him

> Scots wha hae wi' Wallace bled.

A song more animating than ever Tyrtæus sang to the fife before the Spartans. But simplicity in Burns is never stale and unprofitable. In Burns there is no waste of words out of an ill-shouldered sack; no troublesome running backward and forward of little, idle, ragged ideas; no ostentation of sentiment in the surtout of selfishness. Where was I?

> Better none—The later Sydney—Young Vane—
> These moralists could act—and—comprehend!

IMAGINARY CONVERSATIONS: ENGLISH

We might expect as much if "*none were better.*"

>They knew how genuine glory was—put on!

What is genuine is not *put on.*

>Taught us how rightfully—a nation—

Did what? Took up arms? No such thing. *Remonstrated?* No, nor that. What then? Why, "*shone*"! I am inclined to take the *shine* out of him for it. But how did the nation "rightfully *shine*"? In *splendour!*

>Taught us how rightfully a nation shone
>In splendour!

Now the secret is out; make the most of it. Another thing they taught us,

>What strength was.

They did indeed, with a vengeance. Furthermore, they taught us what we never could have expected from such masters,

>What strength was—*that could not bend* [1]
>But in magnanimous *meekness.*

Brave Oliver! brave and honest Ireton! We know pretty well where your magnanimity lay; we never could so cleverly find out your meekness. Did you leave it peradventure on the window-seat at Whitehall? The "later Sydney and young Vane, who could call Milton friend," and Milton himself, were gentlemen of your kidney, and they were all as meek as Moses with their arch-enemy.

>Perpetual emptiness: unceasing change.

How could the *change* be unceasing if the *emptiness* was perpetual?

>No single volume paramount: no *code:*

That is untrue. There is a Code, and the best in Europe: there was none promulgated under our Commonwealth.

>No master-spirit, no determined road,
>And equally a want of books and men.

SOUTHEY. I do not agree in this opinion: for although of late years France hath exhibited no man of exalted wisdom or great worth, yet surely her Revolution cast up several both intellectual

---
[1] Correct quotation: "would not bend," etc.

and virtuous. But, like fishes in dark nights and wintry weather, allured by deceptive torches, they came to the surface only to be speared.

PORSON. Although there were many deplorable ends in the French Revolution, there was none so deplorable as the last sonnet's. So diffuse and pointless and aimless is not only this, but fifty more, that the author seems to have written them in hedger's gloves, on blotting paper. If he could by any contrivance have added to

> Perpetual emptiness unceasing change,

or some occasional change at least, he would have been more tolerable.

SOUTHEY. He has done it lately: he has written, although not yet published, a vast number of sonnets on Capital Punishment.

PORSON. Are you serious? Already he has inflicted it far and wide, for divers attempts made upon him to extort his meaning.

SOUTHEY. Remember, poets superlatively great have composed things below their dignity. Suffice it to mention only Milton's translation of the Psalms.

PORSON. Milton was never half so wicked a regicide as when he lifted up his hand and smote King David. He has atoned for it, however, by composing a magnificent psalm of his own, in the form of a sonnet.

SOUTHEY. You mean on the massacre of the Protestants in Piedmont. This is indeed the noblest of sonnets.

PORSON. There are others in Milton comparable to it, but none elsewhere. In the poems of Shakespeare, which are printed as sonnets, there sometimes is a singular strength and intensity of thought, with little of that imagination which was afterward to raise him highest in the universe of poetry. Even the interest we take in the private life of this miraculous man cannot keep the volume in our hands long together. We acknowledge great power, but we experience great weariness. Were I a poet, I would much rather have written the *Allegro* or the *Penseroso* than all those, and moreover than nearly all that portion of our metre, which, wanting a definite term, is ranged under the capitulary of lyric.

SOUTHEY. Evidently you dislike the sonnet; otherwise there are very many in Wordsworth which would have obtained your approbation.

IMAGINARY CONVERSATIONS: ENGLISH

PORSON. I have no objection to see mince-meat put into small patty-pans, all of equal size, with ribs at odd distances: my objection lies mainly where I find it without salt or succulence. Milton was glad, I can imagine, to seize upon the sonnet, because it restricted him from a profuse expression of what soon becomes tiresome, praise. In addressing it to the Lord Protector, he was aware that prolixity of speech was both unnecessary and indecorous: in addressing it to Vane, and Lawrence, and Lawes, he felt that friendship is never the stronger for running through long periods: and in addressing it to

> Captain, or Colonel, or Knight-at-Arms,

he might be confident that fourteen such glorious lines were a bulwark sufficient for his protection against a royal army.

SOUTHEY. I am highly gratified at your enthusiasm. A great poet represents a great portion of the human race. Nature delegated to Shakespeare the interests and direction of the whole: to Milton a smaller part, but with plenary power over it: and she bestowed on him such fervour and majesty of eloquence as on no other mortal in any age.

PORSON. Perhaps, indeed, not on Demosthenes himself.

SOUTHEY. Without many of those qualities of which a loftier genius is constituted, without much fire, without a wide extent of range, without an eye that can look into the heart, or an organ that can touch it, Demosthenes had great dexterity and great force. By the union of these properties he always was impressive on his audience; but his orations bear less testimony to the seal of genius than the dissertations of Milton do.

PORSON. You judge correctly that there are several parts of genius in which Demosthenes is deficient, although in none whatever of the consummate orator. In that character there is no necessity for stage-exhibitions of wit, however well it may be received in an oration from the most persuasive and the most stately: Demosthenes, when he catches at wit, misses it, and falls flat in the mire. But by discipline and training, by abstinence from what is florid and too juicy, and by loitering with no idle words on his way, he acquired the hard muscles of a wrestler, and nobody could stand up against him with success or impunity.

SOUTHEY. Milton has equal strength, without an abatement of

beauty : not a sinew sharp or rigid, not a vein varicose or inflated. Hercules killed robbers and ravishers with his knotted club; he cleansed also royal stables by turning whole rivers into them : Apollo, with no labour or effort, overcame the Python; brought round him, in the full accordance of harmony, all the Muses; and illuminated with his sole splendour the universal world. Such is the difference I see between Demosthenes and Milton.

PORSON. Would you have anything more of Mr. Wordsworth, after the contemplation of two men who resemble a god and a demi-god in the degrees of power ?

SOUTHEY. I do not believe you can find in another of his poems so many blemishes and debilities as you have pointed out.

PORSON. Within the same space, perhaps not. But my complaint is not against a poverty of thought or expression here and there; it is against the sickliness and prostration of the whole body. I should never have thought it worth my while to renew and continue our conversation on it, unless that frequently such discussions lead to something better than the thing discussed; and unless we had abundant proofs that heaviness, taken opportunely, is the parent of hilarity. The most beautiful iris rises in bright expanse out of the minutest watery particles. Little fond as I am of quoting my own authority, permit me to repeat, in this sick chamber, an observation I once made in another almost as sick :

> When wine and gin are gone and spent,
> Small beer is then most excellent.

But small beer itself is not equally small nor equally vapid. Our friend's poetry, like a cloak of gum-elastic, makes me sweat without keeping me warm. With regard to the texture and sewing, what think you of

> No thorns can pierce *those* tender feet,[1]
> Whose *life* was as the violet sweet !

SOUTHEY. It should have been written " *her* tender feet "; because, as the words stand, it is the *life* of the tender feet that is sweet as the violet.

[1] *Epitaphs and Elegiac Poems.* " Elegiac Stanzas to Sir George Beaumont on the Death of his Sister-in-law." Version now reads : " No thorns can pierce her tender feet," etc.

IMAGINARY CONVERSATIONS: ENGLISH

PORSON. If there is a Wordsworth school, it certainly is not a grammar school. Is there any lower? It must be a school for very little boys, and a rod should be hung up in the centre. Take another sample.

> There is a *blessing* in the air,[1]
> Which *seems* a sense of joy to yield.

Was ever line so inadequate to its purpose as the second! If the blessing is evident and certain, the sense of joy arising from it must be evident and certain also, not merely seeming. Whatever only seems to yield a sense of joy, is scarcely a blessing. The verse adds nothing to the one before, but rather tends to empty it of the little it conveys.

> And shady groves, for recreation *framed*.[2]

" Recreation "! and in groves that are " *framed* "!

> With high respect and gratitude sincere.[3]

This is indeed a good end of a letter, but not of a poem. I am weary of decomposing these lines of sawdust: they verily would disgrace any poetry-professor.

SOUTHEY. Acknowledging the prosaic flatness of the last verse you quoted, the sneer with which you pronounced the final word seems to me unmerited.

PORSON. That is not gratitude which is not " sincere." A scholar ought to write nothing so incorrect as the phrase; a poet nothing so imbecile as the verse.

SOUTHEY. *Sincere* conveys a stronger sense to most understandings than the substantive alone would; words which we can do without, are not therefore useless. Many may be of service and efficacy to certain minds, which other minds pass over inobservantly; and there are many which, however light in themselves, wing the way for a well-directed point that could never reach the heart without it.

PORSON. This is true in general, but here inapplicable. I will

---

[1] *Poems of Sentiment and Reflection.* " To My Sister."
[2] So in early editions of *The Excursion*, altered by Wordsworth later.
[3]
> ... I appear
> Before thee, Lonsdale, and this work present,
> A token (may it prove a monument!)
> Of high respect and gratitude sincere.
> Dedication of *The Excursion*.

SOUTHEY AND PORSON

tell you what is applicable on all occasions, both in poetry and prose : αἰεὶ ἀριστεύειν : without reference to weak or common minds. If we give an entertainment, we do not set on the table pap and panada, just because a guest may be liable to indigestion : we rather send these dismal dainties to his chamber, and treat our heartier friends *opiparously*. I am wandering. If we critics are logical, it is the most that can be required at our hands : we should go out of our record if we were philosophical.

SOUTHEY. Without both qualities not even the lightest poetry should be reprehended. They do not exclude wit, which sometimes shows inexactnesses where mensuration would be tardy and incommodious.

PORSON. I fear I am at my wits' end under this exhausted receiver. Here are, however, a few more *Excerpta* for you. I shall add but few ; although I have marked with my pencil, in these two small volumes, more than seventy spots of sterility or quagmire. Mr. Wordsworth has hitherto had for his critics men who uncovered and darkened his blemishes in order to profit by them, and afterward expounded his songs and expatiated on his beauties in order to obtain the same result ; like picture-cleaners, who besmear a picture all over with washy dirtiness, then wipe away one-half of it, making it whiter than it ever was before. And nothing draws such crowds to the window.

I must make you walk with me up and down the deck, else nothing could keep you from sickness in this hull. How do you feel ? Will you sit down again ?

SOUTHEY. I will hear you and bear with you.

PORSON.
> I on the earth will go plodding on
> By myself cheerfully, till the day is done.

In what other author do you find such heavy trash ?

> How do you live and what is it you do ?

Show me anything like this in the worst poet that ever lived, and I will acknowledge that I am the worst critic. A want of sympathy is sometimes apparent in the midst of poetical pretences. Before us a gang of gipsies, perhaps after a long journey, perhaps after a marriage, perhaps after the birth of a child among them, are found resting a whole day in one place. What is the reflection on it?

> The *mighty* moon;
> This way she looks, *as if at them,*
> And they regard her not!
> *O! better wrong and strife;*
> *Rather vain deeds or evil than such life!* [1]

Mr. Southey! is this the man you represented to me, in our last conversation, as innocent and philosophical? What! better be guilty of robbery or bloodshed than not be looking at the moon? better let the fire go out and the children cry with hunger and cold? The philanthropy of poets is surely ethereal, and is here, indeed, a matter of moonshine.

SOUTHEY. The sentiment is indefensible. But in the stoutest coat a stitch may give way somewhere.

PORSON. Our business is, in this place, with humanity. We will go forward, if you please, to religion. Poets may take great liberties; but not much above the nymphs; they must be circumspect and orderly with Gods and Goddesses of any account and likelihood. Although the ancients laid many children at the door of Jupiter, which he never could be brought to acknowledge, yet it is downright impiety to attribute to the God of Mercy, as his, so ill-favoured a vixen as Slaughter.

SOUTHEY. We might enter into a long disquisition on this subject.

PORSON. God forbid we should do all we might do! Have you rested long enough? Come along, then, to Goody Blake's.

> *Old* Goody Blake was *old* and poor.[2]

What is the consequence?

> Ill-fed she was, and thinly clad,
> And any man who passed her door
> Might see—

What might he see?

> How *poor* a hut she had.

---

[1] Correct version:—
> Behold the mighty moon! this way
> She looks as if at them—but they
> Regard not her:—oh better wrong and strife
> (By nature transient) than such torpid life.
> *Poems of the Imagination.* "Gypsies."

[2] *Poems of the Imagination.* "Goody Blake and Harry Gill."

SOUTHEY AND PORSON

SOUTHEY. Ease and simplicity are two expressions often confounded and misapplied. We usually find ease arising from long practice, and sometimes from a delicate ear without it; but simplicity may be rustic and awkward; of which, it must be acknowledged, there are innumerable examples in these volumes. But surely it would be a pleasanter occupation to recollect the many that are natural, and to search out the few that are graceful.

PORSON. We have not yet taken our leave of Goody Blake.

> All day she spun in her *poor* dwelling,[1]
> And then 'twas three hours' work at night;
> *Alas! 'twas hardly worth the telling.*

I am quite of that opinion.

> But when the ice our streams *did fetter*,

Which was the fetterer? We may guess, but not from the grammar.

> Oh! then how her old bones would shake!
> You would have said, *if you had met her*,

Now, what would you have said? " Goody! come into my house, and warm yourself with a pint of ale at the kitchen fire "? No such naughty thing.

> You would have said, if you had met her,
> *'Twas a hard time for Goody Blake!*

SOUTHEY. If you said only *that*, you must have been the colder of the two, and God had done less for you than for her.

PORSON.

> Sad case it was, *as you may think*,[2]
> As every one who knew her says.

---

[1] Correct version:—

> . . . dwelling:
> And then her three hours' work at night,
> Alas! 'twas hardly worth the telling,
> It would not pay for candle-light.

[2] Correct version:—

> Sad case it was, as you may think,
> For very cold to go to bed;
> And then for cold not sleep a wink.
>
> Oh, joy for her! whene'er in winter
> The winds at night had made a rout;
> And scattered many a lusty splinter
> And many a rotten bough about.
> Yet never had she, well or sick,
> As every man who knew her says,
> A pile beforehand, turf or stick,
> Enough to warm her for three days.

IMAGINARY CONVERSATIONS: ENGLISH

Now, mind ye! all this balderdash is from " Poems purely of the Imagination." Such is what is notified to us in the title-page. In spite of a cold below zero, I hope you are awake, Mr. Southey! How do you find nose and ears? All safe and sound? Are the acoustics in tolerable order for harmony? Listen then.[1] Here follows " An Anecdote for Fathers, showing how the practice of Lying may be taught."[2] Such is the title, a somewhat prolix one: but for the soul of me I cannot find out the lie, with all my experience in those matters.

> Now tell me *had* you rather be?

Cannot our writers perceive that " had be " is not English? " Would you rather be " is grammatical. " *I'd* " sounds much the same when it signifies " I would." The latter with slighter contraction is " I 'ou'd "; hence the corruption goes farther.

SOUTHEY. This is just and true; but we must not rest too often, too long, or too pressingly, on verbal criticism.

PORSON. Do you, so accurate a grammarian, say this? To pass over such vulgarisms; which indeed the worst writers seldom fall into; if the words are silly, idle, or inapplicable, what becomes of the sentence? Those alone are to be classed as verbal critics who can catch and comprehend no more than a word here and there, and who lay more stress upon it, if faulty, than upon all the beauties in the best authors. But unless we, who sit perched and watchful on a higher branch than the word-catchers,* and who live on somewhat more substantial than syllables, do catch the word, that which is dependent on the word must escape us also. Now do me the favour to read the rest; for I have only just breath enough to

---

[1] 1st ed. reads: " Listen then. 'The west that burns like *one* dilated *sun.*' Are you ready for the sublime? Come on. ' Where in a mighty crucible expire The mountains!' It must now be all over with them if they expired. The self-same verse, however, continues to inform us, that, after this operation, they were—What think you? ' Glowing hot.'

" SOUTHEY. Coals of fire are generally on the outside of crucibles. The melting of the mountains is taken from the Holy Scriptures.

" PORSON. And never was there such a piece of sacrilege. Away he runs with them, and passes them (as thieves usually do) into the crucible. Here follows," etc.

[2] *Poems referring to the Period of Childhood.*

* Like word-catchers that live on syllables.—*Pope.*—W. S. L. [Correct version: " Each word-catcher that lives on syllables."]

converse, and your voice will give advantages to the poetry which mine can not.

SOUTHEY (*reads*).

> In careless mood he look'd at me,
>   While still I held him by the arm,
> And said, " At Kilve I 'd rather be
>   Than here at Liswyn-farm."
> Now, little Edward, *say why so,*
>   My little Edward, *tell me why.*

PORSON. Where is the difference of meaning betwixt

> Little Edward, *say why so,*

and

> Little Edward, *tell me why?*

SOUTHEY (*reads*).

> I cannot tell, I do not know.

PORSON. Again, where is the difference between " I cannot tell," and " I do not know " ?

SOUTHEY (*reads*).

> Why, this is strange, said I

PORSON. And I join in the opinion, if he intends it for poetry.

SOUTHEY (*reads*).

> For here are woods, hills smooth and warm ;[1]
> There surely must some reason be.

PORSON. This is among the least awkward of his inversions, which are more frequent in him, and more awkward, than in any of his contemporaries. Somewhat less so would be

> Surely some reason there must be,

or—

> Some reason surely there must be,

or—

> Some reason there must surely be.

Without ringing more changes, which we might do, he had the choice of four inversions, and he has taken the worst.

[1] Correct version : " For here are woods and green-hills warm," etc.

IMAGINARY CONVERSATIONS: ENGLISH

SOUTHEY (*reads*).
>His head he raised : there was *in sight*,
>It caught his eye, he saw it plain,

PORSON. What tautology, what trifling!

SOUTHEY (*reads*).
>Upon the house-top, glittering bright,
>A broad and gilded vane.

PORSON. Can we wonder that the boy saw "*plain*" "a broad and gilded vane," on the house-top just before him?

SOUTHEY (*reads*).
>Thus [1] did the boy his tongue *unlock*,

PORSON. I wish the father had kept the Bramah key in his breeches pocket.

SOUTHEY (*reads*).
>And eased his mind with this reply,[2]

PORSON. When he had written " did unlock," he should likewise have written " and ease," not " and eased."

SOUTHEY (*reads*).
>At Kilve there was no weathercock,
>And that's the reason why.
>O dearest, dearest boy! my heart
>For better lore would seldom yearn,
>Could I but teach the hundredth part
>Of what from thee I learn.

PORSON. What is flat ought to be plain; but who can expound to me the thing here signified? Who can tell me where is the lie, and which is the liar? If the lad told a lie, why praise him so? And if he spoke the obvious truth, what has he taught the father? "The hundredth part" of the lore communicated by the child to the parent may content *him*: but whoever is contented with a hundredfold more than all they both together have given *us*, cannot be very ambitious of becoming a senior wrangler. These, in good truth, are verses
>Pleni ruris et inficetiarum.

>Dank, limber verses, stuft with lakeside sedges,
>And propt with rotten stakes from broken hedges.

---

[1] Correct version: " Then did," etc.
[2] Correct version: " And thus to me he made reply," etc.

SOUTHEY AND PORSON

In the beginning of these I forbore to remark on

Kilve by the *green* sea.

When I was in Somersetshire, Neptune had not parted with his cream-coloured horses, and there was no *green* sea within the horizon. The ancients used to give the sea the colour they saw in it; Homer *dark-blue*, as in the Hellespont, the Ionian, and Ægæan; Virgil *blue-green*, as along the coast of Naples and Sorento: I suspect, from his character, he never went a league off land. He kept usually, both in person and poetry, to the *vada cærula*.

SOUTHEY. But he hoisted purple sails, and the mother of his Æneas was at the helm.

PORSON. How different from Mr. Wordsworth's wash-tub, pushed on the sluggish lake by a dumb idiot! We must leave the sea-shore for the ditch-side, and get down to " the small Celandine." I will now relieve you: give me the book.

Pleasures newly found are sweet,[1]

What a discovery! I never heard of any pleasures that are not.

When they lie about our feet.

Does that make them the sweeter?

February last.

How poetical!

February last, my heart
First at sight of thee was glad;
All unheard-of as thou art,
Thou must needs, *I think*, have had,
Celandine! and long ago,
Praise of which I nothing know.

What an inversion! A club-foot is not enough, but the heel is where the toe should be.

*I have not a doubt but he
Whosoe'er the man might be,*
Who the first with pointed rays
(*Workman worthy to be sainted*)
Set the signboard in a blaze," &c.

Really is there any girl of fourteen whose poetry, being like this,

[1] " To the Small Celandine." *Poems of the Fancy.*

IMAGINARY CONVERSATIONS : ENGLISH

the fondest mother would lay before her most intimate friends ? If a taste for what the French call *niaiserie* were prevalent, he who should turn his ridicule so effectively against it as to put it entirely out of fashion, would perform a far greater service than that glorious wit Cervantes, who shattered the last helmet of knight-errantry. For in knight-errantry there was the stout, there was the strenuous, there was sound homeliness under courtly guise, and the ornamental was no impediment to the manly. But in *niaiserie* there are ordinarily the debilitating fumes of self-conceit, and nothing is there about it but what is abject and ignoble. Shall we go on ?

SOUTHEY. As you heard me patiently when we met before, it is fair and reasonable that I should attend to you, now you have examined more carefully what I recommended to your perusal.[1] But I do not understand your merriment.

PORSON. My merriment is excited now, and was excited on a former occasion, by the fervour of your expression, that " Pindar

---

[1] 1st ed. reads : " perusal.
" PORSON. After a long preamble yon recorder saith,
   'Tis known that twenty years are past since she
Nobody has been mentioned yet, but you shall soon hear who *she* is —
   "(Her name is Martha Ray)
   Gave with a maiden's true good will
   Her company to Stephen Hill,
   And she was blithe and gay,
   While friends and kindred all approved
   Of him whom tenderly she loved ;
   And they had fixed their wedding day."[1]

" Now fifty pounds reward to whosoever shall discover, in any volume of poems, ancient or modern, eight consecutive verses so sedulously purified from all saline particles.

" SOUTHEY. I would not be the claimant.

" PORSON. And pray, Mr. Southey, can you imagine what day of the week that wedding day was ?

" SOUTHEY. I wonder he neglected to specify it. In general he is quite satisfactory on all such dates.

" PORSON. Neither can I ascertain the exact day of the week, entirely through his unusual inadvertence. But the wedding day, sure enough, began with ' The morning that must wed them both.' Odd enough that a wedding should unite *two* persons ! I believe, on recollection, that in the country parts of England such a result of such a ceremony is by no means uncommon. Here in London it is apt to embrace, in due course of time, another or more.

" SOUTHEY. A great deal of bad poetry does not of necessity make a bad poet ; but a little of what is excellent on a befitting subject constitutes a good one.

" PORSON. If ever this poet before us should write a *large* poem (a *great* poem is out of the question), he will stick small particles of friable earth together, and

---

[1] "The Thorn.' *Poems of the Imagination.*

SOUTHEY AND PORSON

would not have braced a poem to more vigour, nor Euripides have breathed into it more tenderness and passion."

SOUTHEY. I spoke of the *Laodamia*.

hang the conglutinated nodules under a thatched roof, the more picturesque and the more interesting (no doubt) for its procumbent elevation.

> "Strange *fits of passion* have I known;[1]
> And I will dare to tell
> But in the lover's ear alone
> What once *to me befell*.

"He has never told lover, or any other man, anything like a *fit of passion*. I wish he could do that.

> "In one of those sweet dreams I slept,
> Kind nature's gentlest boon.

What originality of thought, and what distinctness of expression!

> "My horse moved on; hoof after hoof
> He raised——

What a horse! Did ever another do the like? And never stopped! A Wandering Jew of horse flesh. There's a horse for you! Could any Yorkshire jockey promise more?

> "What fond and wayward thought will *slide*
> Into a lover's head!

Really, are you aware of that, Mr. Southey? But if they must *slide* anywhere, they can nowhere find a piece of harder ice to slide upon.

"SOUTHEY. Certainly there is not much warmth or much invention in several of the *Lyrical Ballads*. This species of poetry can do without them.

"PORSON. Then we can do without this species of poetry. But invention here is; you have never looked deep enough for it. Invention here is, I say again, and a sufficiency for a royal patent. What other man living has produced such a quantity of soup out of bare bones, however unsatisfactory may be the savour? 'O mercy! to myself I cried.' We sometimes say to ourselves, but seldom *cry* to ourselves in moments of reflection. 'If Lucy should be dead.'

"SOUTHEY. Surely this is very natural.

"PORSON. Do not force me to quote Voltaire on the *natural*, and to show you what he called it. If the presentiment had been followed up by the event, the poem, however tedious, had been less bald. In how different a manner has Mad. de Staël treated this very thought, which many others have also entertained! Do me the favour to take down *Corinne*, Excuse my pronounciation. ' Comme je tournais mes regards vers le ciel pour l'en remercier, je ne sçais par quel hazard une superstition de mon enfance s'est ranimée dans mon cœur. *La lune que je contemplais s'est couvert d'un nuage et l'aspect de ce nuage était funestre.*' At the close of the last volume (give it me) we find the consequence. ' Elle voulut lui parler, et n'en eut pas la force. Elle leva ses regards vers le ciel, et vit la lune qui se couvert du même nuage qu'elle avait fait remarquer à Lord Melvil, quand ils s'arrêtèrent sur le bord de la mer an allant à Naples. Alors elle lui montra de sa main mourante, et son dernier soupir fit retomber cette main.' Here you have the poetical; you had before the prose version of the same description.

"SOUTHEY. It is difficult to treat those subjects much better in the *ballad*.

"PORSON. Why then choose them? I will, however, prove to you that it is

---

[1] *Poems Founded on the Affection.* "Lucy."

IMAGINARY CONVERSATIONS: ENGLISH

PORSON. Although I gave way to pleasantry instead of arguing the point with you, I had a great deal more to say, Mr. Southey, than no such a difficult matter to treat them much better, and with a very small stock of Poetry.

"SOUTHEY. I am anxious to see the experiment, especially if you yourself make it.

"PORSON. I have written the characters so minute, according to my custom, that I cannot make them out distinctly in the enclosure of the green curtains. Take up yon paper from under the castor oil bottle; yes that—now read.

"SOUTHEY (*reads*).

I.

"Hetty, old Dinah Mitchell's daughter,
Had left the side of Derwentwater
   About the end of summer.
I went to see her at her cot,
Her and her mother, who were not
   Expecting a new comer.

II.

"They both were standing at one tub,
You might have heard their knuckles rub
   The hempen sheet they washed.
The mother suddenly turned round,
The daughter cast upon the ground
   Her eyes like one abashed.

III.

"Now of this Hetty there is told
A tale to move both young and old,
   A true pathetic story;
'Tis well it happened in my time,
For, much I fear, no other rhyme
   Than mine could spread her glory.

IV.

"The rains had fallen for three weeks,
The roads were looking like beefsteaks
   Gashed deep to make them tender;
Only along the ruts you might
See little pebbles black and white,
   Walking, you'd think—must end here.

V.

"Hetty, whom many a loving thought
Incited, did not care a groat
   About the mire and wet.
She went upstairs, unlocked the chest,
Slipped her clean shift on, not her best;
   A prudent girl was Het.

VI.

"Both stockings gartered, she drew down
Her petticoat and then her gown,
   And next she clapped her hat on.
A sudden dread came o'er her mind,
Good gracious now, if I should find
   No string to tie my patten!

"PORSON. Come, come, do not throw the paper down so disdainfully. I am waiting to hear you exclaim, 'Sume superbiam quæsitam meritis.' Ah, you

SOUTHEY AND PORSON

I said at the first starting of so heavy a runner in his race with Pindar. We will again walk over a part of the ground.

> With sacrifice before the rising morn
> Performed, my slaughtered lord *have I " required,"* [1]
> And in thick darkness, amid shades forlorn,
> Him of the infernal gods *have I " desired."*

I only remember, at the time, that the second and fourth verses terminate too much alike. " Desired " may just as well be where " required " is, and " required " where " desired " is : both are wretchedly weak, and both are preceded by the same words, " have I."

SOUTHEY. He has corrected them at your suggestion ; not indeed much (if anything) for the better ; and he has altered the conclusion, making it more accordant with morality and Christianity, but somewhat less perhaps with Greek manners and sentiments, as they existed in the time of the Trojan war.

PORSON. Truly it was far enough from these before. Acknowledge that the fourth line is quite unnecessary, and that the word " performed " in the second, is prosaic.

SOUTHEY. I would defend the whole poem.

PORSON. To defend the whole, in criticism as in warfare, you must look with peculiar care to the weakest part. In our last Conversation, you expressed a wish that I should examine the verses " analytically and severely." Had I done it severely, you would have caught me by the wrist and have intercepted the stroke. Show me, if you can, a single instance of falsity or unfairness in any of these remarks. If you can not, pray indulge me at least in as much hilarity as my position, between a sick bed and a sorry book, will allow me.

poets are like the curs of Constantinople. They all have their own quarters, and drive away or worry to death every intruder. The mangier they are the fiercer are they. Never did I believe until now that any poet was too great for your praise. Well, what do you think, for we of the brotherhood are impatient to hear all about it ? Zealous creature !

" SOUTHEY. Really I find no cause for triumph.

" PORSON. Nor do I, but my merriment is excited," etc.

[1] See note on 1st Conversation. These lines had been altered by Wordsworth in 1827 to their present version :—

> With sacrifice before the rising morn
> Vows have I made by fruitless hope inspired ;
> And from the infernal Gods, 'mid shades forlorn
> Of night, my slaughtered lord have I required.

IMAGINARY CONVERSATIONS: ENGLISH

SOUTHEY. I must catch the wrist here. The book, as you yourself conceded, comprehends many beautiful things.

PORSON. I have said it; I have repeated it; and I will maintain it: but there are more mawkish. This very room has many things of value in it; yet the empty phials are worth nothing, and several of the others are uninviting. Beside yourself, I know scarcely a critic in England sufficiently versed and sufficiently candid to give a correct decision on our poets. All others have their parties; most have their personal friends. On the side opposite to these, you find no few morose and darkling, who conjure up the phantom of an enemy in every rising reputation. You are too wise and too virtuous to resemble them. On this cool green bank of literature you stand alone. I always have observed that the herbage is softest and finest in elevated places; and that we may repose with most safety and pleasantness on lofty minds. The little folks who congregate beneath you, seem to think of themselves as Pope thought of the women:

The *critic* who deliberates is lost.

SOUTHEY. Hence random assertions, heats, animosities, missiles of small wit, clouds hiding every object under them, forked lightnings of ill-directed censure, and thunders of applause lost in the vacuity of space.[1] I do not find that our critics are fond of suggesting any emendations of the passages they censure in their contemporaries, as you have done in the ancients. Will not you tell me, for the benefit of the author, if there is anything in the *Lyrical Ballads* which you could materially improve?

---

[1] 1st ed. reads: " space. What do you think now of this? ' An ethereal purity of sentiment which could only emanate from the soul of a woman.' [1]
" PORSON. Such criticism is, indeed, pure oil from the *Minerva Press*.
" SOUTHEY. No, indeed; it is train oil, imported neat from Jeffrey's.
" PORSON. Where will you find, in all his criticisms, one felicitous expression? Yet his noxious gas is convertible to more uses than Hallam's caput mortuum that lies under it.
" SOUTHEY. Better is it that my fellow-townsman should ' plod his weary way ' in the Heart of Midlothian, than interline with a sputtering pen the fine writing of Sismondi.
" PORSON. If these fellows know anything about antiquity, I would remind them that the Roman soldier on his march carried not only vinegar, but lard, and that the vinegar was made wholesome by temperate use and proportionate dilution."

---

[1] *Edinburgh Review* on the poems of Felicia Hemans.

SOUTHEY AND PORSON

Porson. Tell me first if you can turn a straw into a walking-stick. When you have done this, I will try what I can do. But I never can do that for Mr. Wordsworth which I have sometimes done for his betters. His verses are as he wrote them; and we must leave them as they are: theirs are not so; and faults committed by transcribers or printers may be corrected. In *Macbeth*, for example, we read,

> The raven himself is hoarse,
> That croaks the fatal entrance of Duncan, &c.

Is there anything marvellous in a raven being hoarse? which is implied by the word " himself ": that is to say, *even* the raven, &c. Shakespeare wrote one letter more: " The raven himself is hoarser."

Southey. Surely you could easily correct in the *Lyrical Ballads* faults as obvious.

Porson. If they were as well worth my attention.

Southey. Many are deeply interested by the simple tales they convey in such plain easy language.

Porson. His language is often harsh and dissonant, and his gait is like one whose waistband has been cut behind. There may be something " interesting " in the countenance of the sickly, and even of the dead, but it is only life that can give us enjoyment. Many beside lexicographers place in the same line *simplicity* and *silliness*: they can not separate them as we can. They think us monsters, because we do not see what they see, and because we see plainly what they never can see at all. There is often most love where there is the least acquaintance with the object loved. So it is with these good people who stare at the odd construction of our minds. Homely and poor thoughts may be set off by facility and gracefulness of language; here they often want both.

Southey. Harmonious words render ordinary ideas acceptable; less ordinary, pleasant; novel and ingenious ones, delightful. As pictures and statues, and living beauty too, show better by *music-light*, so is poetry irradiated, vivified, glorified, and raised into immortal life, by harmony.

Porson. Ay, Mr. Southey, and another thing may be noticed. The Muses should be as slow to loosen the zone as the Graces * are. The poetical form, like the human, to be beautiful, must be succinct.

---

* Zonamque segnes solvere Gratiæ.—W. S. L.

IMAGINARY CONVERSATIONS : ENGLISH

When we grow corpulent, we are commonly said to *lose our figure*. By this loss of figure we are reduced and weakened. So, there not being bone nor muscle nor blood enough in your client, to rectify and support his accretions, he collapses into unswathable flabbiness. We must never disturb him in this condition, which appears to be thought, in certain parts of the country, as much a peculiar mark of Heaven's favour, as idiocy is among the Turks. I have usually found his sticklers, like those good folks, dogmatical and dull. One of them lately tried to persuade me that he never is so highly poetical as when he is deeply metaphysical. When I stared, he smiled benignly, and said, with a deep sigh that relieved us both, "*Ah! you may be a Grecian!*" He then quoted fourteen German poets of the first order, and expressed his compassion for Æschylus and Homer.

SOUTHEY. What a blessing are metaphysics to our generation! A poet or other who can make nothing clear, can stir up enough sediment to render the bottom of a basin as invisible as the deepest gulf in the Atlantic. The shallowest pond, if turbid, has depth enough for a goose to hide its head in.

PORSON. I quoted to my instructor in criticism the *Anecdote for Fathers :* he assured me it is as clear as day ; not meaning a London day in particular, such as this. But there are sundry gentlemen who, like cats, see clearly in the dark, and far from clearly anywhere else. Hold them where, if they were tractable and docile, you might show them your objections, and they will swear and claw at you to show how spiteful you are. Others say they wonder that judicious men differ from them. No doubt they differ ; and there is but one reason for it, which is, because they are so. Again, there are the gentle and conciliatory, who say merely that they can not quite think with you. Have they thought at all? Granting both premises, have they thought, or can they think rightly?

SOUTHEY. To suppose the majority can, is to suppose an absurdity; and especially on subjects which require so much preparatory study, such a variety of instruction, such deliberation, delicacy, and refinement. When I have been told, as I often have been, that I shall find very few of my opinion, certainly no compliment was intended me ; yet there are few, comparatively, whom nature has gifted with intuition or exquisite taste ; few whose ideas have been drawn, modelled, marked, chiselled, and polished, in a *studio* well lighted

SOUTHEY AND PORSON

from above. The opinion of a thousand millions who are ignorant or ill-informed, is not equal to the opinion of only one who is wiser. This is too self-evident for argument; yet we hear about the common sense of mankind! A common sense which, unless the people receive it from their betters, leads them only into common error. If such is the case, and we have the testimony of all ages for it, in matters which have most attracted their attention, matters in which their nearest interests are mainly concerned, in politics, in religion, in the education of their families, how greatly, how surpassingly, must it be in those which require a peculiar structure of understanding, a peculiar endowment of mind, a peculiar susceptibility, and almost an undivided application. In what regards poetry, I should just as soon expect a sound judgment of its essentials from a boatman or a waggoner, as from the usual set of persons we meet in society; persons not uneducated, but deriving their intelligence from little gutters and drains round about. The mud is easily raised to the surface in so shallow a receptacle, and nothing is seen distinctly or clearly. Whereas the humbler man has received no false impressions, and may therefore to a limited extent be right. As for books in general, it is only with men like you that I ever open my lips upon them in conversation. In my capacity of reviewer, dispassionate by temperament, equitable by principle, and, moreover, for fear of offending God and of suffering in my conscience, I dare not leave behind me in my writings either a false estimate or a frivolous objection.

PORSON. Racy wine comes from the high vineyard. There is a spice of the scoundrel in most of our literary men; an itch to filch and detract in the midst of fair-speaking and festivity. This is the reason why I never have much associated with them. There is also another: we have nothing in common but the alphabet. The most popular of our critics have no heart for poetry; it is morbidly sensitive on one side, and utterly callous on the other. They dandle some little poet, and will never let you take him off their knees; him they feed to bursting with their curds and whey. Another they warn off the premises, and will give him neither a crust nor a crumb, until they hear he has succeeded to a large estate in popularity, with plenty of dependants; then they sue and supplicate to be admitted among the number; and, lastly, when they hear of his death, they put on mourning, and advertise to raise a monument or a club-room

IMAGINARY CONVERSATIONS: ENGLISH

to his memory. You, Mr. Southey, will always be considered the soundest and the fairest of our English critics; and, indeed, to the present time, you have been the only one of very delicate perception in poetry. But your admirable good-nature has thrown a costly veil over many defects and some deformities. To guide our aspirants, you have given us (and here accept my thanks for them) several good *inscriptions*, much nearer the style of antiquity than any others in our language, and better, indeed much better, than the Italian ones of Chiabrera. I myself have nothing original about me; but here is an inscription which perhaps you will remember in Theocritus,* and translated to the best of my ability.

INSCRIPTION ON A STATUE OF LOVE.

Mild he may be, and innocent to view,
Yet who on earth can answer for him? You
Who touch the little god, mind what ye do!

Say not that none has caution'd you: although
Short be his arrow, slender be his bow,
The king Apollo's never wrought such woe.

This and one petty skolion, are the only things I have attempted. The skolion is written by Geron.

He who in waning age would moralize,
With leaden finger weighs down joyous eyes;
Youths too, with all they say, can only tell
    What maids know well:

And yet if they are kind, they hear it out
As patiently as if they clear'd a doubt.
I will not talk like either. Come with me;
    Look at the tree!

Look at the tree while still some leaves are green;
Soon must they fall. Ah! in the space between
Lift those long eyelashes above your book,
    For the last look!

SOUTHEY. I cannot recollect them in the Greek.
PORSON. Indeed! Perhaps I dreamt it then; for Greek often plays me tricks in my dreams.

* Where?—W. S. L.

SOUTHEY AND PORSON

SOUTHEY. I wish it would play them oftener with our poets. It seems to entertain a peculiar grudge against the most celebrated of them.

PORSON. Our conversation has been enlivened and enriched by what seemed sufficiently sterile in its own nature; but, by tossing it about, we have made it useful. Just as certain lands are said to profit by scrapings from the turnpike-road. After this sieving, after this pounding and trituration of the coarser particles, do you really find in Mr. Wordsworth such a vigour and variety, such a selection of thoughts and images, as authorise you to rank him with Scott and Burns and Cowper?

SOUTHEY. Certainly not: but that is no reason why he should be turned into ridicule on all occasions. Must he be rejected and reviled as a poet, because he wishes to be also a philosopher? Or must he be taunted and twitted for weakness, because by his nature he is quiescent?

PORSON. No indeed; though much of this quiescency induces debility, and is always a sign of it in poetry. Let poets enjoy their sleep; but let them not impart it, nor take it amiss if they are shaken by the shoulder for the attempt. I reprehended at our last meeting, as severely as you yourself did, those mischievous children who played their pranks with him in his easy-chair; and I drove away from him those old women who brought him their drastics from the Edinburgh Dispensary. Poor souls! they are all swept off! Sydney Smith, the wittiest man alive, could not keep them up, by administering a nettle and a shove to this unsaved remnant of the Baxter Christians.

SOUTHEY. The heaviest of them will kick at you the most viciously. Castigation is not undue to him; for he has snipt off as much as he could pinch from every author of reputation in his time. It is less ungenerous to expose such people than to defend them.

PORSON. Let him gird up his loins, however, and be gone; we will turn where correction ought to be milder, and may be more efficient. Give a trifle of strength and austerity to the squashiness of our friend's poetry, and reduce in almost every piece its quantity to half. Evaporation will render it likelier to keep. Without this process, you will shortly have it only in the form of extracts. You talk of philosophy in poetry; and in poetry let it exist; but let its veins run through a poem, as our veins run through the body, and never be too apparent; for the prominence of veins, in both alike, is a symptom of weakness, feverishness, and senility. On the ground where we are now standing, you have taken one end of the blanket, and I the other; but it is I chiefly who have shaken the dust out. Nobody can pass us without seeing it rise against the sunlight, and observing what a heavy cloud there is of it. While it lay quietly in the flannel, it lay without suspicion.

SOUTHEY. Let us return, if you please, to one among the partakers of your praise, whose philosophy is neither obtrusive nor abstruse. I am highly gratified by your commendation of Cowper, than whom there never was a more virtuous or more amiable man. In some passages, he stands quite unrivalled by any recent poet of this century: none, indeed, modern or ancient, has touched the heart more delicately, purely, and effectively, than he has done in *Crazy Kate*,[1] in Lines on his *Mother's Picture*, in *Omai*, and on hearing *Bells at a Distance*.

PORSON. Thank you for the mention of bells. Mr. Wordsworth, I remember, speaks, in an authoritative and scornful tone of censure, on Cowper's " church-going " bell, treating the expression as a gross impropriety and absurdity. True enough, the *church-going* bell does not go to church any more than I do; neither does the *passing*-bell pass any more than I; nor does the *curfew*-bell cover any more fire than is contained in Mr. Wordsworth's poetry: but the church-going bell is that which is rung for people going to church; the passing-bell for those passing to heaven; the curfew-bell for the burgesses and villagers to cover their fires. He would not allow me to be called *well-spoken*, nor you to be called *well-read*; and yet, by this expression, I should mean to signify that you have read much, and I should employ another in signifying that you have been much read. Incomparably better is Cowper's *Winter* than Virgil's, which is indeed a disgrace to the *Georgics*; or than Thomson's, which in places is grand. But would you on the whole compare Cowper with Dryden?

SOUTHEY. Dryden possesses a much richer store of thoughts, expatiates upon more topics, has more vigour, vivacity, and animation He is always shrewd and penetrating, explicit and perspicuous, concise where conciseness is desirable, and copious where copiousness can yield delight. When he aims at what is highest in poetry, the dramatic, he falls below his *Fables*. However, I would not com-

[1] *The Task*, Bk. i.

SOUTHEY AND PORSON

pare the poetical power of Cowper with his; nor would I, as some have done, pit Young against him. Young is too often fantastical and frivolous; he pins butterflies to the pulpit-cushion; he suspends against the grating of the charnel-house coloured lamps and comic transparencies, Cupid, and the cat and the fiddle; he opens a store-house filled with minute particles of heterogenous wisdom, and unpalatable gobbets of ill-concocted learning, contributions from the classics, from the schoolmen, from homilies, and from farces. What you expect to be an elegy turns out an epigram; and when you think he is bursting into tears, he laughs in your face. Do you go with him into his closet, prepared for an admonition or a rebuke, he shakes his head, and you sneeze at the powder and perfumery of his peruke. Wonder not if I prefer to his pungent essences the incense which Cowper burns before the altar.

PORSON. Young was, in every sense of the word, an ambitious man. He had strength, but wasted it. Blair's *Grave* has more spirit in it than the same portion of the *Night Thoughts;* but never was poetry so ill put together; never was there so good a poem, of the same extent, from which so great a quantity of what is mere trash might be rejected. The worse blemish in it is the ridicule and scoffs, cast not only on the violent and grasping, but equally on the gentle, the beautiful, the studious, the eloquent, and the manly. It is ugly enough to be carried quietly to the grave; it is uglier to be hissed and hooted into it. Even the quiet astronomer,

> With study pale, and midnight vigils spent,

is not permitted to depart in peace, but (of all the men in the world)! is called a " proud man," and is coolly and flippantly told that

> Great heights are hazardous to the weak head,

which the poet might have turned into a verse, if he had tried again, as we will:

> To the weak head great heights are hazardous.

In the same funny style he writes,

> O that some courteous ghost would blab it out,[1]
> What 'tis they are.

---

[1] Correct version :—
"... out
What 'tis you are and shortly we must be."

IMAGINARY CONVERSATIONS : ENGLISH

Courtesy and blabbing, in this upper world of ours, are thought to be irreconcilable; but blabbing may not be indecorous nor derogatory to the character of courtesy in a ghost. However, the expression is an uncouth one; and when we find it so employed, we suspect the ghost cannot have been keeping good company, but, as the king said to the miller of Mansfield, that his " courtesy is but small." Cowper plays in the play-ground, and not in the churchyard. Nothing of his is out of place or out of season. He possessed a rich vein of ridicule, but he turned it to good account, opening it on prig parsons, and graver and worse impostors. He was among the first who put to flight the mischievous little imps of allegory, so cherished and fondled by the Wartons. They are as bad in poetry as mice in a cheese-room. You poets are still rather too fond of the unsubstantial. Some will have nothing else than what they call pure imagination. Now air-plants ought not to fill the whole conservatory; other plants, I would modestly suggest, are worth cultivating, which send their roots pretty deep into the ground. I hate both poetry and wine without body. Look at Shakespeare, Bacon, and Milton; were these your pure-imagination-men? The least of them, whichever it was, carried a jewel of poetry about him, worth all his tribe that came after. Did the two of them who wrote in verse build upon nothing? Did their predecessors? And, pray, whose daughter was the Muse they invoked? Why, Memory's. They stood among substantial men, and sang upon recorded actions. The plain of Scamander, the promontory of Sigæum, the palaces of Tros and Dardanus, the citadel in which the Fates sang mournfully under the image of Minerva, seem fitter places for the Muses to alight on, than artificial rockwork or than faery-rings. But your great favourite, I hear, is Spenser, who shines in allegory, and who, like an aerolite, is dull and heavy when he descends to the ground.

SOUTHEY. He continues a great favourite with me still, although he must always lose a little as our youth declines. Spenser's is a spacious but somewhat low chamber, hung with rich tapestry, on which the figures are mostly disproportioned, but some of the faces are lively and beautiful; the furniture is part creaking and worm-eaten, part fragrant with cedar and sandal-wood and aromatic gums and balsams; every table and mantelpiece and cabinet is covered with gorgeous vases, and birds, and dragons, and houses in the air.

PORSON. There is scarcely a poet of the same eminence, whom I have found it so delightful to read in, or so tedious to read through. Give me Chaucer in preference. He slaps us on the shoulder, and makes us spring up while the dew is on the grass, and while the long shadows play about it in all quarters. We feel strong with the freshness round us, and we return with a keener appetite, having such a companion in our walk. Among the English poets, both on this side and the other side of Milton, I place him next to Shakespeare; but the word *next*, must have nothing to do with the word *near*. I said before, that I do not estimate so highly as many do the mushrooms that sprang up in a ring under the great oak of Arden.

SOUTHEY. These authors deal in strong distillations for foggy minds that want excitement. In few places is there a great depth of sentiment, but everywhere vast exaggeration and insane display. I find the over-crammed curiosity-shop, with its incommodious appendages, some grotesquely rich, all disorderly and disconnected. Rather would I find, as you would, the well-proportioned hall, with its pillars of right dimensions at right distances; with its figures, some in high relief and some in lower; with its statues and its busts of glorious men and women, whom I recognise at first sight; and its tables of the rarest marbles and richest gems, inlaid in glowing porphyry, and supported by imperishable bronze. Without a pure simplicity of design, without a just subordination of characters, without a select choice of such personages as either have interested us or must by the power of association, without appropriate ornaments laid on solid materials, no admirable poetry of the first order can exist.

PORSON. Well, we can not get all these things, and we will not cry for them. Leave me rather in the curiosity-shop than in the nursery. By your reference to the noble models of antiquity, it is evident that those poets most value the ancients who are certain to be among them. In our own earlier poets, as in the earlier Italian painters, we find many disproportions; but we discern the dawn of truth over the depths of expression. These were soon lost sight of, and every new comer passed further from them. I like Pietro Perugino a thousand-fold better than Carlo Maratta, and Giotto a thousand-fold better than Carlo Dolce. On the same principle, the daybreak of Chaucer is pleasanter to me than the hot dazzling noon of Byron.

SOUTHEY. I am not confident that we ever speak quite correctly of

IMAGINARY CONVERSATIONS: ENGLISH

those who differ from us essentially in taste, in opinion, or even in style. If we cordially wish to do it, we are apt to lay a restraint on ourselves, and to dissemble a part of our convictions.

PORSON. An error seldom committed.

SOUTHEY. Sometimes, however. I for example did not expose in my criticisms half the blemishes I discovered in the style and structure of Byron's poetry, because I had infinitely more to object against the morals it disseminated; and what must have been acknowledged for earnestness in the greater question, might have been mistaken for captiousness in the less. His partisans, no one of whom probably ever read Chaucer, would be indignant at your preference. They would wonder, but hardly with the same violence of emotion, that he was preferred to Shakespeare. Perhaps his countrymen in his own age, which rarely happens to literary men overshadowingly great, had glimpses of his merit. One would naturally think that a personage of Camden's gravity, and placed beyond the pale of poetry, might have spoken less contemptuously of some he lived among, in his admiration of Chaucer. He tells us both in prose and verse, by implication, how little he esteemed Shakespeare. Speaking of Chaucer, he says, "he, surpassing all others, without question, in wit, and leaving our smattering poetasters by many leagues behind him,

'Jam monte potitus
Ridet anhelantem dura ad fastigia turbam.'"

Which he thus translates for the benefit of us students in poetry and criticism:

When once himself the steep top-hill had won,
At all the sort of them he laughed anon,
To see how they, the pitch thereof to gain,
Puffing and blowing do climbe up in vain.

Nevertheless we are indebted to Camden for preserving the best Latin verses, and indeed the only good ones, that had hitherto been written by any of our countrymen. They were written in an age when great minds were attracted by greater, and when tribute was paid where tribute was due, with loyalty and enthusiasm.

Drace! pererrati novit quem terminus orbis
Quem-que simul mundi vidit uterque polus.
Si taceant homines, facient te sidera notum;
Sol nescit comitis immemor esse sui.[1]

---

[1] Camden's *Brittania*, i. 34.

SOUTHEY AND PORSON

PORSON. A subaltern in the supplementary company of the Edinburgh sharpshooters, much prefers the slender Italians, who fill their wallets with scraps from the doors of rich old houses. To compare them in rank and substance with those on whose bounty they feed, is too silly for grave reprehension. But there are certain men who are driven by necessity to exhibit some sore absurdity; it is their only chance of obtaining a night's lodging in the memory.

SOUTHEY. Send the Ismaelite back again to his desert. He has indeed no right to complain of you; for there are scarcely two men of letters at whom he has not cast a stone, although he met them far beyond the tents and the pasturage of his tribe; and leave those poets also; and return to consider attentively the one, much more original, on whom we began our discourse.

PORSON. Thank you. I have lain in ditches ere now, but not willingly, nor to contemplate the moon, nor to gather celandine. I am reluctant to carry a lantern in quest of my man, and am but little contented to be told that I may find him at last, if I look long enough and far enough. One who exhibits no sign of life in the duration of a single poem, may at once be given up to the undertaker.

SOUTHEY. It would be fairer in you to regard the aim and object of the poet, when he tells you what it is, than to linger in those places where he appears to disadvantage.

PORSON. My oil and vinegar are worth more than the winter cabbage you have set before me, and are ill spent upon it. In what volume of periodical criticism do you not find it stated, that the aim of an author being such or such, the only question is whether he has attained it? Now, instead of this being the only question to be solved, it is pretty nearly the one least worthy of attention. We are not to consider whether a foolish man has succeeded in a foolish undertaking; we are to consider whether his production is worth anything, and why it is, or why it is not? Your cook, it appears, is disposed to fry me a pancake; but it is not his intention to supply me with lemon-juice and sugar. Pastiness and flatness are the qualities of a pancake, and thus far he has attained his aim; but if he means it for me, let him place the accessories on the table, lest what is insipid and clammy, and (as housewives with great propriety call it) sad, grow into duller accretion and inerter viscidity the more I masticate it. My good Mr. Southey, do not be offended at these

IMAGINARY CONVERSATIONS: ENGLISH

homely similes. Socrates uses no other in the pages of the stately Plato; they are all, or nearly all, borrowed from the artisan and the trader. I have plenty of every sort at hand, but I always take the most applicable, quite indifferent to the smartness and glossiness of its trim. If you prefer one from another quarter, I would ask, where is the advantage of drilling words for verses, when the knees of those verses are so weak that they can not march from the parade?

SOUTHEY. Flatnesses are more apparent to us in our language than in another, especially than in Latin and Greek. Beside, we value things proportionally to the trouble they have given us in the acquisition. Hence, in some measure, the importance we assign to German poetry. The meaning of every word, with all its affinities and relations, pursued with anxiety and caught with difficulty, impresses the understanding, sinks deep into the memory, and carries with it more than a column of our own, in which equal thought is expended, and equal fancy is displayed. The Germans have among them many admirable poets; but if we had even greater, ours would seem smaller, both because there is less haziness about them, and because, as I said before, they would have given less exercise to the mind. He who has accumulated by a laborious life more than a sufficiency for its wants and comforts, turns his attention to the matter gained, oftentimes without a speculation at the purposes to which he might apply it. The man who early in the day has overcome, by vigilance and restraint, the strong impulses of his blood toward intemperance, falls not into it after, but stands composed and complacent upon the cool clear eminence, and hears within himself, amid the calm he has created, the tuneful pæan of a godlike victory. Yet he loves the Virtue more because he fought for her than because she crowned him. The scholar who has deducted from adolescence many hours of recreation, and, instead of indulging in it, has embarked in the depths of literature; he who has left his own land far behind him, and has carried off rich stores of Greek; not only values it superlatively, as is just, but places all those who wrote in it too nearly on a level one with another, and the inferior of them above some of the best moderns.

PORSON. Dignity of thought arose from the Athenian form of government, propriety of expression from the genius of the language, from the habitude of listening daily to the most elaborate orations and dramas, and of contemplating at all hours the exquisite works of art, invited to them by gods and heroes. These environed the aspiring young poet, and their chasteness allowed him no swerving.

SOUTHEY. Yet weakly children were born to Genius in Attica as elsewhere.

PORSON. They were exposed and died. The Greek poets, like nightingales, sing " in shadiest covert hid "; you rarely catch a glimpse of the person, unless at a funeral or a feast, or where the occasion is public. Mr. Wordsworth, on the contrary, strokes down his waistcoat, hems gently first, then hoarsely, then impatiently, rapidly, and loudly. You turn your eyes, and see more of the showman than of the show. I do not complain of this; I only make the remark.

SOUTHEY. I dislike such comparisons and similes. It would have been better had you said he stands forth in sharp outline, and is, as the moon was said to be, without an atmosphere.

PORSON. Stop there. I discover more atmosphere than moon. You are talking like a poet; I must talk like a grammarian. And here I am reminded I found in his grammar but one pronoun, and that is the pronoun *I*. He can devise no grand character, and indeed no variety of smaller: his own image is reflected from floor to roof in every crystallisation of the chilly cavern. He shakes us with no thunder of anger; he leads us into no labyrinth of love; we lament on the stormy shore no Lycidas of his; and even the Phillis who meets us at her cottage-gate, is not Phillis the neat-handed. Byron has likewise been censured for egoism, and the censure is applicable to him nearly in the same degree. But so laughable a story was never told of Byron as the true and characteristical one related of your neighbour, who, being invited to read in company a novel of Scott's, and finding at the commencement a quotation from himself, totally forgot the novel, and recited his own poem from beginning to end, with many comments and more commendations. Yours are quite gratuitous; for it is reported of him that he never was heard to commend the poetry of any living author.

SOUTHEY. Because he is preparing to discharge the weighty debt he owes posterity. Instead of wasting his breath on extraneous praises, we never have been seated five minutes in his company, before he regales us with those poems of his own, which he is the most apprehensive may have slipped from our memory; and he

IMAGINARY CONVERSATIONS: ENGLISH

delivers them with such a summer murmur of fostering modulation as would perfectly delight you.

PORSON. My horse is apt to shy when I hang him at any door where he catches the sound of a ballad; and I run out to seize bridle and mane, and grow the alerter at mounting.

SOUTHEY. Wordsworth has now turned from the ballad style to the philosophical.

PORSON. The philosophical, I suspect, is antagonist to the poetical.

SOUTHEY. Surely never was there a spirit more philosophical than Shakespeare's.

PORSON. True, but Shakespeare infused it into living forms, adapted to its reception. He did not puff it out incessantly from his own person, bewildering you in the mazes of metaphysics, and swamping you in sententiousness. After all our argumentation, we merely estimate poets by their energy, and not extol them for a congeries of piece on piece, sounding of the hammer all day long, but obstinately unmalleable into unity and cohesion.

SOUTHEY. I can not well gainsay it. But pray remember the subjects of that poetry in Burns and Scott which you admire the most. What is martial must be the most soul-stirring.

PORSON. Sure enough, Mr. Wordsworth's is neither martial nor mercurial. On all subjects of poetry, the soul should be agitated in one way or other. Now did he ever excite in you any strong emotion? He has had the best chance with me; for I have soon given way to him; and he has sung me asleep with his lullabies. It is in our dreams that things look brightest and fairest, and we have the least control over our affections.

SOUTHEY. You cannot but acknowledge that the poetry which is strong enough to support, as his does, a wide and high superstructure of morality, is truly beneficial and admirable. I do not say that utility is the first aim of poetry; but I do say that good poetry is none the worse for being useful; and that his is good in many parts, and useful in nearly all.

PORSON. An old woman who rocks a cradle in a chimney-corner, may be more useful than the joyous girl who wafts my heart before her in the waltz, or holds it quivering in the bonds of harmony; but I happen to have no relish for the old woman, and am ready to dip my fork into the little well-garnished *agro-dolce*. It is inhuman to quarrel with ladies and gentlemen who are easily contented; that is, if you will let them have their own way; it is inhuman to snatch a childish book from a child, for whom it is better than a wise one. If diffuseness is pardonable anywhere, we will pardon it in Lyrical Ballads, passing over the conceited silliness of the denomination: but Mr. Wordsworth has got into the same habit on whatever he writes. Whortleberries are neither the better nor the worse for extending the hard slenderness of their fibres, at random and riotingly, over their native wastes; we care not how much of such soil is covered with such insipidities; but we value that fruit more highly which requires some warmth to swell, and some science and skill to cultivate it. To descend from metaphor: that is the best poetry which, by its own powers, produces the greatest and most durable emotion on generous, well-informed, and elevated minds. It often happens that what belongs to the subject is attributed to the poet. Tenderness, melancholy, and other affections of the soul, attract us toward him who represents them to us; and while we hang upon his neck, we are ready to think him stronger than he is. No doubt, it is very natural that the wings of the Muse should seem to grow larger the nearer they come to the ground! Such is the effect, I presume, of our English atmosphere! But if Mr. Wordsworth should at any time become more popular, it will be owing in great measure to your authority and patronage; and I hope that, neither in health nor in sickness, he will forget his benefactor.

SOUTHEY. However that may be, it would be unbecoming and base in me to suppress an act of justice toward him, withholding my testimony in his behalf when he appeals to the tribunal of the public. The reader who can discover no good or indeed no excellent poetry in his manifold productions, must have lost the finer part of his senses.

PORSON. And he who fancies he has found it in all or in most of them, is just as happy as if his senses were entire. A great portion of his compositions is not poetry, but only the plasma or matrix of poetry, which has something of the same colour and material, but wants the brilliancy and solidity.

SOUTHEY. Acknowledge at least, that what purifies the mind elevates it also; and that he does it.

PORSON. Such a result may be effected at a small expenditure of the poetical faculty, and indeed without any. But I do not say that he has none, or that he has little; I only say, and I stake my credit on it, that what he has is not of the higher order. This is proved beyond all controversy by the effect it produces. The effect of the higher poetry is excitement; the effect of the inferior is composure. I lay down a general principle, and I leave to others the application of it, to-day, to-morrow, and in time to come. Little would it benefit me or you to take a side; and still less to let the inanimate raise animosity in us. There are partisans in favour of a poet, and oppositionists against him; just as there are in regard to candidates for a seat in parliament; and the vociferations of the critics and of the populace are equally loud, equally inconsiderate and insane. The unknown candidate and the unread poet has alike a mob at his heels, ready to swear and fight for him. The generosity which the political mob shows in one instance, the critical mob shows in the other: when a man has been fairly knocked down, it raises him on the knee, and cheers him as cordially as it would the most triumphant. Let similar scenes be rather our amusement than our business; let us wave our hats, and walk on without a *favour* in them.

SOUTHEY. Be it our business, and not for one day, but for life, " to raise up them that fall " by undue violence. The beauties of Wordsworth are not to be looked for among the majestic ruins and under the glowing skies of Greece: we must find them out, like primroses, amid dry thickets, rank grass, and withered leaves; but there they are; and there are tufts and clusters of them. There may be a chilliness in the air about them, there may be a faintness, a sickliness, a poverty in the scent; but I am sorry and indignant to see them trampled on.

PORSON. He who tramples on rocks is in danger of breaking his shins; and he who tramples on sand or sawdust, loses his labour. Between us, we may keep up Mr. Wordsworth in his right position. If we set anything on an uneven basis, it is liable to fall off; and none the less liable for the thing being high and weighty.

SOUTHEY. The axiom is sound.

PORSON. Cleave it in two, and present the first half to Mr. Wordsworth. Let every man have his due: divide the mess fairly: not according to the voracity of the labourer, but according to the work. And (God love you) never let old women poke me with their knitting-pins, if I recommend them, in consideration of their hobbling and wheezing, to creep quietly on by the level side of Mr.

SOUTHEY AND PORSON

Wordsworth's lead-mines, slate-quarries, and tarns, leaving me to scramble as I can among the Alpine inequalities of Milton and Shakespeare. Come now; in all the time we have been walking together at the side of the lean herd you are driving to market,

> Can you make it appear
> The dog Porson has ta'en the wrong sow by the ear?

SOUTHEY. It is easier to show that he has bitten it through, and made it unfit for curing. He may expect to be pelted for it.

PORSON. In cutting up a honeycomb, we are sure to bring flies and wasps about us: but my slipper is enough to crush fifty at a time, if a flap of the glove fails to frighten them off. The honeycomb must be cut up, to separate the palatable from the unpalatable; the hive we will restore to the cottager; the honey we will put in a cool place for those it may agree with; and the wax we will attempt to purify, rendering it the material of a clear and steady light to our readers. Well! I have rinsed my mouth of the poetry. This is about the time I take my ptisan. Be so kind, Mr. Southey, as to give me that bottle which you will find under the bed. Yes, yes; that is it; there is no mistake.

SOUTHEY. It smells like brandy.

PORSON (*drinks twice*). I suspect you may be in the right, Mr. Southey. Let me try it against the palate once more; just one small half-glass. Ah! my hand shakes sadly! I am afraid it was a bumper. Really now, I do think, Mr. Southey, you guessed the right reading. I have scarcely a doubt left upon my mind. But in a fever, or barely off it, the mouth is woefully out of taste. If ever your hand shakes, take my word for it, this is the only remedy. The ptisan has done me good already. Albertus Magnus knew most about these matters. I hate the houses, Mr. Southey, where it is as easy to find the way out as the way in. Curse upon the architect who contrives them!

SOUTHEY. Your friends will be happy to hear from me that you never have been in better spirits, or more vivacious and prompt in conversation.

PORSON. Tell them that Silenus can still bridle and mount an ass, and guide him gloriously. Come and visit me when I am well again; and I promise you the bottles shall diminish and the lights increase, before we part.

XXX. ROMILLY AND PERCEVAL

(*Imag. Convers.*, iii., 1828 ; *Wks.*, i., 1846 ; *Wks.*, iii., 1876.)

ROMILLY. Perceval, I congratulate you on your appointment.[1]

PERCEVAL. It is an arduous one, Romilly, and the more after such eloquent men as have preceded me.

ROMILLY. What ! and do you too place eloquence in the first rank among the requisites of a minister ? Pitt, who could speak fluently three hours together[2], came about us like the tide along the Lancashire sands, always shallow, but always just high enough to drown us.

PERCEVAL. Despise him as you may, he did great things.

ROMILLY. Indeed he did : he made the richest nation in the world the most wretched, and the poorest the most powerful.

PERCEVAL. He was unfortunate, I acknowledge it, on the Continent.

ROMILLY. Like the Apparition in the *Revelation*, he put the right foot upon the sea, and the left upon the land, but in such a manner that they could not act in concert.

PERCEVAL. He was placed among the immortals while living.

ROMILLY. And there are clubs expressly formed for the purpose of irrigating this precious plant of immortality with port and claret. They or their fathers sprang up rapidly in their obscurity under the rank litter of the improvident husbandman. He was called *immortal* by those who benefited from him, the word *God* on such occasions being obsolete.

PERCEVAL. I do not go so far as to call him, what some do, heavenly and godlike.

ROMILLY. I do.

PERCEVAL. How ! you ?

ROMILLY. Yes : men who have much to give are very like God ;

---

[1] As Prime Minister, 1809.
[2] 1st ed. reads : " together, and whom speaking made less thirsty than drinking, came," etc.

ROMILLY AND PERCEVAL

and the more so when the sun of their bounty shines on the unworthy no less than on the worthy. However, he was eloquent, if facility in speaking is eloquence. When we were together in the law-courts, it was reasonable enough to consider our tongues as the most valuable parts of us, knowing that their motion or quiescence would be purchased by dignities and emoluments ; but the present times require men of business, men of firmness, men of consistency, men of probity ; and what is first-rate at the bar is but second-rate on the council-board.[1]

PERCEVAL. I should be glad of your assistance, our opinions being in general alike.

ROMILLY. We could not take the same side on civil and criminal causes, neither can we, for the same reason, in the House of Commons. Whichever may win, we will both lead, if you please.

PERCEVAL. I understand you, and cannot but commend your determination. Yet[2], my dear Romilly, although there have been many Whig oppositions, there never has been and (in the present state of things) never will be a Whig ministry. The post regulates the principles.

ROMILLY. A[3] ministry of such virtue as to carry Whig principles into the cabinet, I fear there never will be, however much I wish it. Yet on certain points disconnected from party, there is no reason why we two should disagree : I will support you in your favourite plan.

PERCEVAL. What is that ?

ROMILLY. To soften the rigour of the penal statutes.

PERCEVAL. I once thought it necessary, or at least advisable. My colleagues oppose it, feeling that, if reform is introduced, it may reach at last[4] the Court of Chancery, and tend to diminish the dignity of the first office under the crown.

ROMILLY. In England there is no dignity but what is constituted by possessions. If you would propose a grant of fifty or sixty thousand pounds a-year to the present chancellor, to indemnify him for the losses he would sustain by regulating his court, I am convinced he would not oppose you.

---

[1] 1st ed. reads : " treasury-bench."
[2] From " Yet " to " principles " added in 2nd ed.
[3] From " A " to " Yet " added in 2nd ed.
[4] 1st ed. reads : " last so high as the," etc.

IMAGINARY CONVERSATIONS: ENGLISH

PERCEVAL. The people are turbulent, and might dislike the grant, reasonable as it must appear to any unprejudiced man. But the principal objection is, that an inquiry would exhibit to the world such a mass of what we have been lately taught to call abuses, as must greatly tend to alienate the affections of the people from the institutions of their country.

ROMILLY. Fees are ticklish things to meddle with, forms are venerable, and silk gowns are non-conductors of inquiry into courts of chancery. I confine myself to the criminal statutes; and would diminish the number of capital offences, which is greater in England, I imagine, than the light and heavy put together in the tables of Solon or Numa. Nay, I am ready to believe that Graco himself did not punish so many with blood as we do, although he punished with blood every one indiscriminately.

PERCEVAL. You can adduce no proof, or rather no support, of this paradox.

ROMILLY. A logician will accept many things which a lawyer would reject, and a moralist will attend to some which would be discountenanced by the logician. Let me remark to you that we punish with death certain offences which Draco did not even note as crimes, and many others had not yet sprung up in society. On the former position I need not expatiate; on the latter let me recall to your memory the vast number of laws on various kinds of forgery; and having brought them before you, let me particularly direct your attention to that severe one on fraudulent bankruptcy.

PERCEVAL. Severe one! there at least we differ. If any crime deserves the punishment of death [1], surely this does. Is it not enough that a creditor loses the greater part perhaps of his property, by the misfortune or imprudence of another, without losing the last farthing of it by the same man's dishonesty?

ROMILLY. Enough it is, and more than enough: but lines of distinction are drawn on murder, and even on the wilful and malicious.

PERCEVAL. There indeed they may be drawn correctly. Malice may arise from injury, more or less grievous, more or less recent; revenge may be delayed and meditated a longer time or a shorter, and may be perpetrated with more or less atrocity; but rarely is it brought to maturity in the coolness of judgment. The fraud under consideration not only is afore-thought; it is formed and grounded

[1] 1st ed. reads: "death, that does."

ROMILLY AND PERCEVAL

upon calculation. You remember a trial at Warwick, or rather the report of it, the result of which was, that a sergeant-major, an elderly man, of irreproachable character antecedently, as was proved by the testimony of his superior officer, who had known him for twenty years, was condemned to be hanged (and not by Buller) for stabbing a young reprobate who had insulted and struck him. It was proved that he ran up-stairs for his sword, in order to commit the crime. This hardly was afore-thought, and certainly was uncalculated.

ROMILLY. It is probable that if he had run down-stairs, instead of up-stairs, his life would not have been forfeited; or even if his counsel had proved that the mounting of the stairs could have been performed in five steps, as I am inclined to think it might by an outraged man. But it appeared to the judge, on the evidence before him, and perhaps on thinking more about his own staircase than about the staircase of an ale-house, that time sufficient had elapsed for his anger to subside and cool.

PERCEVAL. We have seen judges themselves who required a longer time for their anger to subside and cool, though sitting at their ease upon the cushion, to deliberate on matters where, if life was not at stake, property and character were; and not the property and character of drunkards and reprobates, but of gentlemen in their own profession, their equals in birth and education, in honour and abilities.

ROMILLY. Dear Perceval, you have forgotten your new dignity; however I will not betray you.[1] We are treating this matter a little more loosely than we should do in parliament, but more openly and fairly. After an acquaintance and, I am proud to say it, a friendship of twenty-seven years, I think you will give me credit for some soundness of principle.

PERCEVAL. If any man upon earth possesses it.

ROMILLY. Then I will offer to you, if not as my opinion, at least as a subject worth reflection and consideration, whether even a virtuous man, about to fall into bankruptcy, may not commit a fraud, such as by our laws and practice is irremissibly capital?

PERCEVAL. There, my dear Romilly, you go too far. The question (you must pardon me) is not only inconsiderate, but contradictory; the thing impossible. Your problem, in other figures,

---

[1] 1st ed. reads: "betray you. Come, you must dip one foot in Lethe or the other will have a thorn in it ere long. We," etc.

is this; whether a man may not be at once vicious and virtuous, a rogue and honest man: for you do not put a case in this manner, whether one who has hitherto been always honest, may not commit a capital crime, and afterward be honest again. A useless question even thus, among those which a wise man need not, and a scrupulous man would not, discuss. For the limits that separate us from offences ought not to be too closely under our eyes: a large space of neutral ground should be left betwixt. Part of mankind, like boys and hunters, by seeing a hedge before them, are tempted to leap it, only because it is one. Whenever we doubt whether a thing may be done, let us resolve that it may not. I speak as a moralist, by no means as an instructor: in the former capacity all may speak to all: in the latter, none to you, Excuse me, however, my dear Romilly, if in this instance I tell you plainly, that the joints of your logic seem to me to have been relaxed by your philanthropy.

ROMILLY. There are questions which may be investigated by two friends in private, and which I would on no account lay before the public in their rank freshness and fulness. In like manner there are substances, the chief nutriment of whole nations, which are poison until prepared. I would appeal to the judgment and the heart together. He is the most mischievous of incendiaries who inflames the heart against the judgment, and he is the most ferocious of schismatics who divides the judgment from the heart. My argument, if it carried such weight with it as to lay the foundation of a law, would render many men more compassionate (which, after all, is the best and greatest thing we can do on earth), and it would render no man fraudulent.

Suppose a young gentleman to have married a girl equal to himself in fortune, and that in the confidence of early affection, or by the improvidence of her parents, or from any other cause, there is no settlement. A family springs up around them: he is anxious to provide for it more amply than his paternal estate or his wife's property will allow: he enters into business: from unskilfulness, from the infidelity of agents, or from a change in the times and in the channels of commerce, he must become a bankrupt: his creditors are inexorable.

PERCEVAL. That may happen: he is much to be pitied: I see no remedy.

ROMILLY. Speaking of those things which arise from our civil institutions, whatever is to be pitied is to be remedied. The greatest evils and the most lasting are the perverse fabrications of unwise policy, but neither their magnitude nor their duration are proofs of their immobility. They are proofs only that ignorance and indifference have slept profoundly in the chambers of tyranny, and that many interests have grown up, and seeded, and twisted their roots, in the crevices of many wrongs. The wrongs in all cases may be redressed, the interests may be transplanted. Prudence and patience do the work effectually.

I must proceed, although I see close before me the angle of divergence in our opinions.

I will not attempt to run away with your affections, Perceval; I will not burst into the midst of your little playful family, beginning to number it, and forgetting my intent, at the contemplation of its happiness, its innocence, its beauty. I will remove on the contrary every image of grief from the house of my two sufferers; I will suppose the boys and girls too young (just as yours are) for sorrow; I will suppose the mother not expressing it by tears, or wringing of hands, or frantic cries, or dumb desperation, or in any other way that might move you; but so devoted to her husband as for his sake to cover it with smiles, and to engulf it in the abysses of a broken heart. Yet I cannot make him, who is a man as we are, ignorant of her thoughts and feelings, ungrateful to her affection, past and present, or indifferent to her future lot. Obduracy and cruelty press upon him from one side, on the other are conjugal tenderness and parental love. A high and paramount sense of justice too supervenes. What he had received with his partner in misfortune, his conscience tells him, is hers; he had received it before he had received anything from his creditors; he collects the poor remains of it, and places them apart. Unused to fallacy and concealment, the unlawful act is discovered; the criminal is seized, imprisoned, brought out before the judge. Sunday, the day of rest from labour, the day formerly of his innocent projects, of his pleasantest walks, of visits from friends and kindred, of greeting, and union, and hospitality, and gladness; Sunday, the day on which a man's own little ones are dearer to him, are more his own, than on other days—Sunday is granted to him. A further act of grace is extended—his widow may bury him, and his children may learn their letters on his tombstone.

IMAGINARY CONVERSATIONS: ENGLISH

PERCEVAL. What can be done? We are always changing our laws.

ROMILLY. A proof how inconsiderately we enact them. I verily do believe that a balloon by flying over the House would empty it; so little sense of public good or of national dignity is left among us.

What I would propose is this: I would, in such cases, deduct the widow's third from the bankrupt's property, and place it in the hands of trustees for the benefit of herself and her children by that marriage.

PERCEVAL. The motion would do you honour.

ROMILLY. I willingly cede the honour to you. We who are out of place are suspected of innovation; or are well-meaning men, but want practice.

XXXI. ELDON AND ENCOMBE

(*Examiner*, Aug. 21, 1836; *Wks.*, ii., 1846; *Wks.*, vi., 1876.)

Eldon. Encombe! why do you look so grave and sit so silent?

Encombe. To confess the truth, I played last evening, and lost.

Eldon. You played? Do you call it playing, to plunder your guest and overreach your friends? Do you call it playing, to be unhappy if you can not be a robber, happy if you can be one? The fingers of a gamester reach farther than a robber's or a murderer's, and do more mischief. Against the robber or murderer the country is up in arms at once: to the gamester every bosom is open, that he may contaminate or stab it.

Encombe. Certainly I have neither stabbed nor contaminated; I have neither plundered nor overreached.

Eldon. If you did not fancy you had some advantages over your adversary, you would never have tried your fortune with him. I am not sorry you lost; it will teach you better.

Encombe. My dear father! if you could but advance me the money!

Eldon. Your next quarter, the beginning of April, is nigh at hand. However, a part, a moiety, forty days after date—who knows!

Encombe. My loss, I am sorry to say, is heavy.

Eldon. Then wait.

Encombe. Losers would willingly: winners have always a spur against the flank.

Eldon. Tell me the amount of the debt.

Encombe. Two thousand pounds.

Eldon. Two—what! thousand—pounds! Pounds did you say? pounds sterling? incredible!

Encombe. Too true!

Eldon. O my son Encombe! O Encombe, my son, my son!

Encombe. I now perceive you pity my condition, and I grieve to have given so tender-hearted a parent so much uneasiness. Those blessed words remind me of the royal psalmist's.

ELDON. I am very near in my misfortunes at least, although God forbid that I should liken myself in wisdom or piety to that good old king, that king after God's own heart, of whom I can discover no resemblance among men, excepting our own most gracious sovran George the Fourth.

ENCOMBE. Filial love suggests to me some advantages of yours over that early light of the Gentiles. You never were guilty of idolatry nor adultery, nor ever kept (*aside*) anything but his money.

ELDON. The Lord exempted me from so horrible a sin as idolatry, by placing me in the happiest and most enlightened (as indeed it was lately) of all the countries upon earth. Adultery and concubinage did you mention! Another vorago, two voragoes, Scylla and Charybdis, of national wealth.

ENCOMBE. Not national, my dear father, but private—unless he must pay for——

ELDON. Hold! hold! No indecent reflections! Son Encombe! do begin to talk more discreetly and more nobly, and call everything private, *national*.

ENCOMBE. Better so, than to make everything national private.

ELDON. The laws will not allow that. A certain latitude, a liberal construction, a privilege here, a perquisite there—these are things which only the malignant would carp at: the wiser of both parties take the same view of them, and shake their heads, leaving such trifles as they found them.

> Hanc veniam petimusque damusque vicissim.

But, son Encombe, I have often had occasion to remark, that persons who have thrown themselves under tribulation by their extravagancies, roll themselves up in a new morality with all the nap upon it, and are profuse in the loan of sympathies. They are furnished with every sort of morality but that particular one which pinched them; and, when they have done an infinity of private mischief, they are inflamed with a marvellous passion for the public good. Is not this somewhat like a man who has the plague about him offering to cure a patient of the hiccup? Another set of them is still more censurable, and, I am sorry to say, a remark of yours reminded me of the offence whereof they are habitually guilty. Draw distinctions,

ELDON AND ENCOMBE

draw distinctions, Encombe! One of the errors to which you alluded in the mention of King David, if indeed it was one, as perhaps it may appear at first sight, was the error of the times and of the country. We can pretend to no positive proof that he cohabited with more than one of his handmaidens, and possibly it was not without some injunction from above, for purposes beyond our reach and unbecoming our discussion. We must close our eyes on those who are under God's guidance; I mean his more especial guidance, for under it we are all, weak and ignorant creatures as we are.

ENCOMBE. I wish I had been rather more especially so; then I should not have come upon you in this disagreeable business.

ELDON. Don't mind that, Encombe! you come not upon me; I step aside from it. The business may be disagreeable to you, and those who played with you. I grieve at the propensity, but I will avert the ruin.

ENCOMBE. My dear father! do not grieve at it, only pay the money.

ELDON. Only pay the money! only pay two thousand pounds! All the moments of my frail life, nearly worn to nothing in the public service, would scarcely suffice me for counting out the sum.

ENCOMBE. Never fear; only give the order: the banker's clerks are clever fellows, and have life enough before them without encroachment upon yours. I know you will pay it, my noble-minded father, you look so relenting and generous.

ELDON. I would not abuse the time of those worthy clerks. The hours we deduct from youth can never be added to age. Time and virtue are the only losses that are irrecoverable.

ENCOMBE. And sometimes two thousand pounds.

ELDON. Ha! you make me laugh. Pity, that with so much ready wit you should not also keep about you a little ready money. Well, now we have recovered our spirits, we will dismiss all further thought about these little pecuniary matters. I promise you, Encombe, you shall hear no more from me about them, justly as I might reprove a moment's indiscretion, which, were you not insolvent, would be serious.

ENCOMBE. One line then.

ELDON. The clever clerks you mention have all got into parliament. A brace or leash of them have been tossed up to the ticking of my woolsack.

IMAGINARY CONVERSATIONS : ENGLISH

ENCOMBE. There are others as clever as they, and left behind. Let me bring the ink.

ELDON. Youths of business in these days will bring their weight in gold, provided they have words as well as figures at their disposal. I would die with the reputation of having been a just and frugal man. You, who have studied the classics, know the value they entertained for the *homo frugi*, and how many virtues that term included. In conscience, in rectitude, I can not do for you what a sense of paternal propriety forced me to refuse your sister. Relying on the benefices in my gift as chancellor, and venturing to fall in love with a clergyman who had nothing, what does she but marry! No other way was left of showing her the imprudence she had committed, than withholding all supplies. Nothing had she from me for the whole year. The bonds of compassion will yearn, Encombe. Fifteen months, scarcely fifteen months, had elapsed, when Lady Eldon made for the baby two flannel dresses, much longer than itself; and, with very few reproaches, very few indeed, I sent her myself a check for twenty pounds, payable at sight. *Bis dat qui cito dat;* so you may say forty. It was worth as much to her who was starving.

His Majesty, in consideration of my infirmities and in commiseration of my afflictions, has been graciously pleased to send me a most noble breast of mutton. The donation would have been more royal had there been capers and crumbs of bread with it. I have enemies, my son! I have enemies who intercepted the fulness of the royal bounty. However, with God's blessing, here is enough for ourselves and the servants on Christmas day; and the superfluity of fat, discreetly husbanded, may light the house until new year's : indeed the evening of that joyous day may be enlivened by it.

If there is anything in phrenology, my dear Encombe, you must surely have a mountainous boss of destructiveness on your cranium.

ENCOMBE. I, my Lord! Why?

ELDON. Otherwise you would never have crumpled so that admirable piece of parchment. It came but this morning, a ticket to a hare. None such is fabricated in our days : it would have served for letters patent to a dukedom, and would have borne wax enough for the great seal. Now! now! now! do discontinue such childishness. Can not you leave entire even the list that was about the

ELDON AND ENCOMBE

hinder legs! I laid it aside for the fruit-trees against the south-wall. Remember, the loss is yours, if you have fewer and smaller apricots. All I can say is, list is exorbitant: neither they who make the liveries, nor they who sell the cloth, throw any in; they have the meanness to think of selling it. Nothing but selling! selling! We are become much too mercantile.

ENCOMBE. I must interrupt once more the wisdom of your experience and reflections. The matter is really urgent.

ELDON. Who is the creditor?

ENCOMBE. The Marquis of Selborough.

ELDON. Tell him I have made up my mind never to pay a gambling debt.

ENCOMBE. Would you wish him to shoot me?

ELDON. Shoot you!

ENCOMBE. Yes, by all that is sacred!

ELDON. I am shocked at your impiety. He dares not shoot you; and no action will lie. Give him my opinion.

ENCOMBE. He would give me his in return, and we should be just where we stood before.

ELDON. This horrid duelling! I have been thinking of our fine walnut-tree. I did indeed hope to derive some advantage from it in my declining years, little as I apprehended they would be obscured and chilled by the eclipse of dignity and the storms of fortune. It was valued at forty pounds: providential if it produce me thirty at present.

ENCOMBE. It will produce you walnuts.

ELDON. My double teeth are gone, and scarcely any two meet of the single. They are like friends to persons out of place: they stand apart and look shy, and only wish they could serve us.

ENCOMBE. Well, my dear father, let us rather think about the payment of the money than about this melancholy matter.

ELDON. Encombe! Encombe! take care of your teeth. In youth we know not the real value of anything; age instructs us. If you lose a finger, the rest remain; if you lose a tooth, believe me you hold the remainder on no valid security. A dissolute life, care, loss of money, late hours, hot liquors, rich gravies, many dishes, French and Rhenish wines, excursions on the sea in yachts, the sea-coast in crowded places, and, above all, the breath of horses on the race-course, are prejudicial to the duration of teeth. Divine

IMAGINARY CONVERSATIONS : ENGLISH

Providence gives us two sets, and makes us suffer acutely at each gift, in order that we may remember it and prize it. Should you happen to hear of anyone desirous to purchase a fine walnut-tree, particularly adapted to duelling pistol stocks, you may tell him of ours near the house, where dear Lady Eldon loves to sit and amuse herself in the summer evenings, and where we enjoy together the sweet reflection of a well-spent life. It might not be amiss to mention that our favourite tree was valued by admeasurement at forty pounds or upward. Mark me, say *or upward*. The virtuous man is observant of truth, even to his serious loss and detriment. There is much envy, much malignity, in the world we live in. It is by no means clear to me (indeed I am inclined to think the contrary) that there was ever a more general or a more intense hostility toward men in office than at present; especially if, by the appointment of the Almighty, they have the honour and happiness to be in the confidence of his Majesty. Seeing this, it would not at all surprise me if some wicked wretch or other, desirous of bringing me and the laws of England into contempt, should insinuate that I would aid and abet, and lend my hand to, the practice of duelling. Could he but see my heart; could he but hear this conversation! God is my judge; I wish only, as a conscientious man, upright in all my dealings, to sell my walnut-tree. I know not whether, if the offer should come through a third party, it might be useful to remark that Lord Chancellor Eldon was in the habit of meditating under this walnut-tree some of his most important decrees, twenty years together. Shakespeare's mulberry was cut up into snuff-boxes, and a guinea has been given for three inches square. I have drawn as many tears as ever he did, and all in the line of duty, and by law. Perhaps I may be remembered a shorter time among men. Certain great ones, to whom the services of my whole life were devoted, seem to have forgotten me already. But fidelity to our word, to our wives, to our God, and to our king, ensures my happiness here and hereafter.

ENCOMBE. Nevertheless, my dear father, your tone and manner are excessively despondent.

ELDON. Not at all, not at all. Another would be vexed at seeing a mere child take his chair in the Court of Chancery: another would tremble at the probable consequences of such inexperience—— Well, well! they may want me yet, and may not have me.

ELDON AND ENCOMBE

ENCOMBE. Could you be insensible to the call of king and country? You shed tears at the very thought: I have touched the tender point, the nerve of patriotism.

ELDON. Lend me your pocket-handkerchief; for mine is a clean one. Thank you; I am truly grateful for your sympathy and attention—— Are you mad, Encombe? why, yours is clean too. Take it back: I must go upstairs for my last. Who is that man at the hall-door?

ENCOMBE. Apparently a beggar.

ELDON. Go away, go away; beggary is contrary to law. I pity you, my good friend, from the bottom of my heart.

BEGGAR. What a cold place his pity comes from! No wonder it has caught the cramp, and limps.

ELDON. George the Third, of happy memory, stood forward a bright example to all future kings. But I am not about to cite him in that high station. By God's appointment he also shone a burning light for the guidance of parents. Being the natural guardian of his blessed Majesty now reigning, he received on his behalf the proceeds of the duchies of Cornwall and Lancaster, together with certain proceeds from the principality of Wales. In twenty-one years, with compound interest of five per cent, his Royal Highness, then prince of Wales, at present our most gracious sovran, might have imbursed, at the hands of his august parent, from the said proceeds, some nine hundred thousand pounds. But, knowing that a virtuous and a religious education is more pleasing to the eyes of our Maker, and more beneficial to the subject, he expended the whole sum on his royal son's education.

ENCOMBE. Nine hundred thousand pounds?

ELDON. A fraction more or less.

ENCOMBE. Impossible!

ELDON. His Majesty himself declared it. Remember, the tutors of princes are lords temporal and spiritual.

ENCOMBE. Oh then, in that case, his Majesty's word may be relied on.

ELDON. I likewise have bestowed on you, son Encombe, an education such as was suitable to your future rank in society. It is beyond my power to throw you back on Parliament. The Houses would not accept my recommendation for your relief.

ENCOMBE. Indeed I am not so mad as to expect it.

IMAGINARY CONVERSATIONS : ENGLISH

ELDON. It is worse madness to expect it from me. The one has a precedent, the other none. But my bowels yearn for you, although you have brought a whole Vesuvius of ashes on my grey hairs.

ENCOMBE. Even our most gracious Regent has played at cards and lost.

ELDON. Cards were invented for the diversion of a king, and therefore of right do belong to kings. Well we know, Encombe, that our most gracious ruler is the least addicted to light and frivolous pleasures : and fairly may we infer that, if he played and lost at cards, it could only be to countenance the subject. Perhaps to encourage the conversion of rags into paper. The colour-man, the glue-man, entered (no doubt) into his calculation. The money he graciously lost was probably won by some faithful old servant, whose family was in poverty and affliction. Delicate as he is in all things, he could not act more delicately in any than in this. That he is the most abstinent of mankind, not only his household, but all around, have incontestable proofs before their eyes. By the sagacity and sound discretion of his royal father, of happy memory, he was precluded from these proceeds of which we already have largely spoken, and consequently he is reported to have incurred sundry debts. In order to defray them, he took a consort.

ENCOMBE. Being, in the eye of God, married already.

ELDON. No, son Encombe, no ; emphatically *no*.

ENCOMBE. My dear father, you always lay the strongest emphasis on that word, especially when, as now——

ELDON. Encombe ! I can not but rejoice and smile at your ready wit. Your uncle Stowell has it also. It lies deeply seated in the family : my mine has never yet been worked : it might not answer. But let me correct your error of judgment, and inform you that what is not in the eye of the law can not be in the eye of God. For God is law, in order, economy, and perfection. Blessed be his holy name ! I shall hardly be accused of flattery in reverting from God to God's vice-gerent ; more especially when my aim is solely your admonition. Imitate him, Encombe, imitate him !

ENCOMBE. I was apprehensive I had imitated him too closely.

ELDON. Take a wife of some substance.

ENCOMBE. He certainly has done that : but I am unambitious of so large a dominion.

ELDON. His royal highness was singularly abstemious and

patriotic in his union. The instant that, by possibility, the hopes of his people were accomplished, he was as chaste toward his consort as his predecessor Edward the Confessor.

ENCOMBE. In consequence of which abstemiousness——

ELDON. Hold! hold! We mortals are short-sighted. God delivered the lady from her perils. Reluctantly should I have pronounced a sentence of blood. But God, in some cases, hath ordained that the axe separate the impure from the pure.

ENCOMBE. Both parties were equally safe, if such be his ordinance.

ELDON. Furthermore, you have the authority of your sovran for denying the validity of lawless obligations. His Majesty, by right, took possession of the Duke of York's effects. His creditors claimed them, pretending not only that they were unpaid for, but also that they existed on the premises at the Duke's decease. Yet his Majesty demurred. The creditors may bring their action : it will lie.

ENCOMBE. For ever.

XXXII. SOUTHEY AND LANDOR

(Wks., ii., 1846 ; *Wks.*, iv., 1876.)

SOUTHEY. Of all the beautiful scenery round King's-weston, the view from this terrace, and especially from this sundial, is the pleasantest.

LANDOR. The last time I ever walked hither in company (which, unless with ladies, I rarely have done anywhere) was with a just, a valiant, and a memorable man, Admiral Nichols, who usually spent his summer months at the village of Shire-hampton, just below us. There, whether in the morning or evening, it was seldom I found him otherwise engaged than in cultivating his flowers.

SOUTHEY. I never had the same dislike to company in my walks and rambles as you profess to have, but of which I perceived no sign whatever when I visited you, first at Lantony Abbey, and afterward on the Lake of Como. Well do I remember our long conversations in the silent and solitary church of Sant' Abondio (surely the coolest spot in Italy), and how often I turned back my head toward the open door, fearing lest some pious passer-by, or some more distant one in the wood above, pursuing the pathway that leads to the tower of Luitprand, should hear the roof echo with your laughter, at the stories you had collected about the brotherhood and sisterhood of the place.

LANDOR. I have forgotten most of them, and nearly all : but I have not forgotten how we speculated on the possibility that Milton might once have been sitting on the very bench we then occupied, although we do not hear of his having visited that part of the country. Presently we discoursed on his poetry ; as we propose to do again this morning.

SOUTHEY. In that case, it seems we must continue to be seated on the turf.

LANDOR. Why so ?

SOUTHEY. Because you do not like to walk in company : it might disturb and discompose you : and we never lose our temper without losing at the same time many of our thoughts, which are loth to come forward without it.

LANDOR. From my earliest days I have avoided society as much as I could decorously, for I received more pleasure in the cultivation and improvement of my own thoughts than in walking up and down among the thoughts of others. Yet, as you know, I never have avoided the intercourse of men distinguished by virtue and genius ; of genius, because it warmed and invigorated me by my trying to keep pace with it ; of virtue, that if I had any of my own it might be called forth by such vicinity. Among all men elevated in station who have made a noise in the world [1] (admirable old expression !) I never saw any in whose presence I felt inferiority, excepting Kosciusco. But how many in the lower paths of life have exerted both virtues and abilities which I never exerted, and never possessed ! what strength and courage and perseverance in some, in others what endurance and forbearance ! At the very moment when most, beside yourself, catching up half my words, would call and employ against me in its ordinary signification what ought to convey the most honorific, the term *self-sufficiency*, I bow my head before the humble, with greatly more than their humiliation. You are better tempered than I am, and readier to converse. There are half-hours when, although in good-humour and good spirits, I would not be disturbed by the necessity of talking, to be the possessor of all the rich marshes we see yonder. In this interval there is neither storm nor sunshine of the mind, but calm and (as the farmer would call it) *growing* weather, in which the blades of thought spring up and dilate insensibly. Whatever I do, I must do in the open air, or in the silence of night : either is sufficient : but I prefer the hours of exercise, or, what is next to exercise, of field-repose. Did you happen to know the admiral ?

SOUTHEY. Not personally : but I believe the terms you have applied to him are well merited. After some experience, he contended that public men, public women, and the public press, may be all designated by one and the same trisyllable. He is reported to have been a strict disciplinarian. In the mutiny at the Nore he was seized by his crew, and summarily condemned by them to be hanged. Many taunting questions were asked him, to which he made no

[1] " Such persons as have made a noise in the world." Addison, " On Medals."

reply. When the rope was fastened round his neck, the ringleader cried, " Answer this one thing, however, before you go, sir ! What would you do with any of us, if we were in your power as you are now in ours ? " The admiral, then captain, looked sternly and contemptuously, and replied, " Hang you, by God ! " Enraged at this answer, the mutineer tugged at the rope : but another on the instant rushed forward, exclaiming " No, captain ! " (for thus he called the fellow) " he has been cruel to us, flogging here and flogging there, but before so brave a man is hanged like a dog, you heave me overboard." Others among the most violent now interceded : and an old seaman, not saying a single word, came forward with his knife in his hand, and cut the noose asunder. Nichols did not thank him, nor notice him, nor speak : but, looking round at the other ships, in which there was the like insubordination, he went toward his cabin slow and silent. Finding it locked, he called to a midshipman, " Tell that man with a knife to come down and open the door." After a pause of a few minutes, it was done : but he was confined below until the quelling of the mutiny.

LANDOR. His conduct as Controller of the Navy was no less magnanimous and decisive. In this office he presided at the trial of Lord Melville. His lordship was guilty, we know, of all the charges brought against him ; but, having more patronage than ever minister had before, he refused to answer the questions which (to repeat his own expression) might incriminate him. And his refusal was given with a smile of indifference, a consciousness of security. In those days, as indeed in most others, the main use of power was promotion and protection : and *honest man* was never in any age among the titles of nobility, and has always been the appellation used toward the feeble and inferior by the prosperous. Nichols said on the present occasion, " If this man is permitted to skulk away under such pretences, trial is here a mockery." Finding no support, he threw up his office as Controller of the Navy, and never afterward entered the House of Commons. Such a person, it appears to me, leads us aptly and becomingly to that stedfast patriot on whose writings you promised me your opinion ; not incidentally, as before, but turning page after page. It would ill beseem us to treat Milton with generalities. Radishes and salt are the *pic-nic* quota of slim spruce reviewers : let us hope to find somewhat more solid and of better taste. Desirous to be a listener and a learner when you discourse on his poetry, I have been more occupied of late in examining the prose.

SOUTHEY. Do you retain your high opinion of it?

LANDOR. Experience makes us more sensible of faults than of beauties. Milton is more correct than Addison, but less correct than Hooker, whom I wish he had been contented to receive as a model in style, rather than authors who wrote in another and a poorer language; such, I think, you are ready to acknowledge is the Latin.

SOUTHEY. This was always my opinion.

LANDOR. However, I do not complain that in oratory and history his diction is sometimes poetical.

SOUTHEY. Little do I approve of it in prose on any subject. Demosthenes and Æschines, Lisias and Isæus, and finally Cicero, avoided it.

LANDOR. They did: but Chatham and Burke and Grattan did not; nor indeed the graver and greater Pericles; of whom the most memorable sentence on record is pure poetry. On the fall of the young Athenians in the field of battle, he said, " The year hath lost its spring." But how little are these men, even Pericles himself, if you compare them as men of genius with Livy! In Livy, as in Milton, there are bursts of passion which can not by the nature of things be other than poetical, nor (being so) come forth in other language. If Milton had executed his design of writing a history of England, it would probably have abounded in such diction, especially in the more turbulent scenes and in the darker ages.

SOUTHEY. There are quiet hours and places in which a taper may be carried steadily, and show the way along the ground; but you must stand a-tiptoe and raise a blazing torch above your head, if you would bring to our vision the obscure and time-worn figures depicted on the lofty vaults of antiquity. The philosopher shows everything in one clear light; the historian loves strong reflections and deep shadows, but, above all, prominent and moving characters. We are little pleased with the man who disenchants us: but whoever can make us wonder, must himself (we think) be wonderful, and deserve our admiration.

LANDOR. Believing no longer in magic and its charms, we still shudder at the story told by Tacitus, of those which were discovered in the mournful house of Germanicus.

IMAGINARY CONVERSATIONS: ENGLISH

SOUTHEY. Tacitus was also a great poet, and would have been a greater, had he been more contented with the external and ordinary appearances of things. Instead of which, he looked at a part of his pictures through a prism, and at another part through a *camera obscura*. If the historian were as profuse of moral as of political axioms, we should tolerate him less: for in the political we fancy a writer is but meditating; in the moral we regard him as declaiming. In history we desire to be conversant with only the great, according to our notions of greatness: we take it as an affront, on such an invitation, to be conducted into the lecture-room, or to be desired to amuse ourselves in the study.

LANDOR. Pray go on. I am desirous of hearing more.

SOUTHEY. Being now alone, with the whole day before us, and having carried, as we agreed at breakfast, each his Milton in his pocket, let us collect all the graver faults we can lay our hands upon, without a too minute and troublesome research; not in the spirit of Johnson, but in our own.

LANDOR. That is, abasing our eyes in reverence to so great a man, but without closing them. The beauties of his poetry we may omit to notice, if we can: but where the crowd claps the hands, it will be difficult for us always to refrain. Johnson, I think, has been charged unjustly with expressing too freely and inconsiderately the blemishes of Milton. There are many more of them than he has noticed.

SOUTHEY. If we add any to the number, and the literary world hears of it, we shall raise an outcry from hundreds who never could see either his excellences or his defects, and from several who never have perused the noblest of his writings.

LANDOR. It may be boyish and mischievous, but I acknowledge I have sometimes felt a pleasure in irritating, by the cast of a pebble, those who stretch forward to the full extent of the chain their open and frothy mouths against me. I shall seize upon this conjecture of yours, and say everything that comes into my head on the subject. Beside which, if any collateral thoughts should spring up, I may throw them in also; as you perceive I have frequently done in my *Imaginary Conversations*, and as we always do in real ones.

SOUTHEY. When we adhere to one point, whatever the form, it should rather be called a disquisition than a conversation. Most writers of dialogue take but a single stride into questions the most

SOUTHEY AND LANDOR

abstruse, and collect a heap of arguments to be blown away by the bloated whiffs of some rhetorical charlatan, tricked out in a multiplicity of ribbons for the occasion.

Before we open the volume of poetry, let me confess to you I admire his prose less than you do.

LANDOR. Probably because you dissent more widely from the opinions it conveys: for those who are displeased with anything are unable to confine the displeasure to one spot. We dislike everything a little when we dislike anything much. It must indeed be admitted that his prose is often too latinized and stiff. But I prefer his heavy cut velvet, with its ill-placed Roman fibula, to the spangled gauze and gummed-on flowers and puffy flounces of our present street-walking literature. So do you, I am certain.

SOUTHEY. Incomparably. But let those who have gone astray, keep astray, rather than bring Milton into disrepute by pushing themselves into his company and imitating his manner. As some men conceive that if their name is engraven in Gothic letters, with several superfluous, it denotes antiquity of family, so do others that a congestion of words swept together out of a corner, and dry chopped sentences which turn the mouth awry in reading, make them look like original thinkers. Milton is none of these: and his language is never a patchwork.[1] We find daily, in almost every book we open, expressions which are not English, never were, and never will be: for the writers are by no means of sufficiently high rank to be masters of the mint. To arrive at this distinction, it is not enough to scatter in all directions bold, hazardous, undisciplined thoughts: there must be lordly and commanding ones, with a full establishment of well-appointed expressions adequate to their maintenance.

Occasionally I have been dissatisfied with Milton, because in my opinion that is ill said in prose which can be said more plainly. Not so in poetry: if it were, much of Pindar and Æschylus, and no little of Dante, would be censurable.

LANDOR. Acknowledge that he whose poetry I am holding in my hand is free from every false ornament in his prose, unless a few bosses of latinity may be called so; and I am ready to admit the full claims of your favourite South. Acknowledge that,

---

[1] Compare with the passage in the Conversation of Marvel and Parker in which Parker sneers at the affectation of Gothic letters, admitting, however, that Milton was not necessarily to be ranked with those guilty of it.

heading all the forces of our language, he was the great antagonist of every great monster which infested our country; and he disdained to trim his lion-skin with lace. No other English writer has equalled Raleigh, Hooker, and Milton, in the loftier parts of their works.

SOUTHEY. But Hooker and Milton, you allow, are sometimes pedantic. In Hooker there is nothing so elevated as there is in Raleigh.

LANDOR. Neither he, however, nor any modern, nor any ancient, has attained to that summit on which the sacred ark of Milton strikes and rests. Reflections, such as we indulged in on the borders of the Larius, come over me here again. Perhaps from the very sod where you are sitting, the poet in his youth sate looking at the Sabrina he was soon to celebrate. There is pleasure in the sight of a glebe which never has been broken; but it delights me particularly in those places where great men have been before. I do not mean warriors: for extremely few among the most remarkable of them will a considerate man call great: but poets and philosophers and philanthropists, the ornaments of society, the charmers of solitude, the warders of civilisation, the watchmen at the gate which Tyranny would batter down, and the healers of those wounds which she left festering in the field. And now, to reduce this demon into its proper toad-shape again, and to lose sight of it, open your *Paradise Lost*.

SOUTHEY. Shall we begin with it immediately? or shall we listen a little while to the woodlark? He seems to know what we are about; for there is a sweetness, a variety, and a gravity in his cadences, befitting the place and theme. Another time we might afford the whole hour to him.

LANDOR. The woodlark, the nightingale, and the ringdove, have made me idle for many, even when I had gone into the fields on purpose to gather fresh materials for composition. A little thing turns me from one idleness to another. More than once, when I have taken out my pencil to fix an idea on paper, the smell of the cedar, held by me unconsciously across the nostrils, hath so absorbed the senses, that what I was about to write down has vanished, altogether and irrecoverably. This vexed me; for although we may improve a first thought, and generally do, yet if we lose it, we seldom or never can find another so good to replace it. The latter-math has less substance, succulence, and fragrance, than the summer crop. I dare not trust my memory for a moment with anything of my own: it is more faithful in storing up what is another's. But am I not doing at this instant something like what I told you about the pencil? If the loss of my own thoughts vexed me, how much more will the loss of yours! Now pray begin in good earnest.

SOUTHEY. Before [1] we pursue the details of a poem, it is customary to look at it as a whole, and to consider what is the scope and tendency, or what is usually called the moral. But surely it is a silly and stupid business to talk mainly about the moral of a poem, unless it professedly be a fable. A good epic, a good tragedy, a good comedy, will inculcate several. Homer does not represent the anger of Achilles as being fatal or disastrous to that hero; which would be what critics call poetical justice. But he demonstrates in the greater part of the *Iliad* the evil effects of arbitrary power, in alienating an elevated soul from the cause of his country. In the *Odyssea* he shows that every obstacle yields to constancy and perseverance: yet he does not propose to show it: and there are other morals no less obvious. Why should the machinery of the longest poem be drawn out to establish an obvious truth, which a single verse would exhibit more plainly, and impress more memorably? Both in epic and dramatic poetry it is action, and not moral, that is first demanded. The feelings and exploits of the principal agent should excite the principal interest. The two greatest of human compositions are here defective: I mean the *Iliad* and *Paradise Lost*. Agamemnon is leader of the confederate Greeks before Troy, to avenge the cause of Menelaus: yet not only Achilles and Diomed on his side, but Hector and Sarpedon on the opposite, interest us more than the "king of men," the avenger, or than his brother, the injured prince, about whom they all are fighting. In the *Paradise Lost* no principal character seems to have been intended. There is neither truth nor wit however in saying that Satan is hero of the piece, unless, as is usually the case in human life, he is the greatest hero who gives the widest sway to the worst passions. It is Adam who acts and suffers most, and on whom the consequences have most influence. This constitutes him the main character; although

[1] Portions of this passage are also in Landor's *Commentary* on the Memoir of Fox.

IMAGINARY CONVERSATIONS: ENGLISH

Eve is the more interesting, Satan the more energetic, and on whom the greater force of poetry is displayed. The Creator and his angels are quite secondary.

LANDOR. Must we not confess that every epic hitherto has been defective in plan; and even that each, until the time of Tasso, was more so than its predecessor? Such stupendous genius, so much fancy, so much eloquence, so much vigour of intellect, never were united as in *Paradise Lost*. Yet it is neither so correct nor so varied as the *Iliad*, nor, however important the action, so interesting. The moral itself is the reason why it wearies even those who insist on the necessity of it. Founded on an event believed by nearly all nations, certainly by all who read the poem, it lays down a principle which concerns every man's welfare, and a fact which every man's experience confirms; that great and irremediable misery may arise from apparently small offences. But will anyone say that, in a poetical view, our certainty of moral truth in this position is an equivalent for the uncertainty *which* of the agents is what critics call the hero of the piece?

SOUTHEY. We are informed in the beginning of the *Iliad* that the poet, or the Muse for him, is about to sing the anger of Achilles, with the disasters it brought down on the Greeks. But these disasters are of brief continuance, and this anger terminates most prosperously. Another fit of anger, from another motive, less ungenerous and less selfish, supervenes; and Hector falls because Patroclus had fallen. The son of Peleus, whom the poet in the beginning proposed for his hero, drops suddenly out of sight, abandoning a noble cause from an ignoble resentment. Milton, in regard to the discontinuity of agency, is in the same predicament as Homer.

Let us now take him more in detail. He soon begins to give the learned and less obvious signification to English words. In the sixth line,

> That on the secret top, &c.

Here *secret* is in the same sense as Virgil's

> *Secretosque* pios, his dantem jura Catonem.[1]

Would it not have been better to omit the fourth and fifth verses, as

[1] *Æn.*, viii. 670.

SOUTHEY AND LANDOR

incumbrances, and deadeners of the harmony? and for the same reason, the fourteenth, fifteenth, and sixteenth?

> That with no middle flight intends to soar
> Above the Aonian mount, while it pursues
> Things unattempted yet in prose or rhyme.

LANDOR. Certainly much better: for the harmony of the sentence is complete without them, and they make it gasp for breath. Supposing the fact to be true, the mention of it is unnecessary and unpoetical. Little does it become Milton to run in debt with Ariosto for his

> Cose non dette mai nè in prosa o in rima.

Prosaic enough in a rhymed romance, for such is the *Orlando* with all its spirit and all its beauty, and far beneath the dignity of the epic.

SOUTHEY. Beside, it interrupts the intensity of the poet's aspiration in the words,

> And chiefly thou, O Spirit!

Again: I would rather see omitted the five which follow that beautiful line,

> Dovelike satst brooding on the vast abyss.

LANDOR. The ear, however accustomed to the rhythm of these sentences, is relieved of a burden by rejecting them: and they are not wanted for anything they convey.

SOUTHEY. I am sorry that Milton (V. 34) did not always keep separate the sublime Satan and " the infernal Serpent." The thirty-eighth verse is the first hendecasyllabic in the poem. It is much to be regretted, I think, that he admits this metre into epic poetry. It is often very efficient in the dramatic, at least in Shakespeare, but hardly ever in Milton. He indulges in it much less fluently in the *Paradise Lost* than in the *Paradise Regained*. In the seventy-third verse he tells us that the rebellious angels are

> As far removed from God and light of heaven
> As from the centre thrice to the utmost pole.

Not very far for creatures who could have measured all that distance, and a much greater, by a single act of the will.

IMAGINARY CONVERSATIONS: ENGLISH

V. 188 ends with the word *repair*; 191 with *despair*.

>   V. 335.   Nor did they not perceive the evil plight
>   *In which they were.*

LANDOR. We are oftener in such *evil plight* of foundering in the prosaic slough about your neighbourhood than in Bunhill Fields.

>   V. 360.   And Powers that erst in heaven sat on thrones.

Excuse my asking why you, and indeed most poets in most places, make a monosyllable of *heaven*[1]? I observe you treat *spirit* in the same manner; and although not *peril*, yet *perilous*. I would not insist at all times on an iambic foot, neither would I deprive these words of their right to a participation in it.

SOUTHEY. I have seized all fair opportunities of introducing the tribrachys, and these are the words that most easily afford one. I have turned over the leaves as far as verse 534,[2] where I wish he had written *Damascus* (as he does elsewhere) for *Damasco*, which never was the English appellation. Beside, he sinks the last vowel in Meröe in *Paradise Regained*, which follows; and should consistently have done the same in Damasco, following the practice of the Italian poets, which certainly is better than leaving the vowels open and gaping at one another.

>   V. 550.[3]   Anon they move
>   In perfect phalanx to the Dorian mood.

Thousands of years before there were phalanxes, schools of music, or Dorians.

LANDOR. Never mind the Dorians, but look at Satan:

>   V. 571.   And now his heart
>   Distends with pride, and, hardening in his strength,
>   *Glories!*

What an admirable pause is here. I wish he had not ended one verse with "*his* heart," and the next with "*his* strength."

SOUTHEY. What think you of

>   V. 585.[4]   *That small infantry*
>   Warred on by cranes.

---

[1] Landor himself did this in *Gebir*, ii. 160, as Mr. Stephen Wheeler reminds me.
[2] As corrected by Crump, verse 584.   [3] Verse 549.   [4] Verse 575.

SOUTHEY AND LANDOR

LANDOR. I think he might easily have turned the flank of *that small infantry*. He would have done much better by writing, not

> For never since created man
> Met such imbodied force as *named with these*
> *Could merit more* than that small infantry
> Warred on by cranes, though all the giant-brood, &c.,

but leaving behind him also these heavy and unserviceable tumbrils, it would have been enough to have written,

> Never since created man,
> Met such imbodied force; though all the brood
> Of Phlegra with the Heroic race were joined.

But where, in poetry or painting, shall we find anything that approaches the sublimity of that description, which begins v. 589 and ends in v. 620? What an admirable pause at

> Tears, such as angels weep, burst forth!

V. 542.[1] But *tempted* our *attempt*. Such a play on words would be unbecoming in the poet's own person, and even on the lightest subject, but is most injudicious and intolerable in the mouth of Satan, about to assail the Almighty.

V. 673.[2] *Undoubted* sign
That in *his* womb was hid metallic ore.

I know not exactly which of these words induces you to raise your eyes above the book and cast them on me: perhaps both. It was hardly worth his while to display in this place his knowledge of mineralogy, or his recollection that Virgil, in the wooden horse before Troy, had said,

> *Uterumque* armato milite complent,

and that some modern poets had followed him.
SOUTHEY.
V. 675.   As when bands
Of pioneers, with spade and pick-axe armed,
Fore-run the royal camp to trench a field
Or cast a rampart.

Nothing is gained to the celestial host by comparing it with the

[1] Verse 642.   [2] Verse 672.

IMAGINARY CONVERSATIONS : ENGLISH

terrestrial. Angels are not promoted by brigading with sappers and miners. Here we are entertained (V. 722)[1] with

> *Dulcet* symphonies . . . and voices *sweet*,

among " pilasters and *Doric* pillars."

V. 745 is that noble one on Vulcan, who

> Dropt from the zenith like a falling star.

LANDOR. The six following are quite superfluous. Instead of stopping where the pause is so natural and so necessary, he carries the words on,

> Dropt from the zenith, like a falling star,
> On Lemnos, the Ægean isle. Thus they relate,
> Erring ; for he, with this rebellious rout,
> Fell long before ; nor aught avail'd him now
> To have built in Heaven high towers, nor did he scape
> By all his engines, but was headlong *sent*
> With his *industrious* crew to build in hell.

My good Milton ! why in a passion ? If he was sent to build in hell, and *did* build there, give the Devil his due, and acknowledge that on this one occasion he ceased to be rebellious.

SOUTHEY. The verses are insufferable stuff, and would be ill placed anywhere.

LANDOR. Let me remark that in my copy I find a mark of elision before the first letter in *scape*.

SOUTHEY. The same in mine.

LANDOR. *Scaped* is pointed in the same manner at the beginning of the Fourth Book. But Milton took the word directly from the Italian *scappare*, and committed no mutilation. We do not always think it necessary to make the sign of an elision in its relatives, as appears by *scape-grace*. In v. 752 what we write *herald* he more properly writes *harald* ; in the next *sovran* equally so, following the Italian rather than the French.

SOUTHEY. At verse 769 [2] we come to a series of twenty lines, which, excepting the metamorphosis of the Evil Angels, would be delightful in any other situation. The poem is much better without these. And in these verses I think there are two whole ones and two hemistics which you would strike out :

[1] Verse 712.   [2] Verse 768.

SOUTHEY AND LANDOR

>   As bees
> In spring-time, when the sun with Taurus rides,
> Pour forth their populous youth about the hive
> In clusters : they among fresh dews and flowers
> Fly to and fro, or on the smoothened [1] plank,
> The suburb of their straw-built citadel,
> New rubbed with balm, expatiate and confer
> Their state affairs. So thick the aery crowd, &c.

LANDOR. I should be sorry to destroy the suburb of the straw-built citadel, or even to remove the smoothened plank, if I found them in any other place. Neither the harmony of the sentence, nor the propriety and completeness of the simile, would suffer by removing all between "*to and fro*," and "*so thick*," &c. But I wish I had not been called upon to "Behold a wonder."

SOUTHEY. (Book II.)

> High on a throne of royal state, which far
> Outshone the wealth of Ormus and of Ind,
> *Or* where the gorgeous east, &c.

Are not Ormus and Ind within the gorgeous East ? If so, would not the sense be better if he had written, instead of "*Or* where," "*There* where " ?

LANDOR. Certainly.

SOUTHEY. Turn over, if you please, another two or three pages, and tell me whether in your opinion the 150th verse,

> In the wide womb of uncreated night,

might not also have been omitted advantageously.

LANDOR. The sentence is long enough and full enough without it, and the omission would cause no visible gap.

SOUTHEY.

> V. 226. Thus Belial, with words clothed in reason's garb,
> Counsel'd *ignoble ease and peaceful sloth*,
> *Not peace.*

These words are spoken by the poet in his own person ; very improperly : they would have suited the character of any fallen angel ;

---

[1] Read : " smoothed."

IMAGINARY CONVERSATIONS : ENGLISH

but the reporter of the occurrence ought not to have delivered such a sentence.

> V. 299. Which when Beelzebub perceived (than whom,
> Satan except, none higher sat) with grave
> Aspect he rose, and in his rising seemed
> A pillar of state. Deep on his front engraven
> Deliberation sat and public care ;
> And princely counsel in his face yet shone
> Majestic, though in ruin : sage he stood,
> With Atlantean shoulders, fit to bear
> The weight of mightiest monarchies.

Often and often have these verses been quoted, without a suspicion how strangely the corporeal is substituted for the moral. However Atlantean his shoulders might be, the weight of monarchies could no more be supported by them than by the shoulders of a grasshopper. The verses are sonorous, but they are unserviceable as an incantation to make a stout figure look like a pillar of state.

LANDOR. We have seen pillars of state which made no figure at all, and which are quite as misplaced as Milton's. But seriously ; the pillar's representative, if any figure but a metaphorical one could represent him, would hardly be brought to represent the said pillar by *rising* up ; as,

> Beelzebub in his *rising* seem'd, &c.

His fondness for latinisms induces him to write,

> V. 329. *What* sit we then projecting peace and war ?

For " *Why sit we ?* " as *quid* for *cur*. To my ear *What sit* sounds less pleasingly than *why sit*.

I have often wished that Cicero, who so delighted in harmonious sentences, and was so studious of the closes, could have heard,

> V. 353.[1] So was his will
> Pronounced among the Gods, and, by an oath
> *That shook heaven's whole circumference, confirm'd.*

Although in the former part of the sentence two cadences are the same :

> So was his will,
> And by an oath.

---

[1] Verse 351.

SOUTHEY AND LANDOR

This is unhappy. But at 402 [1] bursts forth again such a torrent of eloquence as there is nowhere else in the regions of poetry, although *strict* and *thick*, in v. 402, sound unpleasantly.

> V. 594. The parching wind
> Burns frore, *and cold performs the effect of fire!*

The latter part of this verse is redundant, and ruinous to the former.

SOUTHEY. Milton, like Dante, has mixed the Greek mythology with the Oriental. To hinder the damned from tasting a single drop of the *Lethe* they are *ferried* over:

> V. 604.[2] *Medusa* with Gorgonian terror guards
> The ford.

It is strange that until now they never had explored the banks of the other four infernal rivers.

LANDOR. It appears to me that his imitation of Shakespeare,

> From beds of raging fire to starve in ice,

is feeble. Never was poet so little made to imitate another. Whether he imitates a good or a bad one, the offence of his voluntary degradation is punished in general with ill success. Shakespeare, on the contrary, touches not even a worthless thing but he renders it precious.

SOUTHEY. To continue the last verse I was reading,

> And of itself the water flies
> All taste of living wight, as *once* it fled
> The lip of Tantalus.

No living wight had ever attempted to taste it; nor was it *this* water that fled the lip of Tantalus at any time; least of all can we imagine that it had already fled it. In the description of Sin and Death, and Satan's interview with them, there is a wonderful vigour of imagination and of thought, with such sonorous verse as Milton alone was capable of composing. But there is also much of what is odious and intolerable. The terrific is then sublime, and then only, when it fixes you in the midst of all your energies, and not when it weakens, nauseates, and repels you.

> V. 678. God and his son except,
> Created thing not valued he.

---

[1] Verse 412.   [2] Verse 611.

IMAGINARY CONVERSATIONS: ENGLISH

This is not the only time when he has used such language, evidently with no other view than to defend it by his scholarship. But no authority can vindicate what is false, and no ingenuity can explain what is absurd. You have remarked it already in the *Imaginary Conversations*, referring to

The fairest of her daughters, Eve.

There is something not dissimilar in the form of expression, when we find on a sepulchral stone the most dreadful of denunciations against any who should violate it.

Ultimus suum moriatur.

LANDOR. I must now be the reader. It is impossible to refuse the ear its satisfaction at

Thus roving on
In confused march forlorn, the adventurous bands
With shuddering horror pale and eyes aghast,
View'd first their lamentable lot, and found
No rest. Through many a dark and dreary vale
They past, and many a region dolorous;
O'er many a frozen, many a fiery Alp,
Rocks, caves, lakes, fens, bogs, dens, and shades of death,
A universe of death.

Now who would not rather have forfeited an estate, than that Milton should have ended so deplorably,

Which God by curse
Created evil, *for evil only good,*
Where all life dies, death lives.

SOUTHEY. How Ovidian! This Book would be greatly improved, not merely by the rejection of a couple such as these, but by the whole from verse 647 to verse 1007. The number would still be 705; fewer by only sixty-four than the first would be after its reduction.

Verses 1088 and 1089 [1] could be spared. Satan but little encouraged his followers by reminding them that, if they took the course he pointed out, they were

So much the nearer danger,

---

[1] Verses 1008 and 1009.

SOUTHEY AND LANDOR

nor was it necessary to remind them of the obvious fact by saying,

> Havoc and spoil and ruin are my gain.[1]

LANDOR. In the Third Book the Invocation extends to fifty-five verses; of these however there are only two which you would expunge. He says to the *Holy Light*,

> But thou
> Revisit'st not these eyes, that toil in vain
> To find thy piercing ray, and find no dawn,
> So thick a *drop serene* hath quencht their orbs,
> Or dim suffusion veiled. Yet not the more, &c.

The fantastical Latin expression *gutta serena*, for amaurosis, was never received under any form into our language, and a *thick drop serene* would be nonsense in any. I think every reader would be contented with

> To find thy piercing ray. Yet not the more
> Cease I to wander where the Muses haunt, &c.

SOUTHEY. Pope is not highly reverent to Milton, or to God the Father, whom he calls a *school divine*. The doctrines, in this place (V. 80) more scripturally than poetically laid down, are apostolic. But Pope was unlikely to know it; for while he was a papist he was forbidden to read the Holy Scriptures, and when he ceased to be a papist, he threw them overboard and clung to nothing. The fixedness of his opinions may be estimated by his having written at the commencement of his *Essay*, first,

> A mighty maze, a maze without a plan,

and then,

> A mighty maze, *but not* without a plan.

After the seventy-sixth verse I wish the poet had abstained from writing all the rest until we come to 345: and that after the 382nd from all that precede the 418th. Again, all between 462 and 497. This about the Fool's Paradise,

> Indulgences, dispenses, pardons, bulls,

is too much in the manner of Dante, whose poetry, admirable as it

---

[1] Southey is here represented as supposing that verses 1088-89 belong to Satan's speech; actually they are in the speech of Chaos.

IMAGINARY CONVERSATIONS: ENGLISH

often is, is at all times very far removed from the dramatic and the epic.

LANDOR. Verse 586 is among the few inharmonious in this poem.

> Shoots invisible virtue even to the deep.

There has lately sprung up among us a Vulcan-descended body of splay-foot poets, who, unwilling

> Incudi reddere versus,[1]

or unable to hammer them into better shape and more solidity, tell us how necessary it is to shovel in the dust of a discord now and then. But Homer and Sophocles and Virgil could do without it.

What a beautiful expression is there in v. 546, which I do not remember that any critic has noticed,

> Obtains the brow of some *high-climbing* hill.

Here the hill itself is instinct with life and activity.

V. 574. "*But up or down*" in "*longitude*" are not worth the parenthesis.

V. 109. Farewell remorse! all good to me is lost.

Nothing more surprises me in Milton than that his ear should have endured this verse.

SOUTHEY. How admirably contrasted with the malignant spirit of Satan, in all its intensity, is the scene of Paradise which opens at verse 131. The change comes naturally and necessarily to accomplish the order of events.

The Fourth Book contains several imperfections. The six verses after 166 [2] efface the delightful impression we had just received.

> At one slight *bound* high overleapt all *bound*.

Such a play on words, so grave a pun, is unpardonable; and such a prodigious leap is ill represented by the feat of a wolf in a sheepfold; and still worse by

> A thief bent to unhoard the *cash*
> Of some rich burgher, whose substantial doors,
> *Cross-barr'd and bolted fast,* fear no assault,
> In at the window climbs, or o'er the tiles.

---

[1] Hor., *Ars Poet.*, 441.   [2] Verse 181.

SOUTHEY AND LANDOR

LANDOR. This " in at the window " is very unlike the " bound high above all bound "; and *climbing* " o'er the tiles " is the practice of a more deliberate burglar.

> So since into his church lewd hirelings climb.

I must leave the lewd hirelings where I find them ; they are too many for me. I would gladly have seen omitted all between v. 160 and 205.

SOUTHEY.

> Betwixt them lawns or level downs, and flocks
> Grazing the tender herb.

There had not yet been time for flocks, or even for one flock.

LANDOR. At two hundred and ninety-seven commences a series of verses so harmonious, that my ear is impatient of any other poetry for several days after I have read them. I mean those which begin,

> For contemplation he and valour formed,
> For softness she and sweet attractive grace,

and ending with,

> And sweet, reluctant, amorous, delay.

SOUTHEY. Here indeed is the triumph of our language, and I should say of our poetry, if, in your preference of Shakespeare, you could endure my saying it. But, since we seek faults rather than beauties this morning, tell me whether you are quite contented with,

> She, as a veil, down to the slender waist
> Her unadorned golden tresses wore,
> Dishevel'd, but in wanton ringlets waved
> As the vine curls her tendrils ; *which implied*
> *Subjection, but required with gentle sway,*
> *And by her yielded, by him best received.*

LANDOR. Stopping there, you break the link of harmony just above the richest jewel that Poetry ever wore :

> Yielded with coy submission, modest pride,
> And sweet, reluctant, amorous, delay.

I would rather have written these two lines than all the poetry that has been written since Milton's time in all the regions of the earth. We shall see again things equal in their way to the best of them: but here the sweetest of images and sentiments is seized and carried far away from all pursuers. Never tell me, what I think is already on your lips, that the golden tresses in their wanton ringlets implied nothing like subjection. Take away, if you will,

> And by her yielded, by him best received,

and all until you come to,

> Under a tuft of shade.

SOUTHEY. In verse 388 I wish he had employed some other epithet for *innocence* than *harmless*.

Verses 620 and 621 might be spared.

> While other animals *inactive* range,
> And of their doings God takes no account.

V. 660. Daughter of God and *man*, accomplisht Eve!

Surely she was not daughter of *man*: and of all the words that Milton has used in poetry or prose, this *accomplisht* is the worst. In his time it had already begun to be understood in the sense it bears at present.

Verse 674. " *These, then, tho'* "—harsh sounds so near together.

V. 700. *Mosaic;* underfoot the violet,
Crocus, and hyacinth, with rich inlay
Broidered the ground, more coloured than with stone
Of costliest emblem.

The *broidery* and *mosaic* should not be set quite so closely and distinctly before our eyes. I think the passage might be much improved by a few defalcations. Let me read it:

> The roof
> Of thickest covert was inwoven shade,
> Laurel and myrtle, and what higher grew
> Of firm and fragrant leaf; the violet,
> Crocus, and hyacinth.

I dare not handle the embroidery. Is not this sufficiently verbose?

LANDOR. Quite.

SOUTHEY AND LANDOR

SOUTHEY. Yet, if you look into your book again, you will find a gap as wide as the bank on either side of it :

> On either side
> Acanthus and each odorous bushy shrub
> *Fenced up* the verdant wall ; each beauteous flower,
> Iris all hues, roses and jessamin
> Reared *high* their *flourished* heads between, and *wrought Mosaic.*

He had before told us that there was every tree of *fragrant* leaf : we wanted not " each *odorous* shrub " ; nor can we imagine how it *fenced up* a verdant wall : it constituted one itself ; one very unlike anything else in Paradise, and more resembling the topiary artifices which had begun to flourish in France. Here is indeed an exuberance, and " a wanton growth that mocks our scant manuring."

> In shadier bower
> More sacred and sequestered, *though but feign'd,*
> Pan or Sylvanus never slept.   V. 705.

He takes especial heed to guard us against the snares of Paganism, at the expense of his poetry. In Italian books, as you remember, where Fate, Fortune, Pan, Apollo, or any mythological personage is named incidentally, notice is given at the beginning that no harm is intended thereby to the Holy Catholic-Apostolic religion. But harm is done on this occasion, where it is intended just as little.

> On him *who had stole* Jove's authentic fire.

This is a very weak and unsatisfactory verse. By one letter it may be much improved—*stolen,* which also has the advantage of rendering it grammatical. The word *who* coalesces with *had.* Of such coalescences the poetry of Milton is full. In five consecutive lines you find three.

> Thee only extolled, son of thy father's might
> To execute his vengeance on his foes,
> Not so on man ; him through their malice fallen.
> Father of mercy and grace thou didst not doom
> So strictly, but much more to pity inclined.

V. 722.   The God that made *both* sky, air, earth, and heaven.

Both must signify two things or persons, and never can signify more.

IMAGINARY CONVERSATIONS: ENGLISH

From v. 735 I would willingly see all removed until we come to,

> Hail wedded love!

After these eight I would reject thirteen.

In vv. 73 and 74 [1] there is an unfortunate recurrence of sound:

> The flowery roof
> Showered roses which the morn *repaired*. Sleep on,
> Blest *pair!*

and somewhat worse in the continuation,

> And O yet happiest, if ye seek
> *No* happier state, and *know* to *know no more.*

Five similar sounds in ten syllables, beside the affectation of "know to know."

V. 780. To their night watches in warlike parade

is not only a slippery verse in the place where it stands, but is really a verse of quite another metre. And I question whether you are better satisfied with the word *parade*.

V. 813.[2]
> As when a spark
> Lights on a heap of nitrous powder, *laid*
> *Fit for the tun, some magazine to store*
> Against a rumoured war.

Its fitness for the tun and its convenience for the magazine, adapt it none the better to poetry. Would there be any detriment to the harmony or the expression if we skip over that verse, reading,

> Stored
> Against a rumoured war?

LANDOR. No harm to either. The verses 333 and 334 [3] I perceive have the same cesura, and precisely that which rhyme chooses in preference, and Milton in his blank verse admits the least frequently.

> A faithful leader, not to hazard all,
> Through ways of danger by himself untried.

---

[1] Verses 772 and 774.   [2] Verse 814.   [3] Verses 933 and 934.

SOUTHEY AND LANDOR

Presently what a flagellation he inflicts on the traitor Monk!

> To say and straight unsay, pretending first
> Wise to fly pain, professing next the spy,
> Argues no leader, *but a liar traced*.

When he loses his temper he loses his poetry, in this place and most others. But such coarse hemp and wire were well adapted to the stript shoulders they scourged.

> Satan! and couldst thou *faithful* add? O name!
> O sacred name of faithfulness profaned!
> Faithful! to whom? to thy rebellious crew?
> Army of fiends, fit body to fit head,
> Was this your discipline and faith engaged?
> Your military obedience, to dissolve
> Allegiance to the acknowledged Power supreme?
> And thou, sly hypocrite, who now wouldst seem
> Patron of liberty, who more than thou
> Once fawned and cringed?

You noticed the rhyme of *supreme* and *seem*. Great heed should be taken against this grievous fault, not only in the final syllables of blank verse, but also in the cesuras. In our blank verse it is less tolerable than in the Latin heroic, where Ovid and Lucretius, and Virgil himself, are not quite exempt from it.

SOUTHEY. It is very amusing to read Johnson for his notions of harmony. He quotes these exquisite verses, and says, "There are two lines in this passage more remarkably inharmonious."

> This delicious place,
> For us too large, *where thy* abundance wants
> Partakers, and uncropt *falls to* the ground.

There are few so dull as to be incapable of perceiving the beauty of the rhythm in the last. Johnson goes out of his way to censure the best thought and the best verse in Cowley:

> And the soft wings of Peace *cover him* round.

Certainly it is not iambic where he wishes it to be. Milton, like the Italian poets, was rather too fond of this cadence, but in the instances which Johnson has pointed out for reprobation, it produces a fine effect. So in the verse,

> Not Typhon huge, ending in smoky wire.[1]

---

[1] *Sic.* Read: "snaky twine."

IMAGINARY CONVERSATIONS: ENGLISH

It does the same in *Samson Agonistes*:

> Retiring from the popular noise, I seek
> This unfrequented place, to find some ease,
> Ease to the body some, *none to* the mind.

Johnson tells us that the third and seventh are weak syllables, and that the period leaves the ear unsatisfied. Milton's ear happened to be satisfied by these pauses; and so will any ear be that is not (or was not intended by nature to be) nine fair inches long. Johnson is sensible of the harmony which is produced by the pause on the sixth syllable; but commends it for no better reason than because it forms a complete verse of itself. There can be no better reason against it.

In regard to the pause at the third syllable, it is very singular and remarkable that Milton never has paused for three lines together on any other. In the 327th,[1] 328th, and 329th of *Paradise Lost*, are these:

> His swift pursuers from heaven's gates pursue [2]
> The advantage, and descending tread us down,
> Thus drooping, or with linked thunderbolts
> Transfix us to the bottom of this gulf.

Another, whose name I have forgotten, has censured in like manner the defection and falling off in the seventh syllable of that very verse, which I remember your quoting as among the innumerable proofs of the poet's exquisite sensibility and judgment,

> And toward the gate *rolling* her bestial train,

where another would have written

> And rolling toward the gate, &c.

On the same occasion you praised Thomson very highly for having once written a most admirable verse where an ordinary one was obvious.

> And tremble every feather with desire.

Pope would certainly have preferred

> And every feather trembles with desire.

So would Dryden probably. Johnson, who censures some of the

---

[1] Verse 326.   [2] *Sic.* Read: "... gates discern."

SOUTHEY AND LANDOR

most beautiful lines in Milton, praises one in Virgil with as little judgment. He says, " We hear the passing arrow "

> Et fugit *horrendùm stridens* elapsa sagitta.

Now there never was an arrow in the world that made a *horrible stridor* in its course. The only sound is a very slight one occasioned by the feather. Homer would never have fallen into such an incongruity.

How magnificent is the close of this Fourth Book, from,

> Then when I am thy captive.

LANDOR. I do not agree to the use of golden scales, not figurative but real jewellers' gold, for weighing events :

> *Battles* and realms. In these he put two *weights*,
> The sequel each of parting and of fight ;
> The latter *quick* up-flew and *kicked* the beam.

To pass over the slighter objection of *quick* and *kick* as displeasing to the ear, the vulgarity of *kicking the beam* is intolerable : he might as well, among his angels, and among sights and sounds befitting them, talk of *kicking the bucket*. Here again he pays a penalty for trespassing.

SOUTHEY. I doubt whether (Fifth Book) there ever was a poet in a warm or temperate climate, who at some time or other of his life has not written about the nightingale. But no one rivals or approaches Milton in his fondness or his success. However, at the beginning of this Book, in a passage full of beauty, there are two expressions, and the first of them relates to the nightingale, which I disapprove.

> Tunes sweetest his *love-laboured song*. V. 41.

In *love-laboured*, the ear is gained over by the sweetness of the sound : but in the nightingale's song there is neither the reality nor the appearance of labour.

> *Sets off* the face of things. V. 43

is worthier of Addison than of Milton.

> But know that in the soul, &c. V. 100.

IMAGINARY CONVERSATIONS: ENGLISH

This philosophy on dreams, expounded by Adam, could never have been hitherto the fruit of his experience or his reflection.

LANDOR.
>These are thy glorious works, &c. V. 152.[1]

Who could imagine that Milton, who translated the Psalms worse than any man ever translated them before or since, should in this glorious hymn have made the 148th so much better than the original? But there is a wide difference between being bound to the wheels of a chariot and guiding it. He has ennobled that more noble one,

>O all ye works of the Lord, &c.

But in

>Ye mists and exhalations that now rise
>From hill or steaming lake, dusky or gray,
>Till the sun *paint* your fleecy skirts with *gold*, &c.

Such a verse might be well ejected from any poem whatsoever: but here its prettiness is quite insufferable. Adam never knew anything either of paint or gold. But, casting out this devil of a verse, surely so beautiful a psalm or hymn never rose to the Creator.

SOUTHEY. "No fear lest dinner cool" (v. 396) might as well never have been thought of: it seems a little too jocose. The speech of Raphael to Adam, on the subject of eating and drinking and the consequences, is neither angelic nor poetical: but the Sun *supping* with the Ocean is at least Anacreontic, and not very much debased by Cowley.

>So *down they sat*
>And to their viands *fell*.

LANDOR.
>Meanwhile the eternal eye, whose sight discerns
>Abstrusest thoughts, from forth his holy mount
>And from within the golden lamps that burn
>Nightly before him, saw without their light
>Rebellion rising, &c.
>And smiling to his only son thus said, &c. V. 711.

Bentley, and several such critics of poetry, are sadly puzzled, perplexed, and irritated at this. One would take refuge with the first grammar he can lay hold on, and cry *pars pro toto*: another strives hard for another suggestion. But if Milton by accident had written

[1] Verse 153.

both *Eternal* and *Eye* with a capital letter at the beginning, they would have perceived that he had used a noble and sublime expression for the Deity. No one is offended at the words: " It is the will of Providence," or, " It is the will of the Almighty "; yet Providence is that which *sees before;* and *will* is different from *might.* True it is that Providence and Almighty are qualities converted into appellations, and are well known to signify the Supreme Being: but, if the Eternal Eye is less well known to signify him, or not known at all, that is no reason why it should be thought inapplicable. It might be used injudiciously: for instance, the *right hand* of the Eternal Eye would be singularly so; but *smiles* not. The Eternal Eye *speaks* to his only Son. This is more incomprehensible to the critics than the preceding. And truly if that eye were like ours, and the organ of speech like ours also, it might be strange. Yet the very same good people have often heard without wonder of a *speaking* eye in a very ordinary person, and are conversant with poets who precede an expostulation, or an entreaty for a reply, with " *Lux* mea." [1] There is a much greater fault, which none of them has observed, in the beginning of the speech:

> Son! thou in whom my glory I behold
> In full resplendence! *heir* of all my might.

Now an *heir* is the future and not the present possessor; and he to whom he is heir must be extinct before he comes into possession. But this is nothing if you compare it with what follows, a few lines below:

> Let us advise and to this hazard draw
> With speed what force is left, and all employ
> In our defence, *lest unawares we lose*
> *This our high place, our sanctuary, our hill.*

Such expressions of derision are very ill applied, and derogate much from the majesty of the Father. We may well imagine that far different thoughts occupied the Divine Mind at the defection of innumerable angels, and their inevitable and everlasting punishment.

SOUTHEY. The critics do not agree on the meaning of the words,

> Much less for *this* to be our Lord. V. 799.

---

[1] Joannes Secundus, *Basium*, iii., where the phrase occurs in a passage of two verses declared by Landor, in his criticism of Catullus, 1842, to be of such excellence that the two lines " would have been quoted, even from Catullus, as among his best."

IMAGINARY CONVERSATIONS: ENGLISH

Nothing I think can be clearer, even without the explanation which is given by Abdiel in v. 813 :

> Canst thou with impious obloquy condemn
> The just decree of God, pronounced and sworn
> That to *his only Son*, by right endued
> With royal sceptre, every soul in heaven
> *Shall bend the knee?*

V. 860.[1] There are those who can not understand the plainest things, yet who can admire every fault that any clever man has committed before. Thus, *beseeching* or *besieging*, spoken by an angel, is thought proper, and perhaps beautiful, because a quibbler in a Latin comedy says, *amentium haud amantium*.[2] It appears then on record that the first overt crime of the refractory angels was *punning* : they fell rapidly after that.

LANDOR.

> *These tidings carry to the anointed king.* V. 870.

Whatever *anointing* the kings of the earth may have undergone, the King of Heaven had no occasion for it. Who anointed him ? When did his reign commence ?

> *Through the infinite host.* V. 874.

Although our poet would have made no difficulty of accenting "infinite" as we do, and as he himself has done in other places, I am inclined to think that the accent is here on the second syllable. He does not always accentuate the same word in the same place. In v. 889 [3] Bentley and the rest are in a bustle about,

> *Well didst thou* [4] *advise;*
> *Yet not for thy advice or threats I fly*
> *These wicked hosts* [5] *devoted, lest the wrath, &c.*

One suggests one thing, another another ; but nothing is more simple and easy than the construction, if you put a portion of the second verse in a parenthesis, thus,

> Yet (not for thy advice or threats), &c.

SOUTHEY. The archangel Michael is commanded (Book vi., v. 44) to do what the Almighty, who commands it, gave him not strength to

---

[1] Verse 869. [2] Terence, *Andr.* [3] Verse 888.
[4] *Sic.* Read : "thou didst." [5] *Sic.* Read : "wicked tents."

do, as we find in the sequel, and what was reserved for the prowess of the Messiah.

LANDOR. V. 115. " Whose faith and realty," &c. Bentley, more unlucky than ever, here would substitute *fealty*, as if there were any difference between *fealty* and *faith*: *reale* and *leale* are the same in Italian.

SOUTHEY.

> Before thy fellows, ambitious to win, &c. V 160.

Surely this line is a very feeble one, and where so low a tone is not requisite for the harmony or effect of the period. But the battle of Satan and Michael is worth all the battles in all other poets. I wish however I had not found

> A stream of *nectarous* humour issuing.

The *ichor* of Homer has lost its virtue by exposure and application to ordinary use. Yet even this would have been better:

> Forthwith on all sides to his aid *was run*
> By angels.

This Latinism is inadmissible; there is no loophole in our language for its reception. He once uses the same form in his History. " Now was fought eagerly on both sides." Even here the word *it* should have preceded: and the phrase would still remain a stiff intractable Latinism. In the remainder of this Book there are much graver faults, amid highest beauty. Surely it was unworthy of Milton to follow Ariosto, and Spenser, and many others, in dragging up his cannon from hell, although it is not, as in the *Faery Queen*, represented to us distinctly,

> *Ram'd with bullets round.*

LANDOR. I wish he had omitted all from v. 483,

> Which into hollow engines, *long and round*,
> Thick ramm'd at *the other bore*,

down to 525 [1]: and again from 545,[2] " barbed with fire," to v. 627,[3] where the wit, which Milton calls the *pleasant vein*, is worthy of

---

[1] Verse 523.   [2] Verse 546.   [3] Verse 628.

newly-made devils who never had heard any before, and falls as foul on the poetry as on the antagonist.

> Their *armour* helpt their *harm*.

Here *helpt* means *increased*. A few lines above, we find "*Light* as the *lightning* glimpse." We should have quite enough of this description if at v. 628 we substituted *but* for *so*, and continued to v. 644, " They pluckt the seated hills," skipping over all until we reach 654,

> Which in the air, &c.

SOUTHEY. I think I would go much farther, and make larger defalcations. I would lop off the whole from " Spirits of purest light," v. 661,[1] to 831; then (for *He*) reading " God on his impious foes," as far as 843, " his ire." Again, omitting nine verses, to " yet half his strength." The 866th line is not a verse: it is turned out of an Italian mould, but in a state too fluid and incohesive to stand in English. This Book should close with,

> Hell at last
> Yawning received them whole, and on them closed.

LANDOR. The poem would indeed be much the better for all the omissions you propose; if you could anywhere find room for those verses which begin at the 760th, " He in celestial panoply," and end with that sublime,

> He onward came : far off his coming shone.

The remainder, both for the subject and the treatment of it, may be given up without a regret. The last verse of the Book falls " succiso poplite,"

> Remember ; *and fear to transgress*.

Beautiful as are many parts of the Invocation at the commencement of the Seventh Book, I should more gladly have seen it without the first forty lines, and beginning,

> The affable archangel.

SOUTHEY.
> But knowledge is as food, and needs no less
> Her temperance over appetite.

---

[1] Verse 660.

SOUTHEY AND LANDOR

He might have ended here: he goes on thus:

> To know
> In measure what the mind may well contain

Even this does not satisfy him: he adds,

> Oppresses else with surfeit, and soon turns
> Wisdom to folly, as *nourishment to wind*.

Now certainly Adam could never yet have known anything about the meaning of surfeit, and we may suspect that the angel himself must have been just as ignorant on a section of physics which never had existed in the world below, and must have been without analogy in the world above.

LANDOR. His supper with Adam was unlikely to produce a surfeit.

> *At least* our envious foe hath fail'd. V. 139.

There is no meaning in *at least*; " at *last* " would be little better. I would not be captious nor irreverent; but surely the words which Milton gives as spoken by the Father to the Son, bear the appearance of boastfulness and absurdity. The Son must already have known both the potency and will of the Father. How incomparably more judicious, after five terrific verses, comes at once, without any intervention,

> Silence, ye troubled waves! and thou, deep, peace.

If we can imagine any thought or expression at all worthy of the Deity, we find it here. In v. 242 we have another specimen of Milton's consummate art:

> And earth, self-balanced, on her centre hung.

Unhappily he permitted his learning to render him verbose immediately after:

> Let there be light, said God, and forthwith light
> Ethereal, first of things, quintessence pure,
> Sprung from the deep.

The intermediate verse is useless and injurious; beside, according to his own account, light was not " first of things." He represents it springing from " the deep " after the earth had " hung on her centre," and long after the waters had been apparent. We do not want philosophy in the poem, we only want consistency.

SOUTHEY. There is no part of Milton's poetry where harmony is preserved, together with conciseness, so remarkably as in the verses beginning with 312,[1] and ending at 338: but in the midst of this beautiful description of the young earth, we find

> The bush with *frizzled* hair *implicit*.

But what poet or painter ever in an equal degree has raised our admiration of beasts, fowls, and fish? I know you have objected to the repetition of *shoal* in the word *scull*.

LANDOR. *Shoal* is a corruption of *scull*, which ought to be restored, serving the other with an ejectment to another place. Nor do I like *fry*. But the birds never looked so beautiful since they left Paradise. Let me read however three or four verses in order to offer a remark.

> Others, on silver lakes and rivers, bathed
> Their downy breast : the swan with arched neck
> Between her white wings mantling proudly, rows
> Her state with oary feet, yet oft they quit
> The dank, and rising on stiff pennons, tower, &c.

Frequently as the great poet pauses at the ninth syllable, it is incredible that he should have done it thrice in the space of five verses. For which reason, and as nothing is to be lost by it, I would place the comma after *mantling*. No word in the whole compass of our language has been so often ill applied or misunderstood by the poet as this.

SOUTHEY.
> Speed to describe whose swiftness number fails.
> Book viii., v. 38.

Adam could have had no notion of swiftness in the heavenly bodies or the earth: it is among the latest and most wonderful of discoveries.

LANDOR. Let us rise to Eve, and throw aside our algebra. The great poet is always greatest at this beatific vision. I wish however he had omitted the 46th and 47th verses, and also the 60th, 61st, 62nd, and 63rd. There is a beautiful irregularity in the 62nd,

> And from about her shot darts of desire.

---
[1] Verse 313.

SOUTHEY AND LANDOR

But when he adds, " Into *all* eyes," as there were but four, we must except the angel's two : the angel had no occasion for wishing to see what he was seeing.

> He his fabric of the heavens
> Hath left to their disputes, *perhaps to move*
> His laughter.

I can not well entertain this opinion of the Creator's risible faculties and propensities. Milton here carries his anthropomorphism much farther than the poem (which needed a good deal of it) required.

SOUTHEY. I am sorry to find a verse of twelve syllables in 216. I mean to say where no syllables coalesce ; in which case there are several which contain that number unobjectionably.

LANDOR. In my opinion a greater fault is to be found in the passage beginning at verse 286.[1]

> There gentle sleep
> First found me, and with soft oppression seiz'd
> My drowsied sense, untroubled, though I thought
> I then was passing to my former state,
> Insensible, and forthwith to dissolve.

How could he think he was passing into a state of which, at that time, he knew nothing ?

> Daughter of God and man, immortal Eve ! V. 291.

Magnificent verse, and worthy of Milton in his own person : but Adam, in calling her thus, is somewhat too poetical, and too presumptuous : for what else does he call her, but " daughter of God and *me* " ? Now, the idea of *daughter* could never, by any possibility, have yet entered his mind.

> *Affronts* us with his foul esteem
> Of our integrity : his foul esteem
> Sticks no dishonour on our front, but turns
> Foul on himself. V. 328.

The word *affront* is to be taken in its plain English sense, not in its Italian : but what a jingle and clash and clumsy play of words ! In v. 353, I find, " But bid her well be ware," and *be ware* is very properly in two words : so should *be gone*, and *can not*.

[1] Verse 287.

IMAGINARY CONVERSATIONS: ENGLISH

> To the garden of bliss, thy seat prepared. V. 299.

This verse is too slippery, too Italian.

> What thinkest thou then of me and this my state?
> Seem I to thee sufficiently possest
> Of happiness or not, who am alone
> From all eternity; for none I know
> Second to me or like, equal much less. V. 403.

This comes with an ill grace, after the long consultation which the Father had holden with the Son, equal (we are taught to believe) in the godhead.

SOUTHEY.

> And through *all numbers absolute*, though one. V. 421.

I wish he had had the courage to resist this pedantic quibbling Latinism. Our language has never admitted the phrase, and never will admit it.

LANDOR. I have struck it out, you see, and torn the paper in doing so. In verse 576,

> Made so *adorn*, &c.

I regret that we have lost this beautiful adjective, which was well worth bringing from Italy. Here follows some very bad reasoning on love, which (being human love) the angel could know nothing about, and speaks accordingly. He adds,

> In loving thou dost well, in passion not.

Now love, to be perfect, should consist of passion and sentiment, in parts as nearly equal as possible, with somewhat of the material to second them.

SOUTHEY. We are come to the Ninth Book, from which I would cast away the first forty-seven verses.

LANDOR. Judiciously. In the eighty-first you will find a verb singular for two substantives, " the land where flows Ganges and Indus." The small fry will carp at this, which is often an elegance, but oftener in Greek than in Latin, in Latin than in French, in French than in English. Here follow some of the dullest lines in Milton.

> Him, after long debate irresolute
> Of thoughts resolved, his final sentence chose
> Fit vessel, fittest imp of fraud, in whom

SOUTHEY AND LANDOR

> To enter, and his dark suggestion hide
> From sharpest sight : for in the wily snake
> Whatever sleights, *none* would suspicions mark,
> As from his wit and native subtilty
> Proceeding, which in other beasts observed,
> Doubt might beget of diabolic power
> Active within, beyond the sense of brute.

Not to insist on the prosaic of the passage, we may inquire who could be suspicious, or who could know anything about his wit and subtilty ? He had been created but a few days, and probably no creature (brute, human, or angelic) had ever taken the least notice of him, or heard anything of his propensities. " *Diabolic* power " had taken no such direction: and the serpent was so obscure a brute, that the devil himself knew scarcely where to find him. When however he did find him,

> In labyrinth of many a round self-rolled,
> His head the midst, *well stored with subtile wiles,*

he made the most of him. But why had he hitherto borne so bad a character ? Who had ever yet been a sufferer by his wit and subtilty ? In the very next verses, the poet says he was

> Not nocent yet ; but on the grassy herb
> Fearless, unfear'd, he slept.

SOUTHEY. These are the contradictions of a dreamer. Horace has said of Homer, " aliquando bonus *dormitat*." This really is no napping ; it is heavy snoring. But how fresh and vigorous he rises the next moment. And we are carried by him, we know not how, into the presence of Eve, and help her to hold down the strong and struggling woodbine for the arbour. I wish Milton had forgotten the manner of Euripides in his dull reflections, and had not forced into Adam's mouth,

> For nothing lovelier can be found
> In woman than to *study household good*,
> And good works in her husband to promote.

All this is very true, but very tedious, and very out of place.

LANDOR. Let us come into the open air again with her. I wish she had not confessed such a predilection for,

> The smell of sweetest *fennel*. V. 581 ;

IMAGINARY CONVERSATIONS : ENGLISH

for although it is said to be very pleasant to serpents, no serpent had yet communicated any of his tastes to womankind.[1] Again, I suspect you would wish our good Milton a little farther from the schools, when he tells Eve that

> The wife, where danger or dishonour lurks,
> Safest and seemliest by her husband stays,
> Who guards her, or with her the worst endures.

But how fully and nobly he compensates the inappropriate thought by the most appropriate !

> Just then return'd *at shut of evening flowers*.

SOUTHEY.
> To whom the wily *adder*, blythe and glad. V. 625.

I strongly object to the word *adder*, which reduces the grand serpent to very small dimensions. It never is, or has been, applied to any other species than the little ugly venomous viper of our country. Of such a reptile it never could be said that,

> He *swiftly* roll'd
> In *tangles*,

nor that

> Hope elevates, and joy
> Brightens his crest.

Here again Homer would have run into no such error. But error is more pardonable than wantonness, such as he commits in verse 648 :

> *Fruitless* to me, though *fruit* be here to excess.

LANDOR. You have often, no doubt, repeated in writing a word you had written just before. Milton has done it inadvertently in

> While each part,
> Motion, *each* act, won audience ere the tongue, &c. V. 674.

Evidently *each* should be *and*. Looking at the tempter in the shape of an *adder*, as he is last represented to us, there is something which prepares for a smile on the face of Eve, when he says,

> *Look on me*,
> Me, who have toucht and tasted, yet both *live*
> And life more perfect have attained than fate
> Meant me.

---

[1] Landor has forgotten that it is the serpent who is the speaker.

SOUTHEY AND LANDOR

Now certainly the adder was the most hideous creature that ever had crossed her path, and she had no means of knowing, unless by taking his own word for it, that he was a bit wiser than the rest. Indeed she had heard the voices of many long before she had heard his, and as they all excelled him in stateliness, she might well imagine they were by no means inferior to him in intellect, and were more likely by their conformation to have reached and eaten the apple, although they held their tongues. In verse 781,

> She pluckt, she *eat*.
> Earth felt the wound, and nature from her *seat*, &c.

Surely he never wrote *eat* for *ate;* nor would he admit a rhyme where he could at least palliate it. But although we met together for the purpose of plucking out the weeds and briars of this boundless and most glorious garden, and not of overlauding the praises of others, we must admire the wonderful skill of Milton in this section of his work. He represents Eve as beginning to be deceitful and audacious; as ceasing to fear, and almost as ceasing to reverence the Creator; and shuddering not at extinction itself, until she thinks of

> Adam wedded to another Eve.

SOUTHEY. We shall lose our dinner, our supper, and our sleep, if we expatiate on the innumerable beauties of the volume: we have scarcely time to note the blemishes. Among these,

> In her face excuse
> Came prologue and apology less prompt.

There is a levity and impropriety in thus rushing on the stage. I think the vv. 957, 958, and 959, superfluous, and somewhat dull; beside that they are the repetition of 915 and 916, in his soliloquy.

LANDOR. I wish that after 1003,

> Wept at completing of the mortal sin,

every verse were omitted, until we reach the 1821st:[1]

> They sat them down to weep.

A very natural sequence. We should indeed lose some fine poetry; in which however there are passages which even the sanctitude of

[1] 1121st.

IMAGINARY CONVERSATIONS: ENGLISH

Milton is inadequate to veil decorously. At all events, we should get fairly rid of "*Herculean* Sampson." V. 1060.

SOUTHEY. But you would also lose such a flood of harmony as never ran on earth beyond that Paradise. I mean,

> How shall I behold the face
> Henceforth of God or angel, erst with joy
> And rapture so oft beheld ? Those heavenly shapes
> Will dazzle now this earthly with their blaze,
> Insufferably bright. O ! might I here
> In solitude live savage ! in some glade
> Obscured, where highest woods, impenetrable
> To star or sunlight, spread their umbrage broad
> And brown as evening. Cover me, ye pines,
> Ye cedars, with innumerable boughs,
> Hide me, where I may never see them more.

LANDOR. Certainly, when we read these verses, the ear is closed against all others, for the day, or even longer. It sometimes is a matter of amusement to hear the silliness of good men conversing on poetry; but when they lift up some favourite on their shoulders, and tell us to look at one equal in height to Milton, I feel strongly inclined to scourge the more prominent fool of the two, the moment I can discover which it is.

SOUTHEY.

> Long they sat, as *strucken mute*. V. 104.[1]

Stillingfleet says, "This vulgar expression may owe its origin to the stories in romances, of the effect of the magical wand." Nothing more likely. How many modes of speech are called vulgar, in a contemptuous sense, which, because of their propriety and aptitude, strike the senses of all who hear them, and remain in the memory during the whole existence of the language. This is one, and although of daily parlance, it is highly poetical, and among the few flowers of romance that retain their freshness and odour.

LANDOR.

> For what can 'scape the eye, &c. Book x., v. 5.

When we find in Milton such words as '*scape*, '*sdain*, &c., with the sign of elision in front of them, we may attribute such a sign to the wilfulness of the printer, and the indifference of the author in regard

[1] Verse 1064.

SOUTHEY AND LANDOR

to its correction. He wrote both words without it, from the Italian *scappare* and *sdegnare*. In v. 19,[1]

>*Made* haste to *make* appear,

is negligence or worse: but incomparably worse still is,

>And usher in
>The evening cool, when he from wrath *more cool.* V. 95.

SOUTHEY. In 120,[2] he writes *revile* (a substantive) for *rebuke*. In 100 and 131[3] are two verses of similar pauses in the same place.

>I should conceal, and not expose to blame
>By my complaint.

The worst of it is, that the words become a verse, and a less heavy one, by tagging the two pieces together.

>And not expose to blame by my complaint.

I agree with you that, in blank verse, the pause, after the fourth syllable, which Pope and Johnson seem to like the best, is very tiresome if often repeated; and Milton seldom falls into it. But he knew where to employ it with effect: for example, in this sharp reproof, twice over. Verses 143[4] and 146.

>Was she thy God, that her thou didst obey
>Before his voice?

In v. 155 he represents the Almighty using a most unseemly metaphor.

>Which was thy part
>And person.

A metaphor taken from the masks of the ancient stage certainly ill suits " His part and person."

LANDOR. Here are seven (v. 175) such vile verses, and forming so vile a sentence, that, it appears to me, a part of God's malediction must have fallen on them on their way from *Genesis*. In 195,[5] he says,

>Children thou shalt bring
>In sorrow forth, and to thy husband's will
>Thine shall submit: he over thee shall rule.

---

[1] Verse 29.   [2] Verse 118.   [3] Verses 130, 131.
[4] Verse 145.   [5] Verse 194.

IMAGINARY CONVERSATIONS : ENGLISH

The Deity had commanded the latter part from the beginning : it now comes as the completion of the curse.

V. 198 is no verse at all.

> Because thou hast *harkened* to the voice of thy wife.

There are very few who have not done this, *bon-gré mal-gré*, and many have thought it curse enough of itself; poor Milton, no doubt, among the rest.

SOUTHEY. I suspect you will abate a little of your hilarity, if you continue to read from v. 220 about a dozen: they are most oppressive.

> I shall not lag behind, nor err
> The way thou leading.

Such is the punctuation; wrong, I think. I would read,

> I shall not lag behind nor err,
> The way thou leading.

LANDOR. He was very fond of this Latinism : but to *err a way* is neither Latin idiom nor English. From 292[1] to 316, what a series of verses ! a structure more magnificent and wonderful than the terrific bridge itself, the construction of which required the united work of the two great vanquishers of all mankind.

SOUTHEY. Pity that he could not abstain from a pun at the bridgefoot, " by wondrous art *pontifical*." In v. 348 he recurs to the word *pontifice*. A few lines above, I mean v. 315, there must be a parenthesis. The verses are printed,

> Following the track
> Of Satan to the self-same place where he
> First lighted from his wing and landed safe
> From out of chaos, to the outside bare
> Of this round world.

I would place all the words after " Satan," including *chaos*, in a parenthesis; else we must alter the second *to* for *on;* and it is safer and more reverential to correct the punctuation of a great poet than the slightest word. Bentley is much addicted to this impertinence.

LANDOR. In his emendations, as he calls them, both of Milton and of Horace, for one happy conjecture he makes at least twenty

[1] Verse 293.

wrong, and ten ridiculous. In the Greek poets, and sometimes in Terence, he, beyond the rest of the pack, was often brought into the trail by scenting an unsoundness in the metre. But let me praise him where few think of praising him, or even of suspecting his superiority. He wrote better English than his adversary Middleton, and established for his university that supremacy in classical literature which it still retains.

In v. 369 I find " Thou us empower*ed*." This is ungrammatical: it should be empower*edst*, since it relates to time past: had it related to time present, it would still be wrong; it should then be empower*est*. I wonder that Bentley has not remarked this, for it lay within his competence.

SOUTHEY. That is no reason why he omitted to remark it. I like plain English so much that I can not refrain from censuring the phraseology of v. 345, " With joy and tidings fraught," meaning *joyful tidings*, and defended by Virgil's *munera lætitiamque dei*. Phrases are not good, whether in Latin or English, which do not convey their meaning unbroken and unobstructed. The best understanding would with difficulty master such expressions, of which the signification is traditional from the grammarians, but beyond the bounds of logic, or even the liberties of speech. You, who have ridiculed Virgil's *odor attulit auras*, and many similar foolish tricks committed by him, will pardon my animadversion on a smaller (though no small) fault in Milton.

LANDOR. Right. Again I go forward to punctuation. Bentley is puzzled again at v. 368. It is printed with the following:

> Thou hast achieved our liberty, confined
> Within hell-gates till now; thou us empower'd
> To fortify thus far, and overlay
> With this portentous bridge, the dark abyss.

The punctuation should be,

> Thou hast achieved our liberty: confined
> Within hell-gates till now, thou us empoweredst, &c.

I wonder that Milton should a second time have committed so grave a grammatical fault as he does in writing " thou empower*ed*," instead of empower*edst*. V. 380,

> Parted by the empyreal bounds,
> His *quadrature*, from thy orbicular world.

IMAGINARY CONVERSATIONS: ENGLISH

Again the schoolmen, and the crazy philosophers who followed them. It was believed that the empyrean is a quadrangle, because in the *Revelation* the *Holy City* is square. It is lamentable that Milton should throw overboard such prodigious stores of poetry and wisdom, and hug with such pertinacity the ill-tied bladders of crude learning. But see him here again in all his glory. I wish indeed he had rejected " the plebeian angel militant," and that we might read, missing four verses,

> He through the midst *unmaskt* [1]
> Ascended his high throne.

What noble verses, fifteen together!

SOUTHEY. It is much to be regretted that most of the worst verses and much of the foulest language are put into the mouth of the Almighty. For instance, v. 630, &c. I am afraid you will be less tolerant here than you were about the quadrature.

> My hell-hounds, to lick up the draff and filth . . .
> . . . till crammed and gorged, nigh burst . . .
> With suckt and glutted offal.

We are come
> To the other five,
> Their planetary motions and aspects,
> In sextile, square, and trine, and opposite . . .
> Like change on sea and land ; *sideral* blast. V. 693.

Although he is partial to this scansion, I am inclined to believe that here he wrote *sidereal;* because the same scansion as *sideral* recurs in the close of the verse next but one :

> Now *from the* north.

And, if it is not too presumptuous, I should express a doubt whether the poet wrote

> Is his wrath also ? Be it : man is not so.

Not so and *also*, in this position are disagreeable to the ear ; which might have been avoided by omitting the unnecessary *so* at the close.

LANDOR. You are correct. " *Ay me.*" So I find it spelt (v. 813), not *ah me!* as usually. It is wonderful that, of all things borrowed,

---

[1] *Sic.* Read : " *unmarked.*"

SOUTHEY AND LANDOR

we should borrow the expression of grief. One would naturally think that every nation had its own, and indeed every man his. *Ay me!* is the *ahime!* of the Italians. *Ahi lasso!* is also theirs. Our *gadso*, less poetical and sentimental, comes also from them : we need not look for the root.

SOUTHEY. Again I would curtail a long and somewhat foul excrescence, terminating with coarse invectives against the female sex, and with reflections more suitable to the character and experience of Milton than of Adam. I would insert my pruning-knife at v. 871—

> To warn all creatures from thee—

and cut clean through, quite to " household peace confound," v. 908.

LANDOR. The reply of Eve is exquisitely beautiful, especially

> Both have sinned, but thou
> Against God only, I against God and thee.

At last her voice fails her.

> Me, me only, just object of his ire.

Bentley, and thousands more, would read, " Me, only me ! " But Milton did not write for Bentley, nor for those thousands more. Similar, in the trepidation of grief, is Virgil's, " Me, me, adsum qui feci," &c.

> Why stand we longer shivering under fears,
> That show no end but death, and have the power
> Of many ways to die the shortest choosing,
> Destruction with destruction to destroy.   V. 1003, &c.

This punctuation is perhaps the best yet published : but, after all, it renders the sentence little better than nonsense. Eve, according to this, talks at once of hesitation and of choice, " shivering under fears," and both of them " choosing the shortest way," yet she expostulates with Adam why he is not ready to make the choice. The perplexity would be solved by writing thus :

> Why stand we longer shivering under fears
> That show no end but death ? and have the power
> Of many ways to die ! the shortest choose—
> Destruction with destruction to destroy.

If we persist in retaining the participle *choosing*, instead of the

IMAGINARY CONVERSATIONS: ENGLISH

imperative *choose*, grammar, sense, and spirit, all escape us. I am convinced that it was an oversight of the transcriber: and we know how easily, in our own works, faults to which the eye and ear are accustomed, escape our detection, and we are surprised when they are first pointed out to us.

SOUTHEY. I wish you could mend as easily,

> On me the curse aslope
> *Glanced on the ground :* with labour I must earn, &c. V. 1053.

LANDOR. In the very first verse of the Eleventh Book, Milton is resolved to display his knowledge of the Italian idiom. We left Adam and Eve *prostrate ;* and prostrate he means that they should still appear to us, although he writes,

> Thus they, in loneliest plight, repentant *stood*
> Praying.

Stavano pregando would signify *they continued praying.* The Spaniards have the same expression: the French, who never stand still on any occasion, are without it.

SOUTHEY. It is piteous that Milton, in all his strength, is forced to fall back on the old fable of Deucalion and Pyrrha. And the prayers which the son of God presents to the Father in a " golden censer, mixed with incense," had never yet been offered to the Mediator, and required no such accompaniment or conveyance. There are some noble lines beginning at 72; but one of them is prosaic in itself, and its discord is profitless to the others. In v. 86,

> Of that *defended* fruit,

I must remark that Milton is not quite exempt from the evil spirit of saying things for the mere pleasure of defending them. Chaucer used the word *defend* as the English of education then used it, in common with the French. It was obsolete in that sense when Milton wrote; so it was even in the age of Spenser, who is forced to employ it for the rhyme.

LANDOR. This evil spirit which you find hanging about Milton, fell on him from two school-rooms, both of which are now become much less noisy and somewhat more instructive, although Phillpots is in the one, and although Brougham is in the other; I mean the school-rooms of theology and criticism.

SOUTHEY AND LANDOR

SOUTHEY. You will be glad that he accents *contrite* (v. 90) on the last syllable, but the gladness will cease at the first of *rèceptacle*, v. 123.

LANDOR. I question whether he pronounced it so. My opinion is, that he pronounced it *receptàcle*, Latinizing as usual, and especially in Book viii., v. 574,[1]

By *attributing* overmuch to things, &c.

We are strange perverters of Latin accentuations. From *irrìto* we make *ĭrrĭtate*; from *excìto*, *excìte*. But it must be conceded that the latter is much for the better, and perhaps the former also. You will puzzle many good Latin scholars in England, and nearly all abroad, if you make them read any sentence containing *irrito* or *excito* in any of their tenses. I have often tried it; and nearly all, excepting the Italians, have pronounced both words wrong.

SOUTHEY.
    Watchful cherubim, four faces each
Had, *like a double Janus*.

Better left this to the imagination: double Januses are queer figures. He continues,

    All their shape
Spangled with eyes, more numerous than those
Of Argus.

At the restoration of learning it was very pardonable to seize on every remnant of antiquity, and to throw together into one great store-room whatever could be collected from all countries, and from all authors, sacred and profane. Dante has done it; sometimes rather ludicrously. Milton here copies his *Argus*. And four lines farther on, he brings forward *Leucothoë*, in her own person, although she had then no existence.

LANDOR. Nor indeed had *subscriptions*, to articles or anything else: yet we find " but Fate *subscribed* not," v. 182.[2] And within three more lines, " The bird of *Jove*." Otherwise the passage is one of exquisite beauty. Among the angels, and close at the side of the archangel, " *Iris* had dipt her woof." Verse 267, *retire* is a substantive, from the Italian and Spanish.

How divinely beautiful is the next passage! It is impossible

---

[1] Verse 565.   [2] Verse 181.

IMAGINARY CONVERSATIONS : ENGLISH

not to apply to Milton himself the words he has attributed to Eve :

> From thee
> How shall I part ? and whither wander down
> Into a lower world ?

My ear, I confess it, is dissatisfied with everything, for days and weeks, after the harmony of *Paradise Lost.* Leaving this magnificent temple, I am hardly to be pacified by the fairy-built chambers, the rich cupboards of embossed plate, and the omnigenous images of Shakespeare.

SOUTHEY. I must interrupt your transports.

> His *eye* might there command where-ever stood
> City of old or modern fame.

Here are twenty-five lines describing cities to exist long after, and many which his *eye* could not have commanded even if they existed then, because they were situated on the opposite side of the globe. But some of them, the poet reminds us afterward, Adam might have seen in spirit. Diffuse as he is, he appears quite moderate in comparison with Tasso on a similar occasion, who expatiates not only to the length of five-and-twenty lines, but to between four and five hundred.

LANDOR. At v. 480 there begins a catalogue of diseases, which Milton increased in the second edition of the poem. He added,

> Demoniac frenzy, moping melancholy,
> And moonstruck madness, pining atrophy,
> Marasmus, and wide-wasting pestilence !

There should be no comma after " melancholy," as there is in my copy.

SOUTHEY. And in mine too. He might have afforded to strike out the two preceding verses when these noble ones were presented.

> Intestine stone and ulcer, colic pangs,

are better to be understood than to be expressed. His description of old age is somewhat less sorrowful and much less repulsive. It closes with

> In thy blood will reign
> A melancholy *damp* of cold and *dry.*

Nobody could understand this who had not read the strange notions of physicians, which continued down to the age of Milton, in which we find such nonsense as " *adust* humours." I think you would be unreluctant to expunge vv. 624, 625, 626, 627.

LANDOR. Quite : and there is also much verbiage about the giants, and very perplexed from v. 88 to 97.[1] But some of the heaviest verses in the poem are those on Noah, from 717 to 737. In the following we have " *vapour* and *exhalation,*" which signify the same.

> Sea covered sea,
> Sea without shore. V. 750.[2]

This is very sublime : and indeed I could never heartily join with those who condemn in Ovid

> Omnia pontus erant ; deerant quoque litora ponto.

It is true, the whole fact is stated in the first hemisytch ; but the mind's eye moves from the centre to the circumference, and the pleonasm carries it into infinity. If there is any fault in this passage of Ovid, Milton has avoided it, but he frequently falls into one vastly more than Ovidian, and after so awful a pause as is nowhere else in all the regions of poetry.

> How didst thou grieve then, Adam, to behold
> The end of all thy offspring ! end so sad !
> Depopulation !
> *Thee another flood,*
> *Of tears and sorrow a flood, thee also drowned,*
> *And sank thee as thy sons.*

It is wonderful how little reflection on many occasions, and how little knowledge on some very obvious ones, is displayed by Bentley. To pass over his impudence in pretending to correct the words of Milton (whose handwriting was extant) just as he would the corroded or corrupt text of any ancient author, here in v. 895. " To drown the world with man therein, or *beast* " ; he tells us that *birds are forgot*, and would substitute " With man or beast or *fowl*." He might as well have said that *fleas* are *forgot*. Beast means everything that is not man. It would be much more sensible to object to such an expression as *men and animals*, and to ask, are not men animals ? and even more so than the rest, if *anima* has with men a

[1] Verses 688 to 697. [2] Verse 749.

more extensive meaning than with other creatures. Bentley in many things was very acute; but his criticisms on poetry produce the same effect as the water of a lead mine on plants. He knew no more about it than Hallam knows, in whom acuteness is certainly not blunted by such a weight of learning.

SOUTHEY. We open the Twelfth Book: we see land at last.

LANDOR. Yes, and dry land too. Happily the twelfth is the shortest. In a continuation of six hundred and twenty-five flat verses, we are prepared for our passage over several such deserts of almost equal extent, and still more frequent, in *Paradise Regained*. But at the close of the poem now under our examination, there is a brief union of the sublime and the pathetic for about twenty lines, beginning with " All in bright array."

We are comforted by the thought that Providence had not abandoned our first parents, but was still their guide; that, although they had lost Paradise, they were not debarred from Eden; that, although the angel had left them solitary and sorrowing, he left them " yet in peace." The termination is proper and complete.

In Johnson's estimate I do not perceive the unfairness of which many have complained. Among his first observations is this: " Scarcely any recital is wished shorter for the sake of quickening the main action." This is untrue: were it true, why remark, as he does subsequently, that the poem is mostly read as a duty; not as a pleasure. I think it unnecessary to say a word on the moral or the subject; for it requires no genius to select a grand one. The heaviest poems may be appended to the loftiest themes. Andreini and others, whom Milton turned over and tossed aside, are evidences. It requires a large stock of patience to travel through Vida; and we slacken in our march, although accompanied with the livelier singsong of Sannazar. Let any reader, who is not by many degrees more pious than poetical, be asked whether he felt a very great interest in the greatest actors of *Paradise Lost*, in what is either said or done by the angels or the Creator; and whether the humblest and weakest does not most attract him. Johnson's remarks on the allegory of Milton are just and wise; so are those on the nonmateriality or non-immateriality of Satan. These faults might have been easily avoided: but Milton, with all his strength, chose rather to make Antiquity his shield-bearer, and to come forward under a protection which he might proudly have disdained.

SOUTHEY AND LANDOR

SOUTHEY. You will not countenance the critic, nor Dryden whom he quotes, in saying that Milton " saw Nature through the spectacles of books."

LANDOR. Unhappily both he and Dryden saw Nature from between the houses of Fleet-street. If ever there was a poet who knew her well, and described her in all her loveliness, it was Milton. In the *Paradise Lost* how profuse in his descriptions, as became the time and place! in the *Allegro* and *Penseroso,* how exquisite and select!

Johnson asks, " What Englishman can take delight in transcribing passages, which, if they lessen the reputation of Milton, diminish, in some degree, the honour of our country!" I hope the honour of our country will always rest on truth and justice. It is not by concealing what is wrong that anything right can be accomplished. There is no pleasure in transcribing such passages, but there is great utility. Inferior writers exercise no interest, attract no notice, and serve no purpose. Johnson has himself done great good by exposing great faults in great authors. His criticism on Milton's highest work is the most valuable of all his writings. He seldom is erroneous in his censures, but he never is sufficiently excited to admiration of what is purest and highest in poetry. He has this in common with common minds (from which however his own is otherwise far remote), to be pleased with what is nearly on a level with him, and to drink as contentedly a heady beverage with its discoloured froth, as what is of the best vintage. He is morbid, not only in his weakness, but in his strength. There is much to pardon, much to pity, much to respect, and no little to admire in him.

After I have been reading the *Paradise Lost,* I can take up no other poet with satisfaction. I seem to have left the music of Handel for the music of the streets, or at best for drums and fifes. Although in Shakespeare there are occasional bursts of harmony no less sublime, yet, if there were many such in continuation, it would be hurtful, not only in comedy, but also in tragedy. The greater part should be equable and conversational. For, if the excitement were the same at the beginning, the middle, and the end; if consequently (as must be the case) the language and versification were equally elevated throughout; any long poem would be a bad one, and, worst of all, a drama. In our English heroic verse, such as Milton has composed it, there is a much greater variety of feet, of movement, of musical notes and bars, than in the Greek

IMAGINARY CONVERSATIONS: ENGLISH

heroic; and the final sounds are incomparably more diversified. My predilection in youth was on the side of Homer; for I had read the *Iliad* twice, and the *Odyssea* once, before the *Paradise Lost*. Averse as I am to everything relating to theology, and especially to the view of it thrown open by this poem, I recur to it incessantly as the noblest specimen in the world of eloquence, harmony, and genius.

SOUTHEY. Learned and sensible men are of opinion that the *Paradise Lost* should have ended with the words " Providence their guide." It might very well have ended there; but we are unwilling to lose sight all at once of our first parents. Only one more glimpse is allowed us: we are thankful for it. We have seen the natural tears they dropped; we have seen that they wiped them *soon*. And why was it? Not because the world was all before them, but because there still remained for them, under the guidance of Providence, not indeed the delights of Paradise, now lost for ever, but the genial clime and calm repose of Eden.

LANDOR. It has been the practice in late years to supplant one dynasty by another, political and poetical. Within our own memory no man had ever existed who preferred Lucretius, on the whole, to Virgil, or Dante to Homer. But the great Florentine, in these days, is extolled high above the Grecian and Milton. Few, I believe, have studied him more attentively or with more delight than I have; but beside the prodigious disproportion of the bad to the good, there are fundamental defects which there are not in either of the other two. In the *Divina Commedia* the characters are without any bond of union, any field of action, any definite aim. There is no central light above the Bolge; and we are chilled in Paradise even at the side of Beatrice.

SOUTHEY. Some poetical Perillus must surely have invented the *terza rima*. I feel in reading it as a school-boy feels when he is beaten over the head with a bolster.

LANDOR. We shall hardly be in time for dinner. What should we have been if we had repeated with just eulogies all the noble things in the poem we have been reading?

SOUTHEY. They would never have weaned you from the *Mighty Mother* who placed her turreted crown on the head of Shakespeare.

LANDOR. A rib of Shakespeare would have made a Milton: the same portion of Milton, all poets born ever since.

SOUTHEY AND LANDOR

SECOND CONVERSATION

(*Wks.*, ii., 1846; *Wks.*, iv., 1876.)

SOUTHEY. As we are walking on, and before we open our Milton again, we may digress a little in the direction of those poets who have risen up from under him, and of several who seem to have never had him in sight.

LANDOR. We will, if you please: and I hope you may not find me impatient to attain the object of our walk. However, let me confess to you, at starting, that I disapprove of models, even of the most excellent. Faults may be avoided, especially if they are pointed out to the inexperienced in such bright examples as Milton: and teachers in schools and colleges would do well to bring them forward, instead of inculcating an indiscriminate admiration. But every man's mind, if there is enough of it, has its peculiar bent. Milton may be imitated, and has been, where he is stiff, where he is inverted, where he is pedantic; and probably those men we take for mockers were unconscious of their mockery. But who can teach, or who is to be taught, his richness, or his tenderness, or his strength? The closer an inferior poet comes to a great model, the more disposed am I to sweep him out of my way.

SOUTHEY. Yet you repeat with enthusiasm the Latin poetry of Robert Smith, an imitator of Lucretius.

LANDOR. I do; for Lucretius himself has nowhere written such a continuity of admirable poetry. He is the only modern Latin poet who has composed three sentences together worth reading; and indeed, since Ovid, no ancient has done it. I ought to bear great ill-will toward him; for he drove me from the path of poetry I had chosen, and I crept into a lower. What a wonderful thing it is, that the most exuberant and brilliant wit, and the purest poetry in the course of eighteen centuries, should have flowed from two brothers!

SOUTHEY. We must see through many ages before we see through our own distinctly. Few among the best judges, and even among those who desired to judge dispassionately and impartially, have beheld their contemporaries in those proportions in which they appeared a century later. The ancients have greatly the advantage over us. Scarcely can any man believe that one whom he has seen in coat and cravat, can possibly be so great as one who wore a chlamys and a toga. Those alone look gigantic whom Time " *multo aëre sepsit*," or whom childish minds, for the amusement of other minds more childish, have lifted upon stilts. Nothing is thought so rash as to mention a modern with an ancient: but when both are ancient, the last-comer often stands first. The present form one cluster, the past another. We are petulant if some of the existing have pushed by too near us: but we walk up composedly to the past, with all our prejudices behind us. We compare them leisurely one with another, and feel a pleasure in contributing to render them a plenary, however a tardy, justice. In the fervour of our zeal we often exceed it; which we never are found doing with our contemporaries, unless in malice to one better than the rest. Some of our popular and most celebrated authors are employed by the booksellers to cry up the wares on hand or forthcoming, partly for money and partly for payment in kind. Without such management the best literary production is liable to moulder on the shelf.

LANDOR. A wealthy man builds an ample mansion, well proportioned in all its parts, well stored with the noblest models of antiquity; extensive vales and downs and forests stretch away from it in every direction; but the stranger must of necessity pass it by, unless a dependant is stationed at a convenient lodge to admit and show him in. Such, you have given me to understand, is become the state of our literature. The bustlers who rise into notice by playing at leap-frog over one another's shoulders, will disappear when the game is over; and no game is shorter. But was not Milton himself kept beyond the paling? Nevertheless, how many *toupees* and *roquelaures*, and other odd things with odd names, have fluttered among the jays in the cherry orchard, while we tremble to touch with the finger's end his grave close-buttoned gabardine! He was called strange and singular long before he was acknowledged to be great: so, be sure, was Shakespeare; so, be sure, was Bacon; and so were all the rest, in the order of descent. You are too generous to regret that your liberal praise of Wordsworth was seized upon with avidity by his admirers, not only to win others to their party, but also to depress your merits. Nor will you triumph over their folly in confounding what is pitiful with what is admirable in him; rather will you smile, and, without a suspicion of malice, find the cleverest of these good people standing on his low joint-stool with a slender piece of wavering tape in his hand, measuring him with Milton back to back. There is as much difference between them as there is between a celandine and an ilex. The one lies at full length and full breadth along the ground ; the other rises up, stiff, strong, lofty, beautiful in the play of its slenderer branches, overshadowing with the infinitude of its grandeur.

SOUTHEY. You will be called to account as resentful ; and not for yourself, which you never have been thought, but for another : a graver fault in the estimation of most.

LANDOR. I do not remember that resentment has ever made me commit an injustice. Instead of acrimony, it usually takes the form of ridicule ; and the sun absorbs whatever is noxious in the vapour.

SOUTHEY. You think me mild and patient ; yet I have found it difficult to disengage from my teeth the clammy and bitter heaviness of some rotten nuts with which my Edinburgh hosts have regaled me ; and you little know how tiresome it is to wheeze over the chaff and thistle-beards in the chinky manger of Hallam.[1]

LANDOR. We are excellent Protestants in asserting the liberty of private judgment on all the mysteries of poetry, denying the exercise of a decretal to any one man, however intelligent and enlightened, but assuming it for a little party of our own, with *self* in the chair. A journalist who can trip up a slippery minister, fancies himself able to pull down the loftiest poet or the soundest critic. It is amusing to see the labours of Lilliput.

SOUTHEY. I have tasted the contents of every bin, down to the ginger-beer of Brougham. The balance of criticism is not yet fixed to any beam in the public warehouses that offer it, but is held unevenly by intemperate hands, and is swayed about by every puff of wind.

LANDOR. Authors should never be seen by authors, and little by other people. The Dalai Lama is a God to the imagination, a child to the sight : and a poet is much the same ; only that the child excites no vehemence, while the poet is staked and faggoted by his surrounding brethren : all from pure love, however ; partly for himself, partly for truth. When it was a matter of wonder how Keats, who was ignorant of Greek, could have written his *Hyperion*,

---

[1] For the criticisms which provoked Landor see the *British and Foreign Review*, Oct. 1838, " Landor's Pentameron and Pentalogia," an article Landor attributed to Hallam. See also Landor's *Reply to a Reviewer*.

IMAGINARY CONVERSATIONS: ENGLISH

Shelley, whom envy never touched, gave as a reason, " because he *was* a Greek." Wordsworth, being asked his opinion of the same poem, called it scoffingly, a " pretty piece of paganism." Yet he himself, in the best verses he ever wrote, and beautiful ones they are, reverts to the powerful influence of the pagan creed.

SOUTHEY. How many who write fiercely or contemptuously against us, not knowing us at all, would, if some accident or whim had never pushed them in the wrong direction, write with as much satisfaction to themselves a sonnet full of tears and tenderness on our death! In the long voyage we both of us may soon expect to make, the little shell-fish will stick to our keels, and retard us one knot in the thousand. But while we are here, let us step aside, and stand close by the walls of the old houses, making room for the swell-mob of authors to pass by, with their puffiness of phraseology, their german silver ornaments, their bossy and ill-soldered sentences, their little and light parlour-faggots of trim philosophy, and their topheavy baskets of false language, false criticism, and false morals.

LANDOR. Our sinews have been scarred and hardened with the red-hot implements of Byron; and by way of refreshment we are now standing up to the middle in the marsh. We are told that the highly-seasoned is unwholesome; and we have taken in good earnest to clammy rye-bread, boiled turnips, and scrag of mutton. If there is nobody who now can guide us through the glades in the Forest of Arden, let us hail the first who will conduct us safely to the gates of Ludlow Castle. But we have other reasons left on hand. For going through the *Paradise Regained* how many days' indulgence will you grant me?

SOUTHEY. There are some beautiful passages, as you know, although not numerous. As the poem is much shorter than the other, I will spare you the annoyance of uncovering its nakedness. I remember to have heard you say that your ear would be better pleased, and your understanding equally, if there had been a pause at the close of the fourth verse.

LANDOR. True; the three following are useless and heavy. I would also make another defalcation, of the five after " else mute." If the deeds he relates are

Above heroic, *though in secret done*,[1]

---

[1] *Par. Reg.*, i. 15.

SOUTHEY AND LANDOR

it was unnecessary to say that they are

> Worthy to have not remained so long unsung.

SOUTHEY. Satan, in his speech, seems to have caught hoarseness and rheumatism since we met him last. What a verse is

> This is my son beloved, in him, *am* pleased.

It would not have injured it to have made it English, by writing " in him I am pleased." It would only have continued a sadly dull one.

> Of many a pleasant realm—*and province wide*,
> The Holy Ghost, and the power of the Highest. V. 118.

But this is hardly more prosaic than " O what a multitude of thoughts, at once awakened in me, swarm, while I consider what from within I feel myself, and hear," &c. But the passage has reference to the poet, and soon becomes very interesting on that account.

> But to vanquish by wisdom hellish wiles.

It is difficult so to modulate our English verse as to render this endurable to the ear. The first line in the *Gerusalemme Liberata* begins with a double trochee *Canto l'arme*. The word " *But* " is too feeble for the trochee to turn on. We come presently to such verses as we shall never see again out of this poem.

> And he still on was led, but with such thoughts
> Accompanied, of things past and to come,
> Lodged in his breast, *as well might recommend
> Such solitude before choicest society*.
> But was driven
> With them from bliss to the bottomless deep.

This is dactylic.

> With them from | bliss to the bottomless | deep.

> He before had sat
> Among the prime in splendour, now deposed,
> Ejected, *emptied*, gazed, unpitied, shunn'd,
> A spectacle of ruin *or* of scorn, &c. V. 412.

Or should be *and*.

> Which they who ask'd have seldom *understood*,
> And, not well *understood*, as *good* not known.

IMAGINARY CONVERSATIONS: ENGLISH

To avoid the jingle, which perhaps he preferred, he might have written "*as well*," but how prosaic!

LANDOR. The only tolerable part of the First Book are the six closing lines, and these are the more acceptable because they are the closing ones.

SOUTHEY. The Second Book opens inauspiciously. The devil himself was never so unlike the devil as these verses are unlike verses.

> Andrew and Simon, *famous after known*,
> With others though in holy writ not named,
> Now missing him, &c.
> Plain fishermen, no greater men *them call*.

LANDOR. I do not believe that anything short of your friendship would induce me to read a third time during my life the *Paradise Regained*: and I now feel my misfortune and imprudence in having given to various friends this poem and many others, in which I had marked with a pencil the faults and beauties. The dead level lay wide and without a finger-post: the highest objects appeared, with few exceptions, no higher or more ornamental than bulrushes. We shall spend but little time in repeating all the passages where they occur, and it will be a great relief to us. Invention, energy, and grandeur of design, the three great requisites to constitute a great poet, and which no poet since Milton hath united, are wanting here. Call the design a grand one, if you will; you can not however call it his. Wherever there are thought, imagination, and energy, grace invariably follows; otherwise the colossus would be without its radiance, and we should sail by with wonder and astonishment, and gather no roses and gaze at no images on the sunny isle.

SOUTHEY. Shakespeare, whom you not only prefer to every other poet, but think he contains more poetry and more wisdom than all the rest united, is surely less grand in his designs than several.

LANDOR. To the eye. But *Othello* was loftier than the citadel of *Troy;* and what a *Paradise* fell before him! Let us descend; for from *Othello* we *must* descend, whatever road we take; let us look at *Julius Cæsar*. No man ever overcame such difficulties, or produced by his life and death such a change in the world we inhabit. But that also is a grand design which displays the interior workings of the world within us, and where we see the imperishable and

SOUTHEY AND LANDOR

unalterable passions depicted *a fresco* on a lofty dome. Our other dramatists painted only on the shambles, and represented what they found there; blood and garbage. We leave them a few paces behind us, and step over the gutter into the green-market. There are however men rising up among us endowed with exquisiteness of taste and intensity of thought. At no time have there been so many who write well in so many ways.

SOUTHEY. Have you taken breath? and are you ready to go on with me?

LANDOR. More than ready, alert. For we see before us a longer continuation of good poetry than we shall find again throughout the whole poem, beginning at verse 155,[1] and terminating at 224. In these however there are some bad verses, such as

> Among daughters of men the fairest found,
> And made him bow to the gods of his wives.

V. 180,

> Cast wanton eyes on the daughters of men,

is false grammar; " thou *cast* for thou *castedst*." I find the same fault where I am as much surprised to find it, in Shelley.

> Thou lovest, but ne'er *knew* love's sad satiety.

Shelley in his *Cenci* has overcome the greatest difficulty that ever was overcome in poetry, although he has not risen to the greatest elevation. He possesses less vigour than Byron, and less command of language than Keats; but I would rather have written his

> Music, when soft voices die,

than all that Beaumont and Fletcher ever wrote, together with all of their contemporaries, excepting Shakespeare.

SOUTHEY. It is wonderful that Milton should praise the continence of Alexander as well as of Scipio. Few conquerors had leisure for more excesses, or indulged in greater, than Alexander. He was reserved on one remarkable occasion: we hear of only one. Scipio, a much better man, and temperate in all things, would have been detested, even in Rome, if he had committed that crime from which the forbearance is foolishly celebrated as his chief virtue.

You will not refuse your approbation to another long passage

[1] Verse 153.

IMAGINARY CONVERSATIONS : ENGLISH

beginning at verse 260, and ending at 300. But at the conclusion of them, where the devil says that " beauty stands in the admiration only of weak minds,"[1] he savours a little of the Puritan. Milton was sometimes angry with her, but never had she a more devoted or a more discerning admirer. For these forty good verses, you will pardon,

> After forty days' fasting *had remained*.

LANDOR. Very much like the progress of Milton himself in this *jejunery*. I remember your description of the cookery in Portugal and Spain, which my own experience most bitterly confirmed : but I never met with a *bonito* " gris-amber-steamed." This certainly was reserved for the devil's own cookery. Our Saviour, I think, might have fasted another forty days before he could have stomached this dainty ; and the devil, if he had had his wits about him, might have known as much.

SOUTHEY. I have a verse in readiness which may serve as a napkin to it.

> And with these words his temptation pursued,

where it would have been very easy to have rendered it less disagreeable to the ear by a transposition.

> And his temptation with these words pursued.

I am afraid you will object to a redundant heaviness in,

> Get *riches* first—get *wealth*—and *treasure heap* ;

and no authority will reconcile you to roll-calls of proper names, such as

> Launcelot or Pellias or Pellenore,

and

> Quintius, Fabricius, Curius, Regulus,

or again, to such a verse as

> Not difficult, if thou hearken to me.

V. 461,

> To him who wears the regal diadem,

is quite superfluous, and adds nothing to the harmony. Verses 472, 473, 474, 475, and 476 have the same cesura. This, I believe, has

---

[1] There is confusion here: the quotation is verse 220.

never been remarked, and yet is the most remarkable thing in all Milton's poetry.

It is wonderful that any critic should be so stupid as a dozen or two of them have proved themselves to be, in applying the last verses of this Second Book to Christina of Sweden.

> To *give* a kingdom hath been thought
> Greater and nobler done, and to lay down
> Far more magnanimous, than to assume.
> *Riches* are needless then, &c.

Whether he had written this before or after the abdication of Richard Cromwell, they are equally applicable to him. He did retire not only from sovranty but from riches. Christina took with her to Rome prodigious wealth, and impoverished Sweden by the pension she exacted.

The last lines are intolerably harsh:

> *Oftest* better *miss'd*.

It may have been written " often ": a great relief to the ear, and no detriment to the sense or expression. We never noticed his care in avoiding such a ruggedness in verse 401,

> Whose pains have earn'd the *far-fet* spoil.

He employed " far-*fet* " instead of " far-*fetch'd*," not only because the latter is in conversational use, but because no sound is harsher than "*fetch'd*"; and especially before two sequent consonants, followed by such words as " *with that.*" It is curious that he did not prefer " *wherewith* "; both because a verse ending in " *that* " is followed by one ending in " *quite*," and because " *that* " also begins the next. I doubt whether you will be satisfied with the first verse I have marked in the Third Book,

> From that placid aspèct and meek regard.

LANDOR. The trochee in " *placid* " is feeble there, and " *meek regard* " conveys no new idea to " *placid aspèct*." Presently we come to

> Mules after these, camels and dromedaries,
> And wagons fraught with utensils of war.

And here, if you could find any pleasure in a triumph over the petu-

IMAGINARY CONVERSATIONS : ENGLISH

lance and frowardness of a weak adversary, you might laugh at poor Hallam,[1] who cites the following as among the noble passages of Milton :

> Such forces met not, *nor so wide a camp,*
> When Agrican with all his northern powers
> Besieged Albracca, *as romances tell,*
> The city of Gallafron, from whence to win
> *The fairest of her sex, Angelica.*

SOUTHEY. How very like Addison, when his milk was turned to whey. I wish I could believe that the applauders of this poem were sincere, since it is impossible to think them judicious ; their quotations, and especially Hallam's, having been selected from several of the weakest parts when better were close before them ; but we have strong evidence that the opinion was given in the spirit of contradiction, and from the habit of hostility to what is eminent. I would be charitable : Hallam may have hit upon the place by hazard : he may have been in the situation of a young candidate for preferment in the church, who was recommended to the Chancellor Thurlow. After much contemptuousness and ferocity, the chancellor throwing open on the table his *Book of Livings*, commanded him to choose for himself. The young man modestly and timidly thanked him for his goodness, and entreated his lordship to exercise his own discretion. With a volley of oaths, of which he was at all times prodigal, but more especially in the presence of a clergyman, he cried aloud, " Put this pen, sir, at the side of one or other." Hesitation was now impossible. The candidate placed it without looking where : it happened to be at a benefice of small value. Thurlow slapped his hand upon the table, and roared, " By God, you were within an ace of the best living in my gift."

LANDOR. Hear the end.

> His daughter, sought by many prowest knights,
> Both Paynim and the peers of Charlemagne.

SOUTHEY. It would be difficult to extract, even from this poem, so many schoolboy's verses together. The preceding, which also are verbose, are much more spirited, and the illustration of one force by

[1] For another protest by Landor against this opinion of Hallam, see his criticism of Catullus, 1842 : " There is many a critic who talks of harmony, and whose ear seems to have been fashioned out of the callus of his foot," etc.

the display of another, and which the poet tells us is less, exhibits but small discrimination in the critic who extols it. To praise a fault is worse than to commit one. I know not whether any such critic has pointed out for admiration the "*glass of telescope*," by which the Tempter might have shown Rome to our Saviour, v. 42, Book iv. But we must not pass over lines nearer the commencement, v. 10.

> But as a man who had been matchless held
> In cunning, *over-reach'd* where least he thought,
> To salve his credit, and for very spite
> Still will be tempting him who foils him still.

This is no simile, no illustration, but exactly what Satan had been doing.

LANDOR. The Devil grows very dry in the desert, where he discourses

> Of Academicks old and new, with those
> *Surnamed* Peripateticks, and the sect
> Epicurean, and the Stoick severe.

SOUTHEY. It is piteous to find the simplicity of the Gospel overlaid and deformed by the scholastic argumentation of our Saviour, and by the pleasure he appears to take in holding a long conversation with the Adversary.

> Not therefore am I *short*
> Of knowing what I *ought.* He who receives
> Light from above, from the fountain of light.

What a verse v. 287, &c.! A dissertation from our Saviour, delivered to the Devil in the manner our poet has delivered it, was the only thing wanting to his punishment; and he catches it at last.
V. 396.[1]

> Darkness now *rose*
> As daylight sunk, and brought in *lowering* night,
> Her shadowy offspring.

This is equally bad poetry and bad philosophy: the Darkness *rising* and bringing in the Night *lowering;* when he adds,

> Unsubstantial both,
> Privation mere of light—*and absent day.*

---

[1] Verse 397.

IMAGINARY CONVERSATIONS : ENGLISH

How ! privation of its absence ? He wipes away with a single stroke of the brush two very indistinct and ill-drawn figures.

LANDOR.
> Our Saviour meek and with *untroubled* mind,
> After his airy *jaunt*, tho' *hurried sore*,

How " *hurried* sore," if with *untroubled* mind ?

> Hungry and cold, betook him to his rest.

I should have been quite satisfied with a quarter of this.

> Darkness now rose ;
> Our Saviour meek betook him to his rest.

Such simplicity would be the more grateful and the more effective in preceding that part of *Paradise Regained* which is the most sublimely pathetic. It would be idle to remark the propriety of accentuation on *concourse*, and almost as idle to notice that in verse 420 is

> Thou only *stoodst* unshaken ;

and in v. 425,

> Thou *satst* unappalled.

But to *stand*, as I said before, is to *remain*, or to *be*, in Milton, following the Italian. Never was the eloquence of poetry so set forth by words and numbers in any language as in this period.[1] Pardon the *infernal* and *hellish*.

> Infernal ghosts and hellish furies round
> Environ'd thee : some howl'd, some yell'd, some shriekt,
> Some bent at thee their fiery darts, *while thou*
> Satst unappalled in calm and sinless peace.

The idea of *sitting* is in itself more beautiful than of standing or lying down, but our Saviour is represented as lying down, while

> The tempter watcht, and soon with ugly dreams
> *Disturbed* his sleep.

He could disturb, but not appall him, as he himself says in verse 487.

SOUTHEY. It is thought by Joseph Warton and some others that, where the Devil says,

> Then hear, O Son of David, virgin-born,
> For Son of God to me is yet in doubt, &c.,

---

[1] Compare the eulogy of the same passage in Landor's criticism of Catullus, 1842.

SOUTHEY AND LANDOR

he speaks sarcastically in the word *virgin*-born. But the Devil is not so bad a rhetorician as to turn round so suddenly from the ironical to the serious. He acknowledges the miracle of the Nativity; he pretends to doubt its Divinity.

> So saying he caught him up, and *without wing*
> *Of hippogrif*, bore through the air sublime.

Satan had given good proof that his wing was more than a match for a hippogrif's; and if he had borrowed a hippogrif's for the occasion, he could have made no use of it, unless he had borrowed the hippogrif too, and rode before or behind on him,

> *Over* the wilderness—and *o'er* the plain.

Two better verses follow; but the temple of Jerusalem could never have appeared

> Topt with golden *spires*.
> So Satan fell; and straight a fiery globe
> Of angels on full sail of wing flew nigh,
> Who on their plumy vans received *him soft*.

He means our Saviour, not Satan. In any ancient we should manage a little the *ductus literarum*, and, for the wretched words, " *him soft*," purpose to substitute *their lord*. But by what ingenuity can we erect into a verse v. 597?

> In the bosom of bliss and light of light.

In 613 and 614 we find rhyme.

LANDOR. The angels seem to have lost their voices since they left Paradise. Their denunciations against Satan are very angry, but very weak.

> Thee and thy legions; yelling they shall fly
> *And beg to hide them in a herd of swine*,
> Lest he command them down into the deep,
> Bound, and to torment sent before their time.

Surely they had been tormented long before.

The close of the poem is extremely languid, however much it has been commended for its simplicity.

SOUTHEY.
> He, unobserved,
> *Home*, to his *mother's* house, *private* return'd.

IMAGINARY CONVERSATIONS: ENGLISH

Unobserved and *private*; *home* and his "*mother's house*," are not very distinctive.

LANDOR. Milton took but little time in forming the plan of his *Paradise Regained*, doubtful and hesitating as he had been in the construction of *Paradise Lost*. In composing a poem or any other work of imagination, although it may be well and proper to lay down a plan, I doubt whether any author of any durable work has confined himself to it very strictly. But writers will no more tell you whether they do or not, than they will bring out before you the foul copies, or than painters will admit you into the secret of composing or of laying on their colours. I confess to you that a few detached thoughts and images have always been the beginnings of my works. Narrow slips have risen up, more or fewer, above the surface. These gradually became larger and more consolidated: freshness and verdure first covered one part, then another; then plants of firmer and of higher growth, however scantily, took their places, then extended their roots and branches; and among them and round about them in a little while you yourself, and as many more as I desired, found places for study and for recreation.

Returning to *Paradise Regained*. If a loop in the netting of a purse is let down, it loses the money that is in it; so a poem by laxity drops the weight of its contents. In the animal body, not only nerves and juices are necessary, but also continuity and cohesion. Milton is caught sleeping after his exertions in *Paradise Lost*, and the lock of his strength is shorn off; but here and there a prominent muscle swells out from the vast mass of the collapsed.

SOUTHEY. The *Samson Agonistes*, now before us, is less languid, but it may be charged with almost the heaviest fault of a poem, or indeed of any composition, particularly the dramatic, which is, there is insufficient coherency, or dependence of part on part. Let us not complain that, while we look at Samson and hear his voice, we are forced to think of Milton, of his blindness, of his abandonment, with as deep a commiseration. If we lay open the few faults covered by his transcendent excellences, we feel confident that none are more willing (or would be more acceptable were he present) to pay him homage. I retain all my admiration of his poetry; you all yours, not only of his poetry, but of his sentiments on many grave subjects.

LANDOR. I do; but I should be reluctant to see disturbed the order and course of things, by alterations at present unnecessary, or by attempts at what might be impracticable. When an evil can no longer be borne manfully and honestly and decorously, then down with it, and put something better in its place. Meanwhile guard strenuously against such evil. The vigilant will seldom be constrained to vengeance.

SOUTHEY. Simple as is the plan of this drama, there are prettinesses in it which would be far from ornamental anywhere. Milton is much more exuberant in them than Ovid himself, who certainly would never have been so commended by Quinctilian for the *Medea*, had he written

> Where I, a prisoner chain'd, scarce freely draw
> The air imprisoned also. V. 7.

But into what sublimity he soon ascends!

> Ask for this great deliverer now, and find him
> Eyeless in Gaza at the mill with slaves.

LANDOR. My copy is printed as you read it; but there ought to be commas after *eyeless*, after *Gaza*, and after *mill*. Generally our printers or writers put three commas where one would do; but here the grief of Samson is aggravated at every member of the sentence. Surely it must have been the resolution of Milton to render his choruses as inharmonious as he fancied the Greek were, or would be, without the accompaniments of instrument, accentuation, and chaunts; otherwise how can we account for " abandoned, and by *himself given over; in slavish habit, ill-fitted weeds, over-worn and soiled. Or do my eyes misrepresent? Can this be he, that heroic, that renowned, irresistible Samson!* "

SOUTHEY. We are soon compensated, regretting only that the *chorus* talks of " *Chalybian* tempered steel " in the beginning, and then informs us of his exploit with the jaw-bone,

> In Ramath-lechi, *famous to this day*.

It would be strange indeed if such a victory as was never won before, were forgotten in twenty years, or thereabout.

SOUTHEY. Passing Milton's oversights, we next notice his systematic defects. Fondness for Euripides made him too didactic when action was required. Perhaps the French drama kept him in countenance, although he seems to have paid little attention to it, comparatively.

LANDOR. The French drama contains some of the finest didactic poetry in the world, and is peculiarly adapted both to direct the reason and to control the passions. It is a well-lighted saloon of graceful eloquence, where the sword-knot is appended by the hand of Beauty, and where the snuff-box is composed of such brilliants as, after a peace or treaty, kings bestow on diplomatists. Whenever I read a French alexandrine, I fancy I receive a box on the ear in the middle of it, and another at the end, sufficient, if not to pain, to weary me intolerably, and to make the book drop out of my hand. Molière and La Fontaine can alone by their homœopathy revive me. Such is the power of united wit and wisdom, in ages the most desperate! These men, with Montaigne and Charron, will survive existing customs, and probably existing creeds. Millions will be captivated by them, when the eloquence of Bossuet himself shall interest extremely few. Yet the charms of language are less liable to be dissipated by time than the sentences of wisdom. While the incondite volumes of more profound philosophers are no longer in existence, scarcely one of writers who enjoyed in a high degree the gift of eloquence, is altogether lost. Among the Athenians there are indeed some, but in general they were worthless men, squabbling on worthless matters: we have little to regret, excepting of Phocion and of Pericles. If we turn to Rome, we retain all the best of Cicero; and we patiently and almost indifferently hear that nothing is to be found of Marcus Antonius or Hortensius; for the eloquence of the bar is, and ought always to be, secondary.

SOUTHEY. You were remarking that our poet paid little attention to the French drama. Indeed in his preface he takes no notice of it whatsoever, not even as regards the plot, in which consists its chief excellence, or perhaps I should say rather its superiority. He holds the opinion that " a plot, whether intricate or explicit, is nothing but such economy or disposition of the fable, as may stand best with verisimilitude and decorum." Surely the French tragedians have observed this doctrine attentively.

LANDOR. It has rarely happened that dramatic events have followed one another in their natural order. The most remarkable instance of it is in the *King Œdipus* of Sophocles. But Racine is in general the most skilful of the tragedians, with little energy and less invention. I wish Milton had abstained from calling "Æschylus, Sophocles, and Euripides, the three tragic poets unequalled *yet* by any"; because it may leave a suspicion that he fancied he, essentially undramatic, could equal them, and had now done it; and because it exhibits him as a detractor from Shakespeare. I am as sorry to find him in this condition as I should have been to find him in a fit of the gout, or treading on a nail with naked foot in his blindness.

SOUTHEY. Unfortunately it is impossible to exculpate him; for you must have remarked where, a few sentences above, are these expressions. " This is mentioned to vindicate from the *small esteem, or rather infamy*, which in the account of many it undergoes at this day, with other common interludes; happening through the poet's error of intermixing *comick stuff with tragick sadness and gravity*, or intermixing trivial and vulgar persons, which, by all judicious, hath been counted absurd, and brought in without discretion, corruptly to gratify the people."

LANDOR. It may be questioned whether the people in the reign of Elizabeth, or indeed the queen herself, would have been contented with a drama without a smack of the indecent or the ludicrous. They had alike been accustomed to scenes of ribaldry and of bloodshed; and the palace opened on one wing to the brothel, on the other to the shambles. The clowns of Shakespeare are still admired by not the vulgar only.

SOUTHEY. The more the pity. Let them appear in their proper places. But a picture by Morland or Frank Hals ought never to break a series of frescoes by the hand of Raphael, or of senatorial portraits animated by the sun of Titian. There is much to be regretted in, and (since we are alone I will say it) a little which might without loss or injury be rejected from, the treasury of Shakespeare.

LANDOR. It is difficult to sweep away anything and not to sweep away gold-dust with it! but viler dust lies thick in some places. The grave Milton too has cobwebs hanging on his workshop, which a high broom, in a steady hand, may reach without doing mischief. But let children and short men, and unwary ones, stand out of the way.

SOUTHEY. Necessary warning! for nothing else occasions so general satisfaction as the triumph of a weak mind over a stronger. And this often happens; for the sutures of a giant's armour are

IMAGINARY CONVERSATIONS : ENGLISH

most penetrable from below. Surely no poet is so deeply pathetic as the one before us, and nowhere more than in those verses which begin at the sixtieth and end with the eighty-fifth. There is much fine poetry after this; and perhaps the prolixity is very rational in a man so afflicted, but the composition is the worse for it. Samson could have known nothing of the *interlunar cave;* nor could he ever have thought about the light of the soul, and of the soul being *all in every part.*

LANDOR. Reminiscences of many sad afflictions have already burst upon the poet, but instead of overwhelming him, they have endued him with redoubled might and majesty. Verses worthier of a sovran poet, sentiments worthier of a pure, indomitable, inflexible republican, never issued from the human heart, than these referring to the army, in the last effort made to rescue the English nation from disgrace and servitude.

>   Had Judah that day joined, or one whole tribe,
>   They had by this possest the towers of Gath,
>   And lorded over them whom now they serve.
>   But what more oft, in nations grown corrupt
>   And by their vices brought to servitude,
>   Than to love bondage more than liberty,
>   Bondage with ease than strenuous liberty,
>   And to despise or envy or suspect
>   Whom God hath of his special favour rais'd
>   As their deliverer ! If he aught begin,
>   How frequent to desert him ! and at last
>   To heap ingratitude on worthiest deeds !

SOUTHEY. I shall be sorry to damp your enthusiasm, in however slight a degree, by pursuing our original plan in the detection of blemishes. Eyes the least clear-sighted could easily perceive one in

>   For of such doctrine never was there school
>   But the heart of the fool.
>   And no man therein doctor but himself. V. 299.[1]

They could discern here nothing but the quaint conceit; and it never occurred to them that the chorus knew nothing of schools and doctors. A line above, there is an expression not English. For " who believe not the existence of God,"

>   Who *think* not God at all. V. 295.

---
[1] Verse 297.

SOUTHEY AND LANDOR

And is it captious to say that, when Manoah's locks are called "white as down," whiteness is no characteristic of down? Perhaps you will be propitiated by the number of words in our days equally accented on the first syllable, which in this drama the great poet, with all his authority, has stamped on the second; such as *impùlse*, *edìct*, *contràry*, *prescrìpt*, the substantive *contèst*, *instìnct*, *crystàlline*, *pretèxt*.

LANDOR. I wish we had preserved them all in that good condition, excepting the substantive *contest*, which ought to follow the lead of "*conquest*." But " now we have got to the worst, let us keep to the worst," is the sound conservative maxim of the day.

SOUTHEY. I perceive you adhere to your doctrine in the termination of Aristo*teles*.

LANDOR. If we were to say Aris*totle*, why not Themis*tocle*, Empe*docle*, and Peri*cle*? Here, too, *neath* has always a mark of elision before it, quite unnecessarily. From *neath* comes *nether*, which reminds me that it would be better spelt, as it was formerly, *nethe*.

But go on: we can do no good yet.

SOUTHEY.

> That *invincible* Samson, far renowned. V. 341.

Here, unless we place the accent on the third syllable, the verse assumes another form, and such as is used only in the ludicrous or light poetry, scanned thus;

> That invin | cible Sam | son, &c.

There is great eloquence and pathos in the speech of Manoah: but the "*scorpion's tail behind*," in v. 360, is inapposite. Perhaps my remark is unworthy of your notice; but, as you are reading on, you seem to ponder on something which is worthy.

LANDOR. How very much would literature have lost, if this marvellously great and admirable man had omitted the various references to himself and his contemporaries. He had grown calmer at the close of life, and saw in Cromwell as a fault what he had seen before as a necessity or a virtue. The indignities offered to the sepulchre and remains of the greatest of English sovrans by the most ignominious, made the tears of Milton gush from his

IMAGINARY CONVERSATIONS: ENGLISH

darkened eyes, and extorted from his generous and grateful heart this exclamation :

> Alas ! methinks when God hath chosen one
> To worthiest deeds, if he through frailty err
> He should not so o'erwhelm, and as a thrall
> Subject him to so foul indignities,
> Be it but for honour's sake of former deeds.

How supremely grand is the close of Samson's speech !

SOUTHEY. In v. 439 we know what is meant by

> Slewst them many a slain ;

but the expression is absurd : he could not slay the slain. We also may object to

> The use of strongest wines
> And strongest drinks,

knowing that wines were the " strongest drinks " in those times : perhaps they might have been made stronger by the infusion of herbs and spices. You will again be saddened by the deep harmony of those verses in which the poet represents his own condition. V. 590.

> All otherwise to me my thoughts portend, &c.

In verses 729 and 731, the words *address* and *addrest* are inelegant.

> And words *addrest* seem into tears dissolved,
> Wetting the borders of her silken veil ;
> But now again she *makes address* to speak.

In v. 734,

> Which to have united, without excuse,
> I cannot but acknowledge,

the comma should be expunged after *excuse*, else the sentence is ambiguous. And in 745, "what *amends is* in my power." We have no singular, as the French have, for this word, although many use it ignorantly, as Milton does inadvertently.

> V. 934. Thy *fair* enchanted cup and warbling charms.

Here we are forced by the double allusion to recognise the later mythos of Circe. The cup alone, or the warbling alone, might belong to any other enchantress, any of his own or of a preceding age, since we know that in all times certain herbs and certain incantations were used by sorceresses.

The chorus in this tragedy is not always conciliating and assuaging. Never was anything more bitter against the female sex than the verses from 1010 to 1060. The invectives of Euripides are never the outpourings of the chorus, and their venom is cold as hemlock; those of Milton are hot and corrosive.

> It is not virtue, wisdom, valour, wit,
> *Strength, comeliness of shape, or amplest merit,*
> That woman's love *can win or long inherit ;*
> But what it is, is hard to say,
> *Harder to hit,*
> Which way soever men refer it :
> Much like thy riddle, Samson, in one day
> Or seven, *though one should musing sit.*

Never has Milton, in poetry or prose, written worse than this. The beginning of the second line is untrue; the conclusion is tautological. In the third it is needless to inform us that what is not to be gained is not to be inherited; or in the fourth, that what is hard to *say* is hard to *hit;* but it really is a new discovery that it is harder. Where is the distinction in the idea he would present of *saying* and *hitting ?* However, we will not " musing sit " on these dry thorns.

> Whate'er it be, to wisest men and best
> Seeming at first all heavenly under virgin veil, &c.

This is a very ugly mis-shapen alexandrine. The verse would be better and more regular by the omission of "*seeming*" or "*at first,*" neither of which is necessary.

LANDOR. The giant Harapha is not expected to talk wisely : but he never would have said to Samson

> Thou knowst me now,
> *If thou at all art known ;* much I have heard
> Of thy prodigious strength. V. 1031.[1]

A pretty clear evidence of his being somewhat known.

> And black enchantments, some magician's art.

---

[1] Verse 1081.

IMAGINARY CONVERSATIONS: ENGLISH

No doubt of that. But what glorious lines from 1167 to 1179! I can not say so much of these:

> Have they not sword-players and every sort
> Of gymnic artists, wrestlers, riders, runners,
> Jugglers and dancers, antics, mummers, mimics?

No, certainly not : the jugglers and the dancers they probably had, but none of the rest. *Mummers* are said to derive their appellation from the word *mum*. I rather think *mum* came corrupted from them. *Mummer* in reality is *mime*. We know how frequently the letter *r* has obtained an undue place at the end of words. The English mummers were men who acted, without speaking, in coarse pantomime. There are many things which I have marked between this place and v. 1665.

> V. 1634. That to the arched roof gave main support.

There were no arches in the time of Samson: but the mention of the two pillars in the centre makes it requisite to imagine such a structure. V. 1660,

> O dearly bought revenge, yet glorious.

It is Milton's practice to make vowels syllabically weak either coalesce with or yield to others. In no place but at the end of a verse would he protract *glorious* into a trisyllable. The structure of his versification was founded on the Italian, in which *io* and *ia* in some words are monosyllables in all places but the last. V. 1665,

> Among thy slain self-kill'd,
> Not willingly, but tangled in the fold
> Of dire necessity, whose law in death conjoined
> Thee with thy slaughtered foes, in number more
> Than all thy life hath slain before.

Milton differs extremely from the Athenian dramatists in neglecting the beauty of his choruses. Here the third line is among his usually bad alexandrines; and there is not only a debility of rhythm but also a redundancy of words. The verse would be better, and the sense too, without the words "*in death*." And "*slaughtered*" is alike unnecessary in the next. Farther on, the chorus talks about the phœnix. Now the phœnix, although oriental, was placed in the orient by the Greeks. If the phœnix "*no second knows*," it is probable it knows "*no third.*" All this nonsense is prated while Samson is lying dead before them. But the poem is a noble poem, and the characters of Samson and Delilah are drawn with precision and truth. The Athenian dramatists, both tragic and comic, have always one chief personage, one central light. Homer has not in the *Iliad*, nor has Milton in the *Paradise Lost*, nor has Shakespeare in several of his best tragedies. We find it in Racine, in the great Corneille, in the greater Schiller. In Calderon, and the other dramatists of Spain, it rarely is wanting; but their principal delight is in what we call plot or intrigue, in plainer English (and very like it) intricacy and trick. Hurd, after saying of the *Samson Agonistes*, that " it is, as might be expected, a masterpiece," tucks up his lawn sleeve and displays his slender wrist against Lowth. Nothing was ever equal to his cool effrontery when he says, " This critic, *and all such*, are greatly *out in* their judgments," &c. He might have profited, both in criticism and in style, by reading Lowth more attentively and patiently. In which case he never would have written *out in*, nor *obliged to such freedoms*, nor twenty more such strange things. Lowth was against the chorus: Hurd says, " It will be constantly wanting to rectify the wrong conclusions of the audience." Would it not be quite as advisable to drop carefully a few drops of laudanum on a lump of sugar, to lull the excitement of the sufferers by the tragedy? The chorus in Milton comes well provided with this narcotic. Voltaire wrote an *opera*, and intended it for a serious one, on the same subject. He decorated it with choruses sung to Venus and Adonis, and represented Samson more gallantly French than either. He pulled down the temple on the stage, and cried,

" J'ai réparé ma honte, et j'expire en vainqueur ! "

And yet Voltaire was often a graceful poet, and sometimes a judicious critic. It may be vain and useless to propose for imitation the chief excellences of a great author, such being the gift of transcendent genius, and not an acquisition to be obtained by study or labour: but it is only in great authors that defects are memorable when pointed out, and unsuspected until they are distinctly. For which reason I think it probable that at no distant time I may publish your remarks, if you consent to it.

SOUTHEY. It is well known in what spirit I made them; and as you have objected to few, if any, I leave them at your discretion.

IMAGINARY CONVERSATIONS: ENGLISH

Let us now pass on to *Lycidas*. It appears to me, that Warton is less judicious than usual, in his censure of

>   Shatter your leaves before the mellowing year.

I find in his note, " The *mellowing* year could not affect the leaves of the laurel, the myrtle, and the ivy, which last is characterised before as *never sere*." The ivy sheds its leaves in the proper season, though never all at once, and several hang on the stem longer than a year. In v. 88,[1]

>   But now my oar [2] proceeds
>   And listens to the herald of the sea.

Does the oar [2] listen?

>   Blind mouths that scarce themselves know how to hold
>   A sheep-hook. V. 119.

Now although mouths and bellies may designate the possessors or bearers, yet surely the *blind mouth* holding a shepherd's crook is a fitter representation of the shepherd's dog than of the shepherd. V. 145, may he not have written the *gloming* violet? not indeed well; but better than *glowing*.

>   V. 154. Ay me! while thee the *shores* and sounding seas
>   Wash far away.

Surely the *shores* did not.

>   V. 1750. And hears the *inexpressive* nuptial song
>   In the blest kingdoms *meek* of joy and love.

What can be the meaning?

LANDOR. It is to be regretted, not so much that Milton has adopted the language and scenery and mythology of the ancients, as that he confounds the real simple field-shepherds with the mitred shepherds of St. Paul's Churchyard and Westminster Abbey, and ties the two-handed sword against the crook. I have less objection to the luxury spread out before me, than to be treated with goose and mince-pie on the same plate.

No poetry so harmonious had ever been written in our language; but in the same free metre both Tasso and Guarini had captivated the ear of Italy. In regard to poetry, the *Lycidas* will hardly bear a

---

[1] Verse 89. [2] *Sic.* Read: " oat."

comparison with the *Allegro* and *Penseroso*. Many of the ideas in both are taken from Beaumont and Fletcher, from Raleigh and Marlowe, and from a poem in the first edition of Burton's *Melancholy*. Each of these has many beauties; but there are couplets in Milton's worth them all. We must, however, do what we set about. If we see the Faun walk lamely, we must look at his foot, find the thorn, and extract it.

SOUTHEY. There are those who defend, in the first verses, the matrimonial, or other less legitimate alliance, of *Cerberus* and *Midnight*; but I have too much regard for *Melancholy* to subscribe to the filiation, especially as it might exclude her presently from the nunnery, whither she is invited as *pensive*, *devout*, and *pure*. The union of Erebus and Night is much spoken of in poetical circles, and we have authority for announcing it to the public; but *Midnight*, like *Cerberus*, is a misnomer. We have occasionally heard, in objurgation, a man called a son of a dog, on the mother's side; but never was there goddess of that parentage. You are pleased to find Milton writing *pincht* instead of *pinched*.

LANDOR. Certainly; for there never existed the word "pinch*ed*," and never can exist the word " pinc*h'd*." In the same verse he writes *sed* for *said*. We have both of these, and we should keep them diligently. The pronunciation is always *sed*, excepting in rhyme. For the same reason we should retain *agen* as well as *again*.

What a cloud of absurdities has been whiffed against me, by no unlearned men, about the *Conversation* of Tooke and Johnson! Their own petty conceits rise up between their eyes and the volume they are negligently reading, and utterly obscure or confound it irretrievably. One would represent me as attempting to undermine our native tongue; another as modernising; a third as antiquating it. Whereas I am trying to underprop, not to undermine: I am trying to stop the man-milliner at his ungainly work of trimming and flouncing: I am trying to show how graceful is our English, not in its stiff decrepitude, not in its riotous luxuriance, but in its hale mid-life. I would make bad writers follow good ones, and good writers accord with themselves. If all can not be reduced into order, is that any reason why nothing should be done toward it? If languages and men too are imperfect, must we never make an effort to bring them a few steps nearer to what is preferable? If we find on the road a man who has fallen from his horse, and who has three bones dislocated, must we refuse him our aid because one is quite broken? It is by people who answer in the affirmative to these questions, or seem to answer so, it is by such writers that our language for the last half-century has fallen more rapidly into corruption and decomposition than any other ever spoken among men. The worst losses are not always those which are soonest felt, but those which are felt too late.

SOUTHEY. I should have adopted all your suggestions in orthography, if I were not certain that my bookseller would protest against it as ruinous. If you go no farther than to write *compell* and *foretell*, the compositor will correct your oversight: yet surely there should be some sign that the last syllable of those verbs ought to be spelt differently, as they are pronounced differently, from *shrivel* and *level*.

LANDOR. Let us run back to our plantain. But a bishop stands in the way; a bishop no other than Hurd, who says that "Milton shows his judgment in celebrating Shakespeare's comedies rather than his tragedies." Pity he did not live earlier! he would have served among the mummers both for bishop and fool. We now come to the *Penseroso*, in which title there are many who doubt the propriety of the spelling. Marsand, an editor of Petrarca, has defended the poet, who used equally *pensiero* and *pensero*. The mode is more peculiarly Lombard. The Milanese and Comascs invariably say *pensèr*. Yet it is wonderful how, at so short a distance, and professing to speak the same language, they differ in many expressions. The wonder ceases with those who have resided long in the country, and are curious about such matters, when they discover that at two gates of Milan two languages are spoken. The same thing occurs in Florence itself, where a street is inhabited by the Camaldolese, whose language is as little understood by learned academicians as that of Dante himself. Beyond the eastern gates a morning's walk, you come into Varlunga, a pastoral district, in which the people speak differently from both. I have always found a great pleasure in collecting the leaves and roots of these phonetic simples, especially in hill-countries. Nothing so conciliates many, and particularly the uneducated, as to ask and receive instruction from them. I have not hesitated to collect it from swineherds and

SOUTHEY AND LANDOR

Fra Diavolo : I should have looked for it in vain among universities and professors.

SOUTHEY. Turning back to the *Allegro*, I find an amusing note, conveying the surprising intelligence, all the way from Oxford, that *eglantine* means really the *dog-rose*, and that both dog-rose and *honey-suckle* (for which Milton mistook it) " are often growing against the side or *walls* of a house." Thus says Mr. Thomas Warton. I wish he had also told us in what quarter of the world a house has *sides* without *walls* of some kind or other. But it really is strange that Milton should have misapplied the word, at a time when botany was become the favourite study. I do not recollect whether Cowley had yet written his Latin poems on the appearances and qualities of plants. What are you smiling at ?

LANDOR. Our old field of battle, where Milton

> Calls up him who left untold
> The story of Cambuscan bold.

Chaucer, like Shakespeare, like Homer, like Milton, like every great poet that ever lived, derived from open sources the slender origin of his immortal works. Imagination is not a mere workshop of images, great and small, as there are many who would represent it ; but sometimes *thoughts* also are imagined before they are felt, and descend from the brain into the bosom. Young poets imagine feelings to which in reality they are strangers.

SOUTHEY. Copy them rather.

LANDOR. Not entirely. The copybook acts on the imagination. Unless they felt the truth or the verisimilitude, it could not take possession of them. Both feelings and images fly from distant coverts into their little field, without their consciousness whence they come, and rear young ones there which are properly their own. Chatterton hath shown as much imagination in the *Bristowe Tragedie*, as in that animated allegory which begins,

> When Freedom dreste in blood-stain'd veste.

Keats is the most imaginative of our poets, after Chaucer, Spenser, Shakespeare, and Milton.

SOUTHEY. I am glad you admit my favourite, Spenser.

LANDOR. He is my favourite, too, if you admit the expression without the signification of precedency. I do not think him equal

IMAGINARY CONVERSATIONS: ENGLISH

to Chaucer even in imagination, and he appears to me very inferior to him in all other points, excepting harmony. Here the miscarriage is in Chaucer's age, not in Chaucer, many of whose verses are highly beautiful, but never (as in Spenser) one whole period. I love the geniality of his temperature: no straining, no effort, no storm, no fury. His vivid thoughts burst their way to us through the coarsest integuments of language.

The heart is the creator of the poetical world; only the atmosphere is from the brain. Do I then undervalue imagination? No indeed: but I find imagination where others never look for it: in character multiform yet consistent. Chaucer first united the two glorious realms of Italy and England. Shakespeare came after, and subjected the whole universe to his dominion. But he mounted the highest steps of his throne under those bland skies which had warmed the congenial breasts of Chaucer and Boccaccio.

The powers of imagination are but slender when it can invent only shadowy appearances; much greater are requisite to make an inert and insignificant atom grow up into greatness; to give it form, life, mobility, and intellect. Spenser hath accomplished the one; Shakespeare and Chaucer the other. Pope and Dryden have displayed a little of it in their *Satires*. In passing, let me express my wish that writers who compare them in generalities, and who lean mostly toward the stronger, would attempt to trim the balance, by placing Pope among our best critics on poetry, while Dryden is knee-deep below John Dennis. You do not like either: I read both with pleasure, so long as they keep to the couplet. But *St Cecilia's* music-book is interlined with epigrams, and *Alexander's Feast* smells of gin at second-hand, with true Briton fiddlers full of native *talent* in the orchestra.

SOUTHEY. Dryden says, "It were an easy matter to produce some *thousands* of Chaucer's verses *which* are lame for want of half, and sometimes a whole foot, *which* no pronunciation can make otherwise."

LANDOR. Certainly no pronunciation but the proper one can do it.

SOUTHEY. On the opposite quarter, comparing him with Boccaccio, he says, "He has refined on the Italian, and has mended his stories in his way of telling. Our countryman carries weight, and yet wins the race at disadvantage."

LANDOR. Certainly our brisk and vigorous poet carries with him no weight in criticism.

SOUTHEY AND LANDOR

SOUTHEY. Vivacity and shrewd sense are Dryden's characteristics, with quickness of perception rather than accuracy of remark, and consequently a facility rather than a fidelity of expression.

We are coming to our last days if, according to the prophet Joel, " blood and fire and pillars of smoke " are signs of them. Again to Milton and the *Penseroso*.

> V. 90. What worlds, or what vast regions.

Are not *vast regions* included in *world?* In 119, 120, 121, 122, the same rhymes are repeated.

> Thus, night, oft see me in thy pale career,

is the only verse of ten syllables, and should be reduced to the ranks. You always have strongly objected to epithets which designate dresses and decoration; of which epithets, it must be acknowledged, both Milton and Shakespeare are unreasonably fond. *Civil-suited, frownced, kercheft*, come close together. I suspect they will find as little favour in your eyes as *embroidered, trimmed*, and *gilded*.

LANDOR. I am fond of gilding, not in our poetry, but in our apartments, where it gives a sunniness greatly wanted by the climate. Pindar and Virgil are profuse of *gold*, but they reject the *gilded*.

SOUTHEY. I have counted ninety-three lines in Milton where *gold* is used, and only four where *gilded* is. A question is raised whether *pale*, in

> To walk the studious cloisters *pale*,

is substantive or adjective. What is your opinion?

LANDOR. That it is an adjective. Milton was very Italian, as you know, in his custom of adding a second epithet after the substantive, where one had preceded it. The Wartons followed him. Yet Thomas Warton would read in this verse the substantive, giving as his reason that our poet is fond of the singular. In the present word there is nothing extraordinary in finding it thus. We commonly say within the *pale* of the church, of the law, &c. But *pale* is an epithet to which Milton is very partial. Just before, he has written " *pale career*," and we shall presently see the " *pale-eyed priest*."

SOUTHEY.
> With antick pillars massy-proof.

The Wartons are fond of repeating in their poetry the word *massy-*

proof: in my opinion an inelegant one, and, if a compound, compounded badly. It seems more applicable to castles, whose *massiveness* gave *proof* of resistance. *Antick* was probably spelt *antike* by the author, who disdained to follow the fashion in *antique, Pindaricque,* &c., affected by Cowley and others, who had been, or would be thought to have been, domiciliated with Charles II. in France.

LANDOR. Whenever I come to the end of these poems, or either of them, it is always with a sigh of regret. We will pass by the *Arcades*, of which the little that is good is copied from Shakespeare.

SOUTHEY. Nevertheless we may consider it as a *nebula*, which was not without its efficiency in forming the star of *Comus*. This *Mask* is modelled on another by George Peele. Two brothers wander in search of a sister enthralled by a magician. They call aloud her name, and Echo repeats it, as here in *Comus*. Much also has been taken from Puteanus, who borrowed at once the best and the worst of his poem from Philostratus. In the third verse I find *spirits* a dissyllable, which is unusual in Milton.

LANDOR. I can account for his monosyllabic sound by his fondness of imitating the Italian *spirto*. But you yourself are addicted to these quavers, if you will permit me the use of the word here; and I find *spirit, peril*, &c., occupying no longer a time than if the second vowel were wanting. I do not approve of the apposition in

  The *nodding horrour* of whose shady brows. V. 47.[1]

Before which I find
      Sea-girt isles
  That, like to rich and various gems inlay
  The *unadorned* bosom of the deep.

How can a bosom be *unadorned* which already is *inlaid* with gems?

SOUTHEY. You will object no less strongly to

  Sounds and seas with all their finny drove,

sounds being parts of *seas*.

LANDOR. There are yet graver faults. Where did the young lady ever hear or learn such expressions as " Swilled insolence "?[2]

    The *grey-hooded Even*,[3]
  Like a sad votarist in *palmer's weed*,
  Rose from the hindmost *wheels* of Phœbus' wain.

---

[1] Verse 38.   [2] Verse 178.   [3] Verse 188.

SOUTHEY AND LANDOR

Here is Eve a manifest female, with her own proper hood upon her head, taking the other parts of male attire, and rising (by good luck) from under a wagon-wheel. But nothing in Milton, and scarcely anything in Cowley, is viler than

> Else, O *thievish* night,[1]
> Why should'st thou, but for some *felonious* end,
> In thy *dark-lantern* thus close up the stars.

It must have been a capacious *dark-lantern* that held them all.

> That Nature hung in heaven, and fill'd their lamps
> With everlasting oil.

Hardly so bad; but very bad is

> Does a *sable* cloud
> Turn forth her *silver lining* on the night?

A greater and more momentous fault is, that three soliloquies come in succession for about 240 lines together.

> What time the laboured ox
> In his loose traces from the furrow came
> And the swinkt hedger at his supper sat.

These are blamed by Warton, but blamed in the wrong place. The young lady, being in the wood, could have seen nothing of ox or hedger, and was unlikely to have made any previous observations on their work-hours. But in the summer, and this was in summer, neither the ox nor the hedger are at work: that the ploughman always quits it at noon, as Warton says he does, is untrue. When he quits it at noon, it is for his dinner. Gray says:

> The ploughman homeward plods his weary way.

He may do that, but certainly not at the season when

> The beetle wheels her drony flight.

Nevertheless the stricture is captious; for the ploughman may return from the field, although not from ploughing; and *ploughman* may be accepted for any agriculturer. Certainly such must have been Virgil's meaning when he wrote

> *Quos durus arator*
> Observans nido implumes detraxit.[2]

---
[1] Verse 195.　　[2] *Georg.*, iv. 513.

IMAGINARY CONVERSATIONS : ENGLISH

For ploughing, in Italy more especially, is never the labour in June, when the nightingale's young are hatched. Gray's verse is a good one, which is more than can be said of Virgil's.

> Sweet Echo! sweetest nymph! that livest unseen
> *Within* thy airy shell!

The habitation is better adapted to an oyster than to Echo. We must however go on and look after the young gentlemen. Comus says:

> I saw them under a green mantling vine
> Plucking ripe clusters, &c.

It is much to be regretted that the banks of the Severn in our days present no such facilities. You would find some difficulty in teaching the readers of poetry to read metrically the exquisite verses which follow. What would they make of

> And as I | past I | worshipt it ! [1]

These are the true times; and they are quite unintelligible to those who divide our verses into iambics, with what they call *licences*.

SOUTHEY. We have found the two brothers; and never were two young gentlemen in stiffer doublets.

> *Unmuffle*, ye faint stars, &c.

The elder, although " as smooth as Hebe's his unrazor'd lip," talks not only like a man, but like a philosopher of much experience.

> What need a *man* foretell his date of grief, &c.

How should he know that

> Beauty, like the fair Hesperian tree,
> Laden with blooming gold, had need the guard
> Of dragon watch with unenchanted eye
> To save her blossoms and defend her fruit, &c.

LANDOR. We now come to a place where we have only the choice of a contradiction or a nonsense.

> She *plumes* her feathers and lets grow her wings.

There is no sense in *pluming* a plume. Beyond a doubt Milton

---

[1] Verse 302 should read: "And, as I passed, I worshipt. If those you seek,' etc.

wrote *prunes*, and subsequently it was printed *plumes* to avoid what appeared a contrariety. And a contrariety it would be if the word *prune* were to be taken in no other sense than the gardener's. We suppose it must mean to *cut shorter :* but its real signification is to *trim*, which is usually done by that process. Milton here means to *smoothen* and *put in order ; prine* is better. Among the strange unaccountable expressions which, within our memory, or a little earlier, were carried down, like shingle by a sudden torrent, over our language, can you tell me what writer first wrote "*unbidden tears*"?

SOUTHEY. No indeed. The phrase is certainly a curiosity, although no rarity. I wish some logician or (it being beyond the reach of any) some metaphysician would attempt to render us an account of it. Milton has never used *unbidden*, where it really would be significant, and only once *unbid*. Can you go forward with this " Elder Brother " ?

LANDOR. Let us try. I wish he would turn off his " liveried angels," v. 455, and would say nothing about lust. How could he have learned that lust

> By unchaste looks, loose gestures, and foul talk,
> But most by lewd and lavish act of sin, &c.

Can you tell me what wolves are " *stabled* wolves " ? (v. 534).

SOUTHEY. Not exactly. But here is another verse of the same construction as you remarked before :

> And earth's base built on stubble. But come, let's on.

This was done by choice, not by necessity. He might have omitted the *But*, and have satisfied the herd bovine and porcine. Just below are two others in which three syllables are included in the time of two.

> But for that damn'd magician, let him be girt, &c. V. 802.[1]
> Harpies and hydras, or all the monstrous forms, &c. V. 605.

And again

> And crumble all thy sinews. Why, prithee, shepherd. V. 615.

LANDOR. You have crept unsoiled from

> Under the *sooty* flag of Acheron. V. 600.[2]

---

[1] Verse 602. [2] Verse 604.

IMAGINARY CONVERSATIONS: ENGLISH

And you may add many dozens more of similar verses, if you think it worth your while to go back for them. In v. 610, I find " yet " redundant.

> I love thy courage *yet*, and bold emprise.

Commentators and critics boggle sadly a little farther on.

> But in another country, as he said,
> Bore a bright golden flower ; *but* not in this soil.

On which hear T. Warton. " Milton, notwithstanding his singular skill in music, appears to have had a very bad ear." Warton was celebrated in his time for his great ability in raising a laugh in the common-room. He has here shown a capacity more extensive in that faculty. Two or three honest men have run to Milton's assistance, and have applied a remedy to his ear: they would help him to mend the verse. In fact, it is a bad one ; he never wrote it so. The word *but* is useless in the second line, and comes with the worse grace after the *But* in the preceding. They who can discover faults in versification where there are none but of their own imagining, have failed to notice v. 666.

> Why are you | vext, lady, | why do you | frown ?

Now, this in reality is inadmissible, being of a metre quite different from the rest. It is dactylic ; and consequently, although the number of syllables is just, the number of feet is defective. But Milton, in reciting it, would bring it back to the order he had established. He would read it

> Whȳ *āre* yŏu vēxt ?

And then in a faultering and falling accent, and in the tender trochee,

> Lādў | why dŏ yŏu frōwn ?

There are some who in a few years can learn all the harmony of Milton ; there are others who must go into another state of existence for this felicity.

SOUTHEY. I am afraid I am about to check for a moment your enthusiasm, in bringing you

> To those budge *doctors* of the Stoic *fur*,

whom Comus is holding in derision.

SOUTHEY AND LANDOR

LANDOR. Certainly it is odd enough to find him in such company. It is the first time either cynic or stoic ever put on fur, and it must be confessed it little becomes them. We are told that, v. 727,

>And live like Nature's bastards, not her sons,

is taken from the Bible. Whencesoever it may be taken, the expression is faulty; for a son may be a bastard, and quite as surely a bastard may be a son. In v. 732, " the unsought diamonds " are ill-placed; and we are told that Doctors Warburton and Newton called these four lines " exceeding childish." They are so, for all that. I wonder none of the fraternity had his fingers at liberty to count the syllables in v. 753.[1]

>If you let | slip time, like a neglected rose, &c.

I wish he had cast away the *yet* in v. 745.[2]

>Think what; and be advised; you are but young yet.

Not only is *yet* an expletive, and makes the verse inharmonious, but the syllables *young* and *yet* coming together would of themselves be intolerable anywhere. What a magnificent passage! how little poetry in any language is comparable to this, which closes the lady's reply,
>Thou art not fit to hear thyself convinced. Vv. 792-799.

This is worthy of Shakespeare himself in his highest mood, and is unattained and unattainable by any other poet. What a transport of enthusiasm! what a burst of harmony! He who writes one sentence equal to this, will have reached a higher rank in poetry than any has done since this was written.

SOUTHEY. I thought it would be difficult to confine you to censure, as we first proposed. The anger and wit of Comus effervesce into flatness, one dashed upon the other.

>Come, no more;
>This is mere moral babble, and direct
>*Against the canon laws of our foundation.*

He rolls out from the " cynic tub " to put on cap and gown. The laughter of Milton soon assumed a wry, puritanical cast. Even while he had the *molle* he wanted the *facetum*, in all its parts and

---

[1] Verse 743.   [2] Verse 755.

IMAGINARY CONVERSATIONS: ENGLISH

qualities. It is hard upon Milton, and harder still upon inferior poets, that every expression of his used by a predecessor should be noted as borrowed or stolen. Here in v. 822 [1]

> Will bathe the drooping spirits in delight

is traced to several, and might be traced to more. Chaucer, in whose songs it is more beautiful than elsewhere, writes,

> His harte bathed in a bath of blisse.

Probably he took the idea from the bath of knights. You could never have seen Chaucer, nor the rest, when you wrote those verses at Rugby on Godiva [2]: you drew them out of the *Square Pool*, and assimilated them to the tranquillity of prayer, such a tranquillity as is the effect of prayer on the boyish mind, when it has any effect at all.

LANDOR. I have expunged many thoughts for their close resemblance to what others had written whose works I never saw until after. But all thinking men must think, all imaginative men must imagine, many things in common, although they differ. Some abhor what others embrace; but the thought strikes them equally. With some an idea is productive, with others it lies inert. I have resigned and abandoned many things because I unreasonably doubted my legitimate claim to them, and many more because I believed I had enough substance in the house without them, and that the retention might raise a clamour in my court-yard. I do not look very sharply after the poachers on my property. One of your neighbours has broken down a shell in my grotto, and a town gentleman has lamed a rabbit in my warren: heartily welcome both. Do not shut your book, we have time left for the rest.

SOUTHEY. Sabrina in person is now before us. Johnson talks absurdly, not on the long narration, for which he has reason, but in saying that " it is of no use, because it is false, and therefore unsuitable to a good being." Warton answers this objection with great propriety. It may be added that things in themselves very false are very true in poetry, and produce not only delight, but beneficial moral effects. This is an instance. The part before us is copied from Fletcher's *Faithful Shepherdess*. The Spirit, in his thanks-

---

[1] Verse 812.
[2] See the Conversation of Leofric and Godiva for these verses.

SOUTHEY AND LANDOR

giving to Sabrina for liberating the lady, is extremely warm in good wishes. After the aspiration,

> May thy lofty head be crown'd
> With many a tower and terrace round,[1]

he adds,

> And here and there, *thy banks upon,*
> With groves of myrrh and cinnamon.

It would have been more reasonable to have said,

> And here and there some fine fat geese,
> And ducklings waiting for green peas.

The conclusion is admirable, though it must be acknowledged that the piece is undramatic. Johnson makes an unanswerable objection to the prologue : but he must have lost all the senses that are affected by poetry when he calls the whole drama *tediously instructive.* There is indeed here and there prolixity; yet refreshing springs burst out profusely in every part of the wordy wilderness. We are now at the *Sonnets.* I know your dislike of this composition.

LANDOR. In English; not in Italian : but Milton has ennobled it in our tongue, and has trivialised it in that. He who is deficient in readiness of language, is half a fool in writing, and more than half in conversation. Ideas fix themselves about the tongue, and fall to the ground when they are in want of that support. Unhappily Italian poetry in the age of Milton was almost at its worst, and he imitated what he heard repeated or praised. It is better to say no more about it, or about his Psalms, when we come to them.

SOUTHEY. Among his minor poems several are worthless.

LANDOR. True; but if they had been lost, we should be glad to have recovered them. Cromwell would not allow Lely to omit or diminish a single wart upon his face; yet there were many and great ones. If you had found a treasure of gold and silver, and afterward in the same excavation an urn in which only brass coins were contained, would you reject them? You will find in his English *Sonnets* some of a much higher strain than even the best of Dante's. The great poet is sometimes recumbent, but never languid; often unadorned, I wish I could honestly say not often inelegant. But what noble odes (for such we must consider them) are the eighth, the fifteenth, the sixteenth, the seventeenth, and above all the eighteenth ! There is a mild and serene sublimity in the nineteenth.

[1] Verses 934-35.

IMAGINARY CONVERSATIONS : ENGLISH

In the twentieth there is the festivity of Horace, with a due observance of his precept, applicable metaphorically,

> Simplici myrto nihil adlabores.

This is among the few English poems which are quite classical, according to our notions, as the Greeks and Romans have impressed them. It is pleasing to find Milton, in his later days, thus disposed to cheerfulness and conviviality. There are climates of the earth, it is said, in which a warm season intervenes between autumn and winter. Such a season came to reanimate, not the earth itself, but what was highest upon it.

A few of Milton's *Sonnets* are extremely bad: the rest are excellent. Among all Shakespeare's not a single one is very admirable, and few sink very low. They are hot and pothery: there is much condensation, little delicacy; like raspberry jam without cream, without crust, without bread, to break its viscidity. But I would rather sit down to one of them again, than to a string of such musty sausages as are exposed in our streets at the present dull season. Let us be reverent; but only where reverence is due, even in Milton and in Shakespeare. It is a privilege to be near enough to them to see their faults: never are we likely to abuse it. Those in high station, who have the folly and the impudence to look down on us, possess none such. Silks perish as the silkworms have perished: kings as their carpets and canopies. There are objects too great for these animalcules of the palace to see well and wholly. Do you doubt that the most fatuous of the Georges, whichever it was, thought himself Newton's superior? or that any minister, any peer of parliament, held the philosopher so high as the assayer of the mint? Was it not always in a grated hole, among bars and bullion, that they saw whatever they could see of his dignity? was it ever among the interminable worlds he brought down for men to contemplate? Yet Newton stood incalculably more exalted above the glorious multitude of stars and suns, than these ignorant and irreclaimable wretches above the multitude of the street. Let every man hold this faith, and it will teach him what is lawful and right in veneration; namely, that there are divine beings and immortal men on the one side, mortal men and brute beasts on the other. The two parties stand compact; each stands separate; the distance is wide; but there is nothing in the interval.

SOUTHEY AND LANDOR

Will you go on, after a minute or two, for I am inclined to silence?

SOUTHEY. Next to the *Sonnets* come the *Odes*, written much earlier. One stanza in that *On the Morning of the Nativity*, has been often admired. What think you of this stanza, the fourth? But the preceding and the following are beautiful too.

LANDOR. I think it incomparably the noblest piece of lyric poetry in any modern language I am conversant with: and I regret that so much of the remainder throws up the bubbles and fetid mud of the Italian. In the thirteenth what a rhyme is *harmony* with *symphony*! In the eighteenth,

> Swinges the scaly horror of his *folded* tail.

I wish you would unfold the folded tail for me: I do not like to meddle with it.

SOUTHEY. Better to rest on the fourth stanza, and then regard fresh beauties in the preceding and the following. Beyond these, very far beyond, are the nineteenth and twentieth. But why is the priest *pale-eyed*?

LANDOR. Who knows? I would not delay you with a remark on the modern spelling of what Milton wrote *kist*, and what some editors have turned into *kiss'd*; a word which could not exist in its contraction, and never did exist in speech, even uncontracted. Yet they make *kiss'd* rhyme with *whist*. Let me remark again, on the word *unexpressive*, 116, used before in *Lycidas*, v. 176, and defended by the authority of Shakespeare. (*As You Like It.* Act III., 82.)

> The fair, the chaste, the *unexpressive* she.

This is quite as wrong as *resistless* for *irresistible*, and even more so. I suspect it was used by Shakespeare, who uses it only once, merely to turn into ridicule a fantastic *euphuism* of the day. Milton, in his youth, was fond of seizing on odd things wherever he found them.

SOUTHEY.

> And let the base of heaven's deep organ blow. V. 130.

LANDOR. No; I will not: I am too puritanical in poetry for that.

SOUTHEY. The twenty-third, "And sullen Moloch," is grand, until we come to

> The brutish gods of Nile, *as fast*
> Isis and Osiris and the dog Anubis, haste.

IMAGINARY CONVERSATIONS: ENGLISH

As fast as what? We have heard of nothing but the ring of cymbals calling the grisly king. We come to worse in twenty-six,

> So when the sun *in bed*
> Curtain'd with cloudy *red*,
> *Pillows his chin*, &c.
>
> And all about the *courtly table*
> *Bright-harnest* angels sit—in order *serviceable*.

They would be the less *serviceable* by being seated, and not the more so for being harnest.

The Passion. The five first verses of the sixth stanza are good, and very acceptable after the " letters where my tears have *washt a wannish white*." The two last verses are guilty of such an offence as Cowley himself was never indicted for. The sixth stanza lies between two others full of putrid conceits, like a large pearl which has exhausted its oyster.

LANDOR. But can anything be conceived more exquisite than

> Grove and spring
> Would soon unbosom all their echoes mild!

This totally withdraws us from regarding the strange superfetation just below.

The Circumcision, v. 6.

> Now mourn; and if sad *share* with us to *bear*.

Death of an Infant. It is never at a time when the feelings are most acute that the poet expresses them: but sensibility and taste shrink alike, on such occasions, from witticisms and whimsies. Here are too many; but the two last stanzas are very beautiful. Look at the note. Here are six verses, four of them in Shakespeare, containing specimens of the orthography you recommend.

> Sweet Rose! fair flower, untimely *pluckt*, soon vaded,
> *Pluckt* in the bud and vaded in the spring,
> Bright orient pearle, alack too timely shaded!
> Fair creature! *kil'd* too soon by Death's sharp sting.

Again,

> Sweete lovely Rose! ill *pluckt* before thy time,
> Fair worthy sonne, not conquered, but *betraid*.[1]

SOUTHEY. The spelling of Milton is not always to be copied,

---

[1] Kyd, *Spanish Tragedy*, ii.

though it is better on the whole than any other writer's. He continues to write *fift* and *sixt*. In what manner would he write *eighth* ? If he omitted the final *h* there would be irregularity and confusion. Beside, how would he continue ? Would he say the *tent* for the *tenth*, and the *thirtent*, *fourtent*, &c. ?

LANDOR. We have corrected and fixed a few inconsiderate and random spellings, but we have as frequently taken the wrong and rejected the right. No edition of Shakespeare can be valuable unless it strictly follows the first editors, who knew and observed his orthography.

SOUTHEY.

> From thy prefixed seat didst *post*. St. 9, v. 59.

We find the same expression more than once in Milton ; surely one very unfit for grave subjects, in his time as in ours.

Let us, sitting beneath the sun-dial, look at the poem *On Time*.

> Call on the lazy leaden-stepping Hours
> Whose speed is but the weary [1] plummet's pace.

Now, although the Hours may be the lazier for the lead about them, the plummet is the quicker for it.

> And glut thyself with what thy womb devours.

It is incredible how many disgusting images Milton indulges in.

LANDOR. In his age, and a century earlier, it was called strength. The Graces are absent from this chamber of Ilithyia. But the poet would have defended his position with the *horse* of Virgil.

> *Uterumque* armato milite complent.

SOUTHEY.

> Then long eternity shall greet our bliss
> With an *individual* kiss,

meaning *undivided ;* and he employs the same word in the same sense again in the *Paradise Lost*. How much more properly than as we are now in the habit of using it, calling men and women, who never saw one another, *individuals*, and often employing it beyond the person : for instance, " a man's *individual* pleasure," although the pleasure is *divided* with another or with many. The last part,

---

[1] *Sic.* Read : " heavy."

IMAGINARY CONVERSATIONS: ENGLISH

from "When everything," to the end, is magnificent. The word *sincerely* bears its Latin signification.

The next is, *At a Solemn Music.* And I think you will agree with me that a sequence of rhymes never ran into such harmony as those at the conclusion, from " That we on earth."

LANDOR. Excepting the commencement of Dryden's *Religio Laici*, where indeed the poetry is of a much inferior order : for the head of Dryden does not reach so high as to the loins of Milton.

SOUTHEY. No, nor to the knees. We now come to the *Epitaph on the Marchioness of Winchester*. He has often much injured this beautiful metre by the prefix of a syllable which distorts every foot. The *entire* change in the *Allegro*, to welcome Euphrosyne, is admirably judicious. The flow in the poem before us is trochaic : he turns it into the iambic, which is exactly its opposite. The verses beginning

> The God that sits at marriage-feast

are infinitely less beautiful than Ovid's. These.

> He at their invoking came,
> But with a scarce well-lighted flame.

bear a faint resemblance to

> Fax quoque quam tenuit lacrimoso stridula fumo
> Usque fuit, *nullosque invenit motibus ignes*.

Here the conclusion is ludicrously low,

> No marchioness, but now a queen.

In *Vacation Exercise :*

> Driving *dumb silence* from the *portal door*,
> Where he had *mutely sat* two years before.

What do you think of that ?

LANDOR. Why, I think it would have been as well if he had sat there still. In the 27th verse he uses the noun substantive *suspect* for *suspicion;* and why not ? I have already given my reasons for its propriety. From 33 to 44 is again such a series of couplets as you will vainly look for in any other poet.

SOUTHEY. " *On the Ens.*" Nothing can be more ingenious. It was in such subjects that the royal James took delight. I know not what the Rivers have to do with the present, but they are very refreshing after coming out of the Schools.

The Epitaph on Shakespeare is thought unworthy of Milton. I entertain a very different opinion of it, considering it was the first poem he ever published. Omit the two lines,

> Thou in our wonder and astonishment
> Hast built thyself a live-long monument,

and the remainder is vigorous, direct, and enthusiastic; after invention, the greatest qualities of all great poetry.

On the Forces [1] *of Conscience.* Milton is among the least witty of mankind. He seldom attempts a witticism unless he is angry; and then he stifles it by clenching his fist. His unrhymed translation of *Quis multâ gracilis*, is beautiful for four lines only. *Plain in thy neatness* is almost an equivoke; *neat in thy plainness of attire* would be nearer the mark.

LANDOR. *Simplex munditis* does not mean that, nor *plain* in thy " ornaments," as Warton thinks; but, without any reference to ornaments, plain in *attire*. *Mundus muliebris* (and from *mundus munditiæ*) means the toilet; and always will mean it, as long as the world lasts. We now come upon the *Psalms;* so let us close the book.

SOUTHEY. Willingly; for I am desirous of hearing you say a little more about the Latin poetry of Milton than you have said in your *Dissertation.*

LANDOR. Johnson gives his opinion more freely than favourably. It is wonderful that a critic, so severe in his censures on the absurdities and extravagances of Cowley, should prefer the very worst of them to the gracefulness and simplicity of Milton. His gracefulness he seldom loses; his simplicity he not always retains. But there is no Latin verse of Cowley worth preservation. Thomas May indeed is an admirable imitator of Lucan; so good a one, that if in Lucan you find little poetry, in May you find none. But his verses sound well upon the anvil. It is surprising that Milton, who professedly imitated Ovid, should so much more rarely have run into conceits than when he had no such leader. His early English poetry is full of them, and in the gravest the most. The best of his Latin poems is that addressed to Christina in the name of Cromwell: it is

[1] *Sic.* Read: " Forcers."

worthy of the classical and courtly Bembo. But in the second verse *lucida stella* violates the metre : *stella serena* would be more descriptive and applicable. It now occurs to me that he who edited the last *Ainsworth's Dictionary*, calls Cowley *poetarum sæculi sui facile princeps*, and totally omits all mention of Shakespeare in the obituary of illustrious men. Among these he has placed not only the most contemptible critics, who bore indeed some relation to learning, but even such people as Lord Cornwallis and Lord Thurlow. Egregious ass ! above all other asses by a good ear's length ! Ought a publication so negligent and injudicious to be admitted into our public schools, after the world has been enriched by the erudition of Facciolati and Furlani ? Shall we open the book again, and go straight on ?

SOUTHEY. If you please. But as you insist on me saying most about the English, I expect at your hands a compensation in the Latin.

LANDOR. I do not promise you a compensation, but I will waste no time in obeying your wishes. Severe and rigid as the character of Milton has been usually represented to us, it is impossible to read his *Elegies* without admiration for his warmth of friendship and his eloquence in expressing it. His early love of Ovid, as a master in poetry, is enthusiastic.

> Non tunc Ionio quidquam cessisset Homero,
> *Neve* foret victo laus tibi prima, Maro ! [1]

Neve is often used by the moderns for *neque*, very improperly. Although we hear much about the *Metamorphoses* and the *Æneid* being left incomplete, we may reasonably doubt whether the authors could have much improved them. There is a deficiency of skill in the composition of both poems ; but every part is elaborately worked out. Nothing in Latin can excell the beauty of Virgil's versification. Ovid's at one moment has the fluency, at another the discontinuance, of mere conversation. Sorrow, passionate, dignified, and deep, is never seen in the *Metamorphoses* as in the *Æneid ;* nor in the *Æneid* is any eloquence so sustained, any spirit so heroic, as in the contest between Ajax and Ulysses. But Ovid frequently, in other places, wants that gravity and potency in which Virgil rarely fails : declamation is no substitute for it. Milton, in his Latin verses,

[1] Verses 23-24.

often places words beginning with *sc*, *st*, *sp*, &c., before a dactyl, which is inadmissible.

> Ah ! quoties dignæ stupui miracula formæ
> Quæ possit senium vel reparare Jovis.[1]

No such difficult a matter as he appears to represent it : for Jupiter, to the very last, was much given to such reparations. This elegy, with many slight faults, has great facility and spirit of its own, and has caught more by running at the side of Ovid and Tibullus. In the second elegy, *alipes* is a dactyl ; *pes*, simple or compound, is long. This poem is altogether unworthy of its author. The third is on the death of Launcelot Andrews, bishop of Winchester. It is florid, puerile, and altogether deficient in pathos. The conclusion is curious :

> Flebam turbatos Cepheleiâ pellice somnos ;
> *Talia contingant somnia sæpe mihi.*

Ovid has expressed the same wish in the same words, but the aspiration was for somewhat very dissimilar to a bishop of Winchester. The fourth is an epistle to Thomas Young, his preceptor, a man whose tenets were puritanical, but who encouraged in his scholar the love of poetry. Much of this piece is imitated from Ovid. There are several thoughts which might have been omitted, and several expressions which might have been improved. For instance :

> Namque eris ipse *Dei* radiante sub *ægide* tutus,
> Ille tibi custos et *pugil* ille tibi.[2]

All the verses after these are magnificent. The next is on Spring ; very inferior to its predecessors.

> Nam dolus et cædes *et vis*, cum nocte recessit
> *Neve* giganteum Dii me*tuere* scelus.[3]

How thick the faults lie here ! But the invitation of the Earth to the Sun is quite Ovidian.

> Semicaperque deus semideusque caper [4]

is too much so. Elegy the sixth is addressed to Deodati.

> Mitto tibi sanam non pleno ventre salutem,
> Qua tu, distento, *fortē* carere potes.

---

[1] Verses 53-54.   [2] Verses 111-112.   [3] Verses 39-40.   [4] Verse 122.

IMAGINARY CONVERSATIONS: ENGLISH

I have often observed in modern Latinists of the first order, that they use indifferently *forte* and *forsan* or *forsitan*. Here is an example. *Forte* is, *by accident*, without the implication of a doubt, *forsan* always implies one. Martial wrote bad Latin when he wrote " Si *forsan*." Runchenius himself writes questionably to D'Orville " sed *forte* res non est tanti." It surely would be better to have written *fortasse*. I should have less wondered to find *forte* in any modern Italian (excepting Bembo, who always writes with as much precision as Cicero or Cæsar), because *ma forse*, their idiom, would prompt *sed forte*.

        Naso Corallæis mala carmina misit ab agris.[1]

Untrue. He himself was discontented with them because they had lost their playfulness : but their only fault lies in their adulation. I doubt whether all the elegiac verses that have been written in the Latin language ever since, are worth the books of them he sent from Pontus. Deducting one couplet from Joannes Secundus, I would strike the bargain.

        Si modo *saltem*.

The *saltem* is here redundant and contrary to Latinity.

SOUTHEY. This elegy, I think, is equable and pleasing, without any great fault or great beauty.

LANDOR. In the seventh he discloses the first effects of love on him. Here are two verses which I never have read without the heart-ache :

        Ut mihi adhuc refugam quærebant lumina noctem
          Nec matutinum sustinuere jubar.

We perceive at one moment the first indication of love and of blindness. Happy, had the blindness been as unreal as the love. Cupid is not exalted by a comparison with Paris and Hylas, nor the frown of Apollo magnified by the Parthian. He writes, as many did, *author* for *auctor:* very improperly. In the sixtieth verse is again *neve* for *nec;* nor is it the last time. But here come beautiful verses :

        Deme meos tandem, verum nec deme, furores ;
          Nescio cur, miser est suaviter omnis amans.

I wish *cur* had been *quî*. Subjoined to this elegy are ten verses in

[1] Verse 19.

which he regrets the time he had wasted in love. Probably it was on the day (for it could not have cost him more) on which he composed it.

SOUTHEY. The series of these compositions exhibits little more than so many exercises in mythology. You have repeated to me all that is good in them, and in such a tone of enthusiasm as made me think better of them than I had ever thought before. The first of his epigrams, on Leonora Baroni, has little merit: the second, which relates to Tasso, has much.

LANDOR. I wish however that in the sixth line he had substituted *illâ* for *eâdem;* and not on account of the metre; for *eadem* becomes a spondee, as *eodem* in Virgil's " uno *eodemque* igni." And *sibi*, which ends the poem, is superfluous; if there must be any word it should be *ei*, which the metre rejects. The scazons against Salmasius are a miserable copy of Persius's heavy prologue to his satires; and moreover a copy at second-hand: for Ménage had imitated it in his invective against Mommor, whom he calls Gargilius. He begins,

Quis expedivit psittaco suo χαιρε.

But Persius's and Ménage's at least are metrical, which Milton's in one instance are not. The fifth foot should be an iambic. In *primatum* we have a spondee. The iambics which follow, on Salmasius again, are just as faulty. They start with a false quantity, and go on stumbling with the same infirmity. The epigram on More, the defender of Salmasius, is without wit; the pun is very poor. The next piece, a fable of the Farmer and Master, is equally vapid. But now comes the " Bellipotens Virgo," of which we often have spoken, but of which no one ever spoke too highly. Christina was flighty and insane; but it suited the policy of Cromwell to flatter a queen almost as vain as Elizabeth, who could still command the veterans of Gustavus Adolphus. We will pass over the Greek verses. They are such as no boy of the sixth form would venture to show up in any of our public schools. We have only one alcaic ode in the volume, and a very bad one it is. The canons of this metre were unknown in Milton's time. But, versed as he was in mythology, he never should have written

Nec puppe lustrâsses Charontis
Horribiles *barathri* recessus.

IMAGINARY CONVERSATIONS : ENGLISH

The good Doctor Goslyn was not rowed in that direction, nor could any such place be discovered from the bark of Charon, from whom Dr. Goslyn had every right, as Vice-Chancellor of the University, to expect civility and attention.

SOUTHEY. We come now to a longer poem, and in heroic verse, on the *Gunpowder Plot*. It appears to me to be even more Ovidian than the elegies. Monstrosus Typhoeus, Mavortigena Quirinus, the Pope, and the mendicant friars meet strangely. However, here they are, and now come Saint Peter and Bromius.

LANDOR.

> Hic Dolus insortis semper sedet ater *ocellis*.

Though *ocellus* is often used for *oculus*, being a diminutive, it is, if not always a word of endearment, yet never applicable to what is terrific or heroic. In the one hundredth and sixty-third verse the Pope is represented as declaring the Protestant religion to be the true one.

> Et quotquot fidei caluere cupidine veræ.

This poem, which ends poorly, is a wonderful work for a boy of seventeen, although much less so than Chatterton's *Bristowe Tragedy* and *Ælla*.

SOUTHEY. I suspect you will be less an admirer of the next, on *Obitum Præulis Elienses*,

> Qui rex sacrorum illâ fuisti in insulâ
> Quæ nomen Anguillæ tenet,[1]

where he wishes Death were dead.

> Et imprecor neci necem.[2]

Again,

> Sub regna furvi luctuosa Tartari
> Sedesque subterraneas.[3]

LANDOR. He never has descended before to such a bathos as this, where he runs against the coming blackamoor in the dark. However, he recovers from the momentary stupefaction, and there follow twenty magnificent verses, such as Horace himself, who excells in this metre, never wrote in it. But the next, *Naturam non pati*

---

[1] Verses 13-14. [2] Verse 24. [3] Verse 43.

senium, is still more admirable. I wish only he had omitted the third verse.

> Heu quàm perpetuis erroribus acta fatiscit
> Avia mens hominum, tenebrisque immersa profundis
> Œdipodioniam volvit sub pectore noctem.

Sublime as *volvit sub pectore noctem* is, the lumbering and ill-composed word, *Œdipodioniam*, spoils it. Beside, the sentence would go on very well, omitting the whole line. Gray has much less vigour and animation in the fragment of his philosophical poem. Robert Smith alone has more : how much more ! Enough to rival Lucretius in his noblest passages, and to deter the most aspiring from an attempt at Latin poetry. The next is also on a philosophical subject, and entitled *De Idea Platonica quemadmodum Aristoteles intellexit*. This is obscure. Aristoteles *knew*, as others do, that Plato entertained the whimsy of God working from an archetype ; but he himself was too sound and solid for the admission of such a notion. The first five verses are highly poetical : the sixth is Cowleian. At the close he scourges Plato for playing the fool so extravagantly, and tells him either to recall the poets he has turned out of doors, or to go out himself. There are people who look up in astonishment at this *archetypus gigas*, frightening God while he works at him. Milton has invested him with great dignity, and slips only once into the poetical corruptions of the age.

SOUTHEY. Lover as you are of Milton, how highly must you be gratified by the poem he addresses to his father !

LANDOR. I am happy, remote as we are, to think of the pleasure so good a father must have felt on this occasion, and how clearly he must have seen in prospective the glory of his son.

In the verses after the forty-second,

> Carmina regales epulas ornare solebant,
> Cum nondum luxus vastæque immensa vorago
> Nota gulæ, et modico fumabat cœna Lyæo,
> Tum de more sedens festa ad convivia vates, &c.

I wish he had omitted the two intermediate lines, and had written,

> Carmina regales epulas ornare solebant,
> Cum, de more, &c.

The four toward the conclusion,

> At tibi, chare pater, &c.

must have gratified the father as much almost by the harmony as the sentiment.

Southey. The scazons to Salsilli are a just and equitable return for his quatrain; for they are full of false quantities, without an iota of poetry.

Landor. But how gloriously he bursts forth again in all his splendour for Manso; for Manso, who before had enjoyed the immortal honour of being the friend of Tasso.

> Diis dilecte senex! te Jupiter æquus oportet
> Nascentem et miti lustrârit lumine Phœbus,
> Atlantisque nepos; *neque enim nisi charus ab ortu.*
> *Diis superis poterit magno favisse poetæ.*[1]

And the remainder of the poem is highly enthusiastic. What a glorious verse is,

> Frangam Saxonicas Britonum sub marte phalanges.

Southey. I have often wondered that our poets, and Milton more especially, should be the partisans of the Britons rather than of the Saxons. I do not add the Normans; for very few of our poets are Norman by descent. The Britons seem to have been a barbarous and treacherous race, inclined to drunkenness and quarrels. Was the whole nation ever worth this noble verse of Milton? It seems to come sounding over the Ægean Sea, and not to have been modulated on the low country of the Tiber.

Landor. In his pastoral on the loss of Diodati, entitled *Epitaphium Damonis*, there are many beautiful verses: for instance,

> Ovium quoque tædet, at illæ
> Mœrent, inque suum convertunt ora magistrum.[2]

The pause at *Mœrent*, and the word also, show the great master. In Virgil himself it is impossible to find anything more scientific. Here, as in *Lycidas*, mythologies are intermixed, and the heroic bursts forth from the pastoral. Apollo could not for ever be disguised as the shepherd-boy of Admetus.

> Supra caput imber et Eurus
> Triste sonant, *fractæque agitata crepuscula sylvæ.*

Southey. This is finely expressed: but he found the idea not

---

[1] Verses 70-73.   [2] Verses 66-67.

untouched before. Gray and others have worked upon it since. It may be well to say little on the *Presentation of the poems to the Bodleian Library*. Strophes and antistrophes are here quite out of place; and on no occasion has any Latin poet so jumbled together the old metres. Many of these are irregular and imperfect.

Ion Acteâ genitus Creusâ [1]

is not a verse : *authorum* is not Latin.

Et tutela dabit *sŏlers* Roüsi [2]

is defective in metre. This Pindaric ode to Rouse the librarian is indeed fuller of faults than any other of his Latin compositions. He tells us himself that he has admitted a spondee for the third foot in the phaleucian verse, because Catullus had done so in the second. He never wrote such bad verses, or gave such bad reasons, all his life before. But beautifully and justly has he said,

Si quid meremur sana posteritas sciet.[3]

LANDOR. I find traces in Milton of nearly all the best Latin poets, excepting Lucretius. This is singular; for there is in both of them a generous warmth and a contemptuous severity. I admire and love Lucretius. There is about him a simple majesty, a calm and lofty scorn of everything pusillanimous and abject: and consistently with this character, his poetry is masculine, plain, concentrated, and energetic. But since invention was precluded by the subject, and glimpses of imagination could be admitted through but few and narrow apertures, it is the insanity of enthusiasm to prefer his poetical powers to those of Virgil, of Catullus, and of Ovid; in all of whom every part of what constitutes the true poet is much more largely displayed. The excellence of Lucretius is, that his ornaments are never out of place, and are always to be found wherever there is a place for them. Ovid knows not what to do with his, and is as fond of accumulation as the frequenter of auction-rooms. He is playful so out of season, that he reminds me of a young lady I saw at Sta. Maria Novella, who at one moment crossed herself, and at the next tickled her companion, by which process they were both put upon their speed at their prayers, and made very good and happy. Small as is the portion of glory which accrues to Milton from his Latin

---

[1] Verse 60.   [2] Verse 78.   [3] Verse 86.

poetry, there are single sentences in it, ay, single images, worth all that our island had produced before. In all the volume of Buchanan I doubt whether you can discover a glimpse of poetry; and few sparks fly off the anvil of May.

There is a confidence of better days expressed in this closing poem. Enough is to be found in his Latin to insure him a high rank and a lasting name. It is however to be regretted that late in life he ran back to the treasures of his youth, and estimated them with the fondness of that undiscerning age. No poet ever was sorry that he abstained from early publication. But Milton seems to have cherished his first effusions with undue partiality. Many things written later by him are unworthy of preservation, especially those which exhibit men who provoked him into bitterness. Hatred, the most vulgar of vulgarisms, could never have belonged to his natural character. He must have contracted the distemper from theologians and critics. The scholar in his days was half clown and half trooper. College-life could leave but few of its stains and incrustations on a man who had stept forward so soon into the amenities of Italy, and had conversed so familiarly with the most polished gentlemen of the most polished nation.

SOUTHEY. In his attacks on Salmasius, and others more obscure, he appears to have mistaken his talent in supposing he was witty.

LANDOR. Is there a man in the world wise enough to know whether he himself is witty or not, to the extent he aims at? I doubt whether any question needs more self-examination. It is only the fool's heart that is at rest upon it. He never asks how the matter stands, and feels confident he has only to stoop for it. Milton's dough, it must be acknowledged, is never the lighter for the bitter barm he kneads up with it.

SOUTHEY. The sabbath of his mind required no levities, no excursions or amusements. But he was not ill-tempered. The worst-tempered men have often the greatest and readiest store of pleasantries. Milton, on all occasions indignant and wrathful at injustice, was unwilling to repress the signification of it when it was directed against himself. However, I can hardly think he felt so much as he expresses; but he seized on bad models in his resolution to show his scholarship. Disputants, and critics in particular, followed one another with invectives; and he was thought to have given the most manifest proof of original genius who had invented a new form of reproach. I doubt if Milton was so contented with his discomfiture of Satan, or even with his creation of Eve, as with the overthrow of Salmasius under the loads of fetid brimstone he fulminated against him.

It is fortunate we have been sitting quite alone while we detected the blemishes of a poet we both venerate. The malicious are always the most ready to bring forward an accusation of malice: and we should certainly have been served, before long, with a writ pushed under the door.

LANDOR. Are we not somewhat like two little beggar-boys, who, forgetting that they are in tatters, sit noticing a few stains and rents in their father's raiment?

SOUTHEY. But they love him.

Let us now walk homeward. We leave behind us the Severn and the sea and the mountains; and, if smaller things may be mentioned so suddenly after greater, we leave behind us the sun-dial, which marks, as we have been doing in regard to Milton, the course of the great luminary by a slender line of shadow.

LANDOR. After witnessing his glorious ascension, we are destined to lower our foreheads over the dreary hydropathy and flanelly voices of the swathed and sinewless.

SOUTHEY. Do not be over-sure that you are come to the worst, even there. Unless you sign a certificate of their health and vigour, your windows and lamps may be broken by the mischievous rabble below.

LANDOR. Marauders will cook their greens and bacon, though they tear down cedar panels for the purpose.

SOUTHEY. There is an incessant chatterer,[1] who has risen to the first dignities of state, by the same means as nearly all men rise now by; namely, opposition to whatever is done or projected by those invested with authority. He will never allow us to contemplate greatness at our leisure: he will not allow us indeed to look at it for a moment. Cæsar must be stript of his laurels and left bald; or some reeling soldier, some insolent swaggerer, some stilted ruffian,

---

[1] Lord Brougham. See Landor's "Opinions on Cæsar, Cromwell, Milton, and Buonaparte": "No person has a better right than Lord Brougham to speak contemptuously of Cæsar, of Cromwell, and of Milton. Cæsar . . . rose with moderation, and he fell with dignity. Can we wonder at Lord Brougham's unfeigned antipathy," etc. See also Brougham's article in the *Edinburgh Review*, April, 1839.

thrust before his triumph. If he fights, he does not know how to use his sword; if he speaks, he speaks vile Latin. I wonder that Cromwell fares no better; for he lived a hypocrite, and he died a traitor. I should not recall to you this ridiculous man, to whom the Lords have given the *run of the House*—a man pushed off his chair by every party he joins, and enjoying all the disgraces he incurs—were it not that he has also, in the fulness of his impudence, raised his cracked voice and incondite language against Milton.

LANDOR. I hope his dapple fellow-creatures in the lanes will be less noisy and more modest as we pass along them homeward.

SOUTHEY. Wretched as he is in composition, superficial as he is in all things, without a glimmer of genius, or a grain of judgment, yet his abilities and acquirements raise him somewhat high above those more quiescent and unaspiring ones, you call his fellow-creatures.

LANDOR. The main difference is, that they are subject to have their usual burdens laid upon them all their lives, while his of the woolsack is taken off for ever. The allusion struck me from the loudness and dissonance of his voice, the wilfulness and perverseness of his disposition, and his habitude of turning round on a sudden and kicking up behind.